AF539507

ART OF SUCCESSFUL BUSINESS, FAMILY AND SOCIAL LIFE

ART OF SUCCESSFUL BUSINESS, FAMILY AND SOCIAL LIFE

V.S. MAHAJAN
Director
Centre for Indian Development Studies
Chandigarh

DEEP & DEEP PUBLICATIONS PVT. LTD.
F-159, Rajouri Garden, New Delhi - 110 027

ART OF SUCCESSFUL BUSINESS, FAMILY AND SOCIAL LIFE

ISBN 978-81-8450-039-4

Typeset by RAHUL COMPOSERS
358, Sector 16-B, Phase-II, Pocket-B, Dwarka, New Delhi - 110 075

Printed in India at NEW ELEGANT PRINTERS
A-49/1, Mayapuri, Phase-I, New Delhi - 110 064

Published by DEEP & DEEP PUBLICATIONS PVT. LTD.,
F-159, Rajouri Garden, New Delhi - 110 027 • Phone : 25435369, 25440916
E-mail : ddpubs@gmail.com • ddpbooks@yahoo.co.in
Showroom :
2/13, Ansari Road, Daryaganj, New Delhi - 110 002 • Telefax : 23245122

Contents

PART II

THOUGHTS OF HAPPY LIFE

PART III

MARRIAGE BLISS, CHILDREN AND FAMILY VALUES

Introduction

PURPOSE BEHIND THESE WRITINGS

Through these writings an attempt has been made to reach out to the day-to-day problems of our daily life. Problems that often arise in business, employment, family life, children, health, stress, foods, social life, retirement and several other areas have been looked into, both from their positive as well as negative aspects. Ultimately a reasonable view has been stressed for facing them in practical life.

There is certainly no foolproof formula (Mantra) for leading a happy and blissful life. Our daily activities do result in several stresses and strains on us, however it is the way we are able to face them that is far more important for leading a balanced life.

This slim volume spread over four parts, deals with such issues in a concise manner and the main points emerging have been summarized for easy reading and practice.

V.S. MAHAJAN

PART I

Art of Successful Business and Entrepreneurship

How to be a Winner in Business

In the mid-eighties two friends—Ashok and Gopal (not real names)—had joined hands to make money in the booming stock market. Then Chandigarh was just a new entrant into this business and the local (unrecognised) market functioned from a non-descript SCO in Sector 17. Soon a crowd of investors started to get the taste of the booming market. They would collect in the forenoon at this place when bidding would start by the so-called brokers in the prized stocks, which had already shown encouraging response in the market. These speculative deals were based entirely on reports gathered from the press and financial journals. As settlements were made on the spot, people would buy and sell their stocks through these brokers who would get the documents validated later. As deals were made among the local people, and buyers and sellers usually met each other, there was normally no difficulty in settling accounts soon when sellers were paid the money that was due to them.

While this boom lasted only for a limited period, it helped brokers to earn good income and also helped to lay the foundation of a regular local stock market which later started functioning from a more spacious SCO where brokers were registered and started functioning on a regular basis from their cabins in this building.

Both Ashok and Gopal were also able to manage a cabin for themselves and began to function from there on a regular basis. This also provided them a place where they would be available during working days and even late evenings. Soon their work started picking up and they expanded their business by hiring more space as well as expanded their work team by recruiting more office staff.

However, their partnership didn't last for long and it ran into rough weather. Both the friends had different temperaments and adjustment became a problem. Ashok was cool-headed and patiently listened to others in a pleasant and smiling mood, which was greatly appreciated by the clients. Gopal, on the other hand, was short-tempered and would easily lose his cool and often ran into trouble with customers. He often conveyed the impression that he knew far more about the market situation than customers and the latter should accept him without questioning. Of course, this attitude often annoyed customers who didn't argue with him further.

Thus this attitude of Gopal began to work against the interest of the firm and often clients would avoid him and rarely sought advice from him. The employees were also not happy with his attitude and rough behaviour, and thus so long as he was there it became difficult for the firm to have a team of stable employees, which ultimately hit the functioning of this firm adversely.

Gradually the situation came when Gopal himself decided to quit and floated a new firm of his own. This was of course appreciated by Ashok. Gentle and accommodating, he never uttered any harsh word towards Gopal and tolerated his obstructionist attitude with patience.

Of course, Gopal could not be a success in his independent business and soon he quitted the stock market business itself, where he proved to be a big failure. On the other hand, Ashok built up his business step by step and soon his friendly and accommodating attitude paid rich dividend. He also enjoyed very cordial relations with his employees who gave him all possible support, with the result that all possible details of sales, purchases, settlements and other activities connected with the stock market were tackled efficiently by the employees, and customers were thus quite pleased with the functioning of this firm.

Later, the firm shifted to a more spacious accommodation and installed a number of computers and other modern facilities which gave further boost to its business.

Thus the lesson from this story is that in a successful business one has to cultivate patience, perseverance as well as adopt a helpful attitude towards customers, who might be seeking advice for the wise investment of their hard earned money, so that these yielded encouraging returns. And it is only after winning their affection, good will and support that they would stay with the firm subsequently. In fact, gradually there is a sort of multiplying impact from the initial efforts made to win over the customers.

The reverse would happen if the CEO has negative qualities, like Gopal had in the above episode. Had he not moved out, the business was sure to lose its clients and head for a failure.

Thus to be a winner you must understand your customers, their problems and their expectations. In other words, you should be able to influence them through correct advice and guidance. When a customer visits, you should consider it a great honour and treat him with full respect and courtesy and attend to his queries in the best possible way so that he is satisfied with your dealings. He would surely patronize you further. Thus, much would depend on how you behave with a customer.

DON'T TURN HAUGHTY WHEN FORTUNE VISITS YOU

Most of us, when we see fortune knocking at our door, tend to ignore old friends simply because we have risen much higher over them. This is an unethical and most undesirable practice that reflects the negative attitude of our mind, for we have conveniently forgotten the support they had rendered when we ourselves were struggling and frantically looking for customers to establish our business and these people had come to our rescue.

Remember, in business, fortune can change and who knows you may again be facing a difficult situation and think how you would feel when your contemporaries today who are equally prosperous try to ignore you when you call on them or seek their support when your business has run into rough weather. So always think of that situation which would keep you away from a negative attitude and teach you to respect everyone in business.

You should always have a soft corner for those people who every helped you in your heart and render them every possible assistance. They would gratefully appreciate it and bless you and your business.

BUSINESS PREMISES SHOULD HAVE A DESIRABLE LOOK

It is worth-remembering that customers visit those premises where they feel honoured to visit and find the needed facilities. Even a large business house without good environment and proper service would fail to attract customers and if not appropriately modified, it would soon be heading for a downfall.

During the 1950s Panipat (in Haryana) happened to be a major wool centre in North India but many major interested parties especially foreigners would hesitate to visit this place with highly unattractive surroundings and little of comfort available. The town was full of squalor, dirt and flies and there was no good place where one could spend a comfortable night.

These negative aspects of this prosperous wool centre were fully realised by one visionary young businessman who argued with himself that if he could succeed in providing modern facilities, his business would flourish. And that is exactly what he did, though he didn't have the needed financial support this project demanded. He knocked on every possible door and with much effort was able to raise a loan from friends, relatives and banks where he had to pawn his wool factory.

Gradually the dream project began to take shape and after sometime a modest one-storey structure, fully air-conditioned, free from dust and flies having a couple of bedrooms, baths and toilets, and a modern kitchen and dining hall, was raised where foreigners could spend the night in full comfort.

While this project put him under heavy debt, it gradually started paying a rich dividend. Quite a few foreign wool buyers visited Panipat and this gentleman's business expanded briskly. Even the Central Government's excise staff who rarely stayed overnight in Panipat, would now be tempted to visit it more frequently and enjoyed the hospitality of this gentleman who was also able to extract a good concession for his business from these excise barons, which they made good from other parties who would also be queuing up at this place to meet excise officers.

Thus this gentleman's farsightedness and innovative approach paid him over several times and soon he was also able to raise another floor in the premises where he moved the guest house while the ground floor accommodated his office. His fully air-conditioned office added to his efficiency and ensured him and his staff dust and heat-free atmosphere.

Thus it clearly shows that business premises even in a small town would yield rich and lasting dividends provided you are able to cash on this opportunity in time.

BUILD STRONG RELATIONS WITH EMPLOYEES

Another quality of successful business is to encourage warm and personal relations with the employees. While the customer is the king, for he has spared time to visit your premises which is in your interest, but don't forget that it is your employees who run the show and are thus equally important. Ultimately it is their attitude and approach towards customers which matters a lot in attracting business.

If the employees are not prepared to cooperate or are in an indifferent mood and hardly take interest in business, rest assured you are going to lose your customers, even while you try to impose all your authority on the employees. Also remember that authority hardly works ultimately. It might be OK for a while but not in the long-run when it would be resented and turn counter productive. You have to be careful.

But then sit and ponder whose fault it has been in making the employees behave in this manner? Clearly you will realise that it has been by and large yours, when you started treating them just as paid employees and acted in the manner of a boss even before customers and did not spare-scolding them when some error was detected.

Remember they are not inferior persons. They are extremely conscious of their presence and behaviour and know well that without them you would not be able to run a good business. So they don't depend on you. Rather you depend on them. So you must treat them with courtesy and on equal footing, respect them and avoid harsh remarks against them especially in the presence of others.

If they have committed some fault tell them politely about it later. They will appreciate it and fully cooperate with you. Rest assured it is the satisfied members of your team, in which you reposed your full faith and encouraged them for their performance that will ultimately pay your business well. Thus your employees are as important in business as customers.

Both are interrelated, as good business is the outcome of such relationship.

DON'T ADOPT A NEGATIVE ATTITUDE TOWARDS YOUR RIVALS

Most businessmen have their eyes on those business premises around them which attract high clientele. In case they are unable to compete with them they even try to work out a strategy to pull them down, instead of looking into their own deficiencies.

This is a destructive mind set and is totally unhelpful in either destroying the rival's business or extending their own. Rather, through such negative approach they might lose a part of their own business to the rival. Thus, instead of harming the rival's business it might end up in harming your own.

Ultimately customers are not so easily misled by such propaganda. They have their own clear perception about which premises offered them better stuff for their money. Thus the lesson is clear. Ultimately it is the quality of goods and services provided that would attract customers to a particular business house. Thus rival business houses should try to act accordingly if they want to win more customers.

It should also be simultaneously remembered that ultimately it is the volume of goods transacted that would be the best yardstick for measuring the aggregate business prosperity and this is best ensured when all the business firms are doing their level best. The weak who fail to upgrade themselves would automatically disappear and it is generally found that it is these business houses that carry out malicious propaganda against their rivals.

CREATE LONG TERM CONTACTS WITH YOUR CLIENTS

Apart from the quality of turning out a winner in business, it is also important to build long-term relations with customers, which would sustain your business over a long period. In fact, it is the after-sale contact which would play a more important role in getting your goods across the global market.

In our country we have thought very little in this direction. Look at Japan. During the inter-war period when the world faced a long time business depression and several businesses closed down, and a large part of the labour force was thrown out of employment, it were the Japanese products which were able to capture a good share of the world market, for they had a knack of creating a permanent class of clients through their effective after-sale service in a large number of centres set-up in different parts of the globe.

Here their embassies overseas had played an important role in helping their manufacturers in establishing permanent contact with clients through service centres created at important destinations, which provided regular and effective service to their products after their sale and this worked miracles in establishing close links with customers.

This system also helped to know the changes that had occurred in the customers' tastes and thus manufacturers were able to update their products accordingly which helped to expand their overseas market base and they were far ahead of other countries.

Little surprise that while during this prolonged period of world depression the western countries suffered a very high rate of unemployment, Japan on the other hand was the only country where employment actually rose during this period. Their success thus laid in building close customer relations through the magic of after-sale services as well as product upgradation reflecting changes in the global markets, which paid a good dividend.

Thus the lesson is, if our businessmen want to capture a large share of the world market, they will have to adopt production strategies which reflect the taste of global markets.

In brief, the qualities needed to become a successful winner in the modern global market are:

First, improve your personal traits. Acquire qualities of patience and perseverance in dealing with customers, listen to them carefully and attend to their queries in a sincere and convincing tone. Try to develop personal relations with customers.

Second, learn to respect your old friends and colleagues in business even when you are far ahead of them. Always think what would happen if misfortune visits you. Its very thought would make you humble and you will think well of people who are in trouble.

Third, take special care of surroundings your business for customers are very much attracted to the existence of good surroundings as well as well planned and well executed interiors and customer services.

Fourth, see that your employees are a satisfied lot and treat them almost like partners in business. Apart from good working conditions, salary and other benefits, you must also often say words of cheer and appreciation to them. Also expose them to modern training. That will work wonders. Not only their efficiency and outlook would improve, they would feel an integral part of the business and devote their full attention for its growth.

Fifth, never adopt a negative attitude towards your rivals. Instead, try to learn from their positive approach that has made their business far more successful than yours. Apart from trying to adopt these goals in your business, try to adopt other plus points so that your business makes still higher growth compared to others.

Sixth, develop long-term contacts with your clients by offering them after-sales benefits. This would particularly help when you are trying to develop global contacts.

And the adoption of similar other measures would help you to create more business opportunities. Also, don't forget to share a liberal part of these gains with your employees as their bonds in business would be further strengthened in this way.

Road to Becoming a Successful Boss

Whether you are in a small organisation or a big one, in government or in a private sector, there are certain norms which help to become a successful boss, which if properly observed would certainly enhance your popularity and make you a happy and successful man liked by your subordinates, customers and all those with whom you come in contact.

AVOID BOSSISM

The first question you have to ask yourself is whether you would like to behave like a dominating boss who believes in perfect bossism and is drunk in its full power, thinks himself to be the most superior and indispensable person, at least in the organisation, and all others are thought to be subordinates? If you do, you could never be a successful boss. When bossism gets right in your head and you treat others as your subordinates who have to obey your orders without opposition and don't have their voice, or you are not receptive to their view points or suggestions, and don't encourage them to be open-minded, you are certainly strangulating your organisation and it would not be a success.

Your subordinates will try to avoid you, will not show much progress, like to follow go-slow tactics, and not display any creativity, any change, which is so essential in the modern business world where things are moving very fast and if you have to compete successfully, you will have to change a lot in your organisation.

But then it is your stubbornness, born out of the attitude of bossism, which doesn't allow it.

So the first principle for becoming a successful boss is not to act like a literal boss but be flexible and friendly with the subordinates and all those with whom you come in contact. Treat them with dignity and respect and encourage your employees in every possible way, which would enhance the image of your organisation.

ENCOURAGE FAITH AND RELIANCE IN YOUR WORK FORCE

Employees should also be tempted to work hard and put in their best for the success of the business. Give them the security of tenure which, particularly in a private organisation, is very important, for otherwise they would be tempted to move to other organisations, which could disturb the functioning of your organisation.

At the same time security of tenure doesn't mean that it should encourage inefficiency. Rather, with security of job, training, as well as avenues of suitably rewarding the inventive employees, it has been found that employees would work with enthusiasm and dedication for the growth of their organisation.

This is the way how it has worked in Japan where most of the employees do make one or the other original contribution. Some are even highly innovative and come out with new products, marketing and management ideas which enhance the value of their products and services, and they in turn are very suitably rewarded by their firms.

If your organisation also encourages such rewarding policy, every employee would be tempted to hunt for a new idea. Remember, ultimately it is these ideas, which are behind the success of top businesses. There are of course going to be a few black sheep or laggards but then if the majority are hardworking and devoted, it doesn't matter. Ultimately, in any organisation you can't have 100 percent committed employees. It is the solid majority that would enhance the image of the firm as well as put it in the forefront.

While in a big organisation you can't remember the names of your employees, in a medium or small one, you can. It would be a great pleasure if you were to address them by their first name. They would feel important and at the same time you should also give due respect to age as, in the case of a senior employee you should address him with more respect. They would duly remember it and stand by the organisation through thick and thin.

Thus, the second recipe for becoming a successful boss is to have full faith in your employees, encourage them with job security and innovative spirit by holding out suitable rewards.

RESTRAIN YOUR PASSIONS WHEN SOMETHING GOES WRONG

It is fairly common with bosses to let out steam when they find some errant employee, and the volume of steam is directly proportionate to the enormity of the error committed. In fact, some bosses call for the erring person right from the time they enter their office premises and shower all kind of invectives and threaten to throw him out or even hand him over to the police in case he persisted in committing such errors time and again.

It is highly advisable that bosses learnt to restrain their passions at such an occasion and treat the whole situation with a cool and balanced mind. Even if provoked by their colleagues, they should use their own discretion. This will greatly help to diffuse the situation.

Often it has been found that when such a situation is handled with tact and in a cool manner, it would do a lot good to the organisation as well as employees. They would hesitate to commit such an error in future and even feel guilty for such omission and resolve not to repeat it again. When handled in this way with a smile on the face of the chief executive, they would feel not only ashamed of their performance, but would even ensure that in future no other colleague in the firm committed such a blunder.

Thus the lesson is clear. That letting out steam doesn't do any good. It also becomes clear from this episode. The story goes that Punjab's Chief Minister Partap Singh Kairon had a bitter tongue and by frequent nasty use of tongue and behaviour, had antagonized himself with his colleagues and subordinates.

Once it is said that in the heat of anger when he found that some very senior officer had failed to carry out his instructions he sent for him right when he entered his office in the morning and showered on him all the choicest invectives for daring to be so careless. Naturally this officer felt deeply offended and sought his immediate transfer.

The moral is that such behaviour did no good, rather it only antagonized the boss with the senior officer, notwithstanding all the good work that Kairon did for the upliftment of Punjab at a time when it was struggling to build itself after independence.

This is a clear instance of how when a delicate situation is not tactfully handled it can cause misunderstanding and leave behind a bad taste in the mind of the affected person. Subsequently, Kairon had to pay a heavy price for his nasty behaviour when he was shot dead by some aggrieved persons while on his way to Chandigarh from Delhi.

Thus, another lesson is to not let yourself be overpowered by anger when something has gone wrong with your instructions or overall functioning of your organisation due to the negligence of some employees, but try to handle the situation with a cool mind and tact.

Your approach should be to reform the wrong doers so that they not only realise their error, even promise that the same is not repeated in future, rather they improve their performance. Thus efforts should be made to inculcate in the minds of employees that it is their organisation, and whatever they did was for their own organisation. In fact, this motto lies behind the success of any organisation.

SHAPE EMPLOYEES INTO SUCCESSFUL HUMAN RESOURCES

Ultimately, it is the human resources who play a vital role in the success of any organisation. Thus, much would depend upon their efficiency, training, commitment and alertness, and all these factors depend upon how well they are treated and encouraged in their performance by the organisation they work for. So it is all inter-related. Behind any top business is the positive role played by its human resources, their hard efforts and sense of commitment.

Of course, it is not that all the human resources would work in an identical manner. Some are going to be far more active and alert than others. But it's the overall environment which spells success. Under such an environment, those who are lazy and careless are also going to turn out different in the long-run, for in such an organisation they could not afford to be lazy for long.

On the contrary, in an organisation where inefficient manpower dominates, it will certainly pull down even those who are efficient and hard working and thus ultimately bring about the overall ruin of the organisation.

Thus, the top executives should ensure that such a situation does not arise and instead encourage a congenial business and work situation where the human resources are tempted to put in their best and are simultaneously adequately compensated.

Apart from a transparent and well streamlined recruitment policy, the organisation should pay due attention to the training and placement of their selected employees to suitable positions and encourage them to perform their job well without interference. Remember undue interference in the performance of an employee would not be liked and can even harm the organisation if such interference is pushed too far.

There should be regular training programmes for employees which would do them a lot of good and make them familiar with what was happening around and aware of how they themselves need to pick up the best from such training programmes. Thus a periodic exposure to such training and other in house as well as outside programmes would pay a rich dividend to the organisation.

Bill Gates, the richest boss in the world and the owner of the world's biggest IT organisation Microsoft, believes reached this position only with the support and cooperation of the world class employees whom he treats as his colleagues—nothing short of that. Thus, Bill Gates has given top priority in selecting first rate youngsters for his programme and they ultimately with possible incentives, liberal salaries and a strong training programme, turn out to be the best asset for the growth of his company. Little surprise that with such care and efforts made to select and later build up top human resources in the world. Bill Gates is blessed with the world class professionals who turn his organisation into the best possible in the world. It has revolutionized the whole IT industry and is ever on the road to further success.

This shows how it is Bill Gates' innovative approach to shape human resources for excellent performance which has led his company to the top successful position in the world.

Thus the lesson is clear if a boss has to rise to the world position, he would have to treat human resources with dignity, on equal footing and plan his policies and programmes in a way that would ultimately shape these resources into the best possible assets, who feel it a pleasure as well as pride to work for such an organisation.

ENCOURAGE DIALOGUE WITH OTHERS

A boss should not shut himself in the office. He should be accessible to others who want to meet him, particularly outsiders. It would of course be best that he encourages visitors to meet him through prior appointment and this task should be carefully handled by his personal staff who should be easily available to guide visitors as well as brief the boss.

As for the time schedule for visitors, it should be worked out carefully a day earlier and thus the boss should know in advance about who is coming to meet him and the purpose of visit. It would help if the boss were to take spot decision on the problems faced by visitors instead of postponing them which could do harm to the company's reputation.

Personal attention to the needs of visitors would further boost the image of the organisation and people will start having confidence in its management, leadership as well as products. This will also encourage personal touch, improve the image of the company and build its long-term growth.

It is equally essential that while the boss has to plan the time for meeting the outside visitors, he should also devote some time to look into the internal matters of his own organisation, meet the heads of different departments and see for himself how things were progressing, what problems were being faced and what were the possible solutions.

It is the usual practice with big organisations that in the forenoon, all the heads of different departments sit together around the boss and have a stocktaking of their departments which gives an overall idea of the functioning of the firm. In this light some suggestions would emerge and more time is devoted later on to thrash out these problems.

Also, in these meetings an opportunity is thrown to the employees to coordinate their activities with different sections of the organisation. This would thus avoid duplication of efforts if these were there and some closely related departments would find a better opportunity for the coordination of their work.

The boss should at times move out of his office and personally meet the heads of departments. That would help to develop personal contact with them and enable to discuss problems of these departments more effectively, particularly if they have emerged in the larger meeting with different heads of departments in the forenoon. Even otherwise, such personal meetings would familiarise the boss with any shortcoming in the overall coordination of the organisation, which may itself be hindering the work process.

In view of the multiple demand on the time of a boss, it is essential that he wisely rationalizes his time for these meetings, and leaves much of the task of the firm's management and day-to-day affairs to the heads of departments.

Thus the fifth rule is that the boss should draw his daily schedule of work meticulously when he should be conveniently available to outsiders as well as his own firm's heads of departments. He should delegate much of his daily routines to the heads of departments who should look into these problems effectively, instead of taking these to the boss.

DON'T CARRY OFFICE AT HOME

It is fashion with some bosses, though particularly in government departments, to carry important files home. This is an undesirable practice and should be avoided, as home is not meant for office work which should be left behind before the boss leaves for home.

No one at home would appreciate such a load of files and papers and it is very often seen that most of these papers return back to office next day unattended and again clutter the desk of the boss which makes an unpleasant sight.

Bosses should therefore avoid such practice. They should in the very first instance not postpone disposal of a file which should be done during the office time itself so that at home one has free time to relax and mix with the family members, look after the problems of children and share some bright moments with them.

It has been observed that bosses who relax at home, mix with family members and enjoy sound sleep, are fresh, smiling, not easily irritated, keep themselves cool and thus turn out to be successful bosses. Thus, a happy family life is an essential precondition for the success of any organisation. If one were to carry domestic tension to office, it would have an adverse consequence in the functioning of the business.

Most unsuccessful bosses who have played a major role in the downfall of their organisations are also those who were both mentally as well as socially not suited for their positions.

Look at Bill Gates again who, just in his 40s, has turned out to be the most successful boss and also enjoys a happy family life. The same has been true of other successful bosses.

Thus the lesson is to avoid doing office work at home. Just forget it and mix with your family members and relax. This would help you to get over the day's fatigue and induce you to have a sound sleep. After all you also have responsibility towards your family. Remember a happy family life also makes for a happy and successful office.

YOUR FIRM SHOULD HAVE A COMPETITIVE EDGE

To achieve success in business it is also essential that your firm has a competitive edge over others, which can be ensured through high quality products at competitive prices, efficient customer service and the like. Remember, a customer is all the time looking for a product, which is superior to others in quality, and at the same time it is price competitive.

Here again it is Japan, a country that has travelled a long way to achieve these goals. Initially during the pre-second world war period, its products though globally cheap, were often labelled poor in quality. But see what a remarkable change it has made in the post-war period.

Japan has now emerged as the world's top country producing the best quality products through the use of latest world class cost-effective technology. Thus, it has very successfully achieved the twin objectives of quality and competitive price for its products. No surprise that such achievement in its products is now universally recognised and enjoys a high demand, thus earning good profits for its manufacturers and exporters.

Japan has also been for a long time providing effective after-sales service for its products which has helped it enjoy the global trade at a time when very few countries could dream of it.

India on the other hand is yet lagging far behind. Most of our entrepreneurs continue to be obsessed by the idea of making a quick buck (i.e. grow rich overnight) irrespective of the quality of their products. Of course, much of it is a hangover from the past period of import substitution that ruled supreme before the country went global.

Most of our manufacturers are yet drowned in this era and have failed to rise to the occasion, with the result that they are finding it difficult to survive when faced with highly competitive and latest quality-oriented foreign products, and are desperately seeking government assistance. Quite a few of them have already surrendered themselves to the superior foreign firms which of course is an example of coward business behaviour.

Why should not our bosses take up this challenge squarely like Tatas, Ambanis and others and stand on their own and even feel that they are superior to foreign firms in a number of ways, particularly when we have one of the best technical manpower in the world, which has in fact played a major role in the development of several new products in the US and other developed economies.

Thus our businessmen should develop a new outlook towards workers and change the existing business and manufacturing system which is a great hindrance to modernisation. Here lies the challenge before them. Instead of living under the fear of foreign multinationals, they should pick up the challenge and face it squarely with the world class products manufactured at their plants. If Japan could do it and China has done it recently, why not this country?

Thus another business rule is that our bosses should develop a new mind set to face the challenge of global competition by upgrading their technology, skills of workers, management practices and marketing strategies. This challenge should be faced squarely and our manufacturers should develop well thought out strategies for putting forward their products in the global market which should compete with the products already available.

AFTER-SALES SERVICE

It is also essential that for maintaining a close contact with customers and to build a lasting relationship with them, our firms should aim at reliable and effective after-sales service facilities. Even today the primary reason why customers still prefer Japanese products, is that the care taken even after the sale of these products by their manufacturers is unmatched by any other country.

Our firms should not lag behind. Though some of them have already created similar facilities, but they are far behind and thus a lot of effort is yet needed. Other firms that do not have such facilities should create them early. In fact here our foreign missions and embassies can render a lot of help.

In fact, long back when Japan was struggling to gain its foothold in the international market, it had effectively used its foreign offices for helping the local manufacturers and it worked exceedingly well.

Thus, the eighth rule for creating an effective global business is to create a network of after-sales service for the Indian products, which would also provide a feedback of customers' reaction to these products, as to how effectively these could be improvised to fit into their changing needs.

FINANCIAL MATTERS SHOULD HAVE TOP PRIORITY

The boss would have to look closely into the financial matters of the organisation. It has been observed that finance still continues to be the weak point of Indian business. Most of our firms do not pay the close attention needed to this matter which ultimately lands them in trouble.

In fact several business failures in this country have been the result of poor financial management, several of these firms with doubtful intentions have manipulated public funds and landed the shareholders and business in difficulty.

Thus successful and committed bosses should not allow this to happen. They should play a positive role in financial matters and ensure financial reliability and viability of their firms and closely guard the letting of any extraneous consideration to spoil the reputation of their organisation.

Here it would be essential that there exists a strong financial wing in the company managed by qualified and experienced managers who keep day to day reliable accounts of the financial deals of their company and which are audited regularly by a reputed firm of auditors There should also be regular internal audits by experts to weed out possible errors and ensure transparency of accounts.

Thus another rule for the successful boss is that he should ensure a reliable and dependable system of accounting, which is regularly audited by a reputed firm of auditors and thus present a true growth scenario of the firm.

SUMMING UP

Thus summing up the qualities needed for a successful boss, these are the important ones:

Firstly, the boss should avoid bossism. In fact, the word 'I' should be replaced by the word 'we' to denote the collective look in the organisation.

Secondly, the boss should have full faith in employees and encourage them with job security and innovative skills.

Thirdly, the boss should control his anger and tongue, which can cause great damage to the functioning of the firm. He should tackle even a difficult situation with tact and a cool mind, without losing temper. This would build up respect for him from his employees and also encourage better performance in future.

Fourthly, the boss should encourage development of better human relations, which in fact plays a vital role in the success of a modern business unit. This should be done through a well defined and practiced policy. Investment in human resources, as the experience shows, pays very rich dividends in the growth of an organisation.

Fifthly, the boss should encourage meeting with others and not shut himself in his office. He should be accessible to outsiders as well as his own employees. He should also visit the heads of departments to sort out their problems and to be acquainted with the problems they face.

Sixthly, a boss should not carry office work home. He should keep the home free from office matters and have free time with his family members, which in return would help him to lead a more satisfying and healthy career as a boss.

Seventhly, the boss should build up a strong competitive edge for his firm and not bask under traditional mode of functioning, which unfortunately has been the major goal of the majority of firms hitherto. If the business has to survive in the current highly competitive world, it must move into the fast lane of modern business.

Eighthly, the boss should also encourage continuous relations with customers by providing after-sales service for the products of its company, of course where it is possible. This will enhance the value of its products as well as encourage lasting relationship with customers.

Ninthly, though not last, the boss should give top priority to financial matters for it is the financial transparency which is the major guideline for measuring the health of a firm.

How to be a Top Entrepreneur

While most of us dream of climbing to the top position in our business career where there are high rewards, however it is generally less appreciated that reaching that height calls for sustained effort, positive approach, determination as well as a high innovative spirit and clear forward vision, which we generally lack.

This amounts to saying that those who successfully climb to such a height have before them a clear vision or goal and are prepared for a ceaseless struggle to achieve the same.

Thus, it is their total involvement with their work plan to reach the goal before them, unmindful of the efforts needed, that ultimately brings them the desired reward.

This is what it means when we say that things don't happen easily in business as one thinks and the path of climbing to the top position of the business ladder is beset with a lot of effort, hard work and patience.

At the same time, it doesn't mean that unless one has had a high exposure to business education and allied tools, it would be difficult to climb to the top position. Often it is unlike this. While proper exposure to education is an important element for attempting to reach the desired goal, it is not an essential ingredient at the same time. On the other hand, it is observed that people with hardly any exposure to formal business education have made unique contribution.

Thus, climbing to the top position is not what is taught in a formal class room, it is generally acquired through one's efforts and determination. Here vision is of course the foremost. Unless one has vision, howsoever qualified he might be, there is hardly going to be any change in his outlook and functioning.

This also explains why a majority of people just stay where they are, hardly experience any change in their job, professional career and ultimately disappear without contributing anything outstanding. They are the people from the common rung, not made of sterm material, who feel smug and satisfied with their existing position, which has become their long-time routine.

In other words, these people lack vision, are not motivated to change themselves, take for granted what comes their way and are not risk prone.

Contrary to this, there are quite a few of those who are not satisfied with things around them either in business or profession and yearn for a further healthy change which would provide them a competitive edge over their rivals.

It is from such people that there emerges a class of innovators, those who would like to introduce new ideas, new thinking, new products, new situations which are different from the existing ones.

It is ultimately from this class that there emerge those people who while employed in a comparatively low position in a business, hit at some new innovation—a new device which helps to reduce the production cost of a product or helps in marketing a new product with a promising future, something like this,—shoot into limelight through their constant dedication and hard labour.

It is through the process of their thinking and awareness of market realities that even while working they hit upon such innovation which helps to change the production strategy of the firm and gives it an edge over its rivals. And in this process these innovators climb to the top position of the firm's ladder and become indispensable.

The whole history of business is very much the history of these people who with their efforts, mental vision and persistence were able to design new products, cost saving devices, better work situations and the like which ultimately helped their firms to derive immense advantage.

It is the same story of almost all the top business firms which have gradually emerged from a small entity to the global stature with their assets fast multiplying and products gaining global competitiveness.

This is, for instance, the story of Henry Ford who has been named as businessman of the last century by the highly respectable Fortune magazine after months of research.

The magazine said Ford "was a builder of industry that transformed the very land we live on; the first to create a mass market as well as means of satisfying it as great an entrepreneur as we've ever seen. He was a kind of genius that endures."

It continues: "Ford founded the Ford Motor Co. in 1903, at the age of 40. Five years later he introduced the Model T, which remained in production until 1927 as its price fell from $ 850 to $ 290. In 1913, he adopted the moving assembly line for automobile production and drastically lowered the cost of cars."

Thus Ford was a unique innovator who for the first time put the car within the reach of a common man through drastically reducing its cost of production. This shows how Ford's mind was working, when he not only conceptualised, he also motivated his fellow workers to act accordingly and quite a few of them came out with new ideas in cost reduction, quality improvement as well as in their marketing strategy.

Ford also paid his workers the princely wage of $ 5 a day (imagine, in the early part of the last century) and in this way created a big market for his cars when workers with higher earnings could afford to buy these cars. And just imagine he had a very large work force. Thus, during the inter-war period which is considered a very dull business period, he was able to create a unique demand for his own products through his unique thinking and planning.

How creative thinking and forward planning could bring substantial reward is also borne from the example of Bill Gates, last century's superman in information technology, who at the age of 40 became the world's richest man, and prime ministers and ministers of almost all countries were only too anxious to have a meeting with him.

That shows the indispensable position that a young man has acquired. He has successfully built the largest empire of information technology—Microsoft. Bill has intense faith in the young dynamic human resources and believes that his people are the first main resource of his competitive edge.

The same is the story of quite a few business firms in Japan—a country with a humble beginning a little over a century ago has now emerged to the top global position and thus earned universal popularity. Its products are now rated the highest and command a high demand.

What is the secret for this? Foremost it is in the constant search for new technology which embodies improvement over the earlier one. Interestingly Japanese employees themselves have contributed substantially in this area; several of them have helped in introducing cost reducing and sales promoting innovations. In fact Japan is ever on the path of technological change in which quite a few of its own employees have their proud share.

If, on the other hand, a nation is just to copy what others do and hardly puts its mind on bringing new changes, it is certainly not going to be globally competitive, rather would remain a dependent nation.

This is very much true in case of our own country. Here most of our business people are just followers and feel smug and satisfied with the current functioning of business, products and marketing strategy, howsoever out of tune with the world situation. They hardly like to change the technology of production even when we have access to new technology, as they are too lazy and think that even the existing technology would serve the purpose. Thus, the mind set of most of our business men is not attuned to change, much less to develop a new technology.

Thus the lesson is clear. If we want to be globally competitive we would have to change the mind set of our business and people behind it. They should change their attitude towards business as well as technology. Surely people who are behind the existing successful global business, whether in the USA or Japan or elsewhere, are not different from our own people where they too had to struggle hard to establish themselves. Something has been behind such a dramatic transformation which has helped several of them to contribute substantially before putting their business at par with the global level.

Again we come back to Japan. For several years Japan struggled hard with borrowed technology. In fact, this nation was referred to contemptuously as a big borrower/copier who didn't have anything of its own to contribute. And Japan continued to suffer this humiliation for a long time when right up to the second world war period Japanese products were rated poor in quality compared to the western products and 'made in Japan' label signified an inferior product.

In the post-war period we find a dramatic change. No longer western nations dared to label Japanese products in a contemptuous term; rather they themselves have become anxious to learn from Japan's turnaround in technology and its superior products which excel the world over. This country today is an example of the world's top business successes.

How has this happened? Japan, during the last half a century has witnessed dramatic change in the whole process of its production, particularly in the field of technology. No longer are they copiers. They are now original manufactures with their indigenous technology itself undergoing constant change to manufacture still better products and today Japan is much ahead of other countries. It is the joint effort of both, entrepreneurs and their work team.

The whole business environment has undergone a remarkable change where lots of opportunities are offered to the workmen for being innovative in developing new and superior production processes. Even those who do not succeed are encouraged to go ahead and are given special awards for their efforts.

Thus, there has been a chain system in the development of new technology, new work systems, new products, resulting in all around prosperity.

In case India has to change, the lesson is to change its business environment. No longer should the manufacturers feel contented with the imported technology. Instead, they should encourage their own people to develop still superior technology which would bring them high rewards, make their products globally competitive and cost effective.

It is not something impossible. If Japan, China and other Asian countries have gone ahead, why not India? Thus a positive change in business environment must be brought about.

Our businessmen should also learn another lesson. That is, if they have to effectively compete globally they should no longer be dependent on the government support which in fact encourages negative attitude towards business and supports lethargy and even dependence on the administration for survival.

See how our business community has miserably failed to the challenge of foreign players after the economy was thrown open under globalisation, simply because they have been depending too much on the government support and have failed to stand on their own.

They have not encouraged their own employees, despite several of them being fine products from the country's top institutes of technology and management and other pride institutions, to affect suitable changes in the current mode of production, management and marketing, and technology particularly is yet not world class.

The result is what we are witnessing. Foreign products have completely swamped the local economy and the country is running a high balance of payments problem with bulging imports and hardly growing exports because we are not able to produce goods at world competitive costs—and how could it be with non-competitive technology and management?

Our entrepreneurs must change their work culture if they want to survive and their exports should be globally competitive.

They have thus to bring about major changes in their business ethics and environment where human resources will have to play a role similar to one played by the Japanese workmen.

It is noticed that if business changes on dynamic lines and becomes independent of government support and interference, it makes a quick change on modern lines. Here lies the secret of successful business.

SUMMING UP

Successful entrepreneurship is a complex job where it is the vision, environment and determination as well as forward looking colleagues who make the major contribution for its overall success. History is replete with such experiences.

Foremost, it is the spirit of innovation which is an essential ingredient for a successful business. It is the business leadership that emerges from such people who in turn are dedicated, committed and highly forward looking people. They create an environment of successful and lasting business.

Thus, from the efforts of these people there emerges a successful team of workers, who join hands with their leader in taking their business to its supreme heights and thus fill up the gaps which had been ignored earlier. So these entrepreneurs have an intense faith in these people.

India has to learn a lot from the experience of these people and create a class of successful entrepreneurs on the lines similar to other successful economies.

Ultimately this country has to develop its own model of entrepreneurship where an environment has to be created that helps the growth of technology and skills which are comparable with the best available.

PART II

Thoughts of Happy Life

Learn to Smile, You Will be a Happy and Successful Person

Arun was a successful student. He topped in engineering as well as MBA from leading institutes and won quite a few medals and other honours. He was rated very high for his academic worth and succeeded in finding a coveted place in a top multinational firm with a handsome salary and perks.

While Arun was so well endowed with academic gifts, as a social person however he was unsuccessful. He had a rigid attitude towards life that he found hard to change. He rarely smiled and most of the time he wore a grim look which didn't help him, rather it became a positive hindrance in his career for he turned out to be an unsuccessful negotiator with other parties as he would easily lose his cool and was never able to strike his point as successfully as his opponents did, and thus they would ultimately succeed.

This meant a positive loss to the firm he worked for and in due course its CEO would not send Arun to negotiate important deals. Thus others, though less qualified executives, gained an upper hand over Arun.

Not only this, Arun's record or behaviour with his subordinates was equally appalling. They would avoid him and hardly greeted him. Whenever they were called to his office they would use delay tactics for Arun was not the sort of boss who was pleasant to talk to.

With his sullen face he would make an unhappy presence and worse, he would treat his subordinates as an inferior lot and most of the time would behave discourteously with them, even find fault with their functioning and would get angry when any employee even committed a minor mistake. Instead of trying to put him on the right track, he would use foul language and thus the errant employee would almost be in tears.

On the social front he was equally unsuccessful. He hardly had a friend and avoided most social gatherings where he was a misfit. Even if he attended a social function, he would be a lonely person, hardly joined others in conversation, much less displaying the behaviour the occasion demanded. In short, he was a total failure as a man. He was advised by one of his colleagues to change his behaviour and attitude if he wanted to be a successful executive. "See, even after putting in so much of hard work and possessing top academic honours," he added, "you have not risen, while your colleagues, though less qualified, have moved to higher positions. You must seriously think of it, Arun."

Arun of course knew well that his rigid mental attitude and unfriendly behaviour posed a hindrance in his career, but he didn't know how to change this. In fact he found such a change to be a Herculean job. His friend advised him to join lectures delivered by an expert on "how to improve one's personality". Though initially quite reluctant, he ultimately began to attend these lectures and soon found their good impact on him.

He was advised by the expert to learn to smile, which unfortunately he had never done before and initially started practicing right from home. Though he had decided to do it with full earnestness, but he found it very tough going, particularly for a man like him. But gradually with a determined attitude, he moved out of his gloomy and unfriendly frame. He forcefully began to display a smile, which though was not natural for quite sometime. It looked to be so artificial and he himself was quite conscious of this fact. Gradually, however, with practice before the mirror as well as during his morning walks, there was an enormous improvement in his facial expression.

When, for the first time in the morning he greeted his wife with a big smile, she could hardly believe it and looked at him with great curiosity, not believing that he was the same Arun with rigid looks that she never liked and felt relieved during the time he was away from the house. Their weekends were also dull, when they hardly went out.

Surely for this lady to notice such a dramatic change in her husband's attitude was hard to believe. Gradually, Arun was able to convince his wife that he was no longer the old sulking Arun but a new Arun—smiling, happy, cooperative and fun loving.

And gradually he started displaying his new attitude towards his office colleagues and even to his juniors, as well as towards the CEO and customers. Thus there came about a big change in Arun's career, when he started treating everyone with dignity and grace, even his juniors with whom he had been highly rude in the past.

All this worked wonders. Not only Arun became a happy person, full of life, sociable, he also made a wonderful rise in his official career and soon occupied the next higher position which he had failed to earn all these years.

Thus the lesson from this is that it is not your academic degrees and qualifications that would make you a happy person and earn a big career, equally—I would say even more—important is your personality, behaviour and attitude towards life and people around. In other, words, you have to develop a positive attitude towards life and shun its negative aspects with boldness.

While some of us are naturally gifted with a smiling and happy behaviour, several of us might not be so endowed for one reason or the other. It may be due to family circumstances where the rigid attitude of the elders has been responsible in shaping our behaviour. In fact, it is in the childhood period when the foundations of human behaviour are being shaped, that there have been some unpleasant circumstances in the family or in the school career that have moulded our behaviour adversely. Though people do change later on with changed environments, but those of us who do not find such an opportunity, continue to stay in the mental mould developed from childhood.

Thus, it is very important that emphasis should be laid on the development of the child's personality, so that the child doesn't suffer as he grows. Here the role of parents is equally important. Certainly, happy family environments do have a good bearing on moulding the personality of the child.

Unfortunately in modern times under the stress of a competitive life, parents are far more concerned with the child's academic side and less on developing his personality. The result is the kind of unbalanced outcome as witnessed in the case of Arun who, though a very successful scholar, was a big failure as a human being.

Thus parents while looking into the future of their children would have to be careful to ensure that they do not pull children too far towards academic life, much at the cost of developing the child's overall personality or human side.

It is equally important that the business sector should not be all the while concerned with maximizing profit earning aspect, it should be equally concerned with developing the human side and regular programmes are organised for exposing their employees towards personality development and exposure to good public relations which would not only benefit the employees but would equally benefit their business.

See how even a small exposure to human side through lectures delivered by an expert as well as subsequent interaction brought about a remarkable change in the personality of Arun. In fact it changed his entire outlook on life and brought him to the road of success.

People often ask how they should start this process of change when they have never done it before. Though there is no easy answer to this but then it is not difficult either. This calls, first of all, for a determined effort to change your rigid attitude towards life, like Arun did, and secondly, once the new habit has been acquired one should not look back. Even Arun, as we have seen above, had to face this problem but then he changed himself to a large extent and stayed with the change later, never letting his old negative mood to return.

Thus, once you are determined to change your rigid attitude you can certainly make it.

There is nothing like age bar in changing your attitude towards life. Remember the story of Grandma Moses, who belonged to a poor American family and had to struggle throughout her life.

After the death of her husband she was determined to become a top artist, and she had taken this pledge when she was 78, at an age when most of us start looking towards the grave. But she did change the course of her life.

She died at the age of 101, by which time her fame had travelled far and wide. It is said that at an exhibition of her works, as many as one lakh visitors had come. A firm sold more than 35 million greeting cards of Moses in 10 years. Her paintings were highly refreshing to behold. Her death was widely reported in the world press.

Moses' story tells us how with perseverance, effort, zeal, sense of enterprise and vision, you could start any activity at any age and reach the top position. You could even add several healthy years to your life, through commitment to your new enterprise. Possibly the secret behind Grandma's staying satisfied, happy and in good health for nearly two and a half decades after she had reached the age of 78, was her adopting a new mission in life from which she derived high personal satisfaction, pleasure and fame.

So age stands no bar in your moving into the lane of fame provided you have cultivated a pleasant personality and stuck to your life's mission with sturdy commitment and grace. The instance of Grandma Moses, who despite her poverty and lifelong struggle against several hardships, achieved fame, amply bears it. If she could do it, you could as well.

Why Lose Your Cool? Become a Man of Achievement

For a successful life, mental coolness occupies a very significant place. In fact, it can well be termed as the most significant factor, for it is aptly said that through mental coolness you can build up the most successful life career, whether in business or profession or even in public life, where it is the mental coolness that invariably wins. For arriving at momentous decisions, it is again the mental coolness that would work wonders. Equally in international diplomacy, nothing would succeed more than the decision made under such coolness. Even when a classroom lecture is delivered or speech is made in public, it is again the maintenance of mental coolness that would help both in the deliverance as well as its acceptance by the listeners.

Thus mental coolness is a wonderful gift of Nature, and yet how often we miss this coolness and are surrounded by grey feelings which let us down and create an environment far from our liking. In other words, we often miserably fail to be worldly wise and miss opportunities that knock at our door.

And when we wake up it is too late. Possibly at that time, in a flash of awareness we resolve to do better next time. But then when this time again comes we often behave no better and get back to our old negative habits and allow the mind to wander about aimlessly in the dark lanes of life. Thus again our mind is stuck deep in negative behaviour and it stubbornly refuses to be disciplined.

Surely there is something wrong with those of us who have lagged behind in the battle of life compared to those who have become successful. Has Nature endowed them differently compared with laggards? How could that be for Nature never discriminates? It offers equal opportunities to its creatures. It is a different matter that some of us are able to exploit the opportunity favourably while others fail.

So don't blame Nature or your bad luck. There is nothing of this sort. The truth is we have ourselves failed to tap our inner vision to the level needed for winning success in our mission. What are these steps needed which would help to turn our negative feelings to positive success?

While going through the success stories of those who have created for themselves a mature place in history, we get a close glimpse of their greatness. While they too were ordinary folks like us, but then it was their achievement that made them outstanding, and rise above others. Some common traits behind their greatness are as under:

(a) Once having decided to achieve a mission, howsoever difficult, they never gave up even in the face of heavy odds. They remained committed to their goal and never lost its sight, rather every time improved their sights to have even more clear vision. (Both these qualities of clarity of goal and a cool disposition to achieve it, are inter-connected. It is the cool disposition of mind that would help you to build clarity of goal and thus will not lead you into a wrong direction).

(b) These achievers had never displayed any sense of pride in their achievement, accepted criticism far more than praise for their recognition. Thus, avoid displaying a feeling of pride—much less of haughtiness—on your achievement. Acknowledge the good wishes of others and once on the right path, don't falter subsequently. Recognition of your achievement could even encourage rivalry and create hurdles in your path of righteousness which should be faced boldly by further improving your performance. Thus any challenge should be accepted and converted into positive action. In other words, your attitude towards thinking should be positive, and never sullied by negative behaviour.

All these qualities centre around the determination to achieve the goal set before you, even facing hardships and adopting a fearless and positive attitude. Above all, it is the clear and cool mental attitude which would help to achieve the goal which is much beyond your personal interest.

Just look at the example of Mahatma Gandhi who continues to be the most respected leader of this country and is well known the world over. He was an ordinary individual like you and me but it was his deeds, persistent efforts to achieve the goals like non-violence and Ahimsa, for which he fought through the major part of his 78 years of worldly existence, that made him rise much above others and brought universal recognition and appreciation for his missions.

People in millions the world over appreciated his peaceful mode of fighting against the worst kind of tyranny in the society, to bring peace and social justice. Thus, after his long struggle and determination towards his goal against all odds, he could contribute enormously in creating a feeling among the British masters that time had come when they should quit and leave the country gracefully and with dignity, without shedding blood—it was a different thing that a lot of blood had been shed between Hindus and Muslims while migrating from one country to another.

Mahatma Gandhi has trailed a lesson for us and there could not be a better example of a great person. In fact, his deeds and writings inspire all of us and one could find answers to our own failings in the life teachings of the Mahatma.

Take another example of Thomas Alva Edison, the world's greatest inventor whose singular achievement was to vanish darkness from the world through the invention of the electric bulb. That great inventor proved the high benefit of this invention as now people could work at night time and thus life became far easier, safer and comfortable.

And yet this man hardly had any successful schooling. The story goes that his teacher was so disgusted with him that soon after his admission in school, had sent a note to his mother that her son was retarded and dullard and should be withdrawn from the school. Of course his mother took this challenge and began to teach him at home. He was hard of listening.

That was Edison who proved to be a man of great vision and hard work who could work in a laboratory almost for the whole day and night and hardly slept for three/four hours and that too generally in the lab.

He had as many as 1093 patents registered in his name. Besides electric bulb, he has several other inventions to his credit like gramophone, motion picture camera, projector, storage battery, electric pen, advanced telegraph system, electricity generation, dictating machine, a new cement-making process—it is said that much of the cement used in the construction of Panama Canal was from his factory, and several others. He was a versatile genius who could concentrate on several projects simultaneously.

He died in 1931 at the age of 84 and as a mark of respect to his memory, lights were dimmed all over the country. That is the story of his rise from rags to riches through his sheer hard work, patience, extraordinary vision and inborn intelligence, and above all the long peace of mind he enjoyed which developed his high concentrating powers.

More recently we have the story of Jack Kilburn—the inventor of microchip, who was also awarded the Nobel Prize

in Physics along with another scientist who also worked on a similar field. The invention by Kilburn has virtually changed the daily life of people. Like Edison he too has achieved a unique place among the achievers and also has five dozen patents registered in his name. And like Edison again his portrait hangs next to his in the National Inventors Hall of Fame.

Born in 1923 he had a great ambition to take up the Degree of Bachelor in Electrical Engineering from MIT. In 1941 after a long train journey from his home town he had appeared for the entrance test, but failed to make it by just three marks. He returned home highly disgusted but didn't give up his courage. He joined the army during World War II and was posted on a tea plantation in North East India.

After the war he joined the University of Illinois and in 1947 obtained the Degree of Electrical Engineering. It was only in his mid-thirties, when he happened to join a job at the semi-conductor research lab at Texas Instruments Headquarters in Dallas, that he was able to develop his invention of microchip.

During the 1950s, electric circuit designs were growing complex and called for miles and miles of wires and millions and millions of soldered connections. Kilburn was able to develop an electric design that solved this complex 'interconnections problem'.

After thoughtful planning, thinking and designing he ultimately came out with this solution and thus was born the invention of microchip which has enabled the elimination of wires connecting the various elements of electric circuits. In his invention, no wires were required and no soldering was needed for making electrical connections. "In this way, a huge number of components could be compressed into a tiny space. Even a whole computer circuit can be constructed on a chip of the size of a baby's finger nail by using this technique."

Such a path-breaking development was the result of intense thinking, several hours of concentration on a single pursuit that if all the elements of a circuit could be made of the same material (i.e. silicon) then all these could be carved into a single slice of that material. The total development that followed after such long thinking, was primarily responsible for the invention of the microchip (or a little chip of silicon).

This invention has revolutionised several other areas: "Now electronic devices such as high speed computers, powerful enough to run worldwide communication network or steer rockets to the moon have already been fabricated using Kilburn's ideas. In the development of the whole area of information technology—personal computers, mobile phones and internet space programmes, the tiny silicon chip occupies the central place."

Thus this man's vision, hard work in the lab and a sense of perfection have tremendously changed the present day life. This shows how consistent dedication with single mind can help one in achieving the cherished goal.

Similar has been the story of other great people who have left behind lasting impressions. Certainly reading the biographies of these people provides great inspiration for turning our failures into success stories through the subtle approach followed by these seers.

To repeat, these are the qualities for turning one's failures into success:

Have a clear goal before you.

Be persistent in achieving it.

Don't let impediments dishearten you in achieving your cherished dream. Rather, these impediments should spur your effort and performance further.

Don't be overwhelmed with exuberance and be least haughty at your success in case success knocks at your door. Be humble in its acceptance, encourage healthy criticisms and listen to these with care, rather than ignore them in a flush of joy on your success.

Learn to Win Through Determination

Krishna (not real name) met with a major accident when his left leg was hit by a speeding scooter and there were multiple injuries. A kind person—who as the later experience showed was an opportunist and fake sympathiser—called a 3-wheeler and as Krishna was completely immobilized and could not walk, he was bodily lifted by the gentleman and put into the vehicle and driven to the nearby government hospital, where again this gentleman put Krishna on a wheel chair—of course payment for the vehicle was made by Krishna. Later, he took him to the emergency counter, helped him to fill in the admission form, then took him to the X-Ray room where an X-Ray of the injured portion was taken, and all this time the gentleman kept waiting like a dutiful family member.

While waiting for the X-Ray result, the gentleman put Krishna back on the wheel chair and took him to the corridor where he could relax. He kept on enquiring about his pain and whether he needed anything. Krishna thought of informing a close relative about this accident and gave his phone number to the gentleman who promised to do the needful and return soon. Though Krishna had been apprehensive, the gentleman returned soon and also confirmed that the message had been delivered to the relative who would be visiting the hospital soon.

When the X-Ray film was ready, the doctor informed Krishna about the multiple injuries suffered by him and that his left leg would be put under plaster which signaled three months minimum confinement to bed and this could be even longer considering Krishna's advanced age.

Krishna was very much upset for he was very active, and a committed scholar who had a busy schedule of work already planned. Now in view of this development, all this had been disturbed. After his leg was wrapped in plaster he was completely immobilized. Meanwhile he had handed over his entire belongings including his office portfolio which carried important documents, telephone diary, even all the cash he had and his identity card, to the gentleman who had won his full confidence.

Soon on some excuse the gentleman went outside telling Krishna he would be back soon and suggested that he left the latter's belongings with him. But Krishna thought these would be more safe with him than being left where several people were around.

Once gone the gentleman never returned. Krishna waited for him with apprehensive feelings, for if he didn't turn up Krishna would be totally broke, not even having his warm clothes which he had removed while the plaster was put on the injured leg. Also, he didn't have a single penny and his diary which contained phone numbers. Thus he was in great distress and told his story of misery to the attending doctor who was completely surprised for he never thought that the gentleman was a complete stranger.

There was a long wait and no trace of the rascal who after winning the confidence of Krishna and knowing that the latter was completely immobilised after the plaster, found a good opportunity to disappear with all the belongings and cash. Krishna, with much difficulty was able to recall from memory the phone number of one of his friends and requested the doctor to call that number hoping that some help would be available even at that odd time in winter.

Luckily his friend could be contacted and he visited Krishna and the latter requested him to hire a taxi for him to his home town the next morning.

That was done and next day Krishna was with his family who were surprised to see him in that condition. However, once at home there was no problem. Things could be managed well.

But Krishna was determined to get back to the driver's seat at the earliest possible and start attending to his busy schedule. The idea of staying in bed for three months or even more worried him and sent feelings of frustration. Much of his thinking was now concentrated on how to cut short this period of forced confinement and be active and busy like before.

And his determined attitude did pay a good return. Within a period of two and a half months he was able to get back to his earlier active life.

Thus Krishna, with sheer determination and disciplined life was able to conquer his handicap. The lesson from this is that in case one is determined and not overpowered by the adverse impact of such a disturbed situation, as well as not resigned to his fate and keeps his spirits high, there is every chance of his achieving the goal set before him and thus turn the adverse situation into a positive one.

CONQUERING LIFE-LONG PHYSICAL HANDICAP

How even a life-long physical handicap can't only be conquered, even be trained for reaching the highest—possible achievement, becomes obvious from the story of Wilma Rudolph, narrated by Shiv Khera, the famous management Guru, in his book 'You Can Win'. Born in a poor house in Tennessee (USA), she suffered double pneumonia with scarlet fever at the age of 4 years, which left her paralysed with polio and forced her to wear braces and doctors declared she would not be able to walk.

However her mother strengthened her nerves saying that with determination and faith in God she could achieve anything. And that she did. Slowly and steadily she started her journey on the earth again, thus proving the doctors' predicament wrong. Not only this, she was even determined to become the world's fastest track woman in the Olympics, which looked impossible to be fulfilled for a girl who was even forbidden to walk on earth. But then she was quite determined and began her practice in earnest. Of course she faced failures a number of times, but slowly improved her grades using each failure as a stick to try and try again.

Ultimately her persistence and dogged determination did pay rich rewards when her dream was fulfilled in the 1960 Olympics where she emerged the fastest racing woman on this earth and won a record three gold medals in races defeating the world's known athlete Jutta Heine who had never been beaten earlier. It was indeed a miracle that a one-time totally handicapped woman who was written off by the medical experts that she would not be able to walk on this earth, became the fastest runner defeating even the unbeatable athlete with global repute.

The lesson from Wilma Rudolph's story is that with a determined mind and will power, even the most serious handicap could not only be conquered, it could even be turned into achieving the most coveted honour. Thus it depends on the way you look at even your most serious handicap. Instead of depending on others for the rest of your life and feeling frustrated even to the extent that life is a big burden and hardly worth living, you could, with determination and proper encouragement convert it into a very happy and fruitful experience.

Look at Wilma Rudolph. Had she not used her determination to build up her inner strength, she would have been condemned to a life-long handicapped existence, dependent on others. She decided not to bow down to such a life and instead turned her handicap to become the world's fastest runner on earth.

It is also important that in this fight against a serious handicap, positive encouragement should be forthcoming from people who matter. In the case of Rudolph, it was her mother who constantly encouraged her and kindled her inner strength to fight against such a serious handicap as well as saw to it that she got the best training to fulfil her dream.

So, positive attitude of a handicapped person can be developed by words of encouragement and proper guidance by those who sincerely mean them, and are prepared to invest their time and energy to help the victim. On the other hand, false display of sympathy and pity towards the victim, would only cause damage. Such people should be shown the door and the victim should avoid them.

THOSE WHO ARE TERMINALLY ILL

There are people who are declared terminally ill as there is no hope for their treatment and thus they have to stay life-long with such an ailment. These people become quite conscious of this fact and several of them suffer frequently unbearable pain and wish they were put to a permanent end.

However, even here those people who are determined would not waste their time brooding over their ailment, rather they would spend their time of earthly existence on one or the other useful activity, depending on the nature of their ailment.

Recently Khushwant Singh, the famous columnist, had narrated the story of his cousin married to a man who was a scholar but was hit by a disease for which there was no cure, and he knew well that his days were numbered. Instead of brooding and feeling miserable waiting for the knock of death, he utilised this period to complete his pending research work. He confined himself wholly to his room and nobody was permitted to disturb him.

He worked hard to finish his assignments before he died. This shows how even for a person terminally ill, it is possible to devote the available time for undertaking productive activity and in this way, not only to make on effective use of the time available forgetting personal pains and adverse mental feelings, it also helps the victim to leave behind his academic contribution for the posterity.

Thus the running lesson from all the above situations is that it is ultimately determination and will power as well as proper guidance and encouragement from others that would help to overcome any handicap or disease in the best possible manner.

Road to a Positive Life

While there is no set rule to a happy life since much would depend upon an individual's circumstances, upbringing, problems and constraints, nevertheless there are some basic rules that would help to promote a happy and prosperous living.

Interestingly, the foremost factor here is that one should be able to understand himself well and also develop a sincere attachment for himself, his body and mind, and work culture. It is often observed that most distressful people are those who have unfortunately neglected themselves, have hardly bothered for their own welfare and denied the needs that their self cried for. It's not that one has to be an introvert. It simply means that one has to take sufficient care of himself, develop attachment and love for himself.

After all if one's own self is neglected, it becomes the root cause of body degeneration. Most diseases that overtake our system are caused by our own neglect because we have given less importance to our own system and far more to other external elements, which if pushed too far might become the cause of our own suffering.

For instance, if we have been less vigilant of our body system and mental attitude, we might be overtaken by some external factor that starts weighing more heavily on us, leading to all sorts of disturbances of both body and mind, and if allowed to persist for too long might become difficult to root out; and ultimately weigh our system to such an extent that the end result is some form of depression.

Surely before this stage sets in, there is need to avoid the basic causative factor for such an occurrence. Here it is crystal clear that we have neglected our own system, forgotten to develop ourselves and all the love that a healthy body and mind needs.

Thus for most sufferings that follow subsequently and which might be highly physically and mentally painstaking, the beginning is made when we forget to have sufficient care and love for ourselves. Why not think that we mean something to the society and that we have been born with some mission and that we have to preserve ourselves in the perfect possible state to achieve this goal.

Such a feeling would bring in us the needed inner strength and help us towards our goal. For instance, help us to plan better our daily schedule as well as life system.

Depression in such a life style becomes a forgotten chapter. Rather one is endeared with enough strength to fight it out easily even if it were to occur.

The focal point is that the primary role of life should be to build the inner strength which is best done by developing understanding with oneself and loving life, and its preservation in sound condition. Thus, loving and caring oneself should get priority over other things. Once it is achieved, it would also help to achieve several other things in life.

LOVE THY NEIGHBOUR

The second rule for a happy life is to develop a friendly attitude with neighbours who are next door and with whom you are going to come in contact quite often. Otherwise too one would not feel happy by ignoring neighbours and by thinking that no useful purpose would be served by being in close contact with them even when they look forward to it. Such an indifferent attitude would lead us nowhere, rather it might become the cause for the loss of our mental peace and thus not augur well in the long-run.

It is often seen that close relatives in the neighbourhood find themselves at loggerheads, not prepared to forge good relations with one another. In some houses, two brothers' families might seldom communicate with each other, rather even find excuses to pull each other down and unpleasant brawls might be often raked up. The situation often worsens when ladies start dominating the families. Thus even in the case when two brothers might like to have good relations, the same is jeopardized by the unpleasant situation pitched up by ladies or even by children.

On the other hand, if one were to think of the positive side of such a neighbourhood, one would realise that it can turn into an ideal situation where not only good social life of mutual interest would emerge, even difficult situations that families are likely to face would be got over with comparative ease. For instance, in times of emergencies, accidents, harassment and other ugly situations, peaceful coexistence of two families would bring about great relief and timely assistance, which would be lost when families are at loggerheads.

Of course, certain healthy norms of such a relationship should also be well respected by both the families. For instance, excessive interference in the affairs of their families should be avoided. Children in particular should be disciplined. Thus a healthy neighbourly relationship should be built which would definitely be a source of mutual happiness and encouragement. This would also help senior members to find peace which they do need at this age.

SOCIAL LIFE

It is said that man is a social being and for leading a healthy life it is very essential that he should develop social contact, have sincere and lasting friendship with persons he could trust and discuss matters of mutual interest as well as share each other's company during get together, visits to parks and participations in public programmes. To cut down isolation, the company of close friends of the same age group would be appreciated.

Often it is also true that in case you have led an isolated life during your active years and hardly encouraged any lasting friendship or social contact, you are likely to suffer more in your advanced age than those who have been socially active. The latter would face far less difficulty in planning their idle time in old age.

So the lesson is clear. Develop good relations with people who are close to you in case you have not done it already. It is not that you must have the company of those people who are professionally close. Others might even prove more helpful. The point is to develop friendship with other persons who are intellectually close to you, as this would also provide an opportunity to share thoughts on mutual experiences.

Thus a good social life is an essential element of healthy living. If not already existing, make your best attempts to become an active partner of such an environment.

HELP OTHERS

You would derive immense satisfaction in helping others—those who are less fortunate than you. You will not have to go far for this. Right near you, you will find someone needing help in one form or the other. Sometimes even a word of cheer for one in difficulty could bring great relief to the sufferer.

Don't close your eyes in the face of someone needing your help. May be your close relative is nailed down with some handicap and unable to attend to daily routines. You will only understand the sufferer's problem by putting yourself in her/ his position. That would make you realise how harsh life is and how the person is utterly helpless.

The great lady, Mother Teresa, who spent her entire life in helping the suffering humanity in Calcutta and virtually earned the name of "Angel of the poor and sufferers," was deeply touched when she saw a dying beggar on the road side. She brought him to her place and did what she could to relieve his suffering so that the person faced his last days with dignity. She was a living symbol of help to the sufferers and we must cultivate such a spirit at least for helping those who need assistance in the family or in the neighbourhood.

While busy with our own daily chores we might not find time, but surely on weekends and holidays we should snatch time for this. Even during daily routine life, if one wishes one can find time, though brief, for such a noble cause.

In well to do families, young ladies who devote a good part of time to club activities and kitty parties, could as well think of rendering such help. In fact they could form a group among themselves and adopt some poor area for rendering any positive help, may be spreading literacy, encouraging cleanliness, improving sanitation, helping in safe drinking water and the like—all these will do a lot of good to the ignorant members and improve their lot. For these activities, well off ladies should normally face no monetary problem, as being well connected socially they could also get such help from other sources—even pull up the local administration and see that its employees perform their routine duties well and with regularity, which would help to improve the surroundings of the poor people's colonies.

Unfortunately it is the lack of awareness among the poor which is the root cause behind their suffering. Thus they will have to be made aware of the benefits of healthy and clean living and planned families. Here education and women empowerment in particular have been the basic tools for bringing about suitable change. This task could be achieved by ladies from well to do families.

Of course, it does not mean that these ladies would have to give up their present social life. Not at all. They will have to balance their time between the club life and helping the needy. In fact they would soon realise that helping the needy is even more important because here it is the unfortunate members, the deprived sections of the country who stand to benefit from such benevolence. They will earn their deep gratitude.

Also retired people in particular who feel bored of their long hours of idleness could learn a suitable lesson from the life of Col. J.C. Kapoor, a Chandigarh resident, who after retirement as an army medical officer has not been idle at all. In fact like an active army personnel he has been spending long hours in the service of the poor in their huts in Chandigarh's slum area, looking after their diverse needs.

Observations about him are: "Today this rugged, bearded, infantry man has become an excellent allround paramedic and is the honorary chief administrator of eight charitable health-care projects being run in and around Chandigarh in slum and rural areas."

Col. Kapoor doesn't mind doing any odd job so long as it is in the interest of poor people, like sweeping the ambulances, cleaning the bottles and boiling the syringes; wiping the faces of urchins and exhorting the mothers on health, hygiene and family planning. He has even installed improved smokeless Chullhas in practically every Jhugee and even paid for these! He is aptly called "the Saint of Slums".

Let our senior citizens who spend idle hours in the four wall of their houses and find one or other fault in each family member, learn from this young man in his seventies and start doing some constructive activity which would help others—the more needy, as well as themselves by keeping well occupied in social service.

Thus, helping others whether within the family or outside should form an integral part of your life's agenda. This will not only help to spend your spare time productively, it would also provide you with high personal satisfaction.

DEVELOP SOME HOBBY

Have you cultivated any hobby in life? Any? Doesn't matter which, so long as it gives you personal satisfaction and helps you to spend good time. A good hobby is also the best means to spend one's long hours usefully. It is often a lonely person, whose number with advancement in age has been rising, that needs to develop one or the other hobby to keep himself away from the idle mind which could turn into a devil's workshop. In case such a person has not picked up any hobby, he need not despair. One could pick up this even in the late stage. You must know your aptitude, may be listening to music (classical or light), may be playing some instrument, may be watching a particular programme on television, may be gardening, may be outdoor walks, etc.

Thus you will have to know where you find yourself most comfortable. It may not be one single hobby, may be a few. You will have to make up your mind and start doing some constructive activity to keep yourself usefully engaged. And once decided, stick to your schedule. That way you will derive the maximum satisfaction. By wavering or being indecisive, you will miss the real fun in life and might even start experiencing the weight of loneliness.

Thus the best way to shun loneliness is to keep yourself busy with some sort of hobby where age has no bar. Remember the celebrated playwright George Bernard Shaw, who died at the age of 97, started learning more difficult forms of ball room dance at an age of 70 and he did it well. He was a lively person who had a well-developed schedule of work and recreation. You could follow his example.

GUIDELINES

The following guidelines would help you to lead a purposeful and positive life:

First, try to understand yourself well and don't ignore yourself, for such ignorance could lead to lose your interest in yourself and on your welfare, which could lead to harmful consequences.

Second, love your surroundings, which would provide you with maximum satisfaction. Here you should be an active partner and find time to improve them.

Third, be social and friendly with your neighbours. None could be more close to you than neighbours. So develop healthy and fruitful neighbourly relations.

Fourth, find time to help the needy persons. One may be a member of your own family. Snatch time even when you have a busy schedule, to help them—even just speak a word of cheer which would give you personal satisfaction as well as help the sufferer.

Fifth, develop friendship with some like-minded persons, which would stand you in good stead later in life.

Sixth, learn to make the best use of your retirement. To keep busy, either get involved in some social activity or else develop some useful hobby. This will keep you away from idleness which is the biggest curse especially in old age.

Seventh, young ladies in well to do families could become torchbearers in helping the poor. They should take the lead.

PART III

Marriage Bliss, Children and Family Values

Mantras of a Successful Married Life

Marriage is described variously. It is said to be a lasting union between two members of opposite sex. It is a convenient relationship for procreation. Others say, marriage is a license for sex indulgence. Still others add, marriage is a convenient guard against extra-marital relation, and so on. As many people, as many views.

But all these miss the real essence of marriage. It goes far beyond sex, far beyond procreation, far beyond social license for sexual orgies or a convenient guard against extra-marital indulgence. It is of course a lasting (licensed) union between the two members of opposite sex. But then for what purpose? This union is for promoting mutual happiness, welfare as well as bringing sobriety and balance in daily life and thus make life more purposeful, more meaningful.

Before we take up this, let us look closely into the prevailing notions about marriage, as mentioned above. Here the most widely prevalent notion is that marriage is a big license for indulgence in sex. Consequently, some let loose their sexual orgies to the maximum extent. Particularly here it is the male chauvinism that comes to the fore when the man thinks that it is his birth right to have it as often as he desires.

How about the convenience of the partner? That's often brushed aside. Thus a woman becomes a mere tool for satisfying the lust of the male partner. It is not that it is among the poor members alone. But it is very much the case even among the better off members who in fact have far more access to privacy than less privileged members, when a large number of members are huddled together in a small place.

Thus often less fortunate members knowing their limitations would often behave in a more restrained manner than their counterparts from better off families.

Unfortunately, despite social progress, quite a few marriages degenerate into this sort of relationship, where it is often the male members who would forget to discipline their sex. Women, biologically also, have more control over their sexual life and behave in a more restrained manner. But when it comes to male domination or influence she is helpless.

Little surprise that such a situation may sooner or later lead to cracks in the married life when it is again the male partner who may start behaving irresponsibly, subject his wife to physical torture and other humiliation in case she doesn't respond favourable to his overtures.

In case this situation persists, the woman may become a physical wreck or psychological case which would be a good opportunity for some male members to get rid of such a partner since his mind starts functioning on the destructive side. Often other members in the family also cooperate as they feel that a new female member would mean additional wealth.

We often ignore such a situation because it does not surface in the open while engrossed with the so called dowry deaths. It is true that while inadequate dowry, not to the expectations of the family members, might turn out to be the principal factor behind bride torture and burning, at the same time we can't ignore the sex maniac attitude of the male member that might well turn out to be a major factor behind such a situation.

Simultaneously it might not always be the fault of the male member alone. Even some female partners might behave in an irresponsible and callous manner, making the life of the male partner quite difficult. But then these cases are rare. Thus the fault by and large is among the male members.

Behind such irresponsible sexual behaviour there is generally considerable ignorance about sex education among young people. When they start married life with wrong notions, it can hardly be peaceful and happy afterwards. It is likely to turn into a problematic one, giving rise to a number of unhealthy fall outs. Thus the very purpose of marriage leading to a blissful life would be lost.

INPUTS FOR SUCCESSFUL MARRIAGE

Thus to make marriage a success, we have to have some minimum norms. These are the major norms or inputs for a successful married life:

The first and foremost norm for such marriage is the cultivation of mutual understanding between the two partners. It is very important that for a successful marriage both partners appreciate each other's point of view and not try to dominate over one another. When tension is let loose even on a small issue, the situation would certainly not be conducive for happy living.

This should be avoided. In fact, mistakes are a part of life and can be committed by anybody. The line of wisdom is that it should be ignored as far as possible or diplomatically tackled so that the other partner does not feel embarrassed or take it too seriously. It is very likely that once made conscious the other partner would try to avoid making such a mistake next time.

Before marriage, both the partners are generally exposed to different environments. It is rarely that they may have experienced similar environments and enjoyed identical habits and thinking. If this point is well appreciated, the occasion for friction, when one partner does something not to the liking of the other, would be minimized. Normally no partner would go to the other extreme. But even when such an occasion arises it is better to tackle it with care and thoughtfulness, rather than to lose temper. This only helps to complicate the situation and does not bring about any acceptable solution.

(1) Thus the first rule for leading a smooth married life is that both the partners should try to understand each other and gradually adjust to a course of life that is mutually convenient and not impose one's views or behaviour over the other.

There is usually the feeling of hurt which comes in the way of compromise, when things have drifted to an unpleasant pitch. At that stage, one's withdrawing from the scene or getting involved in some alternative activity, though not an easy course, would be of help. Even if the occasion demands one's apology, one should have the grace to tender it which would be the best way out. In fact, what harm is there if a person who has committed the mistake owns it?

(2) Thus the second rule for a happy marriage is that a member who has committed some wrong should have the grace to own it after it has been discovered.

PROBLEMS OF WORKING COUPLES

These days most couples are working, which creates its own problems that need to be sorted out carefully. In case couples are in the same profession, things may become little easier, for they could plan their daily routine more conveniently, which would be a little difficult if they happen to be in different professions.

But either way, unless there is mutual understanding things could go wrong. Thus, planning the day when both members are on the jobs should not be left to chance but discussed and thought out well so that children in particular do not suffer.

In case the working couple has some senior lady member in the family, she could be of help particularly in housekeeping and looking after children since it is no longer safe to keep the house in the care of a servant or lock it up.

But with nuclear family becoming the norm these days, most couples are left to manage things for themselves and they will have to adjust to such a life, where the house insurance will provide the ideal solution. While children could be left in a creche and picked up at a convenient time, the situation becomes little difficult in the case of grown up children who have to be properly guided and cared for, especially so in the case of daughters.

Parents must not ignore such a situation and see that they take adequate care of grown up children, lest they fall into bad society. It is important that there is a close family interaction about the daily activities of their children with parents, say when they gather together to watch a television programme or at dinner time. These meetings held under cordial family atmosphere would not only help the children to appreciate that their parents are very much concerned about their welfare, it would also help to tackle anything going wrong. Children would also not hesitate to discuss their matters when their parents are in an understanding and friendly mood.

Parents should themselves at times visit the institutions where the children are studying and discuss their progress with the teacher's concerned, as well as ensure that they are not on an errant path. If they are, it could be found out at an early stage and thus help in taking up remedial steps.

It is also quite important that children have a change of environment and if weekends are properly planned, these would have a very desirable effect in wooing over the children's confidence and thus keeping them away from bad society which offers a lot of temptation to innocent children. This is all the more important for the working couple where normally they do not have much time for the care of their children.

Thus, weekend picnics or visits would provide a good opportunity for relaxation to the family as well as seeing new places sometimes. In this way children would be usefully engaged and not think of following wrong paths. In fact if such programmes become a regular feature, children would shun away from any unhealthy temptation.

(3) Thus the third rule for a happy married life is that parents should take a keen interest in the welfare of their children and not leave them alone or in the care of educational institutions which is no substitute for parental care.

JOINT FAMILY

We have not yet discarded the institution of joint family. In fact quite a number of families continue to live jointly, though the concept of joint family itself is undergoing considerable change. No longer does it mean a large family of the earlier days, but a modest joint family with few close members like parents, brothers and the like.

And it is also observed that quite a number of young couples still love to stay in such a joint family. Of course, it may look odd for the young daughter-in-law after she enters this household, where she has to adjust to the mood of its members.

But then much will depend on her attitude towards such a situation and how she adjusts. Her husband could also play an important role. Often mother-in-laws are painted differently, but unfortunately the positive role played by a mother-in-law in adjusting to such a situation is rarely brought to the fore. There are still a large number of them who see to it that daughter-in-laws are quite comfortable and treat them like their own daughters.

It is equally important that a daughter-in-law should also have an open understanding attitude towards the family of her husband. If this attitude is there, life would be quite smooth.

One of the major advantages of the joint family is that in case both members are working, they could just walk to their work places without bothering about anything, no locking of the house, no worry about children, no visits to creche. Even their food problem would be greatly solved in a joint family. In fact life becomes a lot smooth in a happy joint family where the couple can enjoy a carefree life, provided they behave like responsible members of the joint family.

(4) Thus the fourth rule of a happy married life is to make the best of the joint family household, if the couple is fortunate to have one. There could be no better opportunity for them.

SEX LIFE

A very significant part of married life—perhaps the most significant—is sex, which unfortunately is not discussed and often one may have wrong notions about it. Thus, one of the major prerequisites of a healthy married life is to understand well its sexual part. It is unfortunate that sex education has never found an honourable place in either schools or colleges.

It is something like taboo, not fit for open discussion. There is a feeling that society must keep it as a closely guarded secret and let couples learn their lessons about it only after marriage. Thus any discussion about it before marriage is not sacred. This is sacrilege, unholy—all sorts of funny notions.

No surprise that with such an attitude about sex education, couples are kept in the dark about it even after their wedding. They might be facing problems of adjustment, with little opportunity to share their peculiar problems with others.

Certainly to avoid occurrence of such a situation, and even otherwise to avoid falling into wrong ways, it is important that sex education is made an integral part of the educational system. There are good books on sex available which are mostly by western authors, to help provide a healthy guide to sexual life. If the couple had read these books, they would derive more pleasure from their sexual life.

There is little to deny that sex is the most important part of married life. It is a natural source of healthy body and mind. In fact it has been seen that most successful people are those who have been happily married.

But sex also has its other side in case it is not appropriately indulged. Thus, there has to be proper understanding about it among both the partners before its indulgence. Some members may be in an awful haste and without understanding the mood of their partners, or preparing them well for it, would start indulging. The result is dissatisfaction on both sides.

Especially females would not like such behaviour and in case often repeated, they would start developing hatred towards their male partners and even stop obliging their husbands.

So once the initial stage of sexual life has been disturbed, it becomes difficult to repair it subsequently.

Then there are those who believe in over-indulgence in sex, which is not a healthy feature, and is likened to over-indulgence in food with equally worse consequence. Nature has its own laws and wants human beings to exercise reasonable restraint on sexual life and not indulge it in an unrestrained manner which can harm both the partners.

There is also a wrong notion that it is the indulgence in sex that is the only salvation of a married life. Though sex is an important part of it but then married life does not end here. Thus, it has to be simultaneously supplemented by other non-sexual inputs. For instance, care and affection that one gives to his partner is equally important for a healthy life.

Here, acts that make your partner lessen the body tension that he/she may be suffering from or make him/her sleep comfortably or other caressing acts, could prove highly productive in married life. Thus one should also learn to move beyond sex to make life a happy and lasting experience.

(5) Thus the next rule of a happy married life is to lead a balanced sexual life to derive the best out of it.

AVOID NAGGING

As said, it is not that married life is always smooth. Certainly when two human beings are face to face, some differences, some problems are bound to arise. Further, it is not that the fault always lies with men. It could as well be with women. Here one of the major tragedies is that quite a few women suffer from the habit of nagging, complaining and criticizing their husbands, which the latter would not appreciate, particularly when the nagging habit persists for too long. In such an extreme stage, it might even end in breaking the contract of marriage itself or some other unpleasant consequences.

How such nagging habit has ended in tragic consequences is revealed from the life history of two of the world's great personalities, Leo Tolstoy and Abraham Lincoln. The former was Russia's biggest writer and the latter the most popular president of the USA. Both were unfortunate to have married spouses who brought about their almost total ruin.

Leo Tolstoy was so much disturbed by the constant nagging of his wife for years that he could no longer bear it and ultimately fled from her when he was around 82. A few days later he died of pneumonia at a railway station and his dying request was that his wife should not be permitted to come into his presence.

Equally tragic was the married life of Abraham Lincoln who for nearly a quarter of century had to suffer the antics of his nagging wife who would even grow violent at times. It was the greatest tragedy of his life and he would avoid his wife's presence as much as was possible. They never had a happy day in their married life.

These two instances of Leo Tolstoy and Abraham Lincoln explain the tragic consequences of incessant nagging, which never does any good to the partner, rather it only ends on a note of mutual bitterness.

(6) Therefore, the sixth rule for a happy married life is that women should avoid the nagging habit which could result in their husband's as well as their own misery.

Thus in brief, there are these six rules for making married life a success:

Rule 1. Try to understand each other and adjust to individual behaviour.

Rule 2. Each partner should have the courage to admit the mistakes committeu by him/her. These should be gracefully owned.

Rule 3. Parents should take keen interest in the welfare of their children and not leave them to others.

Rule 4. While living in a joint family, develop good understanding with other members. Remember there may not be a better opportunity for your freedom as well as care of children than in a joint house.

Rule 5. Lead a balanced sexual life. Read dependable sex literature. It will help you.

Rule 6. Women should avoid the habit of nagging which acts like a cancer in destroying the fabric of a happy married life.

Are We Fair Towards Children?

Often it is the neglect of children both in their childhood as well as during adolescent period, that would lead children into wrong directions and also to having strained relations with their parents when they grow up. Most parents being preoccupied in their mundane affairs hardly find sufficient time to attend to their children, who are thus left to take their own care, which often might not result in healthy consequences.

If a child gets into bad society or becomes a drug addict and even starts stealing money to meet his growing expenditure, mostly on undesirable areas, the blame can't rest entirely on the teachers, school or society. Mainly it is the parents who have not taken sufficient care of their children's upbringing, thinking that they would take their own care and lead a sensible life.

Unfortunately it does not happen that way. The child needs constant care and here nobody could do better than parents. They should keep a careful watch on how the child is performing in school, his homework, his society—in fact all this should be done through a friendly approach and not with an aggressive feeling. Parents get annoyed when the child gets a bad report about his classroom performance, little bothering to know what were the basic reasons behind it.

Invariably it would be found that the child has been neglected by his family, his home work has not been checked, parents have been too busy with their social life or watching TV programmes—often the case with most families these days is that would hardly leave spare time to look into the day-to-day progress of the child. Consequently the child is left to struggle alone and its consequences are reflected in the school report which may even not be taken seriously by busy parents.

Thus it is the cumulative effect of all these factors that has resulted in the overall poor performance of the child. The story is the same, rather worse, when he grows up and is likely to be caught up in bad society. At this stage it would call for a strong and prolonged expensive effort to bring him back to the disciplined path.

The society today is in the grip of drug mafias. The number of drug addicts among school and college going children is on an alarming rise and the neglect of parents helps drug peddlers who are quite popular with the student community and take advantage of the situation. If the child even becomes a part of the terrorist gang, it is hardly any surprise.

It has been clearly demonstrated that children of parents who have been dutiful to their children, though their number has been fast declining, show much better results and are kept away from falling into bad society, and even if they are allured to take to drugs by their friends, they would invariably avoid it. They would also not hesitate to discuss this matter with the friendly parents.

Thus an important lesson is that even while you are helpful towards children, don't be unfriendly, lest the child should develop hatred towards you or would not share with you the information about the company he keeps and whether he has turned into a drug addict.

While there are busy parents unable to find time for their children, on the other hand there are over enthusiastic parents who are ever ready to find fault with their children and punish them for lapses, often in a stern and unbecoming manner. This is borne from the story of such type of a disciplinarian father who became furious when he found butts of cigarettes in the school bag of his child.

He was so furious that without waiting, he gave the child a heavy beating and then after pulling off his clothes, tied him to a tree outside the house which put the child to great shame since he was exposed to public view. But the basic question is, did such a punishment stop the child from smoking? No. Rather he became more aggressive and even took to highly harmful things. Certainly such behaviour of the parent was the highest act of barbarity whereas the child could have been brought to the path of sanity through a better and friendly approach. He could have been told about the harm caused to his health by smoking and offered suggestions to divert his attention to some alternative activity.

Apart from such neglect by parents towards their siblings, the recent adverse social and political environment has also taken its toll on them. In fact the rise of such a vicious atmosphere itself has been due to the high collapse of our educational system and the surrounding social environment where neither parents, nor teachers, nor even text books teach children how to be good and responsible citizens, loyal and patriotic towards the country.

In fact most of the children are not able to cultivate any firm roots for the best part of their early life. No surprise, with such an environment surrounding them, they fall an easy prey to the evils in the society and they do not mind committing even unethical acts like robbery, even dacoity, goondaism, killing of innocent people, molestation of women and children, rape and what not.

Over the long period after gaining independence, we have hardly cared to change our school education system and introduced in its place the vital areas like loyalty and patriotism towards the country. Both these, as experience shows, have been an integral part of societies that have risen to the top position. Here a country like Japan presents a unique example. Their citizens' loyalty and patriotism towards the country is too well known.

For long it has become an integral part of their school education system, and this country was among the very few countries to attain hundred percent literacy within a short period. Even workers here in the early period had made it a rule that before starting the day's work, they would pray for their loyalty towards the country reminding themselves that it was their moral duty to increase its output so that the country prospered.

No surprise that with such commitment and loyalty for their country—a small island nation—Japan rose to the top position, while around 1868 it was hardly in a good position.

And look at where we stand today compared with Japan, even though we are blessed with plenty of natural resources which are denied in the case of Japan and as a result it is forced to import most of its needs. While we promised at the time of independence that we would achieve hundred per cent literacy by the end of the last century, we have shamefully failed and are much behind the target.

The root cause behind most of our ills today is to be found in the neglected human resources, the youth, the children, their education and upbringing.

While the education system has toppled our family system too is in no better state. The sense of intolerance between the children and their parents, has brewed up under such a rootless system. While children have learnt to branch out from their families the moment they are in such position, there are quite a few of them who continue to be its part for one reason or the other.

But the trouble starts brewing after their marriage, where it is generally the mother-in-law who might not be able to pull on well with the modern Bahu (daughter-in-law). At times the intolerance might reach the level when the peace of the house is in jeopardy and ultimately leads to an environment of broken families.

This is what exactly happened in the case of a principal of a reputed college, when his domineering wife's excessive interference with the behaviour of their daughter-in-law, often in the shape of amends to her living style, was not taken kindly. She often complained about this to her husband who for quite sometime avoided interfering. But then the matter came to such a pitch that there was no alternative left other than to leave the house.

They moved to another place and rarely saw their parents. Later on when the husband was transferred to another station, he completely avoided visiting or even writing to his parents. Thus, there was a complete breakdown in their relations, for the son never forgot the insolent behaviour of his mother towards his wife. They even had failed to call when their parents died.

This of course shows the other extreme that a grieved couple might be forced to resort to. The moral of this story is that parents should understand the psyche of their children and try to adjust their own behaviour and outlook in accordance with the changed times as well as to the likes and dislikes of their children, of course within limits. The moment they start imposing themselves, particularly after marriage of their son, the situation could turn out to be intolerable in which even a flexible son might be forced to take the extreme decision, as it happened in the above case.

There are also parents who continue to have a strong hold on their meek siblings even after marriage and the son, in this case, continues to behave in the way he is dictated. This ultimately is likely to end in the neglect of the daughter-in-law, and if she is strong willed, she might ultimately seek divorce or else continue to suffer, even ruin her health and possibly visit her parents if she is welcome. Such a situation is a pitiable one, and could ultimately result in the death of the sufferer.

Some callous in-laws, particularly in the case of business families, even use every opportunity to force the daughter-in-law to bring additional cash from her parents, which could be used in the family business, and in case she fails to oblige, then the family might plan to liquidate her, so that a new bride is bargained for, to add to the family resources. Bride burning instances are often noticed in such families and in most cases the culprits get scot free, thanks to major loopholes in our legal system as well as the corrupt administration.

I have often felt that the mere demonstration by women activists before the houses of the victims or at police stations, would not bring about any positive solution. This system is deep-rooted and needs to be tackled through the creation of strong awareness among the members, particularly husbands, about the life long social curse as well as hate they would suffer from, after committing such heinous acts, and also the mental shock that would hound them later. And here the women activists can play an important role and can even avoid the occurrence of such situations if they keep in close touch with the victims.

Often it is too late when these activists appear on the scene. At this stage no useful purpose can be served as the body has been cremated meanwhile and there is no trace of the victim. This is another curse in the Hindu religion for if the body had been buried, one might be able to get at the real truth.

It is not that living with ones own family is a curse; rather we have prided ourselves in the world for enjoying the best possible joint family system, which has also acted as an insurance against unemployment. Several generations have lived together happily under the same roof. But unfortunately, this situation is fast changing. The earlier concept of joint family is gradually vanishing under the changed environments, the example of which we have witnessed earlier.

There are also examples where mothers have played a positive role in raising their children and putting them on the righteous path, even sacrificed their jobs when employed, so that they could be nearer to their children and guide them closely. Not only that. Even after the children have grown up, entered a job, even got married and had children, they have happily adjusted to the new situation and even seen that their daughter-in-law and grand children have a happy coexistence.

Though such instances are few but they are very much there, which shows that with appropriate education and training as well understanding even today two to three generations can live together happily and enjoy a secure family life. Under such a system, the daughter-in-law would also feel secure and happy that children were well cared for during her absence.

Thus it all depends on tradition, understanding and the degree of tolerance among the family members. Of course, in such cases it is important that senior members are financially secure. Otherwise, even in a happy and understanding family, the situation can arise when the parents feel helpless in depending on their son.

There is a story of a farmer who sold his land and other property so that his son could get the best possible education and then enter into a good profession. In due course his dreams were realised when his son, after completing his education with a good score, was selected for a coveted job. Soon he was also able to get married in a reputed family and settled in the posh area of a growing metropolitan city.

Soon after, the son invited his parents to stay with him which they gladly accepted and thus all of them began to stay under one roof. One day their son brought a puppy and showered every possible care and affection on it. The old parents did not like this, particularly when it shouted the whole day long as well as spoiled the surroundings with its privy and urine.

One day out of anger the father beat up the puppy. The son was very angry when he learnt of this and in anger scolded his father by saying that he continued to remain a villager and didn't know about the city life. He also added that if he were to prefer between his parents and the puppy, he would choose the puppy. That was the last straw and the parents had no alternative other than to shift back to the village the earliest, despite the apologies offered by their son. Thus the lesson is clear that for peace in old age don't depend even on your own son.

Be independent and keep sufficient cash with the bank so that if any eventuality arose, it could be faced honourably without depending on others. This should also be assured equally in the case of the wife for if the husband died she would not have to depend on the son or any other family member.

These are the lessons that follow:

(a) Treat your child with care and dignity and not in a casual manner. Do not load the Bahu, in case your son is married, with advices and interfere unnecessarily in her likes and dislikes, which could backfire with adverse consequences and disturb the family peace.

(b) Remember your child is an asset needing investment of time, energy and resources to bring him up to a worthy human being, and when he grows up he would turn out to be a great asset to the family as well his country.

(c) When the child is under proper care and treated with affection he would not hesitate to disclose about his company, his friends and the types of persons he comes in contact with. Such frank sharing of his activities by the child would help the parents to put him on the right path in case he was drifting to bad company.

(d) Parents should keep close touch with the school where the child is studying, by not only looking into his class performance, but also about his other activities and behaviour. This will help to maintain a close rapport with the teacher concerned and in case there is any deficiency it would be corrected in time.

(e) As the child grows up tremendous changes are likely to occur in his personality, behaviour, demands and aspirations. Parents should appreciate such changes and adjust themselves accordingly. They must understand he is no longer a kid, but a grown up young man who must be treated accordingly. It is also during this age that he is likely to face more challenging situations in his studies, classmates and other persons he comes in contact with. If there is any change in his behaviour and attitude try to understand him and guide him before it is too late.

(f) When he enters life, particularly after marriage, see that he is ready to adjust to the changed circumstances, particularly towards his wife who might find it difficult to adjust to her new life, as she had been used to a different life earlier. Her problems have to be understood and cared for, so that gradually she adjusts to the new environment. Often friction would arise when the mother-in-law fails to appreciate her viewpoint or demand. Here the best course is to let the storm blow out without interference. Soon things would settle down.

(g) In case your son is in business or a local job and your daughter-in-law is also working, they would prefer to stay with the family, particularly so after their child is born, as they know that proper care would be given to the child in their absence. It would be unfair on your part to avoid such a situation even if it meant some inconvenience. Thus try to tackle any delicate situation that arises with care, and rest assured your genuine point of view would be appreciated.

(h) Remember the other side of the story. When your son is staying with you, he becomes a great asset during emergencies. He and his wife equally would be in a better position to help the family as with age mobility generally declines and parents might need frequent help from them in old age. Thus, there is a great advantage in staying together under the same roof for at least two generations.

(i) Also remember to be financially independent in your old age and take care that you have a good bank balance and some regular income yielding assets, so that you have not to seek help from your son or other relatives in case of emergencies. So you have to plan about it well in time.

Declining Basic Family Values

One of the undignified fall-outs from quick modernisation to achieve global standards, particularly during the last quarter of the 20th century, has been rapid decline in human values in which the traditional respect for the senior members has been gradually fading away. While the western society had taken many years to change from traditional mores to modern mores, this change has been far quicker in the underdeveloped world, thanks to the fast development in the communication system, modern industry and services, in fact the whole pattern of life.

I remember in the late fifties, in a television discussion between Bertrand Russell, a great philosopher, thinker and human right activist, and Vijaylaxmi Pandit, who was then India's High Commissioner in Britain,—it was Russell who had all praise for India's extended family system where old members were not only respected, they also enjoyed the company of youngsters, particularly children, which helped them to stay cheerful and healthy even at this stage, whereas it was completely missing in the western society, where old people were pushed to Old People's Homes, deprived of family care and children's company and made to lead a completely isolated and lonely life, which created several problems for them at this age.

Well, that was the situation in the fifties. Meanwhile, there has been a tremendous change in our social framework. Both, population explosion and economic development have thrown families apart weakening the traditional joint-family system and with this, respect and care for old people has also disappeared.

While with the spread of medical facilities and control of epidemics, the average life span has increased and far larger number of senior members survive than it was the case couple of decades ago, but their support system, social life and children's affection and protection have gradually dried up.

Unfortunately this sense of indifference towards elders is far more prevalent among the well-off members of society, than the poor who still take care of their aged members. Here to a large extent, such high indifference has been due to quick changes in social values because of a large flow of income as well as exposure to modernisation.

To take an example. Grandma Luxmi (not real name) born in a middle class family has witnessed a quick rise in the fortune of her family which helped it to move from a small house to a palatial one where both her sons had separate flats of their own and their mother had been allotted a separate self-contained room for her stay and a maid servant was engaged to help her—while her two daughters had been married, it was the youngest one who was still unmarried who stayed with her.

Grandma Luxmi tried to adjust herself to the new life which went on smoothly till her youngest daughter was not married. Soon after her marriage she was left all alone. Though her two sons stayed in the same house, they rarely cared to call on her, being busy in their professions, and thus had hardly any time to visit their mother. It was only when one or the other daughter visited her that her loneliness was broken. Most of the time, however, she was only in the company of the maid servant.

Not used to such a lonely life, it began to weigh on her gradually and she developed a melancholy mood, lost her appetite and for most of the time confined herself to bed and didn't feel like moving around. Her younger son, who was more attached to her, enquired after her health and welfare when he could find time, and now engaged a nurse for her.

But both the nurse and maid servant couldn't be a substitute for her missing family affection, particularly of grand children who rarely visited her, and even the daughter-in-laws did not care. Whenever they visited, they only displayed lip sympathy but there was no affection from their heart.

Grandma Luxmi aged fast, her face became wrinkled and she developed breathing problem. Soon she was found dead while in sleep. She died a lonely death while staying in the midst of her own family.

This shows how modernisation and craze for wealth has brought about a selfish change in our value system where we have become so indifferent even to our near and dear ones, and our children being busy with multifarious attractions of the modern society, have little time to spare for their elders.

It is true that such a sense of neglect with the accumulation of wealth hasn't affected all families. There are exceptions. But by and large it has brought about a perceptible sense of indifference. We fail to realise, being over-occupied with our professional, business and office careers, that all this is not the end of our responsibility. We have, as a matter of fact, a much bigger responsibility to discharge towards our family members; particularly elders who have taken so much trouble in our own upbringing and who, in their old age, depend upon us.

The development of such a feeling would bring about much change in our own outlook and we will derive the mental satisfaction of helping our senior members. It will also trail a lesson for our children, who would learn from us how to respect our elders. We should remember that at one time, we would also be facing such a situation and if we don't train our children accordingly they would also treat us likewise, may be even worse. As it is currently happening in the over-materialistic western society where parents, who have been so indifferent towards their children while they were growing up, and often forced them to leave the comfort and protection of their families and find their own moorings, find themselves neglected.

Little surprise that these children would hardly bother about their parents and the latter too would have kept a track of their children only so long it suited them. It is only at the time of their old age that parents start remembering children when it is in fact too late. Often they have to face a lonely death.

We should learn from the ill effects of such modernisation, and let not our family value system be completely eroded under the current lifestyle. With suitable adjustments and thoughts, we could certainly develop a fair compromise between the two systems, as was done by another family mentioned below.

While Luxmi had to suffer in her old age, it was so different in the case of another Grandma, let us call her Radhika. Her husband had died when she was barely in her early twenties with a load of small four kids, yet to grow up. She belonged to an ordinary middle class family and her husband hadn't left any property or cash for her except some ornaments and family household goods. She was entirely at the mercy of her brother-in-Iaw's family for whom she worked hard to enable her children to grow up.

She didn't lose her patience or cool of mind and tolerated all sorts of situations while staying in a small room with the family of her brother-in-law. Gradually, as the eldest child grew up, he managed a small job and with the income thus earned they decided to stay in a small place of their own.

Gradually the situation took a still better turn and with her patience, hard labour and frugal living the family could get over the major crisis—like the poor monetary situation they faced earlier. Better days visited them and Radhika was able to get her both the daughters married and settled in life. The second son had also managed to find a job after his graduation.

Soon the situation began to change further, and both the sons were married. They made good progress in their jobs and with their combined income they were able to run a comfortable household. They were also able to build their own house soon and continued to stay together like one unit. Grandma Radhika commanded great respect from her daughters in-law as well as grand children. She also took care of the grand children when they were at home.

Gradually, as the family grew up they added another storey to the house which made it possible for both the families to stay separately, and Radhika stayed with the younger son who occupied the ground floor. They still shared the kitchen together. As Radhika grew old, she developed an eye problem ultimately leading to total blindness. Used as she was to the place, she could manage to move around without support. Even then, she could not avoid slipping in the bathroom which resulted in her immobilization. She became bed ridden. But she didn't give up her courage even under these circumstances and tried to manage things herself. To keep her blood circulation and body functioning, she moved her feet and legs while sitting. Her grand children slept close to her and she enjoyed their company and shared with them her life's experience.

With family affection and care, particularly from her grand children, and her own strong will power, she stayed healthy and normal even when faced with adverse body problems. Till the last she was in full senses, and had a peaceful end with her family members and well wishers around her.

See the difference between the two situations, first of Grandma Luxmi and other of Grandma Radhika. It is the care that we can give to our elders that helps them to lead a peaceful and happy old age. We must therefore be considerate to them as well as teach our children to be so.

Thus the lesson is that it is the personal care for elders as well as sharing their company in old age which would do far more good than leaving them alone to the care of others. Remember, it is particularly in old age that elders pine for the love, affection and care from their children and especially of grand children, which would bring them much happiness and solace than anything else.

PART IV

Of Health, Food, Fitness and Retirement

Do You Suffer from an 'Agitated Mind'?

There is old saying, 'Man is what he thinkesth'. In other words, man's exterior is a good reflection of the state of his mind. An agitated mind would certainly be reflected in his actions and behaviour. May be it sends him into a bout of depression, just keeps him brooding over some negative thinking that has got a firm hold on his mind. Or there may be some family, business, or job connected matter that takes hold on his mind. Anything could turn out to be its cause.

But its after effect is quite unhealthy and might even turn out to be disastrous if it is not controlled timely or better counsel is not sought by discussing it with someone in whom you have full faith. Here of course no one could be better than your partner in case you are married and your partner is living. Otherwise it could be some other member of the family or even a friend with whom you have developed close faith, for under such circumstances, it is always advisable to unburden your state of mind and seek guidance or even solace, which would do a lot good.

So the first lesson for those suffering from an agitated mind is, do not keep it to yourself and don't feel shy in discussing it with others, especially those in whom you feel confident. Otherwise you may land on a wrong course. For instance, a visit to an astrologer or soothsayer or some such person for this, would not be advisable. In fact it may prolong your agony. It would be even far better to seek guidance from a medical consultant or a psychologist. But remember, ultimately much would depend on your own will power and inner strength.

It is usually observed that when one is not leading an active life, one is more prone to such brooding, for more the idle mind, more it can encourage negative thinking. So another lesson is you should lead a reasonably active life even when you are not on a job. But remember, a reasonably active life after you have retired would not come forth so easily unless you have planned it well ahead.

Unfortunately, most of us, when in office, fail to think of it feeling why worry, it will take its own course. But that, often does not happen and we are suddenly caught in a state of loneliness and deprived of all those facilities we have been used to and suddenly a vacuum is created.

This state should be avoided. Start thinking about some profitable activity well before hand. It is also observed that those who fail to lead a reasonably active social life and hardly make any friends, also suffer in retirement. Thus, there is need to cultivate dependable friends apart from relatives, whom you can trust and have faith, and who can appreciate your feelings and guide you accordingly.

Otherwise also, the company of your friends of the same age group, say during the morning walk and other programmes, could be a great relief and cut down your loneliness as well as chances of falling into negative thinking.

Intellectuals and writers have been found to be more prone to an agitated mind for the simple reason that for most of the time they keep their mind engaged in one or other kind of thought process and sometimes, depending on the sensitivity of mind, it starts travelling in the wrong direction and thus lands the person in difficulty. So these people have to be more careful and learn to discipline their mind well.

These steps would help to get over an agitated mind and encourage one to cultivate mental peace:

First, as it is said, an empty mind is a devil's workshop, and we should take care of this by a well planned use of time, even after retirement. Here, judicious involvement in the direction in which you have your professional, official, business experience should help. When you are well provided for retirement, money should not be much of a consideration, and you should render any service that suits your convenience. But start planning it when you are in service otherwise it might not be so easy.

Second, even if you have nothing else to do and don't find anything coming up easily, you could even listen to light music or devotional tunes which I have noticed, do help to get along at such moments. If you are staying indoors most of the time, you could develop some hobby which would help to spend your time usefully.

Third, of course, meditation is a good way of conquering the agitated mind. But remember, meditation only helps in case you have learnt to concentrate yourself. Otherwise letting your thoughts wander about aimlessly would do no good. Thus, meditation would be a mere ritual, rather a waste of time. So first you should cultivate concentration of your mind so that you can derive the maximum advantage from meditation.

The best alchemy for a disturbed mind is, of course, to face the reality of the circumstances that have driven you to such negative thinking and view it in correct perspective. By this you will notice that there is a perceptive change in your thinking. Ultimately it is your determined thinking that would create a positive mind. Cultivate such thinking and shun the negative side. This attitude will have to be cultivated slowly and with full determination, along with other helpful ways mentioned above.

Fight Stress Through 'Manoshanti' (Peaceful Mind)

The story goes. A person went to a physician and asked him whether there was any medicine that would bring relief to a disturbed mind. The physician thought for a while and replied—there was no such medicine, for the mind's problems were beyond a physician's domain. They treated only visible body problems and not those which were invisible.

This is where the Nature has left man to conquer the peculiar problems of mind himself, through will power, inner strength and determination. After all man unlike other creatures and animals, is quite different, gifted with a mind to think and act independently. It is through this thinking process that he is able to perceive and plan creative ideas for his development and also of his surroundings.

Thus it is a special gift from Nature, not given to other creatures on this earth. That is what has helped man to create wonderful inventions for improvement of his lot. Thus, we have been blessed with a large number of scientists, engineers and other experts as well as philosophers and scholars, who have improved upon their surroundings and created a new world order.

So, man's capacity to think and change this universe for making it more habitable and comfortable is indeed unique. He is specially gifted to bring such order as a result of his own productive thinking and action.

While there are such people who have contributed towards the welfare and prosperity of this universe, there are also those people whose minds have been filled with negative thoughts of destroying this universe and bring misery and unhappiness to its residents. These were the people who had encouraged major destructive plans, wars and like activities.

Thus, their minds have thrived on viewing with satisfaction the destruction and misery all around. Their actions have brought about major upheavals in this world, which resulted in the killings of millions of people and destruction of every sort of property, created with great labour by others.

We have before us the example of Hitler, whose mind was obsessed with a totally destructive attitude, which ultimately resulted in mass killings and destruction. In fact his mind derived sadistic pleasure in seeing people tortured, sent to gas chambers, and children and women mercilessly slaughtered.

His case was indeed of an extreme mental behaviour. And the pity is that he was successful in creating a large group of followers who felt pleasure in carrying out his destructive plans and dared not oppose him, which shows how people could be hypnotized even by a leader following a totally wrong path.

But in the end, such leaders obsessed with negative thinking have not survived for long, and met their ignoble end. Thus, ultimately victory has been for those who have traversed the positive path.

Thus an uncontrolled mind is like a race horse which, if not put in its place, could cause havoc. The question arises, on how to bring order to a disturbed mind. Since there is no medicine for this, as the physician rightly told a suffering patient, what are the alternative routes to avoid the occurrence of such a situation and bring the sufferer back to a peaceful state?

It is the controlled and positive-oriented thinking that would help to conquer an agitated mind. When any negative thinking has got hold of the mind and is allowed to stay there for long, it finds a good opportunity to have a deep hold on one's thinking and thus its riddance becomes quite a tough job.

So the first lesson is, in case you have a tendency for negative thinking, see that it does not make a permanent niche in your mind. The earlier it is got rid of with your determined action, the better it is.

The wonderful nature has also given man power for such positive approach, provided it is used judiciously. That is, in such a case one has to use positive thinking power and look at the other side of the negative mind. By using a positive approach, you will find that the negative thought that created a hold on you, disintegrates. Thus, the earlier it is done the easier it would be to conquer the negative mind and bring it back to the path of sanity.

Thus, mind is the ultimate source of both positive and negative thinking. It is of course excessive indulgence with negative thinking which brings unhappiness and disturbs the peace of mind. (I am not aware whether Hitler tried to find solace for his disturbed state of mind—and there could be little doubt that he was under extraordinary pressure; however in the case of Stalin, who also followed highly disturbing negative policies, and brought misery and death to a large number of innocent people, he admitted that he found solace in the company of the Indian philosopher Dr. Radhakrishnan, when he was our country's ambassador to that country and called on him.)

Thus it is through awareness and regular practice (like reading the experiences of great people, attending helpful lectures/discourses by experts, even listening to soothing music and depending on other helpful activities), that you can certainly build a positive approach route, which is the only solution for enjoying Manoshanti.

Thus these few steps would help bring the disturbed mind to a peaceful state.

First of all, try to understand—as also stressed earlier—what had brought about such a disturbed state and before it makes a prolonged hold, which will put you to a highly disturbed state, make every attempt to get rid of it. Often it is some foolish and meaningless idea or thinking that starts taking a strong hold on you. Get rid of it immediately through the use of positive forces, which can be thought of. Remember, unless you make a determined effort to switch to a productive alternative route, it might not be an easy job to get rid yourself of such negative thinking.

As a last resort, in case your efforts fail, do consult someone in whom you have faith. Sharing your problem with someone who understands, would itself bring relief to you. And even then don't hesitate to consult an expert—though normally this need would not arise in case you have dealt with it at your level with determination, and which alone would provide a permanent solution.

Remember, the very first occurrence of negative thinking should be tackled as quickly as possible and never let it have a strong hold on you, which would make it more difficult to get rid of.

Secondly, instead of letting your mind concentrate time and again on the same negative thought, start using other means that would divert your attention. For instance, you could listen to music that may prove helpful. Or you could concentrate on some physical activity that would help to divert your attention. You could even start taking interest in gardening or engage yourself in some other physical activity like helping the poor in one way or the other, which would divert your mind and bring you mental peace.

There are a number of social organisations which would be happy to take your help in one or other social activity, where you could spend time as per your convenience. In fact involvement in social welfare work provides a very productive opportunity to forget your negative mood and convert it into a useful opportunity to contribute something for the deserving.

Even if, for one or the other reason, you are unable to participate in outdoor activity, you could divert your depressed mind to an active state through various opportunities available indoors. Apart from listening to music, which should of course be as per your mood and taste, you could indulge in sharing some games with children and reading some light books and magazines which would provide good diversion. I have found that reading biographies of great people is quite helpful on such occasions.

Take care that you eat your food regularly but of course it should be light. Eating regularly will help keep you in good health and also improve your mood when you enjoy it. You could choose items which please your mood. Have plenty of water during the day. That will keep your system in order and also help in bringing a change in your mind.

In other words, a disciplined and socially active life should be led if you want to put your disturbed mind back on the rails. Thus it is you yourself alone, who has to fight this state and seek a permanent solution.

There is yet another tried alchemy which works well—as it has in my case. It is called breath control method. Under this method, when faced with some stress problem, attention is concentrated on the control of breath, for by regulating the breathing system, stress is conversely controlled.

It is noticed that when one is under stress, there is a sudden change in the breathing system as well. The affected person starts breathing fast or in an unregulated manner. Thus, as a result of stress, his whole body chemistry undergoes a drastic change. All this is visible in the disturbed breathing system.

Now the question arises on how to get out of it. That's where the controlled breathing comes into the forefront. Both, its awareness as well as its regular practice would help a lot to reach normal breathing. Remember how we regulate our breathing during the morning walk when most of us do have breathing exercise even though may not practice physical exercise.

The same technique, if practiced regularly, would also bring back our disturbed breathing to its normal shape. It is very important that a controlled breathing stage is reached as early as possible. Simultaneously, the help of drinking plenty of water is also advisable, for once your inside has been disturbed, as it is in the case of stress, it virtually burns the body, and to control it the best remedy is the use of water. More the intensity of stress, the more water is needed. So drink as much water as you can but take it comfortably. Your inside would soon be calm and with the help of conscious breathing, you will find that the situation soon returns to normal.

Thus, when in trouble this route could also be tried. Ultimately one has to decide the route which suits best in one's case. Even a wise combination of routes can be thought of.

Walking to Health

Nature has been quite generous in its gift of greenery to mankind. It has bestowed greenlands rich in trees, bushes, grass, as well as thick forests, where Nature wanted man to make the best of his time and keep in perfect health. This has been the story of our ancestors, who often preferred to live in forests and enjoyed the best possible health and also enjoyed a long and healthy life.

Over time, we have unfortunately destroyed much of Nature's wealth to accommodate our industrial and urban craze. The vast greenlands we had inherited, have now shrunk miserably and they are going to be still under high pressure in days to come, thus ultimately leaving only standing space for humanity, where it would be difficult to find sufficient space to clean our lungs.

Compared globally the situation is probably the worst in our country. The population demon is posing a big threat and ultimately would swallow all the greenlands and forests which we had in rich abundance couple of centuries ago—in fact, the onslaught has been the worst during the last century and currently we are left with a very small green cover which if not protected carefully, would also disappear hardly leaving any green spot.

Under the circumstances, if you can find a green patch around your habitation, you are fortunate and should try to make the best of it before it is under pressure.

Fortunately, our urban areas, though under high population pressure, are yet blessed with some open spaces especially around the residential areas and are yet green and reasonably well maintained.

With a shrinking green cover and growing consumerism, leading to sedentary habits and late retiring to bed, it has made most of us late risers, when it is almost unthinkable to go for a walk or even engage in some exercise. This situation with the so-called globalisation, which has thrown us to the drawing-room comfort of the western society, is proving the worst. It not only affects the youngsters, even senior members are becoming its victims as could be noticed from those who are currently airing their clogged lungs in the air of drawing room suffocation as well as eating late meals.

The result is that with such consumerism and artificial comfort around us, we easily fall victims to several ailments, some of them with dreaded names hardly heard before, and the number of these instances is fast rising. All this leads to frequent visits to clinics and rising medical bills. Thus a kind of vicious syndrome has been created in this area. Also rapid changes in the life style has been causing high damage.

Thus, there is need to pause, and medical clinics should not be there only to thrive on the helplessness of their clients, rather they should advise and guide them about the benefits they would derive by modifying their life style like engaging in regular walks and exercise in the open.

In fact some NGOs should devote themselves in educating people about the harm being done by such rapid changes in the life style they have come to patronise. They should even open clubs of morning walkers and ensure that their members regularly participate and convey a message to their lazy members that it is in their own interest to walk as much as possible, which would do them tremendous good and most importantly, help them to lead happier days.

RIGHT TIME TO GET UP

What should be the appropriate time to wake up in the morning so that it helps you to make the best of a morning walk? There is no fixed time limit. It would vary from person to person. Certainly an early riser has an advantage, for he gets more time to plan his walking schedule. In summer, particularly, it would be problematic if one were to face the sunrise when it starts getting hot and thus is hardly congenial for walking. The situation is so different in winter when one feels invigorated after sun rise, but then it would be rather late for those who are working, though such a situation would ideally suit the senior citizens.

In fact, in winter season, senior people would find it more convenient to change their walking schedule to late afternoons when the environment is most congenial for walking and relaxing in a park.

Thus the schedule of walking would vary from person to person and from season to season.

While initially it would be difficult to form the habit of walking, but once formed it would stay even when one hasn't had enough sleep. Normally, a person conscious about his morning walk, would automatically wake up at the appointed time even without an alarm. It almost becomes an inbuilt habit without needing much effort.

Should one get ready for a walk soon after waking up? This would not be advisable, for the human body takes some time to adjust itself to the post-sleep scenario. Thus a little relaxed mood after waking up and going through toilet would be ideal. It would be better if the toilet habit is shifted to early morning which would be extremely helpful for the body system.

WHAT DRESS SHOULD BE WORN?

Again one has to plan his dress according to convenience and season. Whatever dress is worn, it should be comfortable, protective and conducive for easy walking. The same applies to shoes and socks. Thus, dress and shoes should be helpful for easy walking and should not become a hindrance or burden.

RELAXED MOOD

The purpose of walking should not be just a ritual, but to derive the maximum benefit, one should be in a relaxed mood and not burdened with an uneasy mind. In fact, unhappy thoughts could do much harm.

Thus, an important lesson is to forget all about your worries while starting for a walk and fill your mind with healthy thoughts which stay on for the whole day. Thus, concentrate on the walk alone and enjoy Nature's bounty. Sport a smile on your face and warmly greet the acquaintances you come across.

But simultaneously, avoid hanging around them or discussing business and domestic problems. You will be simply wasting your precious time. Even when others force you, avoid them with tact. Gradually they will understand.

Your sole mission while walking should be to walk erect and with grace, occasionally inhaling the fresh air and exhaling all the rubbish gathered inside your system during the last 24 hours. It would do you much good. You would feel relaxed and your lungs would be ready to help you for the next 24 hours. Your head would also feel light and thus you would be able to attend to difficult jobs during the day with ease and comfort.

Walk at a speed which suits you but see that it is firm and graceful. You will yourself feel happy about it and it would also help you to firm up your leg power which is essential for blood circulation. It would also help to get rid off several ailments, especially blood sugar, which can be effectively controlled through regular walking.

HOW MUCH TO WALK AND THE TIME SPENT

There is no specific rule on how much one should walk and for how long. This again depends on one's convenience. One should of course not walk beyond one's capacity, when he starts feeling tired. Such a walk is not advisable, and can even cause harm.

Your goal should be a comfortable and health promoting walk and not one ending in a burden. If one is used to regular exercises, these could be of further help. But then it should be adjusted to convenience and not over done.

Quite a few people are used to brisk walking, and soon after it, without any pause, start equally strenuous exercises which is not advisable. In fact, this can cause great harm to the body system and might even lead to coronary problems.

TIME GAP BETWEEN WALKING AND EXERCISE

There should be adequate pause between walking and exercise, more so if it has been a vigorous walk. Unless the body temperature comes to normal, there is no point in undertaking exercises, which would only put extra strain on your system. Thus for getting the best out of exercises, the golden rule should be to give your body enough rest after a walk, and only when it has cooled down sufficiently start you exercise. Again after exercise, don't walk home all of a sudden. The body needs some relaxation to absorb the exercise effect.

Both, speed of walking and vigour needed in exercise would also depend on season. During hot weather, light walk and exercise should be preferred, while in winter, one would need brisk walking and vigorous exercise to warm up the system and encourage blood circulation.

WHAT TO DO WHEN UNABLE TO WALK

When walk, for one reason or the other, is not possible, one could yet have a small walk within the house and undertake some light exercise and practice deep breathing in particular. In fact, under such conditions one has more time for practicing deep breathing and doing exercises. Both will help the system enormously to face the day well.

EIGHT GOLDEN RULES

Thus these are the golden rules for walking to health:

First, walking is the best way to health and longevity. Cultivate this habit if not already there. It helps to shake the body's dullness, feeling of lethargy and pumps in fresh air into the lungs and whole body system. Thus, walking must be a priority item on the daily agenda.

Second, form the habit of getting up early morning which would do you a lot of good otherwise too. You will have to slacken your march towards consumerism and late dinner, so that you are able to sleep in time which would help you to wake up for your morning walk.

Third, you must walk with determination and grace, in the park of your liking and spend reasonable time there. Never be in a hurry.

Fourth, before walking, shake-off mental clogs if any so that you enjoy a leisured and tension-free walk to gain the best results.

Fifth, while walking, do greet your acquaintances warmly but, avoid lengthy meetings, particularly on business and family matters. You would be gaining nothing and needlessly wasting time.

Sixth, concentrate on walking. Your movements should be firm, straight and graceful. If you choose on exercise later, do give reasonable gap between the two, to gain appropriate results.

Seventh, do give your body some relief before you start walking home as well as after returning. That is essential for the body to reach normal temperature as well as mood.

Eighth, remember regular walking helps to tone up your system and prepares you to face well several health problems. You will also cut down your medical bills and unnecessary exposure to drugs, which can cause several side effects. It is very aptly said that if you want to avoid a visit to the clinic, visit a park regularly.

The Food We Eat

One of the most important contributing factors towards health is the food we eat. We often tend to ignore this. The ultimate contribution of food to a healthy body depends on these factors: (a) what we eat? (b) how we eat? (c) the time we spend on eating? (d) how much effort we make to regulate our eating habit? (e) whether we have time for relaxation before and after eating?

WHAT WE EAT

What we eat is important, for ultimately it is the balanced diet which provides the maximum calories to sustain the body in a healthy state.

What we eat is very much related to our family's food habits, which are also related to climate as well as availability of different food items. Further what food is available depends on soil and climatic factors.

It is also correct that the food available is also the most important health-contributing food. Being comparatively cheap, one can have it in abundance. So there is normally no dearth of such food.

Thus, people who live in wheat-producing areas would eat little of rice, while it is *vice-versa* in case of people living in rice-producing areas. It is true that with advancement of technology, we can grow other foods in areas not naturally suited for them. But in case we indulge in excess production of foods normally not suitable to the soil, the results can be damaging.

Thus wheat growing areas, if excessively exposed to rice cultivation, would soon face adverse climate and environment conditions. That would be the price paid for going against Nature. Tough Nature would tolerate such a situation within permissible norms, beyond which it would revolt.

Similarly, people staying where they are naturally accustomed to certain foods would find it difficult to change in favour of alternative foods. In fact, it might cause even health problems for them. Thus, the lesson is that balance in Nature should be maintained.

Thus ultimately what we eat bears a close relationship to the local food items available. There should be prudent use of these items to provide both change as well as balanced food.

BREAKFAST

Take the case of breakfast. While wheat-producing areas start with wheat-based items like bread, parothas, chapattis; in the rice growing areas people would have rice preparations in one shape or the other.

It is not that there is rigidity about items and hardly any change is possible. No. There is no such rigidity at all. However, it is only for occasional change that people would switch over to alternative items while normally they would stick to theirs.

MOOD WHILE EATING

While what we eat is important, equally important is our mood during eating. Is it relaxed or tense? Certainly a relaxed mood would help to get the maximum benefit from the food we eat, but under sullen/irritated mood, one is likely to find fault with the food and possibly under such a situation, the food is almost swallowed in hurry without being chewed properly. The after effects of such behaviour could be nasty, though if indulged occasionally, the nasty effect might be small. If such a habit is indulged regularly, the effect could reach a serious level.

With such a nasty mood, even the most balanced food would lose its impact and turn into an unpleasant experience. On the other hand, even a lesser balanced diet eaten under a pleasant mood would prove to be far more beneficial.

Another lesson is to avoid a sullen or angry mood while you are sitting around the breakfast table. In case such a mood persists avoid breakfast and drink some liquids, which will not harm you and postpone your eating to when you find your mood is prepared for it.

HURRIED EATING

Also, eating in great hurry is equally harmful. When you are in such a hurry you don't notice how fast you swallow your food without digesting it properly, and often this task is accomplished simultaneously by gulping more of liquid. That makes the situation still worse. Such liquid will not help in converting the hurriedly swallowed food into the desired shape.

Also, more hurriedly the food is swallowed, more the time it will take to settle down in the stomach. Remember, your stomach does not have teeth, so it is difficult for it to perform the job of the teeth. In fact, if teeth are used wisely, they would help to convert your food into the shape acceptable by the system.

Thus we must learn to have patience while eating and avoid pushing down food without first chewing it well with our teeth. You will notice that there is hardly any saving of time between the fast swallowed food and that eaten with patience and care; but the after effect-or time taken by the body to digest the hurried food is far longer than the well chewed food. Besides, there could be many more harmful effects in case this practice is followed regularly.

Thus in the long-run, it would pay to discipline yourself and avoid hurried meals. It would of course not harm if it is practiced once a while. But don't make it a habit, for its long run consequences are going to be harmful.

REGULAR DIET HABITS

It is equally important that a regular diet habit is formed. The time of one's eating is important as it would ensure the body's needed rest, as well as its capacity to function in a well regulated manner. The system could certainly go astray when you do not have the regulated timing for food.

In the western countries, people are more punctual about the timing for food—breakfast, lunch, dinner—than people in developing countries, though here also, before being exposed to consumerism (like television), they were equally punctual in their food habits.

Thus the trend that is witnessed now is not good. It is often observed that there is no uniformity of timing while eating principal meals. It is especially dinner that is eaten late/very late in the evening, which hardly gives the body sufficient time to digest it. Also, often after dinner we rush straight to bed. Thus, little surprise that we face a disturbed night for the simple reason that we have not allowed the food we have eaten to settle down.

Its harmful effect is noticed in the morning when we get up. The cheerful mood that should be there is often missing and we find our stomach is in a poor shape, either it refuses to clear up or turns loose. Either way we have to put up with it during the day, though normally it should clear in the morning itself and rarely disturb us later in the day.

The victims are only elders this problem is also affecting youngsters, since they are glued to the idiot box watching thrilling programmes late in the evening. This habit not only disturbs their study schedule, it also makes them acquire irregular habits often resulting in poor health.

Thus, children should be taught to avoid watching too much of TV programmes, which can also cause problems with their psyche, thus further adding to the family's troubles.

But then unless parents discipline themselves first, children would not learn. Even now, in several western countries, children retire to their study for a small relaxation after eating their supper early along with family members. They go in for early sleep which helps them to lead a regulated life as well as devote sufficient time to their studies.

We must cultivate some disciplined behaviour among ourselves as well as children and avoid watching TV programmes beyond certain hours and eat our dinner well in time to allow children to retire early.

LACK OF RELAXATION BEFORE AND AFTER FOOD

It is observed that a little relaxation before your principal meal as well after it, will do a lot of good both to your appetite as well as body. Often it is the professionals, business executives and their tribe who carry home their office headache, and though in need for relaxation, fail to find it because their mind is too much preoccupied with ongoing office/business problems.

In fact they do not forget these even when they are on the dining table and often have little time to share with family members.

It is little surprise that with such an unregulated life, they often lose then hunger and fail to derive much benefit even if they are served the best possible food. Often they eat in a hurry, without concentration and rush to the office.

Such a portrait of a young and promising executive is indeed worth pitying. Why on earth can't he be a little more cheerful and relax frequently, which would inject tons of energy in him and equally help him plan his career more successfully? If he starts devoting just 10 minutes before meals to complete relaxation, forget his worries, inhale fresh air and relax his limbs, he would find that he has a feeling of real appetite to enjoy the food. And this would ultimately do a lot of good to both his body as well as business.

Thus we should make a general rule of compulsory relaxation before and after meals, for getting the best out of food as well as for maintaining natural health and personal well-being.

It has been observed that people who are in the teaching profession are able to deliver lectures far better when they are in a relaxed mood than in a tense mood (which could result from hurried and undigested eating).

To sum up we should adopt these guidelines for the food we eat:

Eat food that is available and which the soil in your area can grow easily.

Have a relaxed mood while you are eating. Keep tensions away at least for the time being.

Take a little time to digest your food well before transferring it to the stomach.

Cultivate a regulated diet habit and teach your children to follow it.

To get the best from your food, go in for a short relaxation before and after the meal.

These are simple rules, which would do you and your family members a lot of good.

Make a Healthy Start of the Day with Breakfast

How many among us do really enjoy our morning breakfast? I am afraid not many, for one or the other reason. Especially those who have to rush to their offices or other work place; and also the school and college going students would normally not take kindly to their breakfast. Most of them would generally bump to the breakfast table just at the last minute, and virtually swallow whatever is served without bothering about how much of it is accepted by the body system. There is no time for this and some morsels are yet struggling in the mouth, before they are ready to dash to their schools or colleges.

This certainly is not a healthy way of starting your day, when instead of enjoying the breakfast, one treats it as a mere ritual, just to keep the body system going and nothing beyond that. Such a funny notion should be dispensed with, and instead one should make a firm resolve to be serious about breakfast and make it virtually the principal food of the day, which should thus get the maximum attention among all the foods.

In other words, we should be spending a minimum of half an hour over it. Every bit of item we eat should be got converted into a feast of nourishment and never eaten in hurried or thoughtless way.

We should therefore follow a well thought out menu and enjoy it to our heart's content. These rules would help us to gain the maximum benefit from our breakfast:

The first resolve should be that you should spend a minimum of half an hour on the breakfast table, come what may. Thus breakfast should never be rushed through, which could do a lot of damage to your system and thus upset your very start of the day, when bouts of prolonged nausea would visit you during the day. To avoid such an unpleasant occurrence, resolve to stick to this vital rule which will give you ample time to adjust to a healthy breakfast.

When we resolve for a healthy breakfast, simultaneously we have to observe that while on the breakfast table, your mind should be calm and composed and it should not be encumbered with extraneous thoughts. Thus, your sole objective should be to concentrate on breakfast and enjoy it to the maximum.

Also you should avoid any temptation like reading the newspaper or scanning through some office files, howsoever urgent these might be. These temptations should be just forgotten, otherwise you are not sincere to your breakfast. Your thoughts would be elsewhere while you would be physically eating breakfast. That should be avoided and certainly you can afford to forget the newspaper or office file or some other urgent work at least for this half hour.

Thus the second resolve should be that while on the breakfast table, cultivate a cheerful disposition, a happy mood and a smiling face. That will help to bolster your appetite and make you derive the maximum benefit from whatever you are eating.

Remember, breakfast eaten with sullen mood and in a state when your appetite is not stirred up to your satisfaction, would do no good. Rather when you are in such a state, skip over your breakfast. Even then give time to whatever you choose to eat and never hurry through. In fact, when overcome with such a mood, you should give extra time, which will help to stir up your appetite at least partially.

The third resolution should be to eat or drink what suits your appetite, but it should be healthy and nourishing. It may be difficult in a family, to meet your individual requirements, but if you take the trouble of visiting the kitchen to prepare such stuff yourself, a little earlier to settling on the breakfast table, you would also be enjoying an item of your taste. But it may not be always possible, and you could go in for it only occasionally. Thus, the best way would be to adjust your taste and food habits as per the family needs. That would also reduce the load on the housewife.

Certainly, adjustment to family needs and what is regularly being cooked, would be the best possible solution under such circumstances. Also remember that instead of worrying for an individual item, far more important is the mood in which you eat your breakfast.

You must therefore cultivate a broad approach towards breakfast, eat what is served and enjcy it. This would also become a part of your palate.

Also ensure that whatever you eat or drink is done in a slow and measured way. For instance, while eating a solid food like parothas, don't rush through it. It should be eaten slowly bit by bit, when each bite is thoroughly converted into near liquid form with the help of your teeth before it enter the stomach. Not only this. Even while drinking any liquid— milk or anything else—avoid gulping it in a single sip. Have a slow sip which you will really enjoy and it will also be easily accepted by your system. In short, you must enjoy whatever you eat or drink, and the best way to do it is to invest time in it.

Another very important resolution is to rest awhile after breakfast which may be just for a few minutes. This will help the stomach to adjust itself before you are on your next job. It has been observed that those who have some relaxation after breakfast and also have comparatively light breakfast—but of course not too light either, as to arouse your hunger soon after—are far better prepared to face the battle of life than their counterparts. Thus, relaxation is a great elixir in life.

Ultimately, if these few thoughts are kept in mind and practiced while we are eating breakfast, they would enable us to make our breakfast really a healthy start of the day.

दे रहा काशी का पंडत चढ़ बैठा। गायन पर हावी होने की कोशिश करने लगा। जब एक पहर में उसकी बाँहें चढ़ने लगीं तो हमारे घराने के बारे में औल-बौल बकने लगा। माँ काली साक्षात् सामने बैठकर सँभालती रहीं। उसके निढाल होने और भोर होने तक मेरा गायन चलता रहा। तालियों की गड़गड़ाहट रुक ही नहीं रही थी, किन्तु तबलची पंडत स्टेज के पीछे अपने बाल नोच रहा था, उसके शागिर्द पैर पटक रहे थे। न जाने कब-कैसे उनके लिए मैं म्लेच्छ-मुसलमान हो गया था, जो ख़ब्ती था, ख़ानदानी पागल था और न जाने क्या-क्या गालियाँ मेरे कानों में पिघले हुए सीसे की तरह डाली गईं। मेरे दिमाग़ी ख़लल-ख़ब्तीपन की फिर शुरुआत हो गई। फिर वही दीवानापन, वही फ़क़ीरी-भिखमंगी के दिन शुरू हो गए। बेख़ुद-बेसुध कहीं पड़ा रहता। मन्दिर-मस्ज़िद की सीढ़ियों पर, किसी नदी तट पर। गाँजा-वाँजा भी पीना शुरू कर दिया था। उसी बेख़ुदी-बेसुधी के बरसों में तुम्हारे अब्बू, जमाई ख़ुर्शीद जोगी के अब्बू सिकंदर शाह जोगी की टोली से भेंट-मुलाक़ात-दोस्ती हुई और कमोल के दादू रोबिन बाउल से दोस्ती की गाँठ जुड़ी। बड़े नानू की कहानियाँ ख़त्म ही नहीं होतीं। भले रात ख़त्म हो जाए। आधे सोते-आधे जागते हम सुनते कि सोते, पता ही नहीं लगता।

लेकिन इतना तो तय था कि ख़ब्तीपन बड़ो नानू-नानू से होता शब्बो भाभी तक आ पहुँचा था। क्योंकि शाहीबाग़, अहमदाबाद के बाद हर दुर्घटना उन्हें ज़्यादा मुसलमाँ बनाए जा रही थी और कमोल से उनके मन की दूरी बढ़ती जा रही थी। अभी मुज़फ्फरनगर दंगे में अब्बू की हुई बेतरह पिटाई के बाद शब्बो भाभी बिलकुल अपना आपा खो बैठी थीं। कमोल दा क्या, उन्होंने आश्रम के बच्चों से भी मिलना-जुलना छोड़ दिया था।

उसी वक़्त कमोल दा और भाभी के बीच की झूठी लड़ाई, इस ख़ब्तीपन की आग में पेट्रौल डालने न जाने कहाँ से कालिन्दी मैडम पधार गईं। ऐसे ही कमोल डिप्रेशन में थोड़े गया था। आत्महत्या की कोशिशें यूँ ही थोड़े की थीं। बेचारा कमोल...!

4

खुसरो रैन सुहाग की, जागी पी के संग।
तन मेरा मन पीउ का, दोऊ भये एक रंग।

—अमीर खुसरो

बेचारा कमोल दा! उसे सुआर्यन सेना के लोगों के साथ जब-तब होनेवाली बहसों के पहले किसी ने यह याद नहीं दिलाया था कि उसका धरम क्या है? उसकी जाति क्या है? वैसे भी उसका पूरा नाम कमोल कबीर था। वीरभूम के नामी बाउल रोबिन दादू का पोता और संगीत महाविद्यालय के उस्ताद मदन बाउल का इकलौता चिराग़। स्कूल के रजिस्टर में बाबा ने बाउल की जगह लिखाया कबीर तो वह कमोल बाउल से कमोल कबीर हो गया। हालाँकि उसका बहुत मन था कि नाम ही बदलना है तो अपना नाम वह लालन रख ले लालन कमोल...न...न लालन कबीर...कमल लालन ना...लालन कमोल ही ठीक। या फिर निताई रख ले, निताई कमोल...या मिताई...या कमोल गौर कैसा...कैसा...रहता या कमोल चैतन्य...भीषोण भालो...क्या नाम...कमोल चैतन्य। किन्तु उसके मुँह से बोल ही नहीं फूटता था। ननिहाल चुरूलिया जाता तो उसका मन होता कि वह अपना नाम सीधे नज़रूल इस्लाम ही रख ले। अब मन का क्या? मन तो क्या न क्या सोचता रहता!...क़ैसा...कैसा करता रहता! मन करता कि जब कोई उसका

धरम-जाति पूछे तो वह भी अपने पुरखे लालन फ़क़ीर की तरह चिल्ला कर कहे, "सब पूछते लालन फ़क़ीर हिन्दू या मुसलमान, लालन कहे जानूँ न मैं मेरा क्या संधान।" लेकिन लगता है माँ की तरह उसे भी घुट्टी में पिलाया गया था कि मन को मारो। चुप रहो। जब्त करो। जो बाबा कहें वो सच। जो दादू कहें वो सच। बाक़ी सब झूठ। उसे भालो छेले बनना था, जैसे माँ को भालो बोऊ—अच्छी बहू। दोनों ने केवल सिर हिलाना सीखा था। सपने में भी ना नहीं बोला। कभी मन की बात नहीं कही। बस फिर क्या, सब भालो...भालो...। कमोल खोका ख़ूब भालो। मदन बो ख़ूब भालो। लेकिन कमोल जितना अपनी माँ को जानता था उतना बाबा और दादू क्या जानते। माँ अपने मन के खाते-खतियान में साल-भर का हिसाब लिखती रहती और माँ-मनसा के पूजा के दिनों में सब वसूल लेती। हिसाब-किताब बराबर। कमोल ने एक दिन मूड में माँ की कहानी सुनाई थी।

हमारे गाँव धूरिशा में माँ मनसा की पूजा सावन माह के आख़िरी दिनों में बड़ी धूमधाम से सम्पन्न होती। तीन दिनों तक चलनेवाली इस पूजा में बत्तख़ की बलि चढ़ती थी। ख़ास बात यह थी कि माँ पर माँ मनसा की सवारी आती। वे पूजा-स्थल पर जाकर बाल-फाल फैलाकर झूमने लगतीं। साल-भर चुप रहनेवाली माँ कितना-कितना बोलतीं। बोली-बानी सब बदल जाती। सबका भूत-भविष्य सब बाँचने लगतीं। बाबा-दादू से कितना-कितना साड़ी-सन्देश-रशोगोल्ला सब उसी अवस्था में वसूल लेतीं। बड़ा होने पर मुझे सब समझ में आने लगा था। साल-भर जो भी खाने-पीने-पहनने-ओढ़ने का मन करता, माँ मनसा के सवारी के बहाने सब पूरा कर लेतीं। हिसाब-किताब बरोबर।

कमोल के गप्प में माँ मनसा और माँ अक्सर आया करती थीं। लेकिन अभी तक कमोल अपने मन की बातों को पूरा करने का उपाय नहीं ढूँढ़ पाया था। सचमुच में ख़ूब भालो छेले था। नाटक करना-झूठ बोलना-लोगों की बात काटना सीख नहीं पाया। आदमी को इतना अच्छा भी नहीं बनना चाहिए। दादू ने कहा, कमोल गाना सीखेगा। कमोल सबेरे तीन बजे रियाज़ के लिए हाज़िर। बारहवीं पास करते बाबा ने कहा खोका इंजीनियरिंग पढ़ेगा। कमोल कम्पीटिशन की तैयारी में भिड़ गया। दूसरे साल सिम्बोसिस इन्स्टीट्यूट ऑफ मीडिया एंड कम्यूनिकेशन, पुणे के इंजीनियरिंग कॉलेज

में। साउंड इंजीनियरिंग की ब्रांच भी बाबा की पसन्द से। उसकी क्लास में नामी गायिका पद्म विभूषण विदुषी रागेश्वरी देवी की बेटी शबनम ख़ान। पर्सनाल्टी ऐसी कि सब दो हाथ दूर ही रहते। पाँच फीट सात-आठ इंच ऊँचाई, एकदम देवी माँ जैसा रूप-रंग। ख़ूब बड़ी-बड़ी आँखें। घुटनों तक लम्बे घुँघराले बाल। ख़ूब घनी भौंहें। बस नाक सुतवा नहीं, पहाड़ियों जैसी। उसके ऊपर नानू उस्ताद अय्यूब ख़ान साहब जैसी गम्भीर भाव-भंगिमा। अम्मीजान की देश-विदेश से लाईं एक से एक ड्रेस, एक अलग आतंक का माहौल बना देतीं। करेला पर नीम यह कि ग़ुस्सैल भी। किसी ने न दोस्ती करनी चाही और न उसने किसी को तरजीह दी।

छह-सात माह बाद लाइब्रेरी में मिस ख़ान ने ही आवाज़ दी थी..."ऐ... छेले की नाम...ओ...कमोल जरा-सा मेरी यह प्रॉब्लम देख लो। यानी पहले दिन से आदेश देनेवाली अदा। कमोल बेचारा...उसे तो पैदा होते ही आदेश सुनने की आदत, एकदम नेचुरल...घर जैसी फ़ीलिंग। कोई दिक़्क़त नहीं। कोई ईगो-फिगो नहीं। कोई किन्तु-परन्तु नहीं। मिस ख़ान की पढ़ाई की तकलीफ़ें अब कमोल कबीर—के.के. के ज़िम्मे। जब सेमेस्टर के सारे पेपर्स के.के. नोट्स के सहारे पार हो गए तो मिस ख़ान साहिबा को थोड़ी-थोड़ी गिल्ट-गिल्ट-सी फ़ीलिंग हुई होगी, तो उन्होंने एक अटपटा-सा, अजीबोग़रीब-सा फ़रमान जारी किया, "के.के. सुनो अब से हम तुम्हारे फ्रेंड।" कमोल को थोड़ी देर तक तो समझ में नहीं आया कि यह नया आदेश क्या है? इस पर किस तरह रिएक्शन देना है? बात कुछ खुली, तो उसने सदा की तरह हामी भर दी।

लेकिन दादू-बाबा-माँ और अब मिस ख़ान की हर बात पर हामी भरनेवाला भालो छेले-भालो कमोल इतना भालो भी नहीं था। कुछ बातें अपनी मन की भी किया करता था। जैसे दादू से सात-आठ साल तक जो पक्का गान सीखा था वो सब ध्रुपद-धमार-ख़याल, सबका कमरा बन्द कर रात में रियाज़ किया करता। पढ़ाई-प्रोजेक्ट पूरा कर, कमरे की खिड़की-दरवाज़े बन्द करके सारंगी से शुरू करता। माहौल बनते गायन का रियाज़ शुरू। काफ़ी-बागेश्वरी-जैजैवन्ती से होता आधी रात के राग मालकौंस-विहाग तक पहुँचता। फिर नियम से सो जाता। कभी जल्दी नींद आती तो सबेरे जल्दी उठकर ललित-जोगिया-रामकली-गुणकली, भोर के रागों का रियाज़।

लेकिन उस भोर में बात छुपी नहीं रह गई। उसे ठीक-ठाक याद है कि राग जोगिया के कोमल धैवत पर था कि कोई किवाड़ खटखटाने लगा। पहले धीरे-धीरे फिर जोर-जोर से। उसे उठना ही पड़ा। बड़ी खीझ हुई। न जाने कौन है? अगल-बगल के कमरों के बैचमेट्स तो धूप चढ़े आठ-साढ़े आठ बजे तक सोते थे। बैचमेट्स ही क्यों, लगभग पूरे हॉस्टल का यही हाल था। फिर जैसे-तैसे ब्रश-फ्रश करते ब्रेड-आमलेट भकोसते हाफ पैन्ट्स में ही क्लास में। यह इतना आम मंजर था कि अब कोई चौंकता भी नहीं था। लड़कियों ने भी मान लिया था कि ये नालायक-इडियट्स ऐसे ही हैं। नहीं सुधरनेवाले। अब भालो छेले कमोल ही पूरी ड्रेस में ऑड लगता। बैचमेट्स टीज़ करते। ग़ुस्साते। हार कर कमोल भी हाफ पैन्ट-स्लीपर में ही क्लास जाने लगा।

दरवाज़ा खोलते ही सामने मिस ख़ान। अभी...अभी तो ठीक से उजाला भी नहीं हुआ था। सूर्योदय के ठीक पहले का गहरा अँधेरा। क्यों...कैसे, अभी सोच ही रहा था कि मिस ख़ान उसे हल्के से ठेलते हुए कमरे में अन्दर। घूम-घूमकर कभी सारंगी-कभी तानपूरा-कभी हारमोनियम देखने लगी। अजब-ग़ज़ब मंजर थे। उनका चेहरा स्क्रीन बना हुआ था। उस पर तरह-तरह के रंग आ-जा रहे थे। कभी बैजनी-कभी नीला-जामुनी कभी लाल। चेहरा इन्द्रधनुष में तब्दील होता जा रहा था और आँखें फैलकर कानों तक पहुँच गई थीं। पहली बार भालो कमोल...कमल कबीर उर्फ के.के. मिस ख़ान के सामने नर्वस नहीं था। उसे स्क्रीन के क्षण-क्षण बदलते रंगों को देखकर मज़ा आ रहा था।

कुछ मिनटों के बाद ही मिस ख़ान के मुँह से बोल फूटे। बोल क्या, केवल हँसी के बुलबुले फूटे। वह तो बस हँसे ही जा रही थी। धीरे-धीरे पूरा कमरा उनकी खिलखिलाहट से भर उठा। अपने रोम-रोम से खिलखिलाती मिस ख़ान नीचे चटाई पर बैठ गई और तानपूरा उठा लिया। कोमल धैवत से आग़ाज़ किया। राग जोगिया अपने कोमल ऋषभ-कोमल धैवत के साथ कमरे में ख़ुद पधारकर भक्ति बिखराने लगा...सूरत बिसरे नाहीं मन सो...हृदय उपजे आस दरसन...।

5

तुव गुण रवि उदै कीनो याही तें कहत तुमको बाई उदैपुरी।
अनगिन गुण गायन के अलाप विस्तार सुर जोत
दीपक जो तोलों सों विद्या है दुरी॥
जब जब गावत तब तब रससमुद्र लहरें उपजावत
ऐसी सरस्वती कौन कों फुरी।
जानन मन जान शाह औरंगजेब रीझ रहे याही तें
कहत तुमको विधारूप चातुरी॥

—औरंगजेब

मिस शबनम ख़ान के चेहरे पर खिला इन्द्रधनुष थोड़ा ढीठ हो चला था। एक तो बिना पूछे जब-तब चला आता। और आता तो जल्दी रुख़सत नहीं होता। वे जब के.के. के कमरे में तशरीफ़ लातीं तो चेहरे का वह इन्द्रधनुष साथ-साथ तशरीफ़ लाता और कमरे की दरो-दीवार पर क़ाबिज़ हो जाता। बेशरम इन्द्रधनुष बड़ा मायावी था। मायाजाल फैलाना उसकी फ़ितरत थी। दरो-दीवार से उतरकर वह इन दोनों के वजूद में जज़्ब होने की कोशिश में लगा रहता। दोनों की निगाहों की रंगत बदलने में उसे देर नहीं लगती। उसके बाद वह हॉस्टल का नाचीज़ कमरा अपने को जन्नत का हिस्सा महसूसने लगता। फिर वहाँ जो तानपूरे-हारमोनियम के स्वर गूँजते, जो ताल

और सुर चमचमाते, जो राग और सरगम की लहरें उठतीं, उनकी ख़ुशबू से पूरी कायनात महक उठती। अमीर खुसरो-गोपाल नायक और जयदेव, स्वामी हरिदास-बैजू बावरा और तानसेन, राजा मानसिंह तोमर और बादशाह अकबर, मुहम्मद शाह रंगीले, सदारंग-अदारंग और ख़ुशरंग, वाज़िद अली शाह और विष्णु दिगम्बर पलुस्कर, भातखंडे, उस्ताद बड़े ग़ुलाम अली ख़ाँ और बड़ो बाबा, पंडित ओंकार नाथ ठाकुर और उस्ताद अमीर ख़ाँ, सबके सब उस जन्नत के टुकड़े में हाज़िर हो जाते। दाद देते, झूमते, उन दोनों के आलाप और सुर में सुर मिलाते उसे कोरस बनाते। सबका रोम-रोम गाता, रोम-रोम सुनता। ठीक शब्बो के नानू की सीख की तरह कि नग़मा ऐसा कि रूह सुने और रूह सुनाए। जन्नत के इस टुकड़े पर उस ढीठ धनुक की शरारत से रूहें सुना रही थीं और पूरी कायनात सुन रही थी। खिड़की से चोरी-छिपे झाँकता चाँद सुन रहा था, एड़ियों पर उचक कर ताकते सितारे सुन रहे थे, नदियों-वनस्पतियों की डाकिया हवा कमरे में आलथी-पालथी मार कर सुन रही थी।

सब बदल रहे थे। जैसे पतझड़ के बाद बसंत आया हो। सबसे पहले तो मिस शबनम ख़ान बदलीं। सारा रूखापन, उदासी, ग़ुस्सा, डिप्रेशन सबके सब धीरे-धीरे यूँ ग़ायब हुए मानो हरसिंगार के पौधों पर बरसों बाद नई टहनियाँ, पत्ते और कलियाँ आई हों। उसके नानू तो कहा ही करते थे कि मौसीक़ी रूह के सबसे पाक जज़्बे का बहाव है, उसे पेड़ पर पत्तियों की तरह आना चाहिए। और गुलाबी-नई-नकोरी पत्तियाँ शब्बो की रूह में उतरती-खिलती ही जा रही थीं। यह कमाल के.के. का था। जो काम दवाओं और दुआओं ने नहीं किया, नानू-अब्बू-अम्मू की राग-रागिनियों ने नहीं किया, वह असम्भव काम भालो कमोल के तानपूरे और सुर ने कर दिखाया था। एक जादू था जो घटित हो चुका था। उसे आश्चर्य भी हो रहा था, थोड़ी ईर्ष्या भी हो रही थी और थोड़ा दुलार भी आ रहा था। कमोल...भालो बाबू...।

ईर्ष्या इसलिए कि जिस ख़ानदान में वह पैदा हुई थी वह हिन्दुस्तानी मौसीक़ी के सबसे बड़े-ऊँचे आलिमों का ख़ानदान था। कहते हैं छह महीने की उम्र से ही उसने मौसीक़ी की अपनी समझ दिखलानी शुरू कर दी थी। उसकी रुलाई तानपूरे की झंकार सुनते ही बन्द हो जाती। दो-ढाई साल

की उम्र से ही अम्मू के रियाज़ के समय अलस्सुबह जग जाती। उन्हीं के बगल में बैठ, ध्यान से आरोह-अवरोह को गुनती रहती। कभी-कभी उनके आलाप में अपने तुतली आलाप की युगलबन्दी का मज़ा लेती। दुनिया-भर में हिन्दुस्तानी मौसीक़ी का अलख जगाते, सम्मान बढ़ाते लगातार घूमते रहनेवाले नानू ने उसकी जन्मजात प्रतिभा को पहचाना और पाँच साल की उम्र से बाज़ाप्ता गंडा बाँधकर अपना शागिर्द बनाया। सबसे नन्ही शागिर्द। शायद हिन्दुस्तानी संगीत के इतिहास में बाल गन्धर्व-कुमार गन्धर्व के बाद दूसरी सबसे नन्ही शागिर्द। जिसके मानस की कोशिकाओं में सारी राग-रागिनियाँ सोई पड़ी थीं। केवल सच्चे गुरु के टोहके की ज़रूरत थी। कुछ-कुछ कुमार गन्धर्व वाली चमत्कार-जैसी बात शब्बो में भी थी। लेकिन दरअसल उसके असली गुरु उसके अपने अब्बा हुज़ूर ही थे, क्योंकि चाह कर भी नानू और अम्मू अपनी व्यस्ततम रूटीन से उसके लिए समय नहीं निकाल पाते थे। इसीलिए वह नानू से तो उतना नहीं, किन्तु अम्मू से बहुत नाराज़ रहती थी। वह अब्बू की तालीम को गाँठ में बाँध तो रही थी, किन्तु औरों की तरह उसके मन के कोने में यह बात छुपी थी कि अम्मू, अब्बू से कहीं बड़ी गायिका हैं तभी तो इतना नाम है, इतना सम्मान है। इतने प्रोग्राम्स, इतने इनाम-इक़राम। लेकिन जब अब्बू के पाठ-रियाज़ की बदौलत उसने मात्र पन्द्रह बरस की उम्र में ख़याल गायकी का आउटस्टैंडिंग यंग पर्सन अवार्ड जीता तो उसका नज़रिया बदल गया। दरअसल अब्बू ख़ुर्शीद शाह ने भले ही उस्ताद अय्यूब ख़ान के क़दमों में बैठकर सबसे ऊँची तालीम पाई हो, हिन्दुस्तानी मौसीक़ी के ज़र्रे-ज़र्रे को रोम-रोम में जज़्ब किया हो, किन्तु मंच-प्रदर्शन, बैठकी-समारोह, वाहवाही, देश-विदेश के दौरे, ईनाम-इक़राम, साहब-हुक्काम सब उन्हें बेमतलब के लगते। तालियों की गड़गड़ाहटों से उन्हें घबराहट होती। वे थे ख़ानदानी जोगी और जोगी ही बने रहना चाहते थे। वर्षों के रियाज़-मेहनत-गायन की तालीम का लाभ यह हुआ कि अपने उस्ताद अय्यूब ख़ान की तरह मौसीक़ी के बहाने वे भी रूहानी ख़ुशबू से रूबरू हो गए। वह गाढ़ी ख़ुशबू उनके वजूद पर इस कदर तारी हुई कि दुनिया की हर ख़ुशबू, हर रंग फीका लगने लगा।

लेकिन इस औलिया फ़क़ीर ख़ुर्शीद शाह ने मौसीक़ी की तालीम से एक दुनियावी ईनाम भी हासिल किया था। कोहिनूर जैसे नायाब हीरे से

भी बेशक़ीमती-अनमोल-अपरूप हीरा। दरअसल तालीम के आख़िरी दिनों में उस्ताद अपनी बेटी रागेश्वरी को भी संगीत-समारोहों में साथ ले जाते। जाते तो और शागिर्द भी, लेकिन उनकी कोशिश रहती कि रागेश्वरी को भी एकल गायन का मौका मिले। बढ़ावा तो अन्य शागिर्दों को, ख़ासकर मदन बाउल और ख़ुर्शीद जोगी को भी देते, किन्तु बेटी आख़िर बेटी थी, वह भी इतनी गुणवान। मौक़ा भले अब्बू के कारण मिला हो, लेकिन रागेश्वरी ने मौसीक़ी की दुनिया में अपनी ख़ास जगह, अपनी प्रतिभा के बल पर बनाई। जल्द ही उस्ताद के बिना भी अलग से विदुषी रागेश्वरी देवी को गायन के न्योते आने लगे। उसी सिलसिले में एक बहुत ही नामी, राष्ट्रीय स्तर के संगीत सम्मेलन में गायन के लिए न्योता आया, किन्तु अब्बू को यूरोप दौरे पर निकलना था, सो रागेश्वरी का अकेले ही जाना तय हुआ। किन्तु मौसम बदल रहा था और रागेश्वरी को हरारत-सी थी। हल्का बुख़ार, सर्दी-खाँसी। तब तय यह भी हुआ कि साथ में ख़ुर्शीद जोगी भी जाएँगे। शायद उस्ताद को कुछ अन्देशा रहा हो, या यूँ ही एहतियातन।

लेकिन यात्रा की थकान या बेअसर दवा के कारण रागेश्वरी की हरारत बढ़ गई। अब उस बड़े-विशाल समारोह में अपने घराने और उस्ताद की शान बचाने की ज़िम्मेदारी ख़ुर्शीद पर। मौसीक़ी के एक से एक दिग्गज सामने बैठे हुए। उनके पीछे रसिकों की भारी भीड़। नये गायक का होश फाख़्ता करने को सारा सामान मौजूद था। लेकिन ख़ुर्शीद तो मन से जोगी। उन्हें इस भीड़ के लिए थोड़े गाना था, उन्हें तो बस अपने उस्ताद अय्यूब ख़ान और आदिगुरु गोरखनाथ को सुनाना था। दिन का चौथा पहर था। आँखें मूँदीं। जिन्हें सुनाना था, उन्हें याद किया और उस्ताद का मनपसन्द राग मारवा उठाया। उस्ताद की ही मेरुखंड तकनीक। विलम्बित में 'जाग बावरा' के षडज से ही सारी फुसफुसाहटें बन्द हो गईं। कोमल ऋषभ से तीव्र मध्यम पर पहुँचते चमत्कार-सा हुआ। लगा कि शागिर्द ख़ुर्शीद नहीं बल्कि उस्ताद अय्यूब ख़ान साहब ख़ुद माइक के सामने हों। एकदम सन्नाटा। फिर तो सवा घंटे तक मारवा ही मारवा था, विलम्बित से द्रुत तक। 'गुरु बिन ज्ञान न पावें' के बोल धरती से आकाश तक छा गए। गायन ख़त्म हुआ तो महफ़िल सराबोर हो चुकी थी। सबके हृदय और कंठ भरे-भरे से। सुनने-सुनाने के लिए कोई अवकाश ही नहीं था। उस अपूर्व मारवा के

बाद सभा उठ गई। गरम चादर और गाढ़ी चिन्ता में लिपटी रागेश्वरी के तो मानो होश गुम गए हों। गायन के शुरू होते कोमल ऋषभ से तीव्र मध्यम तक पहुँचते उसके दिल की धड़कन तीव्र से तीव्रतम हो गई। अपने अब्बू की छवि ख़ुर्शीद में उतरते देख आँखें फटी रह गईं। मारवा को यूँ रोम-रोम में उतरता महसूस करना एक अचीन्ही ख़ुशबू में डूबना, सब उसके लिए नया था। उसे सब नया-नकोर, चाँद-चाँदनी में ऊब-डूब करता लग रहा था। सामने मंच पर झूमता-झुमाता ख़ुर्शीद भी नया-नया-सा। मारवा भी बिलकुल नये कलेवर में गाढ़े-सुनहरे शहद-सा टपक रहा था। रस में भीगता सारे रसिकों का वजूद धुल-पुँछकर ज़्यादा हरा, चमचम चमकीला हो निखर आया था। कम-से-कम रागेश्वरी तो यही महसूस कर रही थी। उसे तो मंच पर अब्बू के साथ-साथ आदिगुरु गोरखनाथ भी अपने शिष्यों की भीड़ के साथ दिख रहे थे। रागेश्वरी को अब ज़्यादा आगे-पीछे नहीं सोचना था। वह जिस ख़ुशबू में डूब-उतरा रही थी उसी ख़ुशबू से उसने एक अनोखी वरमाला गूँथी और सामने रस में सराबोर ख़ुर्शीद के गले में डाल दी। अब्बू और आदिगुरु तो आशीर्वाद देने के लिए बैठे ही थे।

शब्बो को सब पता था। लेकिन न जाने क्यों ध्यान से सब उतर गया था। दुनियावी चमक-दमक, इनाम-ओ-इकराम की झमक से आँखों पर पर्दा पड़ गया था। वह अपने अब्बू के अनोखेपन को भूल गई थी। क्या अनोखा औलिया-फ़क़ीर-जोगी अम्मी चुनकर लाई थीं? अब उसके हिस्से में यह बाउल। सब औल-बौल उसके ही ख़ानदान की क़िस्मत में। समय-कुसमय, सोच में डूबती-उतराती, अनोखे रंग में रँगती, बेमतलब खिलखिलाती शब्बो ख़ुद भी औल-बौल, औलिया-बाउल बनती जा रही थी।

अब शब्बो को लग रहा है कि जो होता है अच्छा ही होता है। न वह नानू-अब्बू से ज़िद कर अहमदाबाद के राहत शिविरों में जाती, न वे ख़ौफ़नाक मंजर सामने आते, न वह शॉक्ड होती, न मेंटल ब्लॉक होता, न उसका गायन छूटता, न वह इस इंजीनियरिंग कॉलेज में आती और न इस आउल-बाउल कमोल कबीर से भेंट होती। तब फिर अनजाने में उसकी कलम शबनम के. ख़ान कैसे लिखती?

6

...ये सारे बच्चे तुम्हारी रसोई की चौखट पर कब से खड़े हैं माँ,
धरती का रंग हरा होता है फिर सुनहला फिर धूसर
छप्परों से इतना धुआँ उठता है और गिर जाता है
पर वहीं के वहीं हैं घर से निकाले ये बच्चे—तुम्हारी देहरी पर
सिर टेक सो रहे माँ
ये बच्चे कालाहांडी के
ये आंध्र के किसानों के बच्चे, ये पलामू के पट्टन नरौदा पटिया के
ये यतीम, ये अनाथ, ये बँधुआ
इनके माथे पर हाथ फेर दो माँ...

—अरुण कमल

हुआ कुछ ऐसा कि अब्बू की बेचैनी और साथ-संग चलनेवाली बद्दुआ से नानू भी कम परेशाँ नहीं रहते। एक सिलसिला था जो ख़त्म होने का नाम नहीं ले रहा था। साल-छह महीने पर देश में कहीं न कहीं अनहोनी होती रहती। अब्बूजान और उनके संगी-साथी, जोगियों की टोली वहाँ पहुँचती। घृणा की आँधी और हिंसा की आग पर न जाने कितना इनके जोगिया बाने, मौसीक़ी और निरगुन बानी का असर पड़ता। हाँ! इनके वजूद पर पड़ा असर तो महीनों परेशान करता। नानू को ये सारी क़वायदें बेमतलब लगने

लगी थीं। वे इन क़वायद से कुछ ठोस हासिल करना चाहते थे। कुछ तो हो जिसका कुछ मतलब हो, कुछ तो बात बने।

सोचते-गुनते-बुनते नानू को बड़ो बाबा का बच्चों का आश्रम याद आ गया। हुआ ऐसा था कि 1918 ईस्वी में पहली बड़ी लड़ाई के ख़ात्मे के बाद लाशों के सड़ने से महामारी फैल गई। लाल बुख़ार की ऐसी हवा फैली कि गाँव के गाँव उसकी चपेट में आ गए। एक की अर्थी उठी नहीं कि दूसरे की उठने को तैयार। जला-गाड़ कर आए नहीं कि ख़ुद भी खाट पर। कितने ऐसे भी बदनसीब कि कन्धे तक नहीं मिले...चील-कव्वे-सियार-हुँड़ार खा गए। गाँव के गाँव उजाड़। मातम लू की तरह डोलता रहता। जिधर देखो, कोई-न-कोई मुर्दा और उसके सिरहाने रोता-बिसूरता बच्चा। मरी हुई माँ और सूखी छाती निचोड़ता एक बच्चा।

आख़िर बड़ो बाबा ने राजा साहब को मनाया। राजा साहब आख़िर ठहरे उनके शागिर्द, ना कहते भी तो कैसे। महल के पास का एक खप्परपोश बड़ा मकान सौंपा गया। खाने-कपड़े के इन्तज़ामात हुए और ऐसे अनाथ-टूअर बच्चों का आश्रम शुरू हुआ। कुछ तो एकदम नन्हे-दुधमुँहे बच्चे। बड़ो दादी रुई की बत्ती से उन्हें दूध पिलाया करतीं। लेकिन बड़ो बाबा के पाक साये का असर और कठोर-कठिन रियाज़, आगे चलकर इन अनाथ-यतीम बच्चों के बैंड ने बड़ा नाम-बड़ा जस कमाया।

इस बैंड को शोहरत लखनऊ कॉन्फ्रेंस से मिली जिसके आयोजक थे मशहूर विष्णु नारायण भातखंडे। क़ैसरबाग़ में इस बड़े जलसे का आयोजन होना था। बड़ो बाबा को न्योता आया तो उनकी शर्त थी कि उनके बच्चों के बैंड को भी न्योता दिया जाए। नहीं तो वे भी नहीं आएँगे। आख़िर बच्चों के बैंड को भी न्योता मिला। सबको क़ैसरबाग़ की एक कोठी में ठहराया गया। बच्चे मैहर जैसी छोटी जगह से गए थे। देहाती ही थे। सुबह-सबेरे नहान-निबटान के लिए अपना-अपना लोटा-तामलोट लेकर नदी-नाला, झाड़ी-जंगल ढूँढ़ने लगे। कॉन्फ्रेंस वालों की ठिठोली हो गई। बच्चे मज़ाक बन गए। शाम को कॉन्फ्रेंस शुरू हुआ तो बाहर के छोटे मंच पर बच्चों को बैंड बजाने की इजाज़त दी गई। अब बड़ो बाबा भड़क गए। ऐसे भी ग़ुस्सा तो उनकी नाक पर रहता। ज़िद कि अगर बच्चों को कॉन्फ्रेंस में बजाने की इजाज़त नहीं मिली, तो वे भी नहीं बजाएँगे। बात बिगड़ती देख ख़ुद

भातखंडे साहब ने बड़ो बाबा को मनाया और बच्चों को सिर्फ़ दस मिनट अपना हुनर दिखाने का मौका दिया गया। लेकिन वही लोटा-तामलोट वाले देहाती बच्चे जब अपनी राजकीय पोशाक में मंच पर पहुँचे, तो उनकी छवि देखते बन रही थी। जब खिलंदड़े बच्चों ने अपने साज़ों पर यमन कल्याण छेड़ा तो बड़े-बड़े उस्तादों, पंडितों, ख़ाँ साहबों, राजा-बादशाहों को अपने कानों पर यकीं नहीं हुआ। फिर तो फ़रमाइश पर फ़रमाइश और बच्चे बजाए जाएँ। एक से एक कठिन राग उतने ही सहज-निश्छल भाव से।

बाबा की रियाज़ का चमत्कार, कॉन्फ्रेंस की दूसरी शाम भी बच्चों के बैंड की फ़रमाइश हुई। इतनी तारीफ़-इतनी तारीफ़ कि अब देश में जहाँ कहीं भी संगीत सम्मेलन होता, बड़ो बाबा के न्योते के साथ बैंड के लिए अलग से न्योता आता। बच्चों की तैयारी भी ग़ज़ब। एक वक़्त पच्चीस सौ से ज़्यादा रचनाओं की तैयारी उन बच्चों के पास थी कि सारी रात बजाएँ तब भी ख़ज़ाना ख़ाली न हो। नानू सुनाते-सुनाते ख़ुद भाव-विभोर हो गए। नानू कुछ-कुछ वैसा ही सोच रहे थे। ये दंगे-ये बलवे-ये क़त्लेआम-ये खूँरेजी कुछ-कुछ उस ज़माने की महामारियों की तरह हैं। प्लेग-चेचक-हैजा की तरह रह-रहकर उभर आनेवाले। वे बीमारियाँ बाहरी कारणों से फैलतीं। साइंस ने उनकी काट खोज ली। किन्तु यह जाति-धरमों का अलगाव, कट्टरता, घृणा-हिंसा सब दिमाग़ी कीड़ों के कारण, न जाने कब इनका इलाज हो!

नानू का ख़याल था कि दंगों-बलवों-क़त्लोग़ारत के बाद हर बार कुछ मासूम बच्चे यूँ ही यतीम हो छूट जाते हैं, जैसा बड़ो बाबा ने अपने समय की महामारी में देखा था। लाशों पर रोते-बिलखते, भूखे-प्यासे। राहत शिविरों के बन्द होने के बाद सड़कों पर भीख माँगते। क्यों न हम लोग भी एक आश्रम खोलें। राजा-महाराजा नहीं हुए तो क्या हुआ, अपनी रागेश्वरी रानी तो हैं ही। अपना एक जोड़ा जड़ाऊ कंगन बेच दें तो हमारे सपने को हक़ीक़त बनने से कौन रोक सकता है? नानू ने हालाँकि यूँही हँसी-ठिठोली में कंगन वाली बात कही थी, किन्तु अम्मू ने इसे बहुत संजीदगी से लिया। वैसे भी अम्मूजान को जड़ाऊ कंगनों का बड़ा शौक था। संगीत सम्मेलनों में उनकी धज के ज़रूरी किरदार थे ये कंगन। साड़ी तो सिल्क की सादी ही पहनतीं। ज़्यादातर क्रीम कलर की लाल पाड़ वाली। किन्तु ललाट पर

अठन्नी साइज की लाल टह-टह टिकुली, कानों से लटकते हीरे के बुन्दे, पान से लाल होंठ और कलाइयों में जड़ाऊ कंगन, इन सबके ऊपर दशकों मौसीक़ी की सच्ची इबादत का नूर। ऐसी राजसी धज कि मंच पर पहुँचते सन्नाटा छा जाता। फूल गिरने पर भी आवाज़ होनेवाला सन्नाटा। लेकिन जड़ाऊ कंगन अम्मू की कमज़ोर नस थे। उनकी कोशिश होती कि हर बार कंगन ज़रूर नये हों, ख़ासकर अगर विदेशों में प्रोगाम देने जाना हो तो। इसीलिए नानू के मुँह से निकले बोल ख़ाली नहीं गए। शहर के उत्तरी छोर पर कटहल मोड़ के पास ख़रीदी गई दो एकड़ ज़मीन पर एक सुन्दर-सा आलीशान, बड़ो नाना के नाम पर उस्ताद महताबुद्दीन ख़ान संगीत आश्रम का उद्घाटन ठीक एक वर्ष बाद हो गया।

तो हुआ कुछ ऐसा कि आश्रम खुलने के बाद अब्बू की टीम दो भागों में बँट गई। पहली टीम अब्बू के साथ हादसे के पहले पहुँचने की कोशिश करती। हादसा टल जाए या जानोमाल का कम-से-कम नुक़सान हो, इसके लिए यह टीम अपना जी-जान लगा देती। हादसे के बाद दूसरी टीम जाती जिसमें नानू का कोई मोतबर शागिर्द होता। एक वकील भी संग-साथ जाता ताकि राहत शिविरों से अनाथ हुए बच्चों को क़ानूनन अपनाने में कोई अड़चन नहीं हो।

शुरुआत 1978 में सुन्दरवन के एक द्वीप मोरिछझाँपी के दलित-निम्नवर्णी बांग्लादेशी शरणार्थियों के नरसंहार से बचे बच्चों एवं पश्चिम त्रिपुरा ज़िले के जिरनिया प्रखंड के मन्दई गाँव के हादसे के अनाथों से हुई, जहाँ 8 जून, 1980 की रात को दो-ढाई सौ से ज़्यादा हिन्दू बंगाली शरणार्थियों की एक हिंसक भीड़ ने सामूहिक हत्या कर दी थी। एक साल से पाँच-छह साल की उम्र के सात ऐसे बच्चे अपनाये गए जिनके माँ-बाप दोनों हादसे के शिकार हो गए थे। फिर तो यह भी एक सिलसिला सा ही चल निकला। हर साल-दो साल के बाद बच्चों का आना जारी रहा। तीन साल बाद असम के नेल्ली से बहुत ज़्यादा बच्चे आए। ऐसे भी वहाँ हिंसा के शिकार बंगाली मुस्लिम शरणार्थियों की संख्या भी दो हज़ार से ज़्यादा थी। फिर चौरासी के देश-भर में फैले दंगों से सिक्ख बच्चे-बच्चियाँ। हाशिमपुरा, हज़ारीबाग़, भागलपुर, ये जगहों के नाम नहीं थे। नानू की मानें तो ये हमारी हिन्दुस्तानी तहज़ीब के दामन पर लगे गहरे धब्बे थे।

नब्बे के बाद जम्मू के राहत शिविरों से वन्धामा, प्राणकोट, छापनारी में क़त्ल हुए पंडित परिवार के बच्चे। गहरे लाल-कत्थई काले-काले धब्बों का आकार बढ़ता जा रहा था और हमारे आश्रम में मुरझायी-बुझी सूरत वाले बच्चे-बच्चियों की संख्या।

इन सारे बच्चों में एक बात आम थी कि इनका बचपना इनकी नन्ही मुट्ठियों से फिसल गया था। हादसों के साये लगातार इनका पीछा करते। इन्हें भूख नहीं लगती। जबरन खिलाने पर भी ठीक से खा नहीं पाते। वजन गिरता जाता। ये किसी से मिलना-जुलना नहीं चाहते। इन्हें नींद ही नहीं आती। आती भी तो आधी रात में चिहुँककर उठ जाते और अपने माँ-बाबा को खोजने लगते। किसी के सिर, किसी के पेट, किसी की छाती में दर्द होता रहता। बारह-तेरह साल की उम्र तक रात में बिछावन गीला करते। ये सब गहरे मानसिक सदमे के लक्षण थे, जिससे बाहर निकालना एक बड़ी भारी ज़िम्मेदारी थी। नानू ने मनोचिकित्सक और उनकी चार-पाँच एक्सपर्ट्स की टीम लगा रखी थी जो एक वक़्त बीतते एक तरह से इस आश्रम के सदस्य ही हो गए थे।

लेकिन लगता है कि मौसीक़ी का रियाज़ और पेन्टिंग का अभ्यास ही इन असमय मुरझाये बच्चों का बचपना वापस ला पाया। धीरे-धीरे नानू-अम्मू-अब्बू सबों की मेहनत रंग लाने लगी और बड़ो बाबा जैसा हिन्दुस्तानी मौसीक़ी का बैंड तैयार हो गया, जो धीरे-धीरे संगीत-सम्मेलनों में अपनी जगह बनाने लगा था। शुरुआती दौर में आए बच्चे जवान हो रहे थे। वे न केवल मौसीक़ी बल्कि अपने मन-मुआफ़िक़ अन्य प्रोफेशन में भी सफल हो रहे थे। हरेक बच्चे की सफलता सभी लोगों का सिर फ़ख़्र से ऊँचा कर देती।

सब कुछ एक तरह से ठीक-ठाक ही चल रहा था। तभी गोधरा और गुजरात में कुछ हो गया और वली दकनी का मज़ार बचाने में अब्बू के साथ और शाहीबाग़ के पास स्टेडियम में प्रोग्राम के वक़्त अम्मू के साथ थोड़ी ज़्यादा ज़्यादती हो गई। घर पर मातम छा गया। नानू अपने दौरे से लौटे तो सदा की तरह इस दर्द की दवा भी दर्द में ही ढूँढ़ी। अहमदाबाद के कैम्पों से यतीम बच्चों को आश्रम में लाने की काग़ज़ी कार्रवाई शुरू की गई। टीम निकलने को थी तो शब्बो ने भी ज़िद कर दी। नानू को यह

ज़िद कुछ अच्छी नहीं लगी। लेकिन टीम में जा रही दोनों शिष्याओं ने ढाड़स बँधाया कि वे सब सँभाल लेंगी। नानू ने रोका तो नहीं, किन्तु कुछ खटक रहा था। अहमदाबाद के रिलीफ कैम्पों के हालात कुछ ठीक नहीं थे। शब्बो दिलो-दिमाग़ से बहुत नाज़ुक थी। उम्र ही क्या थी? मौसीक़ी में भले नाम कमाना शुरू कर दिया हो, इंटर की परीक्षा तो इसी साल पास की थी। मुश्किल से सत्रह-अठारह की होगी। ऊपर से बहुत सेन्सिटिव, बहुत जज़्बाती। जिसे अपने अब्बू की मरहम-पट्टी के समय भी एहतियातन कमरे से बाहर भेज दिया जाता। उसे ज़ख़्म-ख़ून-ख़ूँरेजी कुछ भी बर्दाश्त नहीं होता। अजब तरह से शॉक्ड-सी हो जाती। जो फिल्मों में मार-पीट के सीन के वक़्त उठकर बाहर चली जाती हो, वह गुजरात के भयावह मंज़रों को कैसे बर्दाश्त करेगी? नानू को यही सवाल बार-बार परेशाँ कर रहा था।

उधर ट्रेन में दीदी लोगों के बार-बार मना करने के बावजूद पुरानी पत्र-पत्रिकाओं में शब्बो गोधरा-गुजरात की तस्वीरें देखे जा रही थी। जान रही थी कि बर्दाश्त नहीं होगा, सदमा-सा लगेगा। लेकिन शब्बो मज़बूत बनना चाह रही थी कि अपने को मज़बूत दिखाना चाह रही थी यह तो वह ही जाने। साबरमती एक्सप्रेस की धू-धू जलती बोगियाँ, गुजरात की सड़कों-गलियों में हर कहीं आग-ख़ून, नरोदा पाटिया-गढ़ों में छिपे हुए इनसानों की जली हुई देह, गुलबर्गा सोसाइटी-सड़कों पर प्राण की भीख माँगते लोगों की आँसुओं में डूबी तस्वीरें। अपनी रुलाई को जबरन रोकती, दिल की तेज़-तेज़ धड़कनों को अनदेखा करती शब्बो और आगे-और आगे देखे जा रही थी। अन्त में जैसे ही छोटे-छोटे बच्चों के ज़ख़्मी शरीर वाली तस्वीर के पन्ने देखे, उसकी अँतड़ियों में तेज-तेज ऐंठन होने लगी। वह बेसिन की ओर दौड़ी, सब उलट कर बाहर आने लगा।

तबीयत बहुत ख़राब थी, यह तो दिख ही रहा था। केवल उल्टी ही लगातार नहीं हो रही थी, हल्का बुख़ार भी हो आया था। तब भी होटल के कमरे में रुकने को तैयार नहीं थी शब्बो। दीदी लोगों की तो छोड़िए, मोबाइल पर नानू की बात भी काट रही थी। केवल शाहआलम कैम्प भर जाएगी, फिर वहाँ से लौट आएगी। बार-बार एक ही रट। हारकर नानू ने भी हाँ कर दी। हालाँकि सबसे ज़्यादा ख़राब हालत उसी कैम्प की थी। दस हज़ार से ज़्यादा लोग और टॉयलेट केवल बीस-बाईस। गन्दगी हर

जगह बजबजा रही थी। माताएँ क़ब्रग़ाह में बच्चों को जन्म दे रही थीं, तो मर्द भी रातों में डर और जगह की कमी से कब्रों पर सो रहे थे। लगता है अनहोनी तय थी, क्योंकि जब टीम उस कैम्प में पहुँची, तो खुले में जैसे-तैसे ज़ख़्मी बच्चों की पट्टियाँ बदली जा रही थीं। नन्हे मासूम बच्चों के जिस्मों के गहरे खुले ज़ख़्मों पर नज़र पड़ते पथरा-सी गई शब्बो। चेहरा स्याह हो गया। पुतलियाँ थिर हो गईं और कुछ मिनटों के बाद ही ग़श खाकर गिर पड़ी।

7

कूचा ए यार ऐन कासी है
जोगि ए दिल वहां का वासी है
पी के बैराग की उदासी सूं
दिल पे बैराग की उदासी है
ऐ सनम तुझ जबीं ऊपर यह खाल
हिन्दु वे हरिद्वार वासी हैं
ज़ुल्फ़ तेरी है मौज जमुना की
तिल नजुक उस के ज्यों सनासी है
...
ऐ वली जो लिबास तन पे रखा
आशिकां की नजुक लिबासी है—

—वली दकनी

हुआ कुछ यूँ कि नानू की दुलारी शब्बो रानी अब अपने घर, अपने बिस्तर पर थोड़े आराम से थी। तबीयत थोड़ी सँभल गई थी। बुख़ार अब ढलान पर था। केवल नींद ने थोड़ी दूरी बना रखी थी। कभी अम्मू-कभी अब्बू राग सोहनी-राग भैरवी गा-गा कर निंदिया रानी को गुहारते। बड़ी मेहनत से वे पधारतीं। थोड़ी देर के लिए ही सही, पलकें झपकतीं कि कोई ख़ौफ़नाक

मंज़र झपाके से आता और घबड़ाकर फिर निंदिया रानी दूर चली जातीं। नतीजतन नानू-अम्मू सबों ने अपने-अपने प्रोग्राम्स रद्द कर दिए थे। सबके सब शब्बो के बिस्तर के पास। कहानियाँ-क़िस्से-गप्पें। मौसीक़ी नहीं। मौसीक़ी से न जाने क्यों शब्बो का मन उचट गया था। कोई बात नहीं। सब ठीक हो जाएगा। अभी क़िस्से-कहानियाँ ही सही, नानू को उदासी बर्दाश्त नहीं होती। वैसे भी सबों के एक साथ रहने से घर कितना भरा-भरा सा, ख़ुशगवार-सा हो गया था, इसमें उदासी को कहाँ अटना था?

नानू के पास क़िस्से-कहानियों के ख़ज़ाने थे। आपबीती-जगबीती, हर क़िस्म के क़िस्से। लेकिन इन क़िस्सों की रौ में वली दकनी की मज़ार रह-रहकर स्पीड-ब्रेकर बन जा रही थी। नानू को यह समझ में नहीं आ रहा था कि उस मक़बूल शायर ने, जिसने अपनी ज़िन्दगी गुजरात की मुहब्बत में गुज़ार दी। जिसने हिन्दुस्तानी फ़ारसी शायरी को ख़ालिस हिन्दुस्तानी ज़ुबाँ दी, उर्दू की बेशुमार गुंजाइशों और दिलकश ख़ूबसूरती का पता दिया। जिसने अपने कलाम में राम, लखन, और गोविन्द लाल को बार-बार अलग-अलग बहानों से याद किया। गुजरात से ऐसी आशनाई कि वली दकनी से वली गुजराती हो गया। उस साढ़े तीन सौ साल पहले ख़ाकनशीं हुए हरदिल अज़ीज़ शायर से इतना ग़ुस्सा-इतनी घृणा-इतनी नफ़रत कि मज़ार तक खोद दी जाए। उस पर सड़क बनाई जाए-कोलतार बिछाया जाए। नानू को लगता कि यह कोलतार केवल उस मज़ार पर नहीं, समूची हिन्दुस्तानी तहज़ीब पर बिछायी गई है। नानू को यह भी लगता कि कश्मीरी पंडितों की ज़िलावतनी, साबरमती एक्सप्रेस की जलती बोगियाँ और नरोदा-पाटिया में जल कर कोयला हुए इनसानी जिस्म, सब उस कोलतार को और गाढ़ा करते गए हैं।

नानू की ख़ासियत है कि वे बहुत देर तक नाराज़ नहीं रह पाते। किसी से सचमुच का ग़ुस्सा नहीं कर पाते। तुरन्त ही मुस्कुराहट उनके लबों पर थिरक कर ग़ायब हुए ग़ुस्से की चुग़ली कर देती है। नानू को वली दकनी के अशआर याद आ रहे थे, 'हुए हैं राम पीतम के नयन आहिस्ता-आहिस्ता, कि ज्यूँ फाँदे में आते हैं हिरन आहिस्ता-आहिस्ता।' वली को गुजरात से इतनी मुहब्बत कि एक दिन का वियोग बर्दाश्त नहीं, 'गुजरात के फ़िराक़ सों है ख़ार-ख़ार दिल, बेताब है सूनेमन आतिल बहार दिल।' हालाँकि इस

अज़ीम शायर ने काशी को भी कई बहानों से याद किया है। काशी की बात निकले और नानू के जिगरी दोस्त बाबा बिस्मिल्ला ख़ाँ की याद न आए, यह तो हो नहीं सकता। सो क़िस्सा घूमते-घूमते काशी पहुँच गया। कितनी रंगीन-मीठी-शीरीं यादें।

बाबा बिस्मिल्ला ख़ाँ का ध्यान आते नानू के ज़ेहन में ढेरों-ढेर बातें ठेलम-ठेल मचाने लगतीं। उन्हें समझ में ही नहीं आता, कहाँ से शुरू किया जाए। क्या बताया जाए और क्या नहीं बताया जाए। लिहाज़ा नानू ने बिना आगा-पीछा सोचे, जो जी में आया सुनाते चले गए। अमीरुद्दीन नौ साल की उमर से बालाजी मन्दिर के पास बैठकर शहनाई का रियाज़ किया करते। यही वह मन्दिर था जिसके सामने उनके नाना और परनाना ने भी शहनाई बजाई। मेहनताने के तौर पर रोज़ मन्दिर का प्रसाद और अठन्नी मिलती अमीरुद्दीन को। उसी अठन्नी से पक्का महाल की कुलसुम की कचौड़ी दुकान से शुद्ध घी की चार कचौड़ियाँ खाई जातीं और सुलोचना-गीताबाली की फिल्में देखी जातीं। सुलोचना और उसकी फिल्मों के दीवाने थे अमीरुद्दीन। कहते थे कि कलकलाते घी में जब कुलसुम कचौड़ी डालती तो छन्न-छन्न की आवाज़ में सातों स्वरों का आरोह-अवरोह सब दिख जाता। बरस दर बरस बीतते गए, अमीरुद्दीन रियाज़ करते-करते उस्ताद बिस्मिल्ला ख़ाँ हो गए, किन्तु बच्चों-सी निश्छल मुस्कान वही रही, बालाजी मन्दिर वाली। आज 'भारत रत्न' होने के बावजूद रोज़ सुबह-सबेरे जब रियाज़ शुरू करते हैं तो वे बाबा विश्वनाथ और बालाजी मन्दिर की दिशा की तरफ़ मुँह करके बैठते हैं। वे कहते भी हैं कि मैं यहीं से शिवजी को रोज अपनी शहनाई सुनाता हूँ और अपना सलाम भेजता हूँ।

नानू अपनी रौ में थे। बनारस से किसी ने क्या मुहब्बत की होगी जितनी मेरे यार बिस्मिल्ला ख़ाँ ने की। अमेरिका में इनकी शहनाई की धुनों पर झूमते लोगों ने वहीं बसने का न्योता दे डाला। बिना देर किए उस्ताद ने फ़रमाइश की कि मेरी गंगा माई, मंगला माई, बाबा विश्वनाथ और पक्का महाल को ले आइए, हम यहीं बस जाएँगे। यह एक बुजुर्ग के जज़्बात का उफान नहीं, बल्कि अपने मादरे वतन के प्रति सच्ची इबादत और अनगिनत नमाज़ों की ख़ुशबू बोल रही थी। ऐसी फ़रमाइश वही मौसीक़ीकार कर सकता है जिसकी रूह और मौसीक़ी की पाकीज़गी गंगा मैया की डुबकी

से जुड़ी हो, जिसकी शहनाई में अज़ान की कूक फ़िज़ा को रोशन करती हो, जो निहायत नर्मी से यह बतलाता है कि उसकी नमाज़ में सात शुद्ध और पाँच कोमल स्वर हैं।

अपने यार की शहनाई को याद करता हूँ तो अनगिनत नज़ारे नज़रों के सामने तैरने लगते हैं। पहला तो आज़ादी के जश्न की वह अज़ीमुश्शान सुबह, 15 अगस्त, 1947 जब लाल किले पर वह शहनाई राग काफ़ी के साथ अनन्त आकाश को चूमती है। उसके राग के साथ-साथ हमारा तिरंगा, हमारी नवजात आज़ादी, हरेक हिन्दुस्तानी की ख़ुशी आकाश की आख़िरी बुलन्दियों को छूती है। दूसरा नज़ारा ठीक विपरीत। बनारस में हर साल मुहर्रम में जुलूस के आगे-आगे नोहा बजाती, दुख बरसाती उनकी शहनाई। वही गमक-वही मींड़। सुख-दुख में एक समान। यही है हमारा उस्ताद बिस्मिल्ला ख़ाँ, हमारा अमीरुद्दीन-हमारा लँगोटिया।

हुआ कुछ यूँ कि तुम्हारी अम्मू की शादी का न्योता भेजा अपने दोस्त के पास बनारस। लेकिन पहले से उनका यूरोप जाना तय था। टिकट-विकट सब कट चुका था सो आ नहीं सके। लौटकर आए तो उनका फ़रमान आया, भेजो बेटी-जमाई को। यहाँ माई मंगलागौरी के मन्दिर से थोड़ी दूर शीतला घाट है। एक बहुत पुराना रिवाज है कि यहाँ नये जोड़े आकर गंगा माई की पूजा करते हैं। उनसे आँचल फैला अपने गिरहस्त जीवन की दुआ माँगते हैं। गंगा माई आसीसती हैं। काहे नहीं आसीसेंगी। हमारी बेटी-हमारा जमाई है। इतनी सेवा की है मैंने माई की। इतनी बधाइयाँ बजाई हैं। इस बार तो ऐसा बजाऊँगा कि साक्षात् माई को सामने आकर असीसना होगा हमारी बेटी को। 'गंगा द्वारे बाजे बधइया, तोहरे दुआरे बाजे बधइया।'

गंगा मइया से इतना लगाव उस्ताद का कि क्या कहें? कहते हैं कि बार-बार 'बधइया' सुनाता हूँ मियाँ, बड़ी सुरीली हैं हमारी गंगा माई। बहुत पुण्य-बहुत नेमत की बात है कि अगर मन से आसीस दी माई ने और इनका पानी देह से लग गया, तो बस सुर ही सुर होगा भीतर। बस मौसीक़ी की जन्नत होगी। कोई बेसुरा-बेताला नहीं बचेगा। सब एक सुर में होंगे। सारे झगड़े-टंटे ख़त्म। न जाति का झगड़ा, न धरम का रगड़ा। भेजो बिटिया रानी और जमाई राजा को। देखना, ऐसा इन्तज़ाम करना कि चैत्र शुक्ल सप्तमी के एक दिन पहले आप सभी काशी पहुँच जाएँ।

उस चैत्र शुक्ल सप्तमी को बनारस के जितने सुहाने रूप हमने देखे, क्या कोई बरसों में देखेगा। क्या-क्या इन्तज़ामात करके रखा था हमारे जिगरी यार ने। सबसे पहले तो शीतला घाट पर गंगा माई की पूजा और शाम को चैती गायन।

उस शाम का रंग तो अजब-ग़ज़ब था। वैसी ख़ूबसूरत-रंगीन शाम फिर जीवन में नसीब नहीं हुई। पूछ लो अपने अब्बू-अम्मू से। क्या तैयारी थी मेरे यार की। गुलाबबाड़ी नाम से चैती गायन की महफ़िल सजाने का रिवाज था बनारस का। उस रिवाज को हमारे लिए फिर से जगाया गया, खिलाया गया। गुलाबी पंखुड़ियाँ, गुलाबी रंग के बल्ब, गुलाबी रंग का मंच, गुलाबी कपड़ों का शामियाना-कनात, गुलाबी रंग के गावतकिया और ऊपर से गुलाब-जल का छिड़काव। पूरी फ़िज़ा गुलाबी-गुलाबी। रोशनी ऐसी कि गंगा जी की लहरें भी लाल-गुलाबी। फिर चैती और ठुमरी का गायन। सच कहता है मेरा यार कि 'मौसीक़ी की जन्नत से अलग कोई जन्नत नहीं इस जहान में।'

8

ख़ाँचार भीतर अचिन पाखि केमने आसे जाए।
धोरते पारले मनोबेड़ी दिताम ताहार पाये॥
...
मन तुइ रइलि ख़ाँचार आसे
ख़ाँचा जे तोर तैरी काँचा बाँसे
केनदिन ख़ाँचा पड़बे खसे,
फ़क़ीर लालन केंदे कय।

पिंजड़े के भीतर अनचीन्हा पंछी, कैसे आए-जाए?/मैं पकड़ पाता तो मन-बेड़ी डाल देता पंछी के पाँव।/...मन तुझे रही पिंजड़े की आशा, पिंजरा जो तेरे कच्चे बाँस का,/एक दिन पिंजड़ा गिरेगा नीचे, फ़क़ीर लालन रो-रो कह जाए।

—लालन फ़क़ीर

शाहआलम कैम्प हादसे के बाद शब्बो तीन-चार हफ़्तों में पूरी तरह ठीक तो हो गई। अब पूरी तरह बुख़ार-उख़ार सब उतर गया। रातों को नींद ठीक से आने लगी। भूख भी लगने लगी। इसे ही सबों ने ठीक होना मान लिया और रोज़मर्रा के ढर्रे पर लौट गए। लेकिन शब्बो ने यह छुपाया था कि

जले हुए जिस्मों की चिरायंध ने उसका पीछा करना नहीं छोड़ा। अलस्भोर में रियाज़ के लिए जब बैठती है तो क़ब्रों में पैदा हुए नवजात शिशुओं की रुलाई कानों में गूँजने लगती है। कि पलकें मूँदते ही कटे हुए मासूम जिस्मों के ज़ख़्म अपनी आँखें खोल उसे तकने लगते हैं। अब वह शब्बो, जिसने छह माह की उम्र से तानपूरे के साथ रोना-हँसना-किलकारी भरना सीखा था, जिसने अपनी तुतलाहट से अम्मू के आलाप को एक ख़ास दूधिया गंध दिया था, कहते हैं कि जिसकी कोशिकाओं में हज़ारों राग-रागिनियाँ सोई हुई हैं, वही शब्बो रियाज़ से दूर भागने लगी। मौसीक़ी से घबड़ाने लगी। एकदम मन ही उचट गया। आश्रम के मनोचिकित्सकों की हर थेरेपी कुंद पड़ गई। अब्बू के राग विहाग और राग मधुवन्ती ने भी इस बार असर नहीं किया। शायद वली दकनी के ज़मींदोज़ मज़ार पर जमाया गया कोलतार पसरता हुआ दिलो-दिमाग़ तक आ पहुँचा था।

थक-हार कर नानू-अम्मू-अब्बू सबने यह फ़ैसला किया कि ज़बरदस्ती नहीं की जाए। वैसे भी बेमन से की गई इबादत की तासीर भी क्या होगी? अभी आगे की पढ़ाई पर ही शब्बो ध्यान दे। नानू का ख़याल था कि साउंड इंजीनियरिंग पढ़ाई जाए ताकि सुर-ताल, राग-रागिनियों से किसी तरह से नाता जुड़ा रहे। न जाने कब, कौन-सा आलाप, कौन-सी बन्दिश, कोई शुद्ध-कोमल धैवत-निशाद मन की किसी तंत्रिका को छू जाए और अपनी शब्बो फिर से पहले वाली शब्बो में तब्दील हो जाए। तो क़िस्सा-कोताह यह कि नानू की इसी तजवीज़ से मिस शबनम ख़ान मौसीक़ी की दुनिया से सिम्बायोसिस इन्स्टीट्यूट ऑफ मीडिया एंड कम्यूनिकेशन में साउंड इंजीनियरिंग पढ़ने आ गई। कि पढ़ाई पूरी करते ही अपना एक अत्याधुनिक आलीशान रिकॉर्डिंग स्टूडियो खोलना था। अब अन्दर से तो पहले जैसी ही जज़्बाती, मासूम और खिलंदड़ी शब्बो ने न जाने क्यों झूठी अकड़ और ढेर सारी संजीदगी ओढ़कर कैम्पस में कदम रखा।

भालो कमोल ने न जाने कितनी बार मिस शबनम ख़ान से यह कहानी सुनी होगी, किन्तु कभी मिस ख़ान ने उससे यह नहीं पूछा कि वह अपनी रसभरी मौसीक़ी की जन्नत सी दुनिया को छोड़कर पुणे के इस इंस्टीट्यूट में क्यों पहुँचा? मिस ख़ान की अपनी ही कहानी ख़त्म हो, तब न वह कमोल से पूछे। लेकिन कमोल तो सम्पूर्ण भालो, ख़ूब-खूब भालो, उसे किसी से

कोई शिकायत नहीं। वह तो बाउल। बाउल के लिए क्या अच्छा, क्या बुरा! सब समान। सबसे कुछ-कुछ सीखने का। अपने बारे में सोचते रहना भी एक स्वार्थ। हर तरह के स्वार्थ से बाउल को दूर रहने की हिदायत मिली थी लड़कपन से। सो कमोल को मिस ख़ान से भी कोई शिकायत नहीं। मिस ख़ान के कारण कुछ अच्छा-अच्छा भी तो हुआ।

जब नानू-अम्मू-अब्बू सबको मालूम हुआ कि शब्बो की राग-रागिनियाँ फिर से जाग गई हैं, तो उन सबकी ख़ुशी का ठिकाना नहीं रहा। मोबाइल के स्पीकर पर तो उनकी ख़ुशी छलक-छलक जा रही थी। नानू ने उसी दिन पुणे के गन्धर्व महाविद्यालय में बात की। क्लासिकल मौसीक़ी की तालीम की दुनिया में पंडित विनायक राव पटवर्द्धन के इस महाविद्यालय का कोई जवाब नहीं था। एक से एक सितारे गायकों को जन्म देनेवाले इस अज़ीमुश्शान अंजुमन को अपने-आप पर यूँ ही फ़ख़्र नहीं था। वैसे भी नानू ने बताया कि पंडित विनायक राव पटवर्द्धन क़ाबिले-परस्तिश पंडित विष्णु दिगम्बर पलुस्कर के शागिर्द थे, इसीलिए इस अंजुमन पर उनका भी पाक साया है। उनकी भी दुआ है। अब इंजीनियरिंग की पढ़ाई के साथ-साथ सुबह-शाम शब्बो और कमोल की फिर से मौसीक़ी की तालीम की शुरुआत हुई।

शब्बो की ज़िन्दगी में शाहआलम कैम्प के हादसे के बाद जो कुछ बेहतर और ख़ूबसूरत हो रहा था, उन सबके पीछे कमोल था। भालो कमोल। उसका मन तो कमोल का पूरा मुरीद हो गया था। किन्तु झूठी अकड़ और ओढ़ी संजीदगी अभी आगे जाने को तैयार नहीं थी। लेकिन उसके नानू कमोल के बाबा का नाम सुनते ही इतना-इतना ख़ुश हो गए कि शब्बो चौंक-सी गई। फिर नानू शुरू हुए तो कमोल के पूरे ख़ानदान का इतिहास बता डाला। कैसे अपने बड़ो नानू एक बार भटकते-भटकते तारापीठ पहुँच गए। वहाँ से केन्दुली गाँव के जयदेव मेला। एक तरह से बाउल गायकों की राजधानी।

बाउलों से पहली भेंट बड़ो नानू की उर्स मेले से शुरू हुई। कमोल के दादू रोबिन बाउल से हुई जान-पहचान जन्मों की गहरी दोस्ती में बदल गई। दादू रोबिन बाउल ने ही उसके बाद उन्हें सँभाला। उन्हें अजय नदी के किनारे के मोनेर मानुष अखाड़ा ले गए। दिन-रात मौसीक़ी के पाक पानी

से नहलाया। एक औलिया और एक बाउल की इस भेंट ने बहुत करामात किए। दरअसल बाउल हरि जाप भी करते और महान नबी-मौला-अल्लाह को भी पुकारते-टेरते। आदि गुरु लालन शाह फ़क़ीर ने यही सीख दी थी। सहजिया बौद्ध-सूफ़ी और वैष्णव भक्ति की त्रिवेणी यहाँ बहती थी। इनकी रवायत में सूफ़ियों के संग गौर-निताई, चैतन्य-नित्यानन्द शामिल थे।

शब्बो ने इतनी बार यह कहानी बड़ो नानू से सुनी थी कि बाउलों का इतिहास रटा गया था। कहते हैं कि निताई-नित्यानन्द के बेटे बीरभद्र ने ही नेड़ा-नेड़ी को वैष्णव धर्म में दीक्षा दी थी वहीं से बाउल परम्परा की शुरुआत हुई। उधर ख़ुद मिताई-चैतन्य पर चंडीदास का प्रभाव। उन्हीं के गीतों में डूबे रहते। उनका 'सबार ऊपरे मानुष सत्य, ताहार ऊपर किछु नाईं' का फ़लसफ़ा मिताई-निताई से होता लालन तक पहुँचा था और 'मोनेर-मानुष' यानी मन के अन्दर रहनेवाले मानुष की तलाश की व्याकुलता में बदल गया था। इस फ़लसफ़े ने बड़ो नानू को भी अन्दर-बाहर से पूरी तरह बदल डाला।

बड़ो नानू का गोप्पो भी आजोब। वली दकनी से शुरू करेंगे तो अपने यार बिस्मिल्ला ख़ाँ तक पहुँच जाएँगे। वैसे ही बाउलों की बात शुरू करके बीच में जोगियों की कहानी, अब्बू और दादू की कहानी सुनाने लगेंगे। अपनी भटकन के सिलसिले में ही अब्बू के बाबा सिकन्दर शाह जोगी के साथ भी बड़ो नानू उस्ताद महताबुद्दीन ख़ान ने अच्छा-ख़ासा समय गुजारा था। जोगी भी इस पिंड में ही ब्रह्मांड की मौजूदगी को मानते। हूबहू मोनेर मानुष वाली बात। जात-धरम का भेद यहाँ भी नहीं और जोगियों में भी नहीं। दुनियावी चमक-दमक, धन-सम्पत्ति से वास्ता यहाँ भी नहीं, वहाँ भी नहीं। बाउल एक कदम आगे। यहाँ ज़रूरत से ज़्यादा पैसे को अच्छा नहीं माना जाता। आमदनी का एक हिस्सा ग़रीबों में बाँटने का रिवाज। बाउल तो केवल जात-धरम की बराबरी ही नहीं बल्कि धन-सम्पत्ति की बराबरी का सुन्दर ख़्वाब को सँजोए हुए थे।

बड़ो नानू की मानो मन के समाज, मन के लोगों से भेंट हुई हो। महीनों साथ में गुज़ारे। ख़ास बात यह कि गौराई-निताई ने जयदेव के गीत-गोविन्द को अपने भक्ति जतरा से जोड़ा था। वह रवायत बाउलों तक आ पहुँची थी। गीत-गोविन्द बाउल-गान में शामिल था। लेकिन वह अष्टपदी शुद्ध रागों पर

आधारित था। राग भैरवी, विभास, रामकरी,...और...न जाने कौन-कौन! बड़ो नानू पर तो मानो ख़ुशियों की बारिश हो रही हो।

उधर पक्के गान के रसिया कमोल के दादू रोबिन बाउल को तो मानो बैठे-बिठाए मन की मुराद मिल गई हो। मानो भीख के लिए फैलाये दामन में कोहिनूर आ गिरा हो।...कि लालन ख़ुद लौटकर आ गए हों... कि मिताई-निताई। मा...गो...इतने बड़े उस्ताद महताबुद्दीन ख़ान जैसा गान-गुरु ख़ुद चलकर उनके द्वार पर। विश्वास नहीं हो रहा था। ऐसे बड़ो गुरु से रात-दिन सीखने की धुन। मोनेर मानुष अखाड़ा में अब रात होती ही नहीं थी। नींद की भी नींद ग़ायब हो गई थी। सबके सब पक्के गान के झरने में रूह मल-मलकर नहाने में मगन थे। सुनते-सुनते अजय नदी की धारा भी पक्के रागों की शौकीन हो गई। वह भी बड़ो नानू की शागिर्द बन अपनी कलकल को रागों में ढालने लगी। क्या आलम...क्या मंज़र! जैसे जोगियों के यहाँ से बड़ो नानू अपने संगी सिकन्दर शाह जोगी के बेटे ख़ुर्शीद (अब्बू) को शागिर्द बनाने लेकर आ गए, वैसे ही विदा होते वक़्त बाउलों के यहाँ से बन्धु रोबिन बाउल के बेटे मदन को गंडा बाँधकर ले आए।

अब हुआ यूँ कि यह सब अपने प्यारे नानू से सुनकर शब्बो को अपना भालो कमोल ज़्यादा अपना लगने लगा। अपने ही परिवार, अपने ही ख़ानदान का एकदम ख़ासमख़ास अपना। लेकिन वह अभी सब छुपाकर रखना चाहती थी। कुछ तो झूठी अकड़ और ओढ़ी संजीदगी की बाधा, तो कुछ ऐसा कि पहली बार भीतर की खिलंदड़ी शब्बो को अपने इस ख़ासमख़ास के बारे में सोचकर लाज आने लगी थी।

९

प्रथम खरज सुर साधे सोई गुणी जों सुध मुद्रा वाणी गावै।
द्रुत मध विलम्पत लघु गुण पुलित कर दिखावै॥
सप्तसुर तीन ग्राम एकईस मुरछना बाईस सुरत
उनचास कोटितान ताको भेद पावे।
सरस्वती होय प्रसन्न हो सोई शाहजहाँ के श्रवणन को रिझावै।

—शाहजहाँ

ऐसा नहीं था कि भालो कमोल से भेंट होने के बाद केवल मिस शबनम ख़ान ही बदली थीं। बदला तो अपना कमोल भी था। मिस ख़ान के संग-साथ ने उसे अन्दर-बाहर से धीरे-धीरे बदल दिया था। गाँव-कस्बे का थोड़ा-सा झेंपू, थोड़ा ज़्यादा चुप्पा, सबों से आँखें चुरानेवाला, लड़कियों से बहुत-बहुत घबरानेवाला, कमोल के ये सारे मटमैले, धूमिल-धूसर रंग मिस ख़ान की रोशन शख़्सियत की धूप में खोते चले गए। पीछे मुड़कर देखने पर थोड़ी दूर दोराहे पर वह झेंपू कमोल नज़रें चुराता हुआ दिखता। न जाने कब कमोल की चाल-ढाल, बोली-बानी हूबहू मिस ख़ान जैसी होती चली गई। वैसे ही आत्मविश्वास से भरे कदम हवा में तैरते हुए, वैसी ही सीधी-चीरती निगाहें, वैसी ही टनटन आवाज़। एक नया-नकोरा कमोल, मानो लार्वा-प्यूपा को फाड़कर निकली कोई नर-तितली कि तितला अपने सतरंगे पंख फड़फड़ाता परवाज़ भर रहा हो।

उधर मिस शबनम ख़ान की झूठी अकड़ और ओढ़ी संजीदगी की नक़ाब आहिस्ता-आहिस्ता सरकती जा रही थी। दोनों की ग़ैर जानकारी में हौले-हौले यह लेन-देन का व्यापार चल रहा था। एक-दूजे को, एक-दूजे का रंग, रँगे जा रहा था और इसकी ख़बर उन दोनों को ही न थी। उधर इस अदृश्य रंगों की अद्‌भुत रंगबाज़ी को देख सैकड़ों साल के झीने पर्दे के पीछे खड़ा हिन्दवी का पहला महाकवि ख़ुसरो गुनगुनाए जा रहा था, 'आज रंग है, ऐ माँ, रंग है री।' और दोनों पर चढ़ता रंग गाढ़ा होता जा रहा था।

अब हुआ कुछ ऐसा कि दोनों रंगरेज़ों का रंगरेज़ी का कार्य-ब्योपार मौसीक़ी के रियाज़ के साथ परवान चढ़ता गया। एक इतवार चढ़ती रात में इसी रियाज़ के सिलसिले में राग शिवरंजनी के आरोह में ही मिस ख़ान की झूठी अकड़ और ओढ़ी संजीदगी की सारी नक़ाब एक झटके में सरक गई। जज़्बाती शब्बो शिवरंजनी के करुण सुरों में बह चली। आँखें कहना मानना भूल, धार-धार बरसने लगीं। फिर उनके बाद कोई रियाज़ नहीं, राग-रागिनियों का अनुशासन-व्याकरण नहीं, एक अलग तरह के अलौकिक सुर-ताल में दोनों बह चले। आपबीती-जगबीती, जगबीती-आपबीती की एक अलग तरह की मौसीक़ी। अलग, अपूर्व, लय, सुर, ताल। वक़्त क्या, पूरी कायनात अपनी रफ़्तार रोक इस अनोखे संगीत में ऊब-डूब करने लगी।

आज शब्बो बोन्धु कमोल की एक-एक बात जानने को आतुर थी। सब कुछ इतना-इतना जानना चाह रही थी कि कमोल, कमोल न रहे वह शब्बो बन जाए। और शब्बो, शब्बो न रहे वह कमोल हो जाए। बोन्धु कमोल...कि...भालो कमोल...न...कमल कबीर...न...न...कमल बाउल।

शब्बो तो अपने प्यारे नानूजान से कमोल के दादू-बाबा के बारे में बहुत कुछ जान गई थी। दोनों ख़ानदानों की पीढ़ियों के प्यारे-गहरे सम्बन्धों से वह तो वाक़िफ़ थी लेकिन अपने बोन्धु भालो कमोल को इस वाक़िफ़ियत का थोड़ा भी इशारा नहीं किया था। कोई संकेत तक नहीं। यह उसकी झूठी अकड़-ओढ़ी संजीदगी के ही कारण हुआ कि बढ़ती लाज के कारण, यह तो शब्बो को भी नहीं पता! लेकिन इस ख़ास पल में यह सब जानकर कमोल तो भौचक रह गया। उसके प्यारे दादू मिस ख़ान के बड़ो नानू

के बोन्धु थे, शागिर्द थे और उसके बाबा मिस ख़ान के अम्मू-अब्बू के बोन्धु हैं, नानू उस्ताद अय्यूब ख़ान के शागिर्द तो उसका मुँह खुला का खुला रह गया। थोड़ी देर के लिए तो कुछ समझ में ही नहीं आया। उसे अपने कानों पर विश्वास ही नहीं हो रहा था। जब इतना नज़दीक का नाता था तो बेकार में मिस ख़ान से वह इतने महीनों से झेंपता, सकुचाता और ख़ौफ़ खाता रहा।

उसी रात यह बात निकली कि बोन्धु कमोल ने मौसीक़ी की दुनिया क्यों छोड़ी? अब अपने बोन्धु भालो कमोल के सामने चिराग़ था। कहानी उसे ही सुनानी थी। मिस ख़ान...नहीं, शब्बो और उसके साथ कोने में उठँगी हवा, खिड़की पर आलथी-पालथी मारे चाँदनी, झाँकती शिउली-जवा कुसुम की टहनियों और थमे हुए वक़्त को सुनना था। सब ने टकटकी लगा दी थी। सकुचाता कमोल विलम्बित लय में हौले-हौले शुरू हुआ।

तो हुआ कुछ ऐसा था कि बाबा जब उस्ताद अय्यूब ख़ान के यहाँ लगभग दस साल मौसीक़ी की सीख पूरी करके लौटे तो मन में बहुत उमंग थी। लेकिन कोलकाता की हवा ही कुछ अलग थी, कुछ भद्रो-भद्रो जैसी। शास्त्रीय संगीत की दुनिया तो और भी भद्र। वहाँ तो बस कुछ घरानों का वर्चस्व। चक्रवर्ती, बंद्योपध्याय, चट्टोपाध्याय, मुखोपाध्याय जैसे भारी-भरकम नामों ने एक बड़ी मोटी लक्ष्मण रेखा खींच रखी थी जिसमें अज्ञात कुल-शील का प्रवेश वर्जित था। लेकिन सच कहें तो बंगाल क्यों पूरे हिन्दुस्तान में शास्त्रीय संगीत का माहौल कुछ ऐसा ही था। थोड़ा-सा नकचढ़ा एलीट-एलीट सा।

अब बाबा तो बाउल, छोटा लोग। भद्रलोक के बाहर के, ग्राम्य बांग्ला के। वैसे भी पुरूलिया, वीरभूम, वर्धमान, जंगल महाल को कौन बांग्ला मानता था कोलकाता में। दूसरी ओर उनके उस्ताद अय्यूब ख़ान कितने भी बड़े गायक हों, पद्मश्री-पद्म विभूषण हों, न उन्होंने किसी घराने से शिक्षा ली थी, न उन्होंने किसी घराने की शुरुआत की थी। कुछ शुद्धतावादी घराने तो उनकी गायकी को ही शक की नज़र से देख रहे थे, तो उनके शागिर्द की क्या हैसियत? वह भी कोलकाता के नकचढ़े भद्रोलोक में! सो कोलकाता से बाबा को केवल उपेक्षा, हिक़ारत और तिरस्कार ही मिला। वैसे भी बाबा के बाउल संस्कारों ने बहुत बड़े-बड़े सपनों के महल

नहीं बनाए थे। कोई बहुत इनाम-इक़राम, यश-नाम की लालसा नहीं थी। बस इतना चाहते थे कि उनके उस्ताद ने जो नई शुरुआत की थी, उनसे बंगाल भी परिचित हो सके। केवल सदियों से स्थापित राग-रागिनियों की शुद्धता, उनके वादी और संवादी स्वरों के व्याकरण को लेकर कोलाहल नहीं, बल्कि ये राग-रागिनियाँ जिन भावों की वाहक हैं-माध्यम हैं, उनका लोकार्पण। गायक के तप से रागों के भाव की अमूर्तता श्रोता के मन में मूर्त हो सके। उन के हृदय में बस सके। यह कोशिश थी उस्ताद अय्यूब ख़ान और उनके शागिर्दों की। लेकिन हिन्दुस्तानी संगीत के अधिकांश घराने गान-व्याकरण की शुद्धता और उसके दुहराव में उलझकर रह गए थे। वहाँ सारा रियाज़ इस व्याकरण के शुद्ध-शुद्ध दुहराव के द्वार पर दस्तक देता ठिठक गया था। साथ ही वहाँ आँखें मटकाती हुई ईर्ष्या थी, अट्टहास करता द्वेष था, एक-दूसरे को नीचा दिखाने के तरह-तरह की साज़िशें थीं, चक्रव्यूह थे।

वैसे भी मंच से बिना गाये उतारे जाने के अपमान ने उस्ताद अय्यूब ख़ान को तोड़ने के बदले एक नई, कभी न ख़त्म होनेवाली तपस्या की राह दिखलाई थी। कुछ दिनों के शोक और आँसुओं से उबरनेवाला अय्यूब, एक नया, संकल्पबद्ध उस्ताद था जिसे ऐसा गायक बनकर उभरना था जिसके जैसा न सुना गया हो, न गाया गया हो। जिसे भारतीय शास्त्रीय संगीत को दुहराव के दुष्चक्र से बाहर निकाल, आकाश की नई ऊँचाइयाँ देनी थीं। उस्ताद ने हिन्दुस्तानी तहज़ीब के मूल सूत्र समावेशन को पकड़ लिया था। जहाँ भी जो भी अच्छा है, बेहतर है, श्रेष्ठ है उसे जोड़ते जाना है। हालाँकि उनके बाबा उस्ताद महताबुद्दीन ख़ान ने भी अपने गायन में बाउल और जोगी परम्परा की कई बन्दिशों-रागों को शामिल करके इस जोड़ने के सिलसिले की शुरुआत कर दी थी। इसे हमारे बाबा के उस्ताद ने बहुत आगे बढ़ाया। बहुत ऊँचाइयाँ दीं।

अब कई घरानों की ख़ासियत-ख़ुसूसियत को जज़्ब करना इतनी आसान बात भी नहीं थी। सो उस्ताद अय्यूब ख़ान ने रियाज़ को पूरी तवज्जो दी। अपने को तन्हाई में बन्द कर रियाज़ पर एकदम एकाग्र-यकसू हो गए। बरसों-बरस ऐसा रियाज़ कि उनकी हर साँस मुसलसल चलनेवाले एक ख़ामोश रियाज़ में बदल गई। मेरुखंड तानों के अभ्यास ने उन्हें सरगम

एवं पलटों के प्रति इतना सहज कर दिया कि उनकी गायकी भावों को मूर्त करती, रसिकों के मन में आनन्द की वर्षा करती। उनके अपने मादरे-वतन के सच्चे तहज़ीब से जुड़ाव ने कई और कारनामों-उपलब्धियों को जन्म दिया। वे राग-प्रस्तुति के दौरान विलम्बित के लिए एक भक्तिपरक बन्दिश को चुनते तो द्रुत को फारसी की ख़ासकर अमीर ख़ुसरो की कविता या तराने से सजाते, जिससे एक सच्ची हिन्दुस्तानी मौसीक़ी की ख़ूबसूरत छटा प्रकट होती। मंच पर प्रस्तुति के क्रम में वे उत्तर भारतीय और दक्षिण भारतीय रागों का भी सामंजस्य करते। मेरे बाबा और उनके संगी-साथी इस बात के गवाह हैं कि उनके उस्ताद के गले में पाँच हज़ार तानों ने अपना स्थायी घर बना लिया था और जब उनकी तानें एवं सरगम असंख्य चिड़ियों की तरह उड़ते हुए अनन्त आकाश में अपना बसेरा बनाते, तब अनायास सम्मोहित सभा-श्रोता-रसिक ख़ुदी को भूल बेख़ुदी में खोते चले जाते।

अब भौचक होने की बारी शब्बो की थी। अपने प्यारे नानूजान की ख़ासियतों, उनकी तप-तपस्या-रियाज़ की इन गहराइयों-बारीक़ियों की जानकारी उसे भी नहीं थी। उसे तो जन्म से यह सब कुछ सहज-सरल रूप में मिला। इनके पीछे के संघर्ष की कहानी किसी ने बतलाई ही नहीं थी। लेकिन कमोल की कहानी अभी ख़त्म नहीं हुई थी क्योंकि न केवल कोलकाता के भद्रलोक ने बाबा को ठुकराया था, बल्कि बाउलों की बदली दुनिया ने भी उस्ताद मदन बाउल को रोकने में पूरी ताकत लगा दी थी। दरअसल बाउल संगीत अब फैशन में था। बाज़ार में एक बिकाऊ माल। नकली बाउलों ने मंच की सारी जगह हथिया ली थी। बाउल फ़क़ीरों का ग़रीब बाना, पैबन्द लगे कुर्ते, लुंगी, मुरैठा भी ब्रांडेड हो गए थे। महँगे, चमचम चमकीले, रंग-बिरंगे नये बाने में पैबन्द लगाकर उसे 'बाउल बाना' बनाया जाता। पॉप संगीतकार उसे धारण करते ही बाउल हो जाते। भले उन्हें बाउल का अर्थ, परम्परा, दर्शन और गानों का मतलब मालूम न हो। बाउल-मेलों में एकतारा-दोतारा-डुबकी की जगह आधुनिक वाद्ययंत्र तेज़ी से जगह बना रहे थे। वह इबादत की जगह टका कमाने का ज़रिया हो गया था। यहाँ उस्ताद मदन बाउल का क्या काम? बाबा मदन बाउल को भी ऐसे नक़ली और खोखले टका-रुपयों की दुर्गन्ध से भरे माहौल में उल्टी आती। वे वहाँ से भी दूर हो गए। भला हो आपके नानू उस्ताद

अय्यूब ख़ान साहब का कि उन्होंने अपने सभी शागिर्दों को भातखंडे संगीत विश्वविद्यालय से डिग्रियाँ दिलवा दी थीं। इसीलिए बाबा को अपने ही शहर के रोबिन ठाकुर संगीत महाविद्यालय में नौकरी मिलने में दिक़्क़त नहीं हुई। किन्तु एक भारी चिन्ता उन्हें घेरे रहती कि आदि गुरु लालन शाह फ़क़ीर के दस हज़ार गीतों का क्या होगा? एकतारा-दोतारा-डुबकी-खमोक वाले मूल बाउल संगीत का क्या होगा? इनकी रिकार्डिंग कर सुरक्षित तो रखना होगा, इसलिए मौसीक़ी छोड़ कमोल इंजीनियरिंग पढ़ेगा। साउंड इंजीनियरिंग। बस भालो कमोल पुणे आ गया।

10

जो कोई आवे है नज़दीक ही बैठे है तिरे,
हम कहाँ तक तिरे पहलू से सरकते जावें॥

—मीर हसन

एक ख़ुशबू शब्बो और कमोल के इर्द-गिर्द तिरती रहती। एक अलौकिक ख़ुशबू, जिसका न कभी वास लिया गया और न कभी महसूस किया गया। एक अपूर्व रंग उनके चेहरे के नूर में झिलमिलाता रहता। सात रंगों के परे एक ग़ैर दुनियावी रंग, जो न पहले देखा गया, न सुना गया। यह बात सबसे पहले सूरज ने किरणों से कही। फिर किरणों ने समन्दर से, समन्दर ने बादलों से, बादलों ने फूलों से, फूलों ने भँवरों से, भँवरों ने तितलियों से, तितलियों ने ख़ुशबू से, ख़ुशबू ने हवा से और फिर सारी दुनिया को पता चल गया कि शब्बो और कमोल प्यार में हैं। दरअसल दोनों ने वक़्त की तासीर ही बदल दी थी। कब रियाज़ करना है और कब पढ़ाई करनी है, यह उनका मन तय करता, वक़्त नहीं। हाँ! वक़्त बेचारा उनके मन के हिसाब से अपनी रूटीन बदलता रहता। शब्बो केवल सोने के लिए अपने कमरे में जाती, बाकी वक़्त कमोल से साथ ही गुज़ारती। लेकिन यह सोने का वक़्त क्या होगा, यह वक़्त नहीं, उनका मन तय करता।

दूसरी अनोखी बात यह थी कि दोनों रियाज़ कर रहे हों या पढ़ाई, एक-दूजे को निहारते रहते। पलकें खुली हों या बन्द हों, एक-दूजे के चेहरे के नूर में झिलमिलाता वह अपूर्व ग़ैर दुनियावी रंग उनकी पुतलियों में तैरता-डुबकी लगाता रहता। पुतलियों और पलकों की यह रंग-बिरंगी जुगलबन्दी पूरी कायनात को सम्मोहित कर रही थी। हालात कुछ यूँ हो गए थे कि चाँद और सूरज उनकी पलकों पर ही उगते और अस्त होते और तरेगन तो उनकी पुतलियों में ही क़ैद हो सुकून महसूस कर रहे थे।

हुआ कुछ ऐसा कि जब शब्बो, कमोल हो गई थी और कमोल, शब्बो हो गया था, तो रोज़-रोज़ सुबह सात बजे और शाम सात बजे बिना नाग़ा किए वह कौन थी जो कमोल के मोबाइल की बाँसुरी पर टेर भरती, जिस टेर को सुनते कमोल के चेहरे के रंग झरने लगते और वह कमरे के बाहर जा फुसफुसाने लगता! स्वाभाविक था कि शब्बो को यह जानना था। 'कौन' का यह सवाल अब उसके दिमाग़ी सुकून पर भारी पड़ रहा था। कमोल जिस तरह टाल रहा था, सकुचा रहा था, यह देख-सुनकर शब्बो की नाक पर ग़ुस्सा मक्खी की तरह फड़फड़ाने लगा और पुतलियों में चमकते तारे बरसने लगे। इस तरह शब्बो और भालो कमोल के जीवन की रंग-बिरंगी, श्वेत-श्याम कई-कई कहानियों में कालिन्दी की कहानी भी शामिल हुई। जिस तरह चाँद-चाँदनी, बादल, बरसात और फूल कभी पुराने नहीं होते, उसी प्रकार कालिन्दी की कहानी भी एकदम नई-नकोरी थी। कुछ खट्टी, कुछ मीठी, कुछ सोंधी, कुछ तीखी।

हुआ कुछ ऐसा कि एक-डेढ़ साल पहले दूसरे सेमेस्टर की परीक्षा देकर कमोल घर गया हुआ था। मामा के घर शादी थी। माँ केवल उसके आने का इन्तज़ार कर रही थी। दूसरे दिन ही बस से चुरूलिया नानीबाड़ी। बचपन से सारी गरमियों की छुट्टी कमोल ने उसी घर-आँगन-गलियों-अमराइयों-ताल-तलैयों में गुज़ारी थी। सो चुरूलिया का नाम सुनते उसके रोम-रोम में फुरफुरी होने लगती। कमोल के पाँच-पाँच मामा और चार-चार पीसी माँ-मौसी। उसी के उम्र के ढेर सारे ममेरे-मौसेरे भाई-बहन। लगभग डेढ़ दर्जन। धमा-चौकड़ी से न केवल घर बल्कि पूरा मुहल्ला नगाड़े की आवाज़ की तरह गूँजता रहता। मुहल्ले भर के बूढ़े-बूढ़ियों के सिर में दर्द हो जाता। तपती गर्मी की दोपहर में घर से बाहर भयानक लू की चपेट

में न आए, बीमार न पड़े, इसीलिए बिना नागा किसी न किसी की पिटाई होती। डर के मारे बड़े हॉल में सबके सब आँखें मूँदे नींद का नाटक करते। बड़े-बूढ़ों की खर्राटों की आवाज़ सुनते ही एक साथ सब फुरफुरा के जग पड़ते। चिलचिलाती धूप और भूतनी-सी नाचती लू में सारे भाई-बहनों के दो ही प्रिय खेल थे। पहला किसी की भी अमराई में जाकर ढेला चलाकर आम तोड़ना। बदले में बगीचे के बीचोबीच कुएँ के पास झोंपड़ी में आराम कर रहे रखवाले की गालियाँ सुनना। ढेले खाना। दूसरा और भी रोमांचकारी-सनसनी से भरा, किसी पुराने ख़ाली घर-गोदाम-खंडहर में ततैयों के छत्तों को ढेला चलाकर तोड़ने की कोशिश करना। फिर पीछा करते ततैयों के ग़ुस्सैल झुंड के ख़तरनाक डंकों से बचने के लिए सिर पर पाँव रखकर भागना। चूँकि रोज़-रोज़ के अनुभव ने यह बता दिया था कि ढेला चलानेवाले या सबसे पीछे छूट गए या ठेस खा कर लुढ़के भाई-बहनों को ततैया का डंक लगना तय है, इसलिए नौसादर-चूना और लोहे के चाकू की व्यवस्था दादा लोग पहले से कर के रखते। लेकिन लाख नौसादर-लोहा रगड़ा जाए थोड़ी-सी सूजन, थोड़ी सी लाली, चेहरे-बाँह-गरदन-पीठ कहीं न कहीं दिख ही जाती। या फिर सबसे छोटे भाई-बहन की रुलाई लाख पुचकारने पर भी नहीं रुकती और बात खुल जाती। फिर बिना नागा संध्याकालीन पिटाई। इस प्रकार हमारा खट्टा-मीठा-तीखा, डंक और चोटों की मीठी-मीठी दर्द से भरा रोमांचकारी-सनसनीख़ेज़ बचपना इतनी तेज़ी से बीता कि हमें पता ही नहीं चला। लेकिन साथ-साथ खाए डंकों और खजूर की छड़ी की पिटाइयों ने हमारे बीच के नेह-बन्धों को अजीब मज़बूती प्रदान कर दी थी। सो चुरूलिया का नाम सुनते रोम-रोम में फुरफुरी उठने लगती। सारी यादें नींद से जाग, कुलाँचें भरने लगतीं।

इस बार तो दादा की शादी थी। बड़े मामा-मामी के सबसे बड़े बेटे। भारी उमंग-उल्लास का माहौल। ख़ुशी-खिलखिलाहट, गीत-गान से घर-आँगन, आकाश-बातास सब भरे हुए। मामी के मायके से भी बहुत मेहमान आए थे। उन्हीं में कालिन्दी भी थी। मामी की भतीजी, उनके बड़े भाई की बेटी। कोलकाता के सुप्रसिद्ध लोरेटो वीमेन्स कॉलेज की बी.ए. अंग्रेजी ऑनर्स की छात्रा, एन.सी.सी. की फलाँ, जूडो की ढिकाँ, गायन-नृत्य...। बड़ाई की एक लम्बी फ़ेहरिस्त। भालो कमोल का कस्बाई-ग्रामीण संस्कार तो अनजानी

लड़कियों से यूँ ही सकुचाया-दबा-दबा सा रहता। उस पर लोरेटो कॉलेज, एन.सी.सी, जूडो...और न जाने क्या-क्या...बेचारा बोझ से दबता चला गया। वैसे भी कमोल का ख़ूब गोरा भभूका रंग और इंजीनियरिंग कॉलेज की पढ़ाई बड़ी मामी की भाभी को भा गई थी, लेकिन उनकी दुलारी एन.सी. सी. की फलाँ और जूडो की ढिकाँ को कुछ ज़्यादा ही भा गई थी। पहली नज़र में फ़िदा-उदा हो जानेवाली जैसी कुछ बात। चुपके से उस फलाँ-ढेकाँ साँवली-सलोनी कालिन्दी के मन में एक दुर्घटना-सी घट गई थी। जिसकी भले उसके अलावा और किसी को ख़बर न हो, किन्तु कमोल की माँ को थोड़ी-बहुत ख़बर थी। बड़ी मामी ने अकेले में फुसफुसाकर प्रस्ताव रखा था। फुसफुसाकर इसीलिए कि कमोल की पाँच-पाँच मामियाँ और संयोग से सबकी ब्याहने लायक़ भतीजियाँ। सबों का कमोल पर जाना-अनजाना हक़। सबों ने कभी न कभी कमोल की माँ को अकेले में फुसफुसाकर यूँ ही प्रस्ताव दिया था। लेकिन बड़ी मामी एक डेग आगे। भतीजी सशरीर हाज़िर। वह भी बड़ाइयों की लम्बी फ़ेहरिस्त के साथ।

उधर पहली नज़र में फ़िदा-उदा जैसी कालिन्दी का नशा दिन-दुगना रात चौगुना गाढ़ा होता जा रहा था। भालो, दब्बू, झेंपू कमोल पर दुलार-प्यार बढ़ता जा रहा था। शादी घर के भरे-पूरे माहौल में भी, बड़े-बूढ़ों की तरेरती निगाहों को ठेंगा दिखाती कालिन्दी भालो कमोल के इर्द-गिर्द मँडराती रहती। औरों के लिए भाई-बहनों की एक झिलमिली-सी ओट कहने-सुनने भर को तो थी ही। कालिन्दी को भीड़ में कमोल के अलावा कोई और नहीं दिखता। ढीठ इतनी कि कमोल अपने भाइयों के साथ नाश्ता करने बैठता, तो पाटी खींच सामने बैठ उसके ही पत्तल में नाश्ता करने लगती। दोपहर-रात के खाने में भी वही ढिठाई। नानू की डाँट को घुटने तक लम्बे बालों से झटककर उड़ा दिया। एक रात तो हद हो गई। कमोल की ही उम्र की, उसके ही रंग-रूप की मौसेरी बहन कालिन्दी की बगल में हॉल में ढेर सारी महिला मेहमानों के साथ सोई थी। न जाने कैसे कालिन्दी की आँखें खुलीं, आधी नींद में उसे न जाने क्यूँ यह लगा कि बगल में कमोल सोया है। शायद भाई-बहन के एक तरह के रूप-रंग, नाक-नक्श ने धोखा दिया हो। चिहुँक कर चिल्ला पड़ी। पूरे घर भर में जागरण हो गया। ख़ैरियत यह रही कि उस रात भीड़ के कारण कमोल तो छोटे मामा के यहाँ बगल के

मकान में सोने चला गया था। बहुत किरकिरी हुई कालिन्दी की। ख़ूब-ख़ूब डाँट। रात की बात भोर में भूलने की बात हुई थी। लेकिन न बात छुपी और न कालिन्दी पर कोई असर पड़ा। उलटे उसका नशा और गाढ़ा हो गया और झेंपू कमोल थोड़ा और डर गया।

उधर माँ, मौसियों की तरह ऊपर-ऊपर मामियों से मिल्लत रखती। खुल कर हँसती-बोलती, लेकिन दिल से पसन्द नहीं करती। दरअसल नानी शुरू से ही अपनी बेटियों से बहुओं की इतनी-इतनी शिकायतें करती रहतीं कि माँ-मौसी लोग भी क्या करतीं? धीरे-धीरे भाभियों की ओर से उनका भी मन फट गया। एक कभी न भरी जानेवाली दरार। जो हर ननद-भाभी के बीच में पायी ही पायी जाती है। वैसे भी कमोल की शादी एक भाभी की भतीजी से कर के और चार-चार भाभियों को नाराज़ नहीं करना चाहती थी कमोल की माँ। कौन मुँह फूला-फूली वाले माहौल में कल की छुट्टियाँ बरबाद करे। ऊपर से कालिन्दी की ढिठाई ने उनके न के निर्णय को मजबूत ही किया था। संकोच में माँ मामी के मुँह पर सीधे-सीधे तो ना नहीं कह पाई। पढ़ाई के बाद सोचने की बात कहकर टाल दिया। भालो कमोल ने आज तक किसी को न अपनी ओर से कोई बात कही थी, न कालिन्दी से कुछ कह पाया।

सो ब्याह ख़त्म होते कमोल माँ के संग लौट आया, किन्तु लगता है, कालिन्दी पूरी तरह नहीं लौट पाई। उसका बहुत कुछ चुरूलिया में छूट गया था। निगाहों की एक अजीब तरह की ख़ुशबू में ऊब-डूब करती वह कोलकाता तो लौट गई, किन्तु उसके वजूद का बड़ा हिस्सा कमोल के संग पुणे चला आया था, जिसको तलाशने बिना नागा सुबहो-शाम फ़ोन किया करती। कालिन्दी की कहानी ख़त्म होते-होते न जाने क्यों शब्बो का ग़ुस्सा सातवें आसमान पर पहुँच गया। तमतमाहट में उसने कमोल का मोबाइल छीना और जोर से पटक दिया।

इति श्री कालिन्दी कथा प्रथम अध्याय समाप्तम्।

11

अगर तुम राधा होते श्याम
मेरी तरह बस आठों पहर तुम
रटते श्याम का नाम...
चुपके चुपके तुमरे हृदय में
बसता बंशीवाला
और, धीरे-धीरे उसकी धुन से
बढ़ती मन की ज्वाला
पनघट में नैन बिछाए तुम
रहते आस लगाए
और काले के संग प्रीत लगाकर
हो जाते बदनाम...

—क़ाज़ी नज़रूल इस्लाम

कालिन्दी की माँ को समझ में नहीं आ रहा था कि उसकी भीषोण रागी मेये को यह क्या हो गया है? मुहल्ले-कालेज में छेले लोगों को नाकों चने चबवानेवाली उसकी मेये एकाएक कैसे बदल गई? ज़्यादा आगे-पीछे करनेवाले कैसे-कैसे गुंडों-बदमाशों को एक थप्पड़ में ठीक करनेवाली यहाँ कैसी ख़ुद इस लड़के के आगे-पीछे घूम रही है? ठीक है कमोल

बहुत सुन्दर है, इंजीनियरिंग भी कर रहा है, गान-वान भी गाता है, लेकिन उसकी माँ ने अभी तक हाँ तो नहीं बोला है न। फिर इतना लगाव क्यों? मेरे समझाने पर भी नहीं समझ रही। बाबा ने आँखें दिखाईं, फिर भी कमोल के साथ एक ही पत्तल में खाने बैठ गई। मेरी मेये तो ऐसी नहीं थी! बाबा का कहा कभी नहीं टालनेवाली एकाएक ऐसी कैसी हो गई? किसी ने टोना-टोटका तो नहीं कर दिया? नाते-रिश्तेदारों से घर भरा हुआ, कल को अगर यह ब्याह नहीं हुआ तो हम कहीं मुँह दिखाने के लायक नहीं रह जाएँगे। जाति-बिरादरी में तो थू-थू हो जाएगी। इकलौती मेये मेरी, न जाने इसका क्या होगा?

उधर कालिन्दी की कुछ अलग ही चिन्ता, विलग ही फिकिर। क्या है यह खोका, एकदम मम्मीज बॉय। क्षण-क्षण अपनी मम्मी की ओर ताकता रहता है। उन्नीस-बीस से कम का क्या होगा, लेकिन लगता है कि अभी तक दूध के दाँत भी नहीं टूटे हैं। ऐसा भालो छेले तो पूरे कोलकाता में ढूँढ़ने पर नहीं मिलेगा। कैसे-कैसे चंट-चालू-बकबकिया छोकरों से पाला पड़ता रहा है। यह इतना अलग क्यों है? भालो कमोल...नाम ही धरा गया भालो कमोल...वाह रे। कुछ बोलता क्यों नहीं यह खोका। इतना तंग करती हूँ, डाँट ही दे। इसके बदले इसकी ममेरी-मौसेरी बहनें टाँग अड़ाती रहती हैं। धत् तेरे की...इत्ता ओभर प्रोटेक्टेड खोका...इसकी आगे की ज़िन्दगी कैसे चलेगी? इस बदमाश दुनिया को कैसे झेल पायेगा? इसको तो मेरी जैसी ही बीवी चाहिए। माँ और बहनें कब तक आँचल की छाँह दिये रहेंगी।

यह चुप और चुप्पी क्यों? इसकी चुप्पी भी एक रहस्य बन गई है। केवल हिरण के बच्चों की तरह बड़ी-बड़ी आँखों से चकित होकर इधर-उधर निहारता रहता है। लगता है यह भालो खोका पहली बार दुनिया देख रहा हो। बोलता क्यों नहीं? मैं कितना तो बोलती रहती हूँ। अपने कॉलेज के बारे में...टीचर्स और सहेलियों के बारे में...एन.सी.सी. कैम्पस और गणतंत्र दिवस के परेड के बारे में...। किन्तु यह केवल आँखों को कानों तक फैलाकर चुपचाप सुनता रहता है। कुछ बोलता ही नहीं। सुनाती हूँ इसे और इसकी बहनें हुँकारी भरती रहती हैं। बेमतलब का सवाल पूछ-पूछकर बाल का खाल निकालती रहती हैं। मैं बढ़ा-चढ़ाकर, झूठ-सच फेंट-फाटकर गप्प देती हूँ कि कभी तो टोकेगा, झूठ भाँपकर हँस देगा, लेकिन नहीं...

कभी टोकता ही नहीं। मेरा झूठ-सच सब वैसे ही आँखों-कानों से सुनता रहता है। चेहरे पर कोई भाव आने ही नहीं देता। क्या खोका है!

हाँ! टोका इसने। बोल इसके फूटे। आज सीढ़ी के कोने में अकेले में घेर लिया और ज़बरदस्ती मुँह में कैडबरी ठूँस दी। कित्ता तो घबड़ा गया खोका।...छेले मेये से डरे? हद हो गई। लेकिन कितना-कितना मीठा बोला... की कोरछो तुमी?...क्या आवाज़...क्या मिठास...जैसे मधु टपका हो टप टप...।...जैसे बुलबुल ने कुछ गाया हो आ ऽ प आ ऽ प। जैसे फूल की पंखुड़ियों पर अलस्भोर ओस टपकी हो...जैसे दूर कहीं बाँसुरी बजी हो... जैसे घुँघरू खनके हों रुनझुन...रुन...झुन...। किसी छेले की ऐसी मीठी वाणी होगी...यह सपने में भी नहीं सोचा था। ऐसी देवता जैसी आवाज़ सुनकर लगा कि साँस लेना कुछ कठिन हो गया है। जैसे हवा चलते-चलते रुक गई हो! धूप कुछ कुम्हलाती नज़र आई! कोयल जैसी मीठी आवाज़...बस पढ़ा ही था...आज सुनी।...लेकिन यह फिर चुप क्यों हो गया? यह बोलता रहे, मैं सारी ज़िन्दगी सुनती रहूँ। किन्तु यह तो झुक कर मेरी बाँह के नीचे से निकल गया। फिर यह जा...वह जा...ख़ैर! मेरी कैडबरी फेंकी नहीं।

मुझे इसकी वाणी सुननी है। अब इस देववाणी के बिना चैन नहीं। बहनों को फुसलाया कि मुझे नज़रूल संग्रहालय घूमना है। उनका स्मारक भी देखना है। कमोल को ले चलो। बहनों के साथ चलने को तैयार तो हो गया, लेकिन फिर वही चुप्पी। केवल आँखों से चकित भाव से निहारता रहा। हाँ! शायद आँखें ही कुछ बोलती रहीं...कुछ शिकवा...कुछ शिकायत...कुछ डर भी। मुझसे डरता है यह खोका...हद है। इसे तो मालूम ही नहीं कि मैं ही तो इसके सारे डर दूर करूँगी। अपने आँचल से ऐसा ढककर रखूँगी कि धूप का कोना भी नहीं छुए। इसके दूधिया रंग को कभी कुम्हलाने नहीं दूँगी।

मैंने जानबूझ कर नज़रूल और प्रोमिला देवी के ब्याह की बात छेड़ दी। कितना विरोध...कितनी परेशानी...। कुमिल्ला का सेनगुप्ता परिवार कितना स्नेह करता था, 'धूमकेतु' के विद्रोही कवि-सम्पादक क़ाज़ी नज़रूल इस्लाम से। 1922 के दुर्गापूजा विशेषांक में नज़रूल की दीर्घ कविता 'आनन्द माँ का आगमन' ने कैसी धूम मचाई थी। दुर्गा माँ की भारत माँ। कैसे विदेशी

शोषकों का नाश करेंगी हमारी आनन्दमयी माँ। फिर पुलिस का छापे पर छापा। सम्पादक पलायन कर कुमिल्ला में। फिर दीवाली विशेषांक में भीषोण उग्र सम्पादकीय। अन्त में गिरफ़्तारी, 'देशद्रोही' कवि को साल-भर की सज़ा। 1923 में छूट कर आए। उनकी अमर कीर्ति 'अग्निवीणा' इसी साल छप कर आई। इसी साल कवीन्द्र रवीन्द्र ने अपना गीति नाट्य 'बसंत' विद्रोही कवि क़ाज़ी नज़रूल को समर्पित किया। कितना प्यार...कितना दुलार...। पूरा बंगाल क्या, पूरा देश प्यार कर रहा था विद्रोही कवि से, तो सेनगुप्ता परिवार की मासूम किशोरी प्रोमिला कैसे बची रहती? वह भी चुपके से अपना नाम प्रोमिला नज़रूल इस्लाम लिखने लगी थी। विधर्मी संग ब्याह। बहुत बवाल। किन्तु माँ गिरिबाला देवी अपनी बेटी और होनेवाले जमाई के साथ खड़ी रही। कुमिल्ला छोड़ कोलकाता आ गई। किन्तु प्रोमिला की उमर बस सोलह बरस, सिविल मैरेज हो नहीं सकती थी। अठारह होने तक इन्तज़ार कठिन, सो निकाह ही पढ़ा गया। किन्तु प्रोमिला को अपना विश्वास, अपना विचार, अपना धरम मानने से कोई नहीं रोक सका। मुल्ला-मौलवी को डाँटकर भगा दिया नज़रूल ने कि कभी कलमा नहीं पढ़ेगी प्रोमिला। कोई ज़बरदस्ती नहीं चलेगी। उस वक़्त कितने साहस-कितनी हिम्मत की बात थी। इसी चुरूलिया गाँव के नज़रूल और इसी चुरूलिया का नवासा कमोल...कोई मेल नहीं। कहाँ वे शेर-बब्बर, कहाँ यह खरगोश। चुप्पा खरगोश। सारी बहनों को प्रोमिला-कथा कंठस्थ थी, तो इसे क्यों नहीं पता होगी? ख़ूब पता होगी। फिर भी एक बार भी नहीं बोला। बहनें ही पट-पट बोलती रहीं, मैनाओं की तरह, तोतियों की तरह।

कैसे इस भोंदू की मीठी आवाज़ सुनी जाए? बतरस की लालच बढ़ती ही जा रही थी। इसकी बहनें तो कह रही थीं कि बहुत भारी गवैया है। अपने दादू से सात साल गाना सीखा है। ध्रुपद, धमार, ख़याल, ठुमरी, बाउल-गान, नज़रूल गीति...सब के...सब। क्या गाता होगा यह गूँगा...। अगर गाता होगा तो क्या अपूर्वो गान होता होगा वह! बहनें तो कहती हैं कि आँगन में बैठकर गाता है हमारा दादा तो गौशाला से सारी गायें खूँटा तुड़ाकर गान सुनने आ जाती हैं। झूठी कहीं की! फेंकती हैं। गाय गान सुनने आती हैं... हद है...झूठी सब...तानसेन है क्या? किस्से-कहानियों में यह सब होता है, सच में थोड़े ही।

सब ने बहुत मनाया, पीसी माँ, नानी-दादी सब ने। आख़िर में उसकी मम्मी ने डपटकर कहा तो तैयार हुआ। शाम होते बड़े से आँगन में दरी, चादर, गावतकियों की व्यवस्था हुई। धीरे-धीरे आस-पास के घरों से भी लोग जुट गए। कमोल ख़ुद तानपूरा लेकर बैठा, पखावज पर एक भाई। जैसे ही तानपूरे ने झंकार भरी, लगा इन्द्रधनुष झंकृत हुआ हो। लगा मन्द-मन्द बहती बयार एक ठौर दुबक गई हो। सुरमई शाम तो ठिठक ही गई थी। आँगन की कोने की शिउली का पत्ता-पत्ता मानो कान बन गया हो। गुलाब तो गुलाब, उसके कांटे भी कलियों-से दमकने लगे। नज़रूल गीति से शुरुआत हुई। अनुरोध भी यही था। 'जोदि तुमि राधा होते श्याम' गीति के स्वर हवा के रेशे-रेशे को कँपाने लगे। हृदय के अन्दर कोई स्वर्गिक बाँसुरी बजने लगी। तभी सचमुच गौशाला से गायें बरामदे में आकर निःशब्द खड़ी हो गईं। कान-पूँछ सब स्थिर। न जाने कहाँ-कहाँ से कबूतर-मैना और न जाने कौन-कौन से पक्षी आकर छतों पर उतरने लगे। सबों ने मौन धारण कर रखा था। पखावज की ताल और कमोल के सुर एकमेक होकर चारों दिशाओं में थिरक उठे थे। फिर संध्या-राग पीलू 'तुम ही बसत हो प्रियतम प्यारे, तन में मन में नैन लुभाने'। लगा कोई जादू हुआ हो। भाँति-भाँति के चित्र बदलने लगे। जैसे कोई मायावी अपने अदृश्य हाथों से चित्र उकेर रहा हो और मिटा रहा हो। उधर समय भी चुपचाप अपनी गति समेट कर तानपूरे के तारों में दुबक गया था। अद्‌भुत गान से मता कर पृथ्वी के संग पूरा ब्रह्मांड घूमर भरने लगा था। कोने के शिउली-रातरानी के गाछ-पौधे भी घूमर लेने लगे। कुछ ही देर बाद सबकी आँखों के काजल आँसुओं के साथ बह निकले।

अनहद आनन्द के आँसुओं ने न केवल पुरुष-स्त्री बल्कि गाय-गोरू, पंछी-पखेरुओं के कोरों को भी गीला कर दिया। नीलाकाश के नौ लाख तारों ने बहुत धीरज रखा, किन्तु अन्त में उनके आँसू भी ओस बनकर टपक पड़े। मुझे लगा, अन्तस में एक प्राण नहीं, हज़ार-हज़ार प्राण हों और सबके सब बाहर आने को मचल रहे। परम आनन्द में सबों की आँखें मुँदी थीं। पलकें ख़ुशी का बोझ नहीं उठा पा रही थीं। मेरे हज़ार-हज़ार प्राण होंठों पर आकर ठिठके हुए। मेरी विकल और विह्वल पलकें खुलीं, तो अन्य सभी की पलकों को बन्द पाया। न जाने कैसे-कब मेरे होंठ कमोल के होंठों

से जुड़ गए। एक सुघट घटना थी, घट गई। भोंदू कमोल को घबड़ाकर गान तो नहीं रोकना था न! हालाँकि गान रुकने के बाद भी सुर और लय कई पल तक गूँजते रहे...फ़िज़ा में...कानों में...अन्तस में। लेकिन बदमाश कबूतर! सबसे पहले उन्होंने ही गुटर गूँ कर के यह जता दिया कि गान तो बन्द हो गया। फिर गायों की घंटियाँ टनटना उठीं। फिर तो हड़बड़ाहट ही हो गई। पूरे मुहल्ले को एक साथ छूटे हुए काम याद आ गए।

यह सब सपना था कि सच, समझ में नहीं आ रहा। कहीं सच में ऐसा कुछ होता है क्या? यह सपना ही था। लेकिन अन्तस में जो गूँज रहा 'जोदि तुमि राधा होते श्याम'...वो कैसे? मेरे हज़ार-हज़ार प्राण क्यों उमड़ रहे? मैंने मधु के...अमृत के घड़े में होंठ लगाकर पीने की जो कोशिश की उसकी अमृत-धार से मेरे रोम-रोम आप्लावित हैं। लगता है सब सपना ही है, क्योंकि परम आनन्द के इन पलों में विषाद की एक काली छाया भी मेरे तन-मन-प्राण पर क्यों छाती जा रही है...।

क्या है यह? हर्ष और विषाद एक साथ क्यों? क्यों यह अमृत-कलश... यह भोंदू-भालो-कमोल मुझे मिल नहीं सकता? क्या मेरे प्राणों की विकल पुकार अनसुनी रह जाएगी? लेकिन लगता है सच तो यही है। बाकी सब सपना था। क्योंकि इसकी माँ की आँखों में तो मेरे लिए बस सूनापन ही झलकता है। कोई लगाव...उछास...प्रेम...स्नेह नहीं। हाँ! वहाँ नकार ही है...। हाँ होती तो आँखें चुगली करतीं। सब बता देतीं, लेकिन वहाँ बस उचाट है...रेत है...। अब मेरी आँखें जितनी उमड़ लें। हृदय में हूक मर्मान्तक उठ-उठकर उसे मसलकर पीड़ा पहुँचाती रहे। लेकिन सच तो बस यही है। अब इस भोंदू-भालो-कमोल के बिना...इसकी मधु सी मोहक वाणी और दैवी गान के बिना जीना क्या और मरना क्या? यह जीवन तो चुम्बन के उस अमोल, नन्हे से पल में ही पूर्ण हो गया। मेरा सम्पूर्ण जीवन उसी अमृत-कलश में समा गया। अब बस यह छाया जीवन...कमोल बिना प्राणविहीन...। इसे कब तक ढो पाऊँगी? क्या अमृत न मिला तो किसी विष को गले लगाऊँगी?

12

तेग़ मुन्सिफ़ हो जहाँ, दार-ओ-रसन हों शाहिद,
बेगुनाह कौन है उस शहर में क़ातिल के सिवा॥

—अली सरदार जाफ़री

[तेग़ = तलवार, मुन्सिफ़ = न्यायकर्ता, दार-ओ-रसन = फाँसी का फंदा, शाहिद = मौके पर मौजूद गवाह]

कुछ ही वर्ष पहले की तो बात है, जब पुणे से वह मनहूस ख़बर आई थी। हम सबों के नानू उस्ताद अय्यूब ख़ान की हत्या हो गई। पंडित विष्णु दिगम्बर पलुस्कर और उनके शागिर्द पंडित विनायक राव पटवर्द्धन से जुड़े शहर पुणे में नानू की हत्या? हर साल की तरह एक संगीत-समारोह में भाग लेने गए थे नानू। और हमेशा की तरह ही अपने पुराने साथी डॉ. मांजरेकर के घर ठहरे थे। डॉ. मांजरेकर की भी अजीब हस्ती। मेडिकल की ऊँची पढ़ाई करने के बाद भी प्रैक्टिस नहीं करते थे। उनका कहना था कि देह के रोगों का इलाज तो कोई भी डॉक्टर कर देगा, मुझे तो मन की, दिलो-दिमाग़ की बीमारियाँ ठीक करनी हैं। लोगों के दिमाग़ में बसे हुए अन्धविश्वास, भूत-प्रेत, जिन्न-चुड़ैल, ओझा-गुनी, पीर-फ़क़ीर जैसे बैक्टीरिया-वायरस को ख़त्म करना है। उनसे इस देश में हज़ारों सालों से फैली बीमारियों को दूर भगाना है। उन्होंने क़रीब पच्चीस-तीस साल पहले

'वैज्ञानिक चेतना विकास समिति' का गठन किया था। दशकों के अथक मेहनत के बाद उनका संगठन न केवल महाराष्ट्र बल्कि अन्य राज्यों में भी सक्रिय हो गया था। शहरों में कॉलेज-यूनिवर्सिटी के बच्चे-बच्चियाँ 'अन्धविश्वास विरोधी' जत्थे निकालते थे। वे डॉ. मांजरेकर की वैज्ञानिक चेतना के सन्देश को सुदूर गाँवों तक फैलाने की कोशिश कर रही थीं। उनके ही आन्दोलन के दबाव से राज्य विधानसभा ने जादू-टोना विरोधी विधेयक पारित किया था। लेकिन दूसरी ओर उन्हें नापसन्द करनेवालों की संख्या भी बहुत बड़ी थी और लगता है वह दिन दूनी-रात चौगुनी बढ़ती ही जा रही थी। नानू ने ही कभी बातचीत के दौरान बताया था कि उन्हें अक्सर धमकी भरे फ़ोन, चिट्ठियाँ, ई-मेल आते रहते हैं। लेकिन मांजरेकर साहब ठहरे ज़िन्दादिल, हौसले वाले, उन्होंने कभी सरकार की सिक्यूरिटी रखने की पेशकश को मंजूर नहीं किया। मौत का तो एक दिन मुक़र्रर है। उसके लिए इतनी बेचैनी क्यों, परेशानी क्या? वह मुक़र्रर दिन आ ही गया। हत्यारे दरअसल उन्हें ही मारने आए थे। दोनों साथी, नानू और डॉक्टर साहब सुबह-सबेरे टहल कर लौट रहे थे कि घर में घुसने के पहले गोलियाँ चलने लगीं। ख़बर यह भी थी कि केवल दोस्त को बचाने के लिए नानू ने गोलियाँ नहीं खाई थीं बल्कि हत्यारे उन्हें भी पहचानते थे। उन पर गोली चलाते समय कुछ शुद्ध-उद्ध करने की बात चिल्ला-चिल्लाकर कही गई थी कि इन म्लेच्छों से माँ शारदे के मन्दिर को शुद्ध करना है। चश्मदीदों की गवाही में भी यह शुद्धता वाली बात आई थी। अख़बारों ने भी इसे बॉक्स में छापा था।

कुछ देर तक तो किसी को यह समझ में ही नहीं आया कि किस शुद्धि की बात हो रही है? न अम्मू, न अब्बू, न शब्बो भाभी, न कमोल को। किसे म्लेच्छ कहा जा रहा था और किससे सरस्वती माँ के मन्दिर को पवित्र करने की बात की जा रही थी? नानू उस्ताद अय्यूब ख़ान जिन्होंने अपनी पूरी ज़िन्दगी हिन्दुस्तानी मौसीक़ी की इबादत में गुज़ारी थी। जिन्होंने ख़याल गायकी को अलग इत्तिहाद-एका का रंग दिया। जो बड़े ग़ुलाम अली ख़ाँ की तरह जब हरि ओम तत्सत् गाते तो लगता बन्द पलकों की ओट में स्वयं भगवान विष्णु शेषशय्या पर लेटकर आनन्दित हो रहे हों। और पंडित जसराज की तरह मेरो अल्लाह

मेहरबान गाते तो द्रुत तक पहुँचते-पहुँचते कब अल्लाह ओम में तब्दील हो जाते और ओम अल्लाह में कि रसिकों को फ़र्क़ करना मुश्किल हो जाता। तो क्या वह गला, जो माँ सरस्वती-औढरदानी शिवशंकर और अल्लाह-मौला को एक ही साँस में याद कर रहा था वह किसी म्लेच्छ का था? आज जब उस संत गायक की आवाज़ सदा-सदा के लिए बन्द कर दी गई थी, तो क्या शुद्ध हो गया था? आख़िर क्या शुद्ध होना था? कैसे शुद्ध होना था? और किनसे शुद्ध होना था? बात अभी तक पूरी खुली नहीं थी।

आख़िर नानू-अम्मू के ख़ानदान को कितना जानते थे गोली मारनेवाले या मारने की सुपारी देनेवाले? इस खाँटी हिन्दुस्तानी परिवार में कोई कुछ दिन आकर रहे, फिर कहे कि ये म्लेच्छ हैं, विधर्मी हैं—इन्हें कहीं और चले जाना चाहिए...। हिन्दुस्तानी तहज़ीब से अलग क्या थी इनकी मुसलमानी? रियाज़ में डूबे रहना ही उनकी इबादत थी। मौसीक़ी ही पूजा और मौसीक़ी ही पाँचों वक़्त की नमाज़ थी। हिन्दोस्ताँ में मौसीक़ी को इबादत मानने का रिवाज बहुत पुराना रहा है। इस ख़ानदान से तो कभी किसी ने नहीं पूछा था, किन्तु सहारनपुर घराने के डागरों के पूर्व उस्ताद अल्ला बन्दे ख़ाँ से उनके छोटे बेटे रहीमुद्दीन ख़ान ने एक बार पूछा था कि उन्हें नमाज़ वग़ैरह में दिलचस्पी क्यों नहीं है? उन्होंने बड़ी संजीदगी से जवाब दिया था कि मेरा मज़हब मेरे गान से अलग नहीं है। मेरी लिए यही इबादत, यही नमाज़, यही मौला की पुकार है। गान में तो हर पल डूबा ही रहता हूँ, फिर अलग से नमाज़ की क्या ज़रूरत है?

अगर भारतीय संगीत को सारे म्लेच्छों के स्पर्श से मुक्त होना था, इसे परम पवित्र और शुद्ध करना था, वेद माता की जय बोलते हुए पुनः सामगान-मार्गीगान-प्रबन्धगान की ओर पीछे लौटना था, तो बहुत ही मेहनत की ज़रूरत थी। पहले तो एक टाइम-मशीन का जुगाड़ करना था, जिसमें बैठकर प्राचीन काल में पहुँचा जा सके। उस वक़्त के जो संगीतकार शक और पुलिन्द रागों को भारतीय संगीत से जोड़ रहे थे उन्हें कड़ाई से मना करना था। दरअसल अशुद्धि की शुरुआत हमारे उन्हीं नालायक पूर्वजों ने की। फिर जिन्होंने सालाग सुद प्रबन्ध गान से ध्रुपद का विकास किया, उन्हें भी रोकने की आवश्यकता थी क्योंकि

प्रबन्ध गान की इस गंगोत्री से निकली ध्रुपद की गंगा को मध्यकाल के मैदानी भाग में पहुँचते गन्दा हो जाना था। हर निर्झर की धारा का अशुद्ध होना उसकी नियति है, जिसकी शुरुआत तेरहवीं सदी में देवगिरि के महान गायक गोपाल नायक और दिल्ली के अमीर ख़ुसरो का मेल होते हो गई। चुपके से ईरानी संगीत का इत्र भारतीय शास्त्रीय संगीत के गंगाजल में आन मिला। रूहानी ख़ुशबू और पाकीज़गी का अदभुत मेल, जिसे आगे ही बढ़ना था। किन्तु शुद्धीकरण के हिसाब से बहुत भारी दण्ड के भागी थे ये दोनों। फिर बादशाह हुसैन शाह शिर्क़ी और बाबा रामदास, उधर स्वामी हरिदास, राजा मानसिंह तोमर, बादशाह अकबर, बैजू बावरा, उस्ताद तानसेन सभी दोषी हैं। ख़ासकर उस्ताद तानसेन जिनकी गोद में पलकर ध्रुपद गान जवान हुआ और जिन्होंने उसके सोलहो श्रृंगार से उसे सजाया। सबसे ज़्यादा सज़ा के भागी वही थे। फिर उसी मुग़ल ख़ानदान के बादशाह मोहम्मद शाह रँगीला और उनके दरबार के नियामत ख़ाँ सदारंग और उनके भतीजे फ़िरोज़ ख़ाँ अदारंग, जिन्होंने ध्रुपद को ख़याल-ख़्वाब और कल्पनाओं की ऊँचाई दी, उसे सजाया बन्दिशों के बोलों से। इस तरह एक नयी गायकी-ख़याल गायकी की बाज़ाफ्ता शुरुआत की। हिन्दुस्तानी मौसीक़ी के मुकुट में एक नया कोहिनूर जड़ा गया। फिर क्या ज़रूरत थी अवध के बादशाह वाज़िद अली शाह 'अख़्तर पिया' को, कि उन्होंने कृष्ण की याद में सैकड़ों ठुमरियाँ रचीं! शास्त्रीय गायन में एक नया रंग जोड़ा। फिर उन्हें गाया-गवाया। कत्थक में ढाल ख़ुद नाचा-नचवाया। असली शिकायत कृष्ण-कन्हैया से थी। इस साँवले-सलोने यशोदा मैया के लल्ला ने पागल बनाकर छोड़ दिया संतों-कवियों-संगीतकारों को। जायसी, रहीम ख़ानख़ाना, रसख़ान, हब्बा ख़ातून और न जाने कौन-कौन...एक लम्बी सूची पागलों की जिन्होंने कृष्ण के प्यार में पड़कर अजर-अमर भजन-गान-कविता रच डाली। अगर ये सभी म्लेच्छ थे तो इनकी रचनाएँ भी अशुद्ध थीं। इन सबको भी समझाना पड़ेगा कि यह सब वापस लीजिए। हमें आपकी, आपके कवित्त, आपके भजन और आपके गान की ज़रूरत ही नहीं है। हमें शुद्ध-पवित्र सामगान-प्रबन्ध गान ही चाहिए। उससे आगे की म्लेच्छों की रचना और उनका गान, वादन, नाच, कुछ भी नहीं।

लेकिन बात यहीं ख़त्म हो जाती, तो मेहनत भी थोड़ी कम करनी पड़ती। अभी तो टाइम-मशीन को और भी दौड़ना था। मुख्य रूप से मन्दिर-मठों में गूँजनेवाले ध्रुपद और वीणावादन-बीनकारी को सँजोकर रखनेवाले डागर परिवार की भी समझाइश करनी थी कि म्लेच्छ होकर ख़ानदान की कई-कई पीढ़ियों को अपनी ज़िन्दगी बर्बाद करने की क्या ज़रूरत थी? डागर बन्धु नसीर अमीनुद्दीन और नसीर मोइनुद्दीन को क्या ज़रूरत पड़ी थी कि पूरी दुनिया में ध्रुपद की रूहानी रोशनी फैलाएँ? किसने कहा था कि पेरिस में जाकर ध्रुपद सोसाइटी की स्थापना करें और उसे हिन्दुस्तानी तहज़ीब का प्रतीक बना दें! लेकिन बड़े ग़ुलाम अली ख़ाँ का हरिओम तत्सत् और डागर बन्धुओं का ब्रह्मा तुम्हीं, विष्णु तुम्हीं का गान, उनके जीवन भर के सुर-लय के नाद, ब्रह्मांड के अनहद नाद में जाकर समा गए थे। उसे कैसे नष्ट किया जा सकेगा? और बड़ो बाबा अलाउद्दीन ख़ाँ के माँ शारदा की आराधना के गान, बाबा बिस्मिल्लाह ख़ान का रोज़ सुबह-सबेरे शहनाई की सुर से भगवान शिव को भेजा गया सलाम, इन सबका क्या? सच कहें तो अमीर ख़ुसरो से लेकर शबनम के. ख़ान तक हज़ारों-हज़ार उस्तादों-ख़ान साहबों ने केवल मौसीक़ी से मुहब्बत की, इबादत की ओर ईश्वर और अल्लाह में फ़र्क़ नहीं किया। सारे उस्तादों-ख़ान साहबों का गान एक ध्वनि ऊर्जा है जिसे कभी नष्ट ही नहीं होना था। सबके सब अन्तरिक्ष में एक साथ मौजूद थे। किस छलनी से इन्हें छाना जाए? कैसे इन सारी अशुद्धियों को बिलगाया जाए? अब शुद्धि हो तो कैसे हो? इसीलिए शुद्धि-उद्धि की बात कुछ समझ में नहीं आ रही थी।

अभी तो कड़वा सच यह था कि नानू की मिट्टी पुणे से पहुँच गई थी। अकथ दुख में सुबकते समूचे परिवार को अपने गान से अपने उस्ताद की विदाई करनी थी। फ़िज़ा में फैलती रागभैरवी की वेदना ज़र्रे-ज़र्रे में पैवस्त होती जा रही थी। सभी विकल-विह्वल-व्याकुल। रोते-रोते आँसू आँखों में सूख गए थे। हवा-धूप-पानी, पंछी-पखेरू सब स्तब्ध। सब मौन। लगा बड़ो बाबा अलाउद्दीन ख़ाँ, बड़े नानू महताबुद्दीन ख़ाँ, उनके दोस्त बिस्मिल्ला ख़ाँ, पंडित विष्णु दिगम्बर पलुस्कर, पंडित विष्णु नारायण भातखंडे, सबके सब वहीं हों। भैरवी के सुर में सुर मिलाते। अपने प्रिय की विदाई बेला का साक्षी बनते। भैरवी के मौन होते अब्बू ने गोरखवाणी को सुर दिया।

'जल बिच कवल, कवल बिच कलियाँ, भँवर बास न लेता है/इस नगर के दस दरवाज़े नित जोगी फेरी देता है/तन की कुण्डी मन का सोंटा, ज्ञान की रगड़ लगाता है/पाँच पच्चीस बसे घट भीतर उनके घोंट पिलाता है/शून्य घर शहर, शहर घर बस्ती, कौन सूता कौन जागे है/शरण मच्छिन्दर गोरख बोले, एक अखंडी छाया है।'

13

सहेला रे!
आ मिल गाएँ
सप्त स्वरन के भेद सुनाएँ
जनम-जनम को संग न भूलें
अबके मिलें सो बिछुर न जाएँ।

—किशोरी अमोनकर

नानू की उम्र हो चली थी, किन्तु इस तरह जाएँगे ऐसा तो उनके दुश्मन ने भी ख़्वाब में नहीं सोचा होगा। वैसे फ़क़ीराना तबीयत के अपने रियाज़ में डूबे रहनेवाले नानू का कोई क्या दुश्मन होगा? हाँ भातखंडे स्कूल के गायक नानू को पसन्द नहीं करते थे। वे पंडित श्रीराम नाथ ठाकुर को नानू से बड़ा गायक मानते थे। इस बात की जानकारी नानू को थी, किन्तु उन्होंने इस बात को वजाहत तलब नहीं माना, कभी भी अपनी ओर से कोई टिप्पणी नहीं की। उनका मानना था कि अगर मौसीक़ी इबादत है, तो इस बन्दगी में बड़ा क्या और छोटा क्या! नानू जाने के बाद ज़्यादा याद आ रहे थे। उनकी छोटी से छोटी बातें आँखें नम करे जा रही थीं। अम्मू, अब्बू, कमोल, शब्बो भाभी को तो छोड़िए, आश्रम के बच्चों तक का खाना-पीना, पढ़ना-लिखना सब छूट-सा गया था। पूरी फ़िज़ा सोगवार थी और हर सूरत मातमी।

इस सोग और मातम के घने अन्धकार में रोशनी की हल्की-सी किरण दिखी थी। नानू की विदाई ख़ानदान के रिवाज के अनुसार गायन के साथ करनी थी। इस बहाने लगभग दस वर्षों से चुप्पी के कोहरे में डूबी अम्मू, चंद लम्हों के लिए ही सही, बाहर तो आई थीं। हालाँकि वह विलाप ही था, अम्मू के लिए वह गायन नहीं था। किन्तु हम लोगों के लिए एक अनोखे एहसास से रूबरू होना था। हमारा रोम-रोम उस करुण गान में भीग रहा था। हमें मालूम था कि अगले ही पल इस आवाज़ को फिर से गुम हो जाना था। वली दकनी की ज़मींदोज़ मज़ार के पास के शाही बाग स्टेडियम में उत्पात्तियों ने उस दिन कितना बड़ा नुक़सान किया था, इसका एहसास उन्हें कभी नहीं होगा। चुप्पी के जंगलों में अम्मू का गुम जाना न केवल इस ख़ानदान के लिए बल्कि हिन्दुस्तानी मौसीक़ी के लिए एक बहुत बड़ा नुक़सान था। एक ऐसा नुक़सान जिसकी भरपाई होती नहीं दिख रही थी। हो सकता है, अगले दस-एक साल शब्बो भाभी इसी तरह डूब कर रियाज़ करती रहें तो अपनी अम्मू की ऊँचाई को छू सकें। नानू यूँ ही अपनी रागेश्वरी बिटिया को स्वरहंस पर विचरनेवाली गान-सरस्वती नहीं कहा करते थे! लेकिन गान-सरस्वती की बुलन्दी तक पहुँचने के लिए अम्मू ने पिछले पाँच दशक तक जो रियाज़ किया था या नानू ने करवाया था वह भी अनोखा था। अठारह-अठारह घंटों का रियाज़। सुबह—भैरव, दोपहर—सारंग, ढलती दोपहर—भीमपलासी, शाम—श्री और रात में दरबारी कान्हड़ा। नानू ही की तरह और घरानों से भी बहुत कुछ सीखा अम्मू ने। उन्होंने बड़ी मेहनत से आगरा घराने, भेंडी बाज़ार घराने और ग्वालियर घराने की ख़ासियत-ख़ुसूसियत को अपने गायन में शामिल किया।

इस सिलसिले में हुआ कुछ यूँ कि पुणे की ही एक मौसीक़ी की महफ़िल में आगरा घराने के उस्ताद अनवर ख़ाँ से लाचारी तोड़ी और अहीर तोड़ी का ख़याल सुनकर अम्मू उनके कदमों में झुक गईं। उस्ताद की गंडाबद्ध शागिर्दा बनकर उनसे इन रागों की तालीम हासिल की। उसी प्रकार भेंडी बाज़ार घराने की विदुषी अंजनीबाई मालपेकर से मीड़ की दिलफ़रेब ख़ूबसूरती का राज़ हासिल किया। दरअसल उनके जादुई गायन का असली राज़ यह था कि नानू ने उन्हें राग-रागिनियों के आगे ख़ुद को नज्र करने-सुपुर्द करने, पूरी तरह समर्पण करने का बीजमंत्र दिया था।

राग-रागिनियों के आगे अपने वजूद की पूरी सुपुर्दगी, उन लम्हों में उन्हीं की इबादत में खो जाने की नसीहत दी थी। दरअसल रागों में एहसासों को ज़ाहिर करने की ग़ैर महदूद-असीमित ताकत होती है। मनोयोग से किये गए रियाज़ से रागों की दुआ फलती है। नानू ने यह भी बतलाया था कि रागों के दो स्वरों के बीच जो वक़्फ़ा-अन्तराल होता है उसमें एहसासों का पूरा समन्दर लहराता है। यह मौसीक़ीकार का रियाज़ तय करता है कि उस लहराते समन्दर की कितनी लहरों का उपयोग वह उस वक़्फ़े में कर पाता है। रागों की तरह हर बन्दिश में तरक़्क़ी की सम्भावना होती है। गायन के वक़्त बन्दिश की तरक़्क़ी की राह आसमान तक जा पहुँचे, इसके लिए ज़रूरी है ख़ुद को भूलना। ख़ुदी को भूलकर ही लाफ़ानी—अनन्त की राह पर आगे बढ़ा जा सकता है। 'मैं', 'मेरा रियाज़', 'मेरी तैयारी', 'मेरा मीड़', 'मेरी गमक', ये सब बड़ी बाधाएँ हैं। इन्हें छोड़कर आगे बढ़ना होगा।

नानू का सबक़ यह भी था कि ज़ेहन में राग की जो तस्वीर उभरे उसी की परस्तिश-आराधना करनी है। ऐसी परस्तिश जो आपको ज़ेहनी ख़ुशियों से सराबोर कर दे। आनन्द का एक समन्दर आपके आगे लहराये, तभी तो रसिक-सामईन भी रस में भीगेंगे। अम्मू ने एक तरह से अपना पूरा जीवन नानू की सारी सीख को अमली जामा पहनाने में ही गुज़ारा। मंच पर कभी रोशनी अपने चेहरे की ओर नहीं रखतीं। एक बार जो आँखें मूँदकर सुर के समन्दर में डूबतीं तो फिर पूरा गायन ख़त्म करके ही आँखें खोलतीं। वे अपने नयेपन-ताज़गी और तख़्लीक़-सृजनशीलता का तआरुफ़ रागों की बढ़त और फ़ितरत में देतीं। भाव की अनूठी क़सीदाकारी, सुर का कसाव, लय की धड़कन सब मिलकर जज़्बाती गायन के ऐसे अनोखे भावलोक का सृजन करते कि क्या रसिक और क्या अरसिक, सब उसमें डूबते-उतराते।

अम्मू किसी भी समारोह में जाने के पहले पूरी तैयारी करतीं। मंच पर उसी तैयारी के अनुसार गातीं। कभी भी फ़रमाइश पर नहीं गातीं। ग्रीन रूम में किसी से मुलाक़ात नहीं करतीं। उस प्रोग्राम में और कौन-कौन आया है न उनके बारे तफ़्तीश करतीं और न किन्हीं से मिलना पसन्द करतीं। गायन में डूबी होतीं तो कितने ही बड़े तीसमारख़ाँ सामने बैठे हों उन्हें नहीं पहचानातीं, क्योंकि इबादत के वक़्त किसी और के साथ दुआ-सलाम

नहीं हो सकता। फ़रमाइश किसी लाट साहब या किन साहब बहादुर की है, इसकी कभी उन्हें फ़िक्र नहीं रहती। उनका मानना था कि मौसीक़ी की बस्ती का बाशिंदा दुनियावी गोरखधन्धे की परवाह नहीं किया करता।

लेकिन दुनियावी गोरखधन्धे वाले उन्हें नकचढ़ी, घमंडी और सनकी मानते। इधर अम्मू के मन में भी मौसीक़ी की दुनिया के इन धन्धेबाज़ों के लिए एक गाँठ पड़ी हुई थी। एक ग़ुस्सा, एक बेचैनी, एक कातर दुख मन के एक गहरे कोने में पल रहा था। इन्हीं लोगों ने उनके दादू उस्ताद महताबुद्दीन ख़ान को बावला बना कर बरसों दर-दर भटकने को विवश किया था। उन्हें शोहरत की बुलन्दियों से भीख माँगनेवालों की क़तार में पहुँचाने की जुर्रत इन्हीं जैसे धन्धेबाज़ों और उनकी गन्दी सियासत ने की थी। उनके अब्बू को भी शुरुआत में इन्हीं लोगों ने ज़लील कर मंच से उतरने को मजबूर किया था। फिर उनकी ज़िन्दगी के दस-एक सुनहरे साल तन्हाई में बीते थे। वे चाहकर भी इन वाक़िआत को भूल नहीं पाती थीं। इसीलिए मौसीक़ी की इबादत के माहौल में जब ग्रीन रूम में मिलने की इल्तजा की जाती या गायन के दौरान कोई फ़ालतू की फ़रमाइश आती, तो न चाहते हुए भी उनका ग़ुस्सा फट पड़ता। अब धन्धेबाज़ जो समझें, समझते रहें। सामईन की मुहब्बत उनके साथ थी। वे सभी उनके साथ बेख़ुदी के समन्दर में डुबकी लगाने और रूहानी ख़ुशी पाने को बेक़रार रहते। इसीलिए अम्मू को इज़्ज़त बख़्शना और उन्हें न्योतना धन्धेबाज़ों की मजबूरी थी।

नानू की मिट्टी की विदाई होते, अम्मू फिर से चुप्पी के घने कोहरे में खो गईं। हम सभी ग़म के भीगे कम्बल को अपने वजूद से दूर नहीं कर पा रहे थे। इसी ग़मअंगेज़ माहौल में वह दिखी। कालिन्दी अपने शौहर के साथ सोग जाहिर करने आई। यूँ अचानक हमारे शहर में कालिन्दी का होना ही ख़ासकर कमोल के लिए अजब परेशानी का सबब हो गया। एक तो शब्बो भाभी ख़ानदान में होनेवाले हर हादसे के बाद बेहद चिड़चिड़ी हो जातीं। एकाएक पाँचों वक़्त की नमाज़ी हो जातीं। बेमतलब कमोल दा पर चीखतीं-चिल्लातीं। ऐसे नाज़ुक मौकों पर कमोल बच्चों के आश्रम में अपना ठीहा बना लेता। अब पहले से भड़की हुई आग में घी की तरह कालिन्दी का आश्रम में यूँ पहुँचना। न जाने आगे क्या होनेवाला था?

14

नींद मिट्टी की, महक सब्जे की, ठंडक
मुझको अपना घर बहुत याद आ रहा है

—अब्दुल अहद साज़

क्या घरों की भी अपनी ख़ास शख़्सियत होती है, अपना मुकम्मल व्यक्तित्व? क्या घरों का भी लोगों की तरह मूड बदलता है? चेहरे के हाव-भाव बदलते हैं? कभी गुनगुनाते-खिलखिलाते, कभी दुखी-हताश-निराश, आँसुओं में डूबे हुए? औरों के बारे में तो नहीं मालूम लेकिन अपनी बालकोनी से सामने अम्मू के घर 'मौसीक़ी-मंज़िल' के इतने-इतने रूप पिछले दो दशकों में देखे हैं कि वह घर, घर नहीं, जीता-जागता इन्साँ ही नज़र आता है,... वह भी बहरूपिया। क्या-क्या रूप दिखाया इस 'मौसीक़ी-मंज़िल' ने हमें।

जब बड़ो नानू महताबुद्दीन ख़ान थे तो क्या जलवे थे 'मौसीक़ी-मंज़िल' के। क्या चमक, क्या दमक। मानो क्षीरसागर की अगम गहराई से निकला कोई मोती हो, ख़ूब सुफ़ेद-आबदार। दिन-रात आठों पहर दूधिया रोशनी छिटकती रहती। रात के तीसरे पहर से ही जब बड़ो नानू रियाज़ शुरू करते तो पूरा 'मौसीक़ी-मंज़िल' ही कभी तानपूरा, कभी पखावज, कभी वेणु बनकर उनकी संगत शुरू कर देता। जब तक बड़ो नानू घर पर रहते, उन्हीं की तरह हँसता-खिलखिलाता-मुस्कुराता रहता 'मौसीक़ी-मंज़िल'।

बड़ो नानू के गुजरने के बाद थोड़े दिनों की उदासी, आँसुओं से डबडबाई आँखें, फिर लगा मानो नानू अय्यूब ख़ान की शख़्सियत इसने ओढ़ ली हो। दमक सुफ़ेद से सुनहरी हो गई। मानो सोने की परत चढ़ा दी गई हो। उन दिनों बेशक़ीमती अनमोल धरोहर की तरह दिखने लगा था 'मौसीक़ी-मंज़िल'। लेकिन पहले वाली, बड़ो नानू के समय वाली मुलायमियत नहीं, थोड़ा कठोर, गुरु-गम्भीर हो गया था वह। एकदम नानू की तरह। लेकिन नानू जब भी अपने प्रोग्राम्स की वजह से लम्बे समय तक बाहर रहते या विदेश चले जाते, तो यह भी चुपके से अपनी वफ़ादारी बदल लेता और अम्मू के ख़ेमे में दाख़िल हो जाता। मानो जन्म-जन्म से उनका ही शागिर्द हो। फिर 'मौसीक़ी-मंज़िल' का रूप-रंग सब अम्मू जैसा ही। पल में तोला, पल में माशा। एकदम दीवार-घड़ी के पेंडुलम की तरह इस छोर से उस छोर तक डोलता हुआ। सुबह-सुबह रियाज़ की पाकीज़गी की तरह सुफ़ेद-गुलाबी, तो दुपहर में किसी शागिर्द की ग़लती पर लाल भभूका। शाम को सुरमई, तो रात में चाँदनी की तरह दूधिया। वाह रे! तिलिस्मसाज़-जादूगर-मायावी 'मौसीक़ी-मंज़िल'। इसके आगे तो बड़े-बड़े अय्यार-बहुरूपिये पानी भरें।

अम्मू-शब्बो भाभी के सोलह घंटे रियाज़ वाले मौसम में तो इसका रूप-रंग न केवल रागों के हिसाब से बदलता बल्कि इसकी ज़ुल्फ़ों में बिखरी फूलों की क्यारियों से आनेवाली ख़ुशबू भी बदल जाती। राग भैरव के साथ भोर के आकाश का पहला जागरण 'मौसीक़ी-मंज़िल' की नाज़ुक पलकों पर ही होता। राग परज सुस्त रात की विह्वल नींद को दूर से भगाता दिखता। राग कान्हड़ा के साथ वह भी घने अन्धकार में भटक रही अभिसारिका-सी रात की तरह अपनी मंज़िल भूलता नज़र आता। राग भैरवी रंगविहीन असीम की चिरविरह वेदना की तरह इसके चेहरे की हर लकीर पर छलक-छलक पड़ती।

ख़ूबसूरत भी तो किसी से कमतर नहीं था 'मौसीक़ी-मंज़िल'। आख़िर गांधीवादी आर्किटेक्ट विलफ्रेड लॉरेन्स, लॉरी बेकर साहब ने ख़ुद डिजाइनिंग की थी। इसकी ज़िन्दगी की नींव रखी थी। वहीं तिरुअनन्तपुरम् में संगीत-समारोह में बड़ो नानू के गायन के बाद ग्रीन-रूम में सकुचाते-झिझकते मिलने पहुँचे थे लॉरी बेकर। शायद 1967-68 की बात रही होगी। गप्प-शप्प

के दौर में बड़ो नानू ने अपनी ख्वाहिश, अपने ज़ेहन के गर्भ में बरसों से पल रहे स्वप्न-शिशु का ज़िक्र कर दिया, जिसे बेकर साहब ने उसे बड़ी संजीदगी से सहेज लिया। कहना मुश्किल है कि इस 'मौसीक़ी-मंज़िल' की अम्मा कौन है और बाबा कौन? बड़ो नानू और लॉरी बेकर साहब दोनों के ख़्वाब एक हो गए। दोनों की पाकीज़गी के रंग में रँग गया वह स्वप्न-शिशु। दोनों ने साथ-साथ मिलकर, उस शिशु को हौले-हौले ज़मीन पर उतारा। मानो चाँद पर चरखा कातती बूढ़ी नानी ने अपनी गोरी-गुलाबी नातिन-नवासी को चन्द रोज के लिए ज़मीं पर भेजा हो।

मुग़ल और राजपूताना शैली का अनोखा संगम था 'मौसीक़ी-मंज़िल'। चुनार के लाल पत्थर और मकराना, राजस्थान के संगमरमर की ग़ज़ब की जुगलबन्दी, मेहराबों-गुम्बदों की सजावट, ख़ूब खुलापन, भरपूर धूप-हवा की आमद-रफ़्त। जयपुर हवा-महल की तरह जालीदार खिड़कियाँ, गलियारे, छज्जा। ख़ूब ऊँची छत, मोटी दीवारें, जो हिन्दुस्तानी फन्ने तामीर की ख़ासियत थी उसे फिर से नया जीवन दिया बेकर साहब ने। आगे-पीछे बगीची। फूलों और फलदार पेड़ों की घूमर-झूमर नाच के नज़ारे। बायीं और छोटी-सी पोखरी, रंगीन मछलियों और कमोल-कुमुदिनी से भरी-भरी। गरमी की दोपहर में वक़्त गुजारने की ख़ास जगह। दायीं ओर जाड़े की धूप सेंकने के लिए खुली जगह, हरी घास का नदी-सा फैलाव। किनारे चमेली-बेली की लताओं-लतरों-बेलों से सजे मड़वे। सामने रसोई का पिछला दरवाज़ा, ताकि चाय-कहवे-पकौड़ियों की सजी-धजी पालकी को ज़्यादा दूर की यात्रा नहीं करनी पड़े।

सबसे नीचे के तल्ले पर बैठकख़ाना, शागिर्दों की तालीम के लिए बड़ा हॉल, बड़ो नानू और नानू की कोठरियाँ, बावर्चीख़ाना, बड़ा-सा आँगन और डाइनिंग हॉल। पहली मंज़िल पर कोठरियाँ ही कोठरियाँ, छज्जों, गलियारों से भरी-पूरी। तीसरी मंज़िल पर सजावटी गुम्बद। चन्द कोठरियाँ बावर्ची-ड्राइवर-मुलाजिमों के लिए और फूलों की क्यारियाँ। पूरे दो साल लगे इसे तामीर करने में। एक चाँद-चाँदनी से ख़्वाब को हक़ीकत में तब्दील होने में। बड़ो नानू ने न जाने कितने संगीत-समारोहों के न्योतों को ठुकराया होगा, कितनी बार अपनी छाती पर पत्थर रखा होगा, उसकी गिनती नहीं। जब मजबूरी हद से ज़्यादा बढ़ जाती, किसी भी हाल में इनकार के लिए

जगह नहीं बचती, तो हज़ार हिदायतों के साथ नानू को ज़िम्मेवारी सौंप कर जाते। लॉरी बेकर साहब की तो जैसे लौ लग गई थी। वे कभी भी प्रकट हो जाते। कभी-कभी महीने में दो-दो बार। बड़ो नानू ने सोचा होगा कि उनकी यह मानस-संतान, यह स्वप्न-शिशु उनकी तरह ही होगा। हू-ब-हू उनकी सच्ची प्रतिलिपि, नक़्ले-तहरीर। लेकिन हाय! यह बेवफ़ा 'मौसीक़ी-मंज़िल' तो बहुरूपिया निकला। वली दकनी की मज़ार वाले हादसे के बाद अपना आब, अपनी चमक, अपना रंग खो दिया और नानू के क़त्ल के बाद तो अपने चेहरे पर कालिख ही मल ली।

15

हसिबा खेलिबा गाइबा गीत,
हबकि न बोलिबा ढबकि न चलिबा
धीरे धरिबा पाँव,
गरब न करिबा सहजै रहिबा भ्रणत गोरख राँव॥

—गोरखनाथ

'मौसीक़ी-मंज़िल' पर छाई उदासी-हताशा और शोक का स्याह रंग वहाँ से उतरकर रहवासियों की रूह पर छाया था, कि उनकी रूहों से ही उठकर वहाँ तक पहुँचा था...कौन जाने? हाँ! इतना तो साफ़-साफ़ दिख रहा था कि नानू के क़त्ल ने 'मौसीक़ी-मंज़िल' की शख़्सियत को बदलकर रख दिया था। अम्मू के गायन के गले की रूँध और शब्बो भाभी के चिड़चिड़ेपन की तो आदत-सी पड़ गई थी इसे। इनकी तो बड़ो नानू की रुख़सती और वली दकनी के मज़ार के हादसे के बाद भी आमद हुई थी। किन्तु इस बार का असर बहुत गहरा था। सयाने तो सयाने, बेटी बुलबुल को भी इसने अबकी अपनी चपेट में ले लिया था। उसका हँसना-खिलखिलाना, उछलना-कूदना, मुहल्लों के बच्चों को इकट्ठा कर खेलना-झगड़ना, छोटी पोखरी में पैर डाल छप-छप करना, फुलवारी में तितलियों की पकड़ा-पकड़ी से ऊब पीछे के बगीचे में गिलहरी बन अमरूद-शहतूत के पेड़ों पर चढ़ना-फिसलना...ये सबके सब गुम हुए थे। मानो किसी और जन्म की

बातें हों। मानो 'मौसीक़ी-मंज़िल' ने ये मंज़र कभी देखे ही न हों। मानो बुलबुल बेटी ने जन्म की घुट्टी के साथ ही अपने नानू उस्ताद ख़ुर्शीद शाह जोगी से गंडा बँधवा लिया हो और उन्हीं की तरह सुख-दुख के एहसास से आज़ाद हो गई हो। उन्हीं की तरह संजीदा और पुरसुकून। मानो गंगोत्री से उतरते ही बाल भागीरथी के पैरों में ज़ंजीरें बाँध दी गई हों।

वैसे अब्बू ख़ुर्शीद शाह जोगी और साथी कमोल बाउल को ऊपर-ऊपर से देखने पर कुछ पता नहीं चलता था। ख़ूब ग़ौर से देखने पर यह एहसास होता कि 'मौसीक़ी-मंज़िल' की स्याही उनकी पुतलियों के रस्ते सीधे उनकी रूहों तक जा पहुँची थी। अब उनकी रूहों में झाँकने का ताब सबकी नज़रों को कहाँ हासिल था? वैसे भी उन दोनों का मानो उस घर से आबोदाना ही उठ गया हो। दोनों का मंज़िले-मक़सूद अब पूरी तरह आश्रम हो गया था—'उस्ताद महताबुद्दीन ख़ान संगीत आश्रम'।

बड़ो नानू की पलकों से ही झरे इस ख़्वाबनुमा आश्रम-रियाज़तगाह की न केवल तस्वीरकशी बल्कि तामीर की ज़िम्मेदारी भी ख़ुद ही बढ़कर लॉरी बेकर साहब ने ही उठाई थी। ख़्वाब ही इतना पाक था कि किसी की भी पुतलियों में तारे झिलमिलाने लगते, धनक खिल उठते और लॉरी बेकर साहब तो ठहरे गाँधी बाबा के पट्ट शिष्य...वैष्णव जन तो तेने कहिये रे... नरसी मेहता की वाणी के मूर्त रूप। दंगों में यतीम हुई अधखिली फूलों-कलियों को फिर से मिट्टी-पानी-खाद-हवा-आकाश सब मुहैया कराना, घायल मन बीमार तन वाली कलियों-फूलों को सँवारना कोई आसान काम नहीं। क्षिति-जल-पावक-गगन-समीर सबों की भरपूर मौजूदगी ही उपचार का माहौल बनाएगी, इस हक़ीक़त से बड़ो नानू और बेकर साहब दोनों अच्छी तरह से वाक़िफ़ थे। इसलिए थोड़ा ज़्यादा ही खुला-खुला, ज़्यादा आकाश, ज़्यादा हवा, ज़्यादा धूप और चहुँओर फैली हरियाली, इन सबों ने मिलकर रियाज़तगाह को एक ख़ास शख़्सियत के रूप में सँवारा था।

छात्रावासों की हरेक कोठरी-छज्जे के लिए भरपूर धूप-हवा, बरामदे के फैलाव और खुलेपन का ख़ास ध्यान रखा गया था। हरेक कोठरी अपने छज्जे के साथ मुकम्मल थी, पूरी आज़ाद और बरामदे के ज़रिये औरों से जुड़ी हुई भी। बच्चे हों और उनके दौड़ने-धूपने के लिए हरे-भरे मैदान न हों, अमरूद-आम-शहतूत के बागान न हों, पानी और मछलियाँ

न हों, तितलियाँ और गौरैया न हों तो कैसे बच्चे और कैसा बचपना। ये सारे स्वप्न पलकों की कोरों से उतरकर हौले-हौले ज़मीं पर हक़ीक़त का रूप ले सकें, इसके लिए बड़ो नानू, नानू, अम्मू-अब्बू और कमोल सबने दिन-रात कितनी मेहनत की, यह किसी से छिपा नहीं है। बेकर साहब ने न केवल चुनार-मकराना बल्कि स्थानीय पत्थरों का भी भरपूर उपयोग किया था, इसलिए यह आश्रम अपने नाम के मुआफ़िक़ शाही नहीं, सादगी की अलामत-प्रतीक बन गया।

आश्रम में अब्बू और कमोल की लगभग स्थायी रिहाइश ने माहौल में चमक-सी भर दी थी। ग़म को भूलने के लिए दोनों ने काम में अपने को झोंक दिया। सोलह घंटे की रूटीन तैयार की गई थी। रियाज़ के साथ-साथ बच्चों के साथ खेलना-ख़ाना-तैरना सब कुछ। आश्रम सचमुच में रियाज़तगाह में तब्दील हो गया। संजीदगी के भीतर पैठी हुई सुकून की ख़ुशबू से लबरेज़। कमोल को भी पहली बार अब्बा हुज़ूर यानी अपने ससुर साहब के साथ इतने इत्मीनान से रहने की मोहलत और मौक़ा मिला था। 'मौसीक़ी-मंज़िल' में भी एक छत के नीचे ही वे रहते थे, किन्तु अपनी-अपनी दिनचर्या, मसरूफ़ियत में मशग़ूल। यूँ भी अब्बू घर पर रहते ही कितना थे? इधर इकतारे में झंकार हुई, उधर अपने जोगी संगी-साथियों के संग घर-शहर से बाहर। कुछ वली दकनी के मज़ार को ज़मींदोज़ होने से रोकने के दरम्याँ पैरों पर हुए ज़ुल्म और अभी-अभी घटी क़त्ल की इस अनहोनी ने यह मोहलत मुहैया करवा दी थी। चन्द दिनों में ही कमोल, अब्बू का प्रतिरूप दिखने लगा। मानो वे ससुर-दामाद नहीं, बाप-बेटे हों। अब्बू की गोरखवाणी और नोखी-अनोखी कहानियों ने एक नई-नकोरी दुनिया के द्वार खोल दिये। एक सच्चे-सुच्चे जोगी और एक मासूम बाउल की रूहानी ख़ुशबुओं ने रियाज़तगाह में अनोखी फ़िज़ा क़ायम कर दी।

16

यहु मन सकती यहु मन सीव,
यहु मन पाँच तत्त्व का जीव
यहु मन लै जै उनमन रहै
तो तीन लोक की वार्ता कहै॥

—गोरखनाथ

आश्रम-रियाज़तगाह में लाख अपने को झोंकने के बावजूद रह-रहकर उन दोनों पर उदासी हावी हो जाती। अब्बू और कमोल की दो दुखी रूहें कब तक एक-दूसरे से बेगानी और बेनियाज़ रहतीं? उनके दरमियान उम्र और पीढ़ी की बालू की दीवार थी, वह बहुत तेज़ी से घसक रही थी। वैसे भी कमोल को यहाँ अब्बू और गाँव में अपने बाबा की दिनचर्या में कोई फ़र्क़ नहीं दिख रहा था। दोनों अलस्सुबह तीन बजे जग जाते। स्नान-ध्यान, भजन-कीर्तन करते। जोगी और बाउल दोनों मन के अन्दर सत्य की तलाश कर रहे थे। उसी में डुबकी लगाकर वे मुहब्बत से लबरेज़ हो उठते। लेकिन केवल ख़ुद की ख़ुशी का कोई मतलब तो नहीं था, यह भी एक तरह स्वार्थ...एक तरह की ख़ुदग़र्ज़ी थी...। इसीलिए लफ़्ज़े-मुहब्बत को फैलाकर उसमें पूरे ज़माने को समाने की कोशिश की जा रही थी।

अब्बू का नज़रिया एकदम साफ़ था। मज़हब और सियासत के दो पाटों के बीच इनसानियत सदियों से पिसती रही है। तवारीख़ के पन्ने इसके गवाह हैं। लोभ-लूट-ग़रूर में डूबे इनसान के भेष में दरिन्दे मज़हब, नस्ल, रंग, जाति के नाम पर अपने से कमज़ोरों की क़त्लोग़ारत करते आ रहे हैं। अपनी रूह को दरिन्दगी के एहसास से बचाने के लिए तरह-तरह की थ्योरी-उसूल गढ़ते रहे हैं। झूठे और मक्कारी से भरे उसूल। तुम्हारे नानू और उनके साथी का क़त्ल कोई एकाएक घटी घटना नहीं है। इन्हीं सिलसिलों का एक छोटा-सा हिस्सा है। इन्साँ का ज़्यादा पाक, ज़्यादा मज़हबी, ज़्यादा सच्चा होने का झूठा ग़रूर कब उसे इनसान से दरिन्दा बना देता है, उसे पता भी नहीं चलता। नफ़रत के हल से नफ़रत की मिट्‌टी तैयार कर, नफ़रत का ही बीज बो, नफ़रत की फ़सल काटनेवाले सियासतदाँ-पंडित-मुल्ला-पादरी, गुरु-पीर-मुर्शिद, स्वामी-बाबा-औलिया लोगों ने जन्नत-सी धरती को धधकता हुआ जहन्नुम बना रखा है।

इस्लाम में पैग़म्बर मुहम्मद साहब के शुरुआत के तीस वर्षों में क़ायम बराबरी-सादगी-जनतांत्रिक रुझान पाने की ग़ैर तारीखी कोशिशें बार-बार होती रही हैं। कभी ख़ारिजी, कभी इब्न तैय्मिय्याह, कभी मुहम्मद इब्न अब्द अल-वहाब और अब इस्लामिक स्टेट। इन लोगों ने केवल अपने को ही सच्चा-पाक-ख़ालिस माना। शेष मुसलमानों को ग़लत-पापी-काफ़िर मानकर लाशें बिछाईं। मक्का और मदीना जैसी पाक जगहों को भी ख़ून-मवाद से नहलाने में इन्हें झिझक नहीं हुई। ये ख़ुद और ख़ुद की थ्योरी की पाकीज़गी के ग़रूर में इतने अन्धे हुए कि वे अदना सा इन्साँ भी नहीं रहे, इसका इन्हें एहसास ही नहीं। समय की सूई पीछे की ओर नहीं खिसकाई जा सकती। बहरहाल इस्लाम के इस छोटे से कट्‌टरवादी तबके की हैवानियत पूरी दुनिया के लिए ख़तरा तो है ही, लेकिन ज़रूरत थी इनकी साफ़-साफ़ पहचान कर धीरे-धीरे समाज से किनारे करना, किन्तु सियासतें यहाँ भी बाज़ नहीं आ रहीं। उनकी शैतानी चाल पूरे इस्लाम को ही आतंकी पहचान देने की है। यह है एक शातिर सियासती चाल। वही नफ़रत की मिट्‌टी में नफ़रत के बीज। नफ़रत की कटती फ़सल से खड़ी धुन्ध के सामने शिया-सुन्नी अहमदिया मस्जिदों में फटते आरडीएक्स और सैकड़ों नमाज़ियों की लाशों का बहता लहू भी जान-बूझकर ओढ़ी नासमझी

के धुन्ध को साफ़ नहीं कर पाता। मज़हब को ही आतंकी कहने का जुमला ज़ुबान पर चढ़ता गया—काग़ज़ काले किए जाते रहे। चैनल्स चीखते रहे, सोशल मीडिया बिजली की गति से दौड़ता रहा।

हमेशा चुप-चुप रहनेवाले अब्बू को ख़ुद ही एहसास हो गया कि ग़म को ग़लत करने के चक्कर में कुछ ज़्यादा ही बोल गए। इतने लफ़्ज़ तो कभी-कभी हफ़्तों में ख़र्च नहीं होते थे। न जाने क्यों इतने लफ़्ज़ आज एक लम्हे में बह गए। अच्छा नहीं हुआ। मन बोझिल-सा हो गया। उदासी दूर होने के बदले और गहरी हो गई। शायद नफ़रत और दरिन्दगी की बात बार-बार दुहराने से उसकी मौजूदगी का एहसास मन को होने लगा। इसलिए कर्म तो क्या, मन और वचन से भी इन बुरी बातों से दूर रहने की सलाह बड़े-बुज़ुर्ग देते रहते हैं।

आख़िर जब चुप्पी भारी होने लगी, तो कमोल ने नानू की ग़मी के दिन से ही मन को मथ रहे सवाल को अब्बू के सामने रख दिया, कि "अब्बू! जब भारी दंगों की ख़बर आपके इकतारे को हो जाती है तो नानू के क़त्ल की ख़बर उसे और आपको क्यूँ न हुई?"

कोठरी में पसरी हुई चुप्पी और गाढ़ी हो गई। अब्बू का बदन इस सवाल को सुनते ही एकबारगी थरथरा गया। कमोल को भी अफ़सोस होने लगा कि फ़ालतू-सी बात अब्बू के सामने क्यों रख दी? वह शर्म से और अब्बू उदासी में गड़े जा रहे थे। तभी शाम की रुख़्सती और अँधेरे की आमद ने पर्दा-सा टाँग दिया।

आख़िर थोड़ी देर में अँधेरे की ओट से ही अब्बू की आवाज़ आई कि पहले छह माह-साल भर पर कभी-कभी वारदातें हुआ करती थीं। महीनों-सालों ज़मीन तैयार की जाती तब नफ़रत की फ़सल बड़ी मुश्किल से उग पाती। किसी मुहर्रम, रामनवमी, दशहरे के जुलूस या पाक-नापाक गोश्त से दराँती का काम किया जाता तब जाकर कहीं फसल कट पाती थी। इसीलिए साल-छह महीने में कभी-कभी इकतारा काँपता तो हम उस कम्पन के सन्देश को बाँच पाते। अब तो लगता है कि नफ़रत किसी खर-पतवार की तरह हर कहीं फैलती-पसरती जा रही है। इसे काटने के लिए भी ख़ास मुहूर्त का इन्तज़ार नहीं किया जा रहा। कहीं भी, कभी भी दस-बीस इन्साँ की खाल ओढ़े दरिन्दे इकट्ठा हो लिए, किसी भी

ग़ैर मज़हबी को उसके पहनावे, बोली, खान-पान...यानी किसी न किसी बहाने ज़बह कर दिया...फिर कोई मज़हबी-सियासी नारा लगाते, बिना किसी शर्म-लाज-लिहाज़, बिना हैवानियत के एहसास के, छाती फुलाकर ख़रामा-ख़रामा निकल लिए।

अब ऐसे माहौल में हमारा इकतारा दिन-रात काँपता रहता है। उसकी तरंगों को पढ़ना ही कठिन हो गया है। हम और हमारे जोगी साथी सभी के सभी इतने लाचार तो कभी भी नहीं हुए थे।

...इस बार की चुप्पी भीगे कम्बल की तरह भारी होती जा रही थी। थोड़ी देर में अब्बू के सुबकने की आवाज़ ने कमोल के पाँव तले की ज़मीन खिसका दी। तभी अब्बू के उस रात के आख़िरी कुछ लफ़्ज़ सुनाई पड़े, "हमें माफ कर दो बरख़ुरदार।"

17

वो सोज़ो-दर्द मिट गए, वो ज़िन्दगी बदल गई,
सवाले-इश्क है अभी, ये क्या किया ये क्या हुआ।

—फ़िराक़ गोरखपुरी

बीती रात अन्धकार और विषाद की मोटी चादर के सहारे कमोल नींद की गहराई में उतरता चला गया। अब्बू और कमोल के बीच कल साँझ ढले दबे पाँव अँधेरे के साथ-साथ हताशा-उदासी-दुख और अन्त में आँसू कमरे में चोरी-छिपे घुस आए। इन सबों की ठेलमठेल भीड़ ने कमरे की हवा को बोझिल बना दिया। साँसें तक लेना कठिन हो गया तो बेचारे भूख-प्यास की क्या बिसात? जल्दी सोए तो नींद भी जल्दी खुल गई। शायद ख़ाली पेट ने नींद के दरवाज़े पर दस्तक दी हो। बहरहाल, अभी चहुँओर अँधेरा ही था, किन्तु रियाज़ वाले हॉल में रोशनी थी और कुछ आवाज़ें भी आ रही थीं।

कमोल जब हॉल में पहुँचा तो वहाँ का नज़ारा ही कुछ और था। अब्बू नाच रहे थे। अ...ब्बू नाऽच रहे थे? जिनके पैरों में हड्डियाँ कम, स्टील प्लेटें ज़्यादा थीं...जिन्हें वली दकनी मज़ार हादसे के बाद चलने में भी कठिनाई थी...वे नाच रहे थे। अद्भुत दृश्य। पहले कत्थक-भरत नाट्यम् जैसी भाव-भंगिमा-पद चालन। फिर धीरे-धीरे गति बढ़ी। तेज़ गति

की मुद्राएँ-पद चालन। न जाने उस नृत्य की तरंगों ने ही कुछ कहा...जिसे कानों ने नहीं, मन ने सुना और कमोल की उँगलियाँ पखावज पर थिरकने लगीं। पखावज के ताल और अब्बू के पद-तालों में मानो प्रतियोगिता हो रही हो...अब अब्बू गोल-गोल घुमेर भरने लगे। ध्यान आया कि उन्होंने सूफ़ियाना चोग़ा पहन रखा था...उनके पैरों की गति से ज़्यादा चोग़े के घेरे की गति थी। थोड़ी ही देर में उस घेरे की चक्रदार गति में अब्बू के पैर खो-से गए...लग रहा था, वे बिना पैरों के, फ़र्श से एक फ़ीट ऊँचे, हवा में लट्टू की भाँति नाचे जा रहे हों...तभी कभी अल्लाह...हू...तो कभी शिव-शिव की आवाज़ उस घुमेर से आने लगी।

पखावज के ताल अब उस रूहानी नाच की लय-गति पकड़ नहीं पा रहे थे। तभी अब्बू से कमोल की आँखें मिलीं, न जाने क्या इशारे हुए... पखावज वहीं छोड़...कमोल की देह भी अब्बू के साथ उस घूमर नाच का हिस्सा होने की कोशिश करने लगी। लय-गति पकड़ने में कमोल की देह लड़खड़ाती, तो न जाने कहाँ से अब्बू की सजग बाँहें उसे थामने और सही लय साधने में मदद करने को हाज़िर हो जातीं। नतीजतन कुछ ही देर में अब्बू और कमोल की नृत्य-लय एक हो गई। मानो दो देह नहीं, एक ही देह घुमेर भर रही हो...या दो देह पर एक ही रूह...एक ही मन नाचे जा रहा हो।...बूँद में बूँद समानी...। देह तो वहाँ थी ही नहीं...क्षिति, जल, पावक, गगन और समीर ही थे कभी-कभी अलग-अलग...कभी एक-दूजे से जुड़ते।...राख की तरह उदासी-निराशा-हताशा सब धीरे-धीरे झर रही थी। अब घुमेर की गति, ओझल से घेरे में कपास-सी, रुई के फाहे-सी तैर रही थी। समय सेमल के फटे फल की तरह इस हवाई तैराकी को चुपचाप निहारे जा रहा था। धीरे-धीरे कमोल के होश खो गए।

दुबारा दिन चढ़े जब कमोल की नींद खुली, तो उसने अपने को हॉल के एक कोने में पाया...चादर-तकिया सहित...। तो क्या रात वह यहीं सो गया था...अलस्सुबह का वह रूहानी रक़्स क्या केवल एक ख़्वाब था?...फिर पैरों में थकान-सी क्यूँ है?...पिंडलियाँ चढ़ी-चढ़ी-सी मानो दस किलोमीटर की दौड़ में शामिल हुई हों। लेकिन देह रुई-सी हल्की और मन धूप से ज़्यादा चमकीला। कमोल ख़्वाब और हक़ीक़त की कशमकश में उलझकर रह गया।

दिन रविवार का था। बच्चों की धमा-चौकड़ी मन की ख़ुशी को हवा दे रही थी। रियाज़ के बाद खान-पान, उसके बाद बड़े बच्चों के साइंस-मैथ के होमवर्क निपटाने की ज़िम्मेदारी कमोल के कन्धों पर ही थी। दसवीं-बारहवीं के गणित के जिन सवालों को देख अपने स्कूल के समय में जाड़ा-बुख़ार चढ़ आता था, फिर से उन्हीं से दो-दो हाथ। चूँकि बच्चे स्कूल में न पिछड़ें, सो पूरी शिद्दत से कमोल जूझता। नतीजतन दैत्य से भयावह दिखनेवाले कठिन-जटिल अलजेब्रा, कैलकुलस, वेक्टर, ज्योमेट्री... और न जाने क्या...क्या...सब देखते-देखते सर्कस के बौने बन जाते... हँसने-हँसाने...गुदगुदानेवाले। बच्चे भी उसे देख-देख उन सवालों से वैसे ही खिलदंड़ अन्दाज़ में पेश आने लगे। उस दुपहर-तिपहर तो रुई-सी देह और सोने से मन ने जटिल सवालों को मानो हलवा बना दिया हो...जीभ पर रखिए और घुलकर सीधे पेट में। तभी अब्बू के कमरे से राग भीम पलासी गूँजने लगा। यानी तीसरा पहर हो चला था। तभी कालिन्दी आती दिखी।

कमोल और बच्चों के होमवर्क का कार्य-व्यापार बड़े से ड्राइंग रूम में ही चल रहा था। कमोल ने अपने लैपटॉप को प्रोजेक्टर से जोड़ रखा था। दीवार की स्क्रीन पर सवाल और हल करने के तरीक़े सारे बच्चों को एक साथ दिख रहे थे जिससे वे नोट्स ले रहे थे। बीच-बीच में हाहा-हीही-धमाचौकड़ी भी।

नानू की ग़मी के बाद कालिन्दी आती रही थी। शायद यह तीसरी-चौथी बार हो। साथ में गुप्ता साहब भी रहते...उसके शौहर।...ग़मी को लेकर सारी औपचारिक...रस्मी बातें हो चुकी थीं...कई-कई बार। शौहर साहब...गुप्ता साहब को सवाल पूछने की थोड़ी ज़्यादा ही आदत थी। मानो दो-तीन मुलाक़ातों में ही सब कुछ जानने को आतुर हों। नानू, बड़ो नानू-अम्मू-अब्बू सबके बारे में...खोद-खोदकर। अब्बू का घर, उनके बाबा... कमल के बाबा...घर-द्वार। इतने सवालों से तो कोई भी घबरा जाए। यह तो मातम में डूबा घर था...लोग सोगवार, लेकिन उनको तो केवल अपने सवालों की पड़ी रहती।...मेहमान क्या ऐसे मातमपुर्सी करते हैं? लेकिन वे इशारों-एहसासों से नासमझ बन, जबरन गले पड़ना चाहते थे। नतीजतन उन्हें देखते ही चिढ़ होने लगती। हालाँकि हर बार कालिन्दी नज़रों से... और कभी-कभी हाथ दबाकर भी बरजने की कोशिश करती। वे थोड़ी देर

के लिए शान्त होकर बैठ जाते। लेकिन पाँच-सात मिनट के बाद फिर शुरू हो जाते। नतीजतन पिछली बार किसी ने उनसे बात नहीं की। अब्बू उठकर अपने रियाज़ के लिए चले गए। कमोल चाय-पानी की व्यवस्था में व्यस्त दिखने की कोशिश करने लगा। कालिन्दी सब समझ गई थी। चाय पी, दोनों विदा हो गए।

कालिन्दी आती दिख रही थी। आज एकदम नई-नवेली बोंगो बोधु की तरह वेशभूषा। शायद जन्मदिन हो या विवाह की वर्षगाँठ।...क्या शृंगार... क्या सजधज...बड़ी-सी लाल बिन्दी पर डिजाइनदार टिकुली, कज्जलपेटिका से आकर्ण नयन, कानों में नीरडोल, गले में सीताहार, पट्टीहार और सिक तीनों। पट्टीहार और सिक के चमचमाते स्वर्ण की आभा उसके गुलाबी गालों को एक तीसरा ही रंग दे रही थी जिसके लिए किसी भाषा में अभी कोई शब्द जन्मा नहीं था। बालूचरी की बालारूण साड़ी जिसकी किनारी कुसुम्भ-केसर रंग की थी। जिसके आँचल पर कृष्ण-राधा-गोपियों का महारास सजीव-चंचलायमान था। कलाई में मोयूरमुख बाला, मांताशा, शांखा, पोला, लोहाबांधानों सबके सब मौजूद थे अपना-अपना मृदुराग छेड़ते हुए। पैरों उँगलियों-अँगूठों से एड़ी तक चमचमाती चाँदी की बिछिया। हथेलियों, पैरों और तलवों में आलता। सुपारी से तैयार वही आलता जिसे कभी कृष्ण ने राधारानी के तलवों में मला था।

आज कालिन्दी अकेले आई थी। पहले कमोल बच्चों के होमवर्क में व्यस्त दिखने की कोशिश करता रहा...लेकिन देखा कि कालिन्दी एकटक उसे ही देखे जा रही है, तो न जाने कैसा-कैसा लगने लगा...एकदम चुरूलिया जैसा...। लैपटॉप समेट...बच्चों को खेलने भेज, वह कालिन्दी से मुख़ातिब होने की कोशिश करने लगा...। लेकिन वह कोशिश ही होकर रह गई। ऐसे अकेले में दोनों कभी मिलेंगे, ऐसा तो ख़्वाब में भी कमोल ने नहीं सोचा था। न जाने कब बीच के दस-एक साल कहाँ ग़ायब हो गए...। वह फिर से किशोर भालो कमोल में तब्दील हो गया और कालिन्दी...फिर से कोलकत्ता लोरैटो वीमेन्स कॉलेज की शोख़-अल्हड़, मनबढ़, साँवली-सलोनी किशोरी दिखने लगी। वहीं चुरूलिया नानूबाड़ी-सा माहौल...। वही भालो कमोल का झेंपना-सकुचाना...। वही कालिन्दी के होंठों पर शरारत-भरी हँसी...। अभी कोई कुछ बोलता-सुनता तब तक

अब्बू की कोठरी में गायन की आवाज़ फिर से गूँजने लगी। वही तीसरे पहर का राग भीमपलासी—'रंग सो रंग मिलाए/साँझ सज छाई माई री/ अँखियन सिंगार लाई/साँझ जराए बिरहन को मन/मोरी अँखियन में सावन लाई, माई रे।' गायन की तासीर या ड्राइंग रूम में बिखरे जादू का असर कि आँखें सचमुच डबडबाने लगीं। जादू और गाढ़ा हुआ। कालिन्दी की डबडबाई आँखों के जल में डुबकी लगा पुतलियों की राह से निकली अनगिनत तितलियाँ उनके दरमियान फड़फड़ाने लगीं...फिर एक-एक कर भालो कमोल के चेहरे-गरदन-कन्धे-बालों पर उतरने लगीं। लगा अब कालिन्दी अपनी जगह से उठेगी और इन तितलियों को समेटेगी, तभी दूर से गुप्ता आते दिखे और जादू एक झटके में टूट गया।

18

हुदूदे-ज़ात से बाहर निकल के देख ज़रा,
न कोई ग़ैर, न कोई रक़ीब लगता है॥
(हुदूदे-ज़ात: व्यक्ति की सीमाओं से)

—सौदा

क्या संयोग हुआ कि ड्राइंग रूम में सामने के दरवाज़े से गुप्ता साहब और अन्दर की ओर से अब्बू एक साथ तशरीफ़ लाये। न जाने अब्बू को कैसे इल्म हुआ कि कमोल और कालिन्दी वहाँ बहुत देर से अकेले हैं और यह तनहाई गुप्ता को खटक सकती है, जो कमोल के लिए शर्मिन्दगी और ग़ैरों के लिए चिमिगोइयों का सबब बन सकती है। बहरहाल, गुप्ता साहब को देखकर न जाने क्यों कमोल को कुछ अच्छा न लगा...यह बेमज़ा-सा... अच्छा न लगना क्यों...इसका जवाब भी कमोल के पास नहीं था।...अब कालिन्दी...उनकी बीवी यहाँ देर से आई हुई थी तो उन्हें तो आना ही था...इसमें अच्छा लगने...न लगनेवाली बात क्या...? लेकिन कमोल का मन ढिठाई से अपनी बात पर अड़ा था...कि अच्छा नहीं लगा...दरअसल गुप्ता साहब के क़दमों की चाप आने के पहले के लम्हों में जो तितलियाँ थीं,...कमरे में...वजूद पर...पुतलियों में, और मन उनके रंगों में डूबने-डूबने को हो ही रहा था कि जादू टूट गया। दरअसल यही वो बात थी जिसकी

पर्देदारी थी...और मन झूठमूठ रटे जा रहा था कि कुछ अच्छा नहीं लगा। लेकिन कमोल की झेंपी-सी नज़र जब अब्बू की ओर उठी, तो उठी ही रह गई। देखना निरखने में तब्दील हो गया। अब्बू की शख़्सियत थोड़ी बदली-सी नज़र आ रही थी। चाल भी बड़ी सँभली हुई-सी। लड़खड़ाहट कम...कम क्या, बिलकुल ख़त्म-सी हो गई हो, ऐसा महसूस हुआ...और तो और देह का रोम-रोम खिला-खिला सा लगा, जैसे एक नूर-सा छलकने को हो, यानी अलस्सुबह का वह रूहानी रक़्स कोई ख़्वाब न था। कमोल के निरखने का दायरा बढ़ा। अब उसके ख़ुर्दबीन के निशाने पर कालिन्दी थी। पहले उसकी निगाहों ने उन जादुई तितलियों के परवाज़ के निशाँ ढूँढ़ने की कोशिश की, किन्तु वहाँ प्लीज़ डोन्ट ट्रेसपास का साइनबोर्ड टँगा था। मजबूरन मुआयने की दिशा बदल गई। दस-एक साल के गुज़रने का असर वजूद पर साफ़-साफ़ दिख रहा था। कमर का घेरा काफ़ी बढ़ गया था... वजन भी बीस-बाईस किलो से ज़्यादा ही...। आँखों के नीचे गहरे काले घेरे, जिसे मेकअप की पच्चीकारी भी नहीं छुपा पा रही थी...चेहरा भरा-भरा, बड़ा-सा और रंग तब से ज़्यादा दबा हुआ...क्या हो गया चुरूलिया वाली चुलबुली, शाख़-सी लचकती लहीम-शहीम-सी साँवली-सलोनी को...साफ़ है, अपना ख़याल नहीं रख रही थी कालिन्दी।...माँ नहीं बनने का शोक, कि कुछ और...क्या जाने?

कालिन्दी की तुलना में बहुत ही लम्बे-तगड़े थे गुप्ता। छह फ़ीट के आसपास, पाँच फ़ुट दस-ग्यारह से तो एकदम कम नहीं। साथ में बैठी पाँच फ़ीट दो इंच की कालिन्दी ग़ज़ब दिख रही थी, बिलकुल पिद्दी-सी। ख़याल भी ख़ूब रखा था अपने जिस्म का गुप्ता ने। जिम-विम ख़ूब किए जाने का सबूत बाँहों के डोले-शोले सुना रहे थे। एकदम फ़िट फ़ाइटर जैसी शख़्सियत...रंग भी दूधिया गोरा...नाक एकदम तीखी...आँखें नीली...सुनहरे बाल...। वाह! क्या बात...जर्मन इतिहास के पन्नों से निकला शुद्ध नार्डिक आर्यन हमारे समय में चहलक़दमी कर रहा था। लेकिन चेहरे के दाहिने हिस्से में कुछ दाग़दार...एग्जिमा-सा...न, एग्जिमा ही था...चाँद पर धब्बा...।

बहरहाल अब सब आमने-सामने थे। चाय-पानी भी आ चुका था। आज अब्बू भी गप्प-शप्प के मूड में थे। अभी तक तो दो-तीन मुलाक़ातों में गुप्ता ही सवाल पर सवाल करते रहे थे, लेकिन आज अब्बू को भी कुछ पूछना

था। दरअसल अब्बू और कमोल दोनों के दिलों में यह सवाल कब से कुलबुला रहा था कि नानू की ग़मी के बाद यह जोड़ा एकाएक इस शहर में नमूदार कैसे हुआ? लेकिन गुप्ता साहब के पास बहुत ही ठोंकापीटा जवाब मौजूद था। उन लोगों की कम्प्यूटर ट्रेनिंग की एक एकेडमी थी... सुआर्यन कम्प्यूटर ट्रेनिंग एकेडमी। ऑटोनॉमस, किन्तु आई.एस.ओ. 9001 सर्टिफाइड। देश-भर में एक सौ बहत्तर ब्रांचेज थीं। छात्रों और प्रोफेशनल्स के लिए कुछ अपग्रेडेड, कुछ कम्पीटिशन ओरियन्टेड कोर्सेज़ चलाए जाते हैं। बहुत डिमांड में रही है यह एकेडमी। बस, पूर्वी भारत और नॉर्थ ईस्ट के कुछ छोटे-छोटे राज्य छूटे थे जहाँ इसकी ब्रांचेज़ खोली जानी थीं। उसी सिलसिले में बड़ा बाज़ार के हरिओम टावर में नई ब्रांच अगले हफ़्ते शुरू होनी है।

अब इतने चुस्त-दुरुस्त जवाब के बाद शक-शुबहे की कोई गुंजाइश नहीं थी...या छोड़ी नहीं गई थी। बात कालिन्दी ने आगे बढ़ाई कि बिजनेस अपनी जगह पर ठीक ही है, किन्तु हम भी आप लोगों की तरह कुछ पुण्य कमाना चाहते हैं। आश्रम के इन यतीम बच्चों में से सीनियर्स को फ्री कम्प्यूटर ट्रेनिंग देना चाहते हैं ताकि कल इन्हें अपने पैरों पर खड़े होने में थोड़ी मदद मिल सके...लेकिन...।

कालिन्दी का यह 'लेकिन' थोड़ा ज़्यादा ही लम्बा खिंच गया तो गुप्ता ने बात की डोर थाम ली, कि एक ट्रस्ट जो हमारी एकेडमी को संचालित करता है वह थोड़ा धार्मिक क़िसम का है। क्षमा चाहूँगा कि हम आप लोगों की तरह विशाल हृदय-उदार लोग नहीं हैं। हमारे ट्रस्ट के नियम-क़ायदे थोड़े बँधे-बँधे से हैं। अब कैसे कहूँ...हमारी शर्त आप लोगों को थोड़ी छोटी-हल्की लग सकती है...लेकिन हम अपने ही धर्म के बच्चों को एडमिशन देते हैं और फ्री ट्रेनिंग भी उन्हें ही देने की शर्त से हम बँधे हैं।

ड्राइंग रूम में एकदम सन्नाटा छा गया...अब्बू की तो जैसे साँसें रुक गई हों। कितना बेशर्म था यह शख़्स...इसके चेहरे पर तो पश्चात्ताप का कोई निशान भी नहीं था। हाँ! कालिन्दी के चेहरे पर हवाइयाँ उड़ रही थीं। यह तो मानो हमारी और हमारे आश्रम की रूह पर ठोकर मारने की तैयारी कर के आया था। हमारे तनाव से बेख़बर वह बड़े आराम से चाय पीने लगा। अब उसके चाय सुड़कने की बेलज्ज आवाज़ कमरे में गूँजने लगी।

मिनटों में चाय ख़त्म कर उसने बात सँभालने की कोशिश की—मैंने तो कालिन्दी को पहले ही कहा था कि ट्रस्ट की शर्तें आप लोगों को पसन्द नहीं आएंगी। लेकिन इसे ही पुण्य कमाने की बड़ी हड़बड़ी थी। क्षमा कीजिएगा! हमारा उद्देश्य आप लोगों के हृदय को पीड़ा पहुँचाने का कदापि नहीं था। उस बात को भूल जाइए...कुछ दूसरी बात करते हैं...ख़ुर्शीद साहब...आप मुसलमान होकर गेरुआ वस्त्र क्यों पहनते हैं?

...ख़ुर्शीद साहब...? कमोल क्या...लगा पूरा आश्रम ही चौंक पड़ा हो। अब्बू को आज तक किसी ने इस तरह नाम से पुकारा हो, कमोल को याद नहीं आ रहा था। मौसीक़ी की दुनिया में वे उस्ताद जोगी साहब के नाम से जाने जाते थे। दोस्त-संगी-साथी 'जोगी दादा' या 'जोगी साहब' पुकारते। शब्बो भाभी और कमोल के हमउम्र तो उन्हें बाबा या अब्बू ही बुलाते थे।...कमोल तो भूल ही गया था कि अब्बू का नाम ख़ुर्शीद शाह जोगी है।

लेकिन गुप्ता का सवाल दरअसल बदले हुए माहौल का सवाल था। जो हज़ार-हज़ार बार अलग-अलग जगह जोगियों को घेरकर पूछा जा रहा था। अब्बू को सब ख़बर थी फिर भी वैसे ही मुस्कुराते मुख़ातिब हुए, "लगता है, अपने मुल्क और पाक कल्चर की रवायतों से आप पूरी तरह वाक़िफ़ नहीं हैं बरख़ुरदार। हम जोगी हैं और बेटा कमोल, बाउल। जोगी और बाउल न हिन्दू होते हैं और न मुसलमाँ। वे बस जोगी और बाउल ही होते हैं। हम जोगियों के गुरु गोरखनाथ और दादा मछन्दरनाथ ने न पूजा करने से मना किया और न नमाज़ पढ़ने से। वही सीख बाउलों को लालन शाह फ़क़ीर ने दी। दरअसल इबादत के हर दिखावे से हमारे गुरुओं को तकलीफ़ थी। वे भीतर के रहगुज़र के राही और रहनुमा थे। दिल के भीतर शिव और शक्ति को, पाँच तत्त्वों की मौजूदगी को महसूस किया और महसूस करवाया। हम भी भीतर-बाहर भटकते-आवारागर्दी करनेवाले गुरु गोरख के चेले हैं। उस पर से मौसीक़ी से मुहब्बत हो गई...एक तो करेला...ऊपर से नीम चढ़ा...। पागलपन और बढ़ गया है। अब सुर की बहार में ही मौला और ईश्वर की पुकार सुनाई देती है। लेकिन मौज में आते हैं तो पहाड़ी मन्दिर में शिव से भेंट कर आते हैं और पुरानी मोती मस्ज़िद में नमाज़ भी अदा कर आते हैं। वैसे कभी-कभी मन्दिर-मस्ज़िद घूमने-भटकने से फ़ायदा भी होता है। गुरुओं की वाणी पर विश्वास बढ़

जाता है क्योंकि इन जगहों पर सच्ची इबादत कभी महसूस ही नहीं हुई। सच ही कहा है कि इबादत करते हैं जो लोग जन्नत की तमन्ना में, इबादत तो नहीं है इक तरह की तिजारत है। इसीलिए हम जोगी इन तिजारती मज़हबों की सरहदों से बँधे नहीं हैं।

अब आप ही तय कर दीजिए कि हम अपने गुरु गोरखनाथ की रवायत का गेरुआ बाना पहनें कि नहीं...अपना इकतारा बजाते भरथरी के गीत के साथ सुरसती-शिव-विष्णु के भजन गायें कि नहीं?...सुरों पर सवारी कर मौला को पुकारें कि नहीं?

दरअसल बरख़ुरदार, आजकल हमसे ये सवाल थोड़े ज़्यादा ही पूछे जा रहे हैं...कभी मन्दिर के दरवाज़े पे...कभी मस्ज़िद की सीढ़ियों पे...। आप नई पीढ़ी के लोग ही मिलकर तय कर दीजिए। हमें तो इस उम्र में कुछ समझ में नहीं आ रहा, हम क्या बदलें...कैसे बदलें कि आप लोगों को अच्छा लगे।

गुप्ता साहब बुरी तरह सकपका गए। पहली बार हल्की-सी झेंप उनके चेहरे से झाँक रही थी। गुप्ता दम्पती अब उठ लिए। एकेडमी के उद्घाटन का कार्ड थमाया। आने की औपचारिक प्रार्थना की और चल दिए।

19

आदमीयत और शै है, इल्म है कुछ और चीज़,
कितना तोते को रटाया, पर वो हैवाँ ही रहा।

—जज्बी

उस शाम का वाक़या बहुत ही मायूस करनेवाला था, जिसका साया बहुत दिनों तक पीछा करता रहा। अब्बू ने तो जैसे चुप्पी ही साध ली। बस हाँ-हूँ से काम चलाते रहे। मानो उस शाम ज़्यादा ख़र्च हुए लफ़्ज़ों का हिसाब-किताब दुरुस्त कर रहे हों। हाँ! गुप्ता साहब की बकवास से एक फ़ायदा हुआ था। कमोल को कुछ नये आइडिया मिले थे। एक तो आश्रम के सीनियर बच्चों के लिए कम्प्यूटर ट्रेनिंग अपने ही परिसर में शुरू करने का। दूसरा कि कम्प्यूटर ट्रेनिंग और साइंस कोचिंग से आश्रम के लिए कुछ कमाई करने का। वैसे भी नानू अब रहे नहीं, अम्मू-शब्बो का मौसीक़ी के किसी प्रोग्राम में आना-जाना बन्द-सा हो गया था, न देश-विदेश के मंच, न दूरदर्शन, न आकाशवाणी। यानी कि आमदनी के सारे रास्ते बन्द और आश्रम के ख़र्च, बच्चों की बढ़ती उम्र, ऊँची क्लास के कारण बढ़ते जा रहे थे। वैसे भी राशन-पानी, दूध-अंडे, कपड़े-ड्रेस पर ही कौन-सा ख़र्च घट रहा था।

कमोल, 'मौसीक़ी-मंज़िल' के बगलगीर सिन्हा अंकल के बेटे मयंक के साथ, अपनी योजनाओं के बारीक़ ब्योरों में ज़्यादा ही मशग़ूल हो

गया। वैसे मयंक आजकल ख़ाली ही था। उसने कम्प्यूटर प्रोफेशन के ज़रिये बैंगलुरू-हैदराबाद-सिंगापुर-सिलिकॉन वैली की परिक्रमा पूरी कर ली थी। लगभग दस साल का, एक दहाई का चक्र पूरा हो चुका था। कहते हैं कि रिसेशन के कारण उसकी कम्पनी में छँटनी हुई थी। किन्तु मयंक की मस्ती-बेफ़िक्री देखकर लगता कि जैसे ख़ुद ही थोड़ा ब्रेक चाह रहा हो। परिवार बैंगलुरू में...बच्चों की पढ़ाई...वैसे उनका ननिहाल वहीं था...शायद मिसेज अपना जॉब जारी रखना चाह रही थीं...। यानी कमोल और मयंक की आज़ादी के रंग कुछ यकसाँ थे। लिहाज़ा प्लानिंग कुछ ज़्यादा ही लम्बी, पूरे आराम से खरामा-खरामा चल रही थी। अभी और लम्बी खिंचती, अगर वह वीडियो मैसेज कमोल के मोबाइल पर नुमायाँ नहीं हुआ होता।

सन्देश जिस अनजाने नम्बर से आया था, ट्रू कॉलर उसकी पहचान नहीं कर पा रहा था, लेकिन वह वीडियो था बहुत भयानक। सुआर्यन कम्प्यूटर ट्रेनिंग एकेडमी की टी-शर्ट पहने चार-पाँच युवाओं की टीम आश्रम के सीनियर बच्चों से उनके स्कूल में रिसेस के ख़ाली समय में मिल रही थी। लेकिन ख़तरनाक बात यह थी कि मज़हब के बुनियाद पर बच्चों को छाँटकर बात की जा रही थी।...गुप्ता ने उस दिन अब्बू से कहा था, हमारे धर्म के बच्चे...। आश्रम की नींव में ही बारूद भरने की कोशिश। न जाने कोने में ले जाकर बच्चों को कौन-सी घुट्टी...कौन-सा ज़हर भरा जा रहा था...। वीडियो में कोई आवाज़ तो नहीं सुनाई पड़ रही थी, लेकिन खिलती कलियों में गन्दे नाखून गड़ाने की कोशिशें साफ़ दिख रहीं थीं।...मज़हबी बन्दिशों, कट्टरताओं, बाहरी दिखावों, नफ़रतों, झूठी पाकीज़गी और श्रेष्ठता के गन्दे ग़ुरूर से आज़ाद समाज...सच्चे जोगियों-बाउलों-हिन्दुस्तानियों का सच्चा-सुच्चा समाज...जिसके गढ़ने का ख़्वाब बिखरता नज़र आने लगा...। ग़ुस्सा और दुख का इतना तीखा एहसास कमोल ने एक साथ कभी महसूस नहीं किया था...उसकी देह थरथरा रही थी...और आँखें आँसुओं से डबडब...। अभी सामने गुप्ता होता तो ज़रूर पिट जाता।...लेकिन कमोल ने ख़ुद ही ख़ुद को संयत...शान्त किया।...बाउल के लिए दुख क्या और सुख क्या...जो अपने ग़ुस्से पर...अपने मोह-मद पर क़ाबू न रख सके...वह भी बाउल क्या?

कमोल के बाउलपना ने समझाया कि इस छोटे से झटके की सीख यह है कि जिस ट्रेनिंग और कोचिंग क्लासेज के लिए मयंक के साथ कच्छप गति से पंचवर्षीय प्लानिंग की जा रही है उसे बिना देर किए तुरन्त शुरू किया जाए। वीडियो मयंक को फॉरवर्ड कर मैराथन बैठकें की गईं। डीपीएस-डीएवी के साइंस के नये शिक्षकों से बार-बार मिला गया। नेट पर और बाज़ार में घूम-घूमकर कम्प्यूटर्स की ख़रीद की गई। नतीजतन एक हफ़्ते की मेहनत रंग लाई और आश्रम की चहल-पहल एकाएक पहले से दोगुनी-चौगुनी हो गई। अम्मू के हाथों नये क्लासेज का उद्घाटन हुआ। अब संगीत आश्रम में कार्यक्रम हो और गान न हो, यह कैसे हो सकता था? वैसे भी आश्रम को काली निगाहों से बचाने के लिए मंगल गान के कवच की ज़रूरत थी। आज उल्टा हुआ, अम्मू ने तानपूरा सँभाला और शब्बो भाभी के साथ अब्बू ने राग भैरवी की बन्दिशें पेश कीं...मंगल गीत गाओ बजाओ...के बोलों से आश्रम झूमने लगा। दोनों ऐसे डूबे कि समाँ-सा बँध गया। अन्त शब्बो भाभी की एकल प्रस्तुति राग भैरवी की ही ठुमरी...आया करे जरा कह दो साँवरिया से...आया करे मन भाया करे...। कमोल क्या हर कोई...आश्रम का छोटा-छोटा बच्चा भी समझ रहा था कि यह दिल से उठी पुकार किसके लिए है? इस ख़ुलूसे-दिल की पुकार का असर इतना गहरा था कि कमोल की आँखें बिना पूछे धार-धार बरसने लगीं। उधर टेरनेवाले की आँखें भी कोई कम नहीं थीं...वे भी गंगा-जमुना सी बहाने लगीं...। अब बारी आश्रम के बच्चों की थीं। बड़े-छोटे, सारे के सारे, महीनों से अपने प्यारे कमोल दादा की तन्हाई को...उनके दुख को बिना कहे-सुने अपने-अपने दिलों में सँजोए आ रहे थे। आज शब्बो भाभी की टेर में उन सबों की भी बेआवाज़ टेर शामिल थी...और खारे आँसुओं की धार में उनकी आँखों की धाराएँ भी।...गिले-शिकवे सब धुल रहे थे।... काली स्याही मद्धिम पड़ रही थी...शायद राहत भरे दिन आनेवाले थे...।

20

बफैजे-मसलहत ऐसा भी होता है ज़माने में,
कि रहज़न को अमीरे-कारवाँ कहना ही पड़ता है।

—जगन्नाथ आज़ाद

आजकल आश्रम-रियाज़तगाह गुले-गुलज़ार था। कमोल-मयंक की अथक मेहनत की पुरख़ुलूस पुकार से ख़ुशियाँ हौले-हौले उतरी थीं, उनके अनगिनत रंग चाँदनी की तरह चहुँओर बिखरे थे। अब तो आश्रम और 'मौसीक़ी-मंज़िल' के बीच के फ़ासले भी मिट गए थे। अम्मू अक्सर शाम को आने लगी थीं। ख़ासकर बच्चियों के साथ, उनके हॉस्टल में समय गुज़ारने में उन्हें अच्छा लगता। बुलबुल तो कम्प्यूटर और साइंस क्लासेज के बहाने अपने बाबा के पास ज़्यादा से ज़्यादा वक़्त बिताने की हसरत पूरी कर रही थी। शब्बो भाभी भी भोर में रियाज़ के बाद एक चक्कर लगातीं, किन्तु उनकी आरज़ू थी कि कमोल 'मौसीक़ी-मंज़िल' को भी अपना वक़्त दें। उनकी नई टीम के काम को देखें...एकाध माह में देश-भर में शुरू होनेवाले उनके प्रदर्शनों को कोऑर्डिनेट करने में मदद करें।

दरअसल, नानू की ग़मी के बाद देश-भर में फैले उनके शागिर्द, गुरु भाई-बहनें लगातार 'मौसीक़ी-मंज़िल' पहुँच रहे थे। अपने मरहूम अज़ीज़ की जानिब अपनी श्रद्धा-अक़ीदत ज़ाहिर करने और ग़मज़दा परिवार का सोग

बाँटने। इसी सिलसिले में शब्बो भाभी की एक अनोखी तमन्ना, 'सिस्टरहुड' ने जन्म लिया। मौसीक़ीकारों-कलाकारों का एक ऐसा ग्रुप जिसमें सिर्फ़ स्त्रियाँ हों। बड़ो नानू के ही मौसीक़ी के घराने की कई बेटियाँ, जो अब अलग-अलग विधाओं में अपना नाम रोशन कर रही थीं, वे सब उम्र के किसी न किसी पड़ाव पर शब्बो भाभी के साथ ख़ूब हिली-मिली रही थीं। ग़मी के इस सोगवार मौक़े ने यह अवसर मुहैया करवा दिया। इत्तिफ़ाक़न वे एक साथ आ जुटीं। सिस्टरहुड के ख़्वाब को साथ-साथ देखा, महसूस किया। ख़ूब सोच-विचार कर एक साथ आने का फ़ैसला लिया गया। सात बहनों की टीम 'सिस्टरहुड'। गायन शबनम के. ख़ान के ज़िम्मे, तो तबले पर श्रावणी मजूमदार, पखावज शिल्पा देशपांडे के हाथ में, सितार की सितारा माया तलवलकर, बाँसुरी के साथ सुतपा चटर्जी, वायलिन की राइजिंग स्टार महिमा शंकर और कत्थक-क्वीन माधवी पांडेय, इन सात बहनों की मिलीजुली संतान 'सिस्टरहुड'। इस टीम के बनने की ख़बर भर से क्लैसिकल संगीत के आयोजकों में खलबली मच गई। कहाँ कुछ माह से 'मौसीक़ी-मंज़िल' मौसीक़ी के दायरे से एकदम ग़ायब था। नतीजतन आमदनी के रास्ते बन्द। कहाँ अब प्रोग्राम्स के लिए होड़ाहोड़ी। इतनी आपाधापी, इतनी हड़बोंग, डेट्स के लिए मारामारी, फ़ीस के रुपयों का हिसाब-किताब। ऐग्रीमेंट के हिसाब से सिस्टरहुड की सिस्टर्स के खातों में उनका ट्रान्सफर...बाबा रे! इतना गड्डमगोल! यह सब भालो कमोल के बस की बात नहीं थी।

कुछ इसी तरह की परेशानियाँ अब आश्रम के कोचिंग में भी आ रही थीं। न जाने कब मयंक के मन में सुआर्यन कम्प्यूटर ट्रेनिंग एकेडमी से होड़ लेने का ख़याल आया! उसने पूरी ताक़त लगा दी। शहर के सारे स्कूल-कॉलेजों में भेंट-मुलाक़ात। हर कहीं बचपन का कोई-न-कोई साथी मिला। उसका स्थानीय होना और उस पर आई.टी. की जन्नत सिलिकॉन वैली रिटर्न होना सुआर्यन के प्रचार-प्रसार के हर हथकंडे पर भारी पड़ा। नतीजतन आश्रम की रौनक़, चहल-पहल दिन-दूनी बढ़ती गई। एक तरफ़ आश्रम के बच्चे-बच्चियों का एक्सपोजर बढ़ रहा था। एक से एक ज़हीन बच्चे-बच्चियों से हो रही दोस्ती पढ़ने-जानने की ललक जगा रही थी, तो दूसरी तरफ़ मैनेजमेंट की परेशानियाँ सामने आने लगीं। बैचेज की रूटीन,

फ़ीस के हिसाब-किताब, टीचर्स के पेमेंट्स...बाबा रे! यहाँ भी कमोल के होशो-हवास फ़ाख़्ता थे। अब मयंक को ही कुछ सोचना था। कार्य-व्यापार उलझाया उसी ने था, तो रास्ता भी तो उसे ही निकालना था। कमोल के सामने ही सारा नाटक हुआ। मिसेज़ मयंक से स्काइप पर झूठे-सच्चे वादे, गिड़गिड़ाहट, भालो कमोल के चेहरे से उड़ती हवाइयाँ, आश्रम के मासूम बच्चों का फ़्यूचर; यानी नौटंकीबाज मयंक के नाटक के कई-कई एपिसोड, एक-एक कर सब आज़माया गया। एक बार में बैंगलुरू, अपने प्यारे मैके में लगी-लगाई नौकरी छोड़कर कौन आना चाहेगा, यह मयंक ख़ूब अच्छी तरह जानता था। इसलिए हर दो-तीन दिनों पर नौटंकी की पटकथा में नमक-मिर्च का डोज़ बढ़ाया जाता। असर बढ़ाने के लिए शब्बो भाभी और उनके सिस्टरहुड के मैनेजमेंट में हो रही परेशानी उनकी ही ज़ुबानी बखान करवाई गई। नारीवाद का झंडा बुलन्द किया गया। हाथ-पैर जोड़कर अम्मू से भी ख़ास न्योता दिलवाया गया। अब इतने हथकंडों के सामने तो कोई भी परास्त हो जाए। वो तो बीबी थीं, भारतीय नारी को हथियार तो डालना ही था। कम्पनी में लम्बी छुट्टी की दरख़्वास्त डाली, पति की गम्भीर बीमारी का बहाना और बच्चों के साथ हाज़िर। आई.आई.एम. की पढ़ाई का कमाल, हफ़्ते-दस दिनों में आश्रम के कोचिंग्स के साथ-साथ 'सिस्टरहुड' के मैनेजमेंट की समस्याओं को राह दिखाई गई। एक और राहत।

किन्तु अब्बू इन नई हलचलों से वैसा लगाव महसूस नहीं कर रहे थे। वैसा क्या, एक तरह से देखा जाए तो अपने को बिलकुल अलग-थलग रखे हुए थे। अपनी उसी पुरानी रूटीन पर बदस्तूर क़ायम। सबेरे तीन बजे उठना, स्नान-ध्यान कर अपना रियाज़, फिर बच्चे-बच्चियों को मौसीक़ी की तालीम। फिर शाम को इसी रूटीन का दुहराव। कम्प्यूटर, मैथ्स-फ़िज़िक्स की कोचिंग बच्चों की मौसीक़ी की तालीम में आड़े न आए, इसका बहुत बारीक़ी से कमोल को ध्यान रखना पड़ रहा था। कोचिंग्स की आमदनी आश्रम के ख़र्च के लिए व्यावहारिक ज़रूरत थी, इससे उन्हें इनकार नहीं था। किन्तु आश्रम बड़ो नानू-नानू ने मौसीक़ी को नज़्र किया था। इसे भी हमेशा याद रखने की आवश्यकता थी। कभी-कभी कम्प्यूटर कोचिंग क्लासेज़ की ओर अम्मू के साथ टहलते चले भी गए, किन्तु कोई ख़ास दिलचस्पी नहीं दिखाई।

हाँ! एक फ़र्क़ अब्बू के रूटीन में आया था। आजकल अक्सर मोबाइल पर किसी से लम्बी गुफ़्तगू करते दिख जाते। बीच-बीच में दो-तीन दिनों के लिए ग़ायब भी हो जाते। ऑन-लाइन टिकट्स का इन्तज़ाम भी ख़ुद ही कर ले रहे थे। कुछ पता ही नहीं चल रहा था कि क्या चल रहा था? कहाँ आ-जा रहे हैं? एक दिन यूँ ही कमोल ने तफ़्तीश की तो टाल गए। फिर दस-एक दिन के बाद उन्हें रात में परेशाँ देखा, तो कमोल ने ज़िद ठान ली। एकदम बालहठ। हारकर अब्बू को हथियार डालना पड़ा। उन्होंने अपना फ़िक्र बाँटना शुरू किया। मसला सुआर्यन का था। तुम लोग कम्प्यूटर ट्रेनिंग एकेडमी की साज़िशों से आश्रम को बचा कर ख़ुश हो रहे थे। हो सकता है यह शतरंज की बिसात पर उनकी ही छोटी-सी चाल रही हो। दरअसल यह एकेडमी और ऐसी दर्जनों तंज़ीमें-संस्थाएँ सुआर्यन वालों के लिए मुखौटे भर थे। अब्बू थोड़ी देर के लिए रुके। कुछ सोचने लगे। लगा समझाने को वाजिब लफ़्ज़ों की तलाश कर रहे हों। फिर तफ़सील से सुआर्यन की तस्वीर खींची कि यह कोई एक तंज़ीम या संस्था नहीं बल्कि एक ख़ास तरह का नज़रिया है। ख़ास तरह के ख़याल का सिलसिला, जो एक नस्ल और एक ही मज़हब के नेशन-स्टेट को मुकम्मल शक्ल देना चाहता रहा है। कुछ-कुछ इस्लामिक देशों की तरह। इनके नेशन-स्टेट की तस्वीर में भी ग़ैर-मज़हबियों के लिए जगह थोड़ी तंग है। साझी तहज़ीब और मिली-जुली विरासत की बात करनेवालों को ये अपना सबसे बड़ा दुश्मन मानते हैं। इन्होंने मज़हब और सियासत को फेंटफाट कर एक बड़ा ज़हरीला मिक्सचर तैयार किया है। ये अपनी सुविधा से कभी मज़हबी, कभी सियासी हो जाते हैं। अपने कट्टर नज़रिये की नुक़्ताचीनी को देश-मज़हब सबकी नुक़्ताचीनी साबित कर देते हैं। सारे मज़हबों और अलग फिलॉसफी-अलग नज़रिये को इज़्ज़त बख़्शने की इस देश की पुरानी तहज़ीब और उसकी रूह को ही ग़लत साबित करने पर तुले हैं।

ये इसे सेकुलर और विदेशों से उधार माँगी विचारधारा मानते हैं। जबकि, बरख़ुरदार, उल्टे इनके पुरखों में से एक ने 1931 में रोम की यात्रा की थी और इटली से नेशन और जर्मनी से नस्ल के मिथ को उधार माँग कर लाया था। वही यूरोप की ख़ास नेशन-स्टेट का फ़लसफ़ा, जिसकी बुनियाद एक नस्ल, एक भाषा और एक मज़हब पर खड़ी थी और जिसके लिए एक

स्थायी दुश्मन होना ज़रूरी शर्त थी। और मज़ाक़ की बात यह कि यूरोप के फिलॉसफरों वाल्तेयर से लेकर मैक्समूलर-नीत्शे तक ने हिन्दुस्तान से, वेदों और मनुस्मृति से कई मिथक उधार लिए। ख़ासकर वेदों की प्राचीनता, आर्यों की श्रेष्ठता, वर्णव्यवस्था की शुद्धता के मिथ ने उन सबों के नज़रिया गढ़ने में बड़ी भूमिका निभाई। इन मिथकों के सहारे यूरोप ने अपने 'ग़ैर' और 'ग़ैर से नफ़रत' के उसूलों पर धार चढ़ाई, जिसके सहारे उनके सियासतदानों ने यूरोप की तहज़ीब और सियासत से यहूदियों को धीरे-धीरे किनारे किया और आख़िर में नाज़ियों ने उसे हॉलॉकॉस्ट तक पहुँचाया।

अब्बू थोड़ा रुके। आँखें बन्द कीं। ज़्यादा बोलना अब्बू को अच्छा नहीं लगता। ज़्यादा बोलना ख़ूब आक्रमक होकर बोलना भी उन्हें हिंसा का ही एक रूप लगता। किन्तु हमें बात पूरी सुननी थी। अब्बू फिर...आगे सुनाइये अब्बू...। अब्बू ने बात आगे बढ़ाई...दिक़्क़त है कि इस देश में आज़ादी की लड़ाई और आज़ादी मिलने के बाद उसके गढ़ने के जुनून में इस नज़रिये को कुछ ख़ास तवज्जो नहीं मिली। विदेशी पौधा इस देश की मिट्टी पकड़ नहीं पा रहा था। किन्तु अब वक़्त बदल गया है। वह ज़हरीला पौधा छतनार गाछ में तब्दील हो गया है। ये तरक़्क़ीपसन्द, गंगा-जमुनी तहज़ीब को जीनेवाले एक्टिविस्टों, लेखकों-शायरों-अफ़सानानिगारों के क़त्ल में भी गुरेज़ नहीं कर रहे। ये लोग पुणे में ख़ान साहब और उनके साथी की हत्या करने के पहले महाराष्ट्र और कर्नाटक में कई हत्याओं को अंजाम दे चुके थे।

खिड़की के बाहर अँधेरा आज ज़्यादा घना ज़्यादा काला...कोलतार-सा दिख रहा था। हवा भी गुम हो गई थी। लग रहा था कि सहम कर कहीं थम गई हो। हमारी साँसें भी भारी हो रही थीं। पेशानी पर पसीना और चेहरे पर चिन्ता-तनाव साफ़ झलक रहे थे। लेकिन बात पूरी करने की हमारी गुज़ारिश अब्बू टाल नहीं पा रहे थे।

तुम्हारे नानू की हत्या के तुरन्त बाद गुप्ता और कालिन्दी का इस शहर में आमद कोई एकेडमी खोलने के लिए नहीं बल्कि हमारा ध्यान भटकाने, हमारी गतिविधियों पर नज़र रखने और इस शहर के बाअसर लोगों में अपनी पैठ बनाने के लिए हुई है। ताकि कल को हत्या की जाँच प्रभावित की जा सके। यह कोई अटकलबाज़ी नहीं है। हमारे पुणे और बैंगलुरू के

साथी बहुत खोजबीन के बाद इस नतीजे पर पहुँचे हैं। यह इनकी पुरानी कार्यशैली है। इसलिए तुम्हारा-शब्बो का अलग-अलग व्यस्त होना और आश्रम में एकाएक बहुत चहल-पहल बढ़ना मुझे अच्छा नहीं लग रहा है। क्या शब्बो बेटी के 'सिस्टरहुड' की एकाएक बाज़ार में माँग का बढ़ना कुछ चौंकाता नहीं है? यहाँ कोचिंग की यह चहल-पहल। रुपये-पैसे की इतनी आमद कुछ अच्छी नहीं लग रही है। इबादत की जगह...मौसीक़ी का पाक मुक़ाम...यहाँ बाज़ार के गन्दे पाँव ठीक नहीं हैं बेटा। मुझे कई तरह के अन्देशे सताते रहते हैं। वे ध्यान भटकाने के लिए और भी कई हथकंडे अपना रहे हैं...अपनाएँगे। किन्तु मेरे अपनों का उस स्वर्णमृग के पीछे भागना बड़े हादसे का संकेत दे रहा है।

तस्वीर पूरी तरह साफ़ हो गई थी। एक तरफ़ सुआर्यन कम्प्यूटर ट्रेनिंग एकेडमी का भव्य उद्घाटन और लगभग हर हफ़्ते होनेवाले फंक्शन का मायने समझ में आने लगा। इन कार्यक्रमों में शहर के सारे असरदार लोग, ख़ासकर पुलिस महकमे के हाकिमों की ख़ास आवभगत का मतलब भी खुला। यूनिवर्सिटी-कॉलेजों-स्कूलों में ख़ास मज़हब के युवाओं के बीच सुआर्यन की टी-शर्ट, पीले अंगवस्त्र, कच्छप भगवान के लॉकेट वाली चेन और चेहरे के दाहिने हिस्से पर एग्ज़िमा जैसे टैटू के नये-नये फैशन के भी अर्थ खुल रहे थे।

रात गहरी हो रही थी। आश्रम के दरख़्त की मोटी टहनी पर इत्मीनान से सोये चाँद को निगलने आते अजगर की फुत्कार हमारे नींद में सुराख़ कर रही थी।

21

बच गए वो सह लिए जिसने तेरे ज़ुल्म-ओ-सितम,
मिट गए वो जिस पे तेरी मेहरबानी हो गई।

—मजरूह सुल्तानपुरी

अब्बू की संजीदा बातों ने हमारी ख़ुमारी उतार दी। छोटे-छोटे मोर्चे की क्षणिक जीत को पानीपत की चौथी-पाँचवों लड़ाई की ऐतिहासिक विजय मान हम एक नशे में धुत्त थे। चारों तरफ़ चाँद-चाँदनी और बासंती बयार नज़र आ रही थी। मगर अब्बू की मानें तो यह सुआर्यन की बड़ी रणनीति की गड्डियों का छोटा सा पत्ता भर था। अब नशा फटा तो पता चला कि न केवल चिलचिलाती धूप थी बल्कि तेज़ लू भी चल रही थी। हमारी टीम ने अब तक गुप्ता के दाहिने गाल के एग्जिमा—उस जैसे टैटू—के फैलाव पर ध्यान नहीं दिया था। न भगवान कच्छप महाराज के लॉकेट के वितरण के प्रभाव को आँकने की कोशिश की थी। हमारी पूरी टीम आश्रम के कोचिंग क्लासेज और 'सिस्टरहुड' की कोशिशों में ही मगन थी।

अब्बू, गुप्ता के दाहिने गाल के एग्जिमा को दिलो-दिमाग़ में फैले 'ग़ैर' से आठों पहर नफ़रत के गाढ़े ज़हर का बाहरी लक्षण मान रहे थे। एक साइको सोमैटिक बीमारी, जो नफ़रत को मुहब्बत में बदले बिना कभी ठीक नहीं होनी थी।...अब यह मनोदैहिक रोग था या नहीं, किन्तु इतना तो

सच था कि यह एग्जिमा, सिबोरिक डॅर्मटाइटिस था, जो कई कारणों से फैल सकता था, जिसमें बैक्टीरियल इन्फेक्शन से लेकर आनुवांशिकी और मानसिक तनाव तक शामिल थे। किन्तु गुप्ता अपनी सुआर्यन जागरण सेना के नये नौजवानों, अपने प्रतिबद्ध सैनिकों को प्रबोधन-सत्र में यह उद्‌बोधित करता कि उसके पावन हृदय में जो देशप्रेम का उबलता ज्वार है उसी की एक लहर उफान मार चेहरे पर आ छलकी है। यह और कुछ नहीं, अपने धर्म, जाति और राष्ट्र से असीम प्रेम का प्रतीक भर है। एकाग्रता से निरखिए तो इसमें अपने अखंड राष्ट्र का नक्शा दिखेगा और दिखेंगी सूर्योदय की सुनहरी किरणें। जिस दिन आप सबों के दाहिने गाल पर यह नक्शा खिलेगा उसी दिन यह माना जाएगा कि आप राष्ट्र, अपने धर्म, अपनी जाति के सच्चे सैनिक हैं। सेनानायक के उद्‌बोधन के पश्चात् एक अनूठे अनुष्ठान की पवित्र-पावन प्रक्रिया प्रारम्भ होती जिसमें हर सैनिक अपने सेनानायक के हृदय से हृदय और दाहिने गाल से दाहिने गाल का स्पर्श करवाता। ताकि सबके हृदय में सेनानायक माननीय गुप्ता जी की तरह देशभक्ति का ज्वार उफन सके और दाहिने गाल पर उसका निशान शीघ्रातिशीघ्र प्रकट हो। जब तक यह चमत्कार सम्भव नहीं होता तब तक एग्जिमानुमा टैटू से काम चलाना था। अब न जाने कब से कितने-कितने राज्यों के कितने-कितने शहरों में न जाने कितने-कितने माननीय शर्मा जी-वर्मा जी-सिंह जी-तिवारी जी अपने पावन उद्‌बोधनों से देश की नई पीढ़ी को प्रबोधित कर रहे थे उन सबका आकलन एक अदने से तुच्छ मानव के बस की बात नहीं थी। हाँ! यह और बात थी कि पड़ोसी देशों में भी मज़हबी जुनूनी इसी आशय की बातें अपने लफ़्ज़ों-मुहावरों में समझाकर अपने मज़हब, अपनी नस्ल, अपनी क़ौम से अक़ीदत की क़समें खिलाये जा रहे थे।

यूरोप-अमेरिका में नस्ल, रंग और नेशन के जलवे थे। सब जगह एक बात कॉमन थी कि सबका अपना-अपना एक ग़ैर, एक स्थायी दुश्मन था जिससे बिना नफ़रत किए, बिना दुश्मनी निभाये अपने नेशन, अपने मज़हब अपनी क़ौम से मुहब्बत हो ही नहीं सकती थी और इस ग़ैर, पक्के दुश्मन के ख़त्म होते ही ज़मीं पर जन्नत का उतर आना तो पहले से ही तय था।

थोड़ा सा गूगल बाबा को खँगालने और तीन-चार वर्षों की पत्रिकाओं-अख़बारों के बंडल देखने के बाद भयावह मंज़र के कुछ नज़ारे दिखे। देश

के नक्शे में लगभग हर हिस्से पर इनके ख़ूनी पंजों की छाप दिख रही थी। आश्चर्य यह था कि इनके भक्तों की संख्या रक्तबीज की तरह बढ़ती गई थी। भक्त पत्रकार-लेखक-शायर अपनी लेखनी के चमत्कार से इनके हत्या के कार्यक्रमों को भी धार्मिक आभा से ढकने की कोशिश करते दिख रहे थे। 'ग़ैर' से नफ़रत और उसकी पूर्णाहुति के लिए पवित्र-पावननुमा नये मिथक, नयी कहानियाँ गढ़ी गईं, जिसमें भगवान कच्छप महाराज की कहानी थोड़ी ज़्यादा ही पवित्र और पावन थी। बिना स्नान किए इनका नाम भी ज़ुबान पर लाना मना था। इससे पुण्य-क्षय की आशंका थी। अब कच्छप बाबा हैं तो जल के देवता, किन्तु पृथ्वी उनकी ही पीठ पर टिकी है और सोलह अवतारों की कथा तो सोलह बुधवार को ही सुनी-सुनाई जा सकती थी, नहीं तो वही पुण्य-क्षय...। बाबा बहुत ही प्रतापी जीवन्त देवता, जो कलियुग में सब देवताओं से ज़्यादा प्रभावी बताये गए हैं। कई-कई कहानियाँ कही-सुनी जा रही थीं कि फ़लाँ ने सोलह बुधवार विधि अनुसार भगवान् कच्छप महाराज का व्रत रखा तो शादी के अठारह साल बाद पुत्र रत्न की प्राप्ति हुई, फलाँ को गड़ा ख़जाना मिला और ढेकाँ को पक्की सरकारी नौकरी मिली, वह भी ऊपरी आमदनी वाली। व्रत भी कितना आसान था। बस सूर्योदय के पहले उठ, पीले वस्त्र धारण कर, पीले रंग के गरम पानी से स्नान करना था। गर्मी में थोड़ी परेशानी तो हो सकती थी, किन्तु वह व्रत भी व्रत क्या जिसमें व्रतधारी को थोड़ा कष्ट न हो। तत्पश्चात् नये पीले वस्त्र धारण कर दो पहरों का निर्जला उपवास करना और 'भगवान कच्छप माहात्म्य' नामक ग्रंथ का आद्योपान्त सस्वर पाठ करना था। तीसरे पहर से स्वयं अपने हाथों मिट्टी के पीले बर्तनों में पीली मिट्टी के ही चूल्हे पर प्रसाद तैयार करना था। लकड़ियाँ पीले जल से धोकर पहले ही सुखा लेनी थीं। भगवान को उड़द से थोड़ा ज़्यादा ही स्नेह था, अतः उड़द के बड़े, उड़द की खिचड़ी एवं उड़द का हलवा। प्रसाद में बस इतना ही। साथ में कुछ पीले रंग के फल-फलाहार। किन्तु कुछ परहेज़ भी थे जैसे प्रसाद से खट्टे पदार्थों यथा इमली-खटाई आदि का स्पर्श सर्वथा वर्जित था तथा व्रतधारी को लाल मिर्ची से सोलह बुधवार दूर रहना था और व्रत के दिन चौबीस घंटों में वायु विकार नहीं होना चाहिए। वरना न केवल व्रत भंग होगा बल्कि भगवान के भयानक श्राप का भी प्रकोप हो सकता है। शाम

को भगवान के मन्दिर में प्रसाद चढ़ाकर व्रतधारी को उपवास तोड़ना था। मन्दिर की आवश्यकता का निवारण भी हो रहा था। धीरे-धीरे हर चौक-चौराहे, गली-कूचे में भगवान कच्छप महाराज के बड़े-छोटे मन्दिर उग आए थे, कुछ फुनगने की तैयारी में थे।

अब हमारा शहर चूँकि समुद्र तट के नज़दीक था और चारों ओर से नदी-नालों से घिरा हुआ, सो यहाँ भगवान् कच्छप महाराज की लोकप्रियता थोड़ा ज़्यादा ही प्रसारित हुई। वैसे भी शहर की पुरानी बस्तियों में महाराज के प्राचीन मन्दिरों के एकाध खंडहर भी थे (या ऐसा प्रवचनों में बताया जा रहा था) जिससे प्रमाणित होता था कि उनकी पूजा आदि काल से प्रचलित रही है। मध्य अवधि में कलियुग के प्रभाव से मन्द पड़ी थी, किन्तु पुनः मानवता के बन्द नेत्र खुल गए थे और उन्होंने अपने उद्धारक को पहचान लिया था। इसी बीच बॉलीवुड ने 'जय कच्छप बाबा' फिल्म बनाई जो माता-बहनों की कृपा से सुपर-डुपर हिट रही। अब क्या था? धरती से गगन तक भगवान् कच्छप महाराज, कच्छप माता, कच्छप बाबा के जैकारों की गूँज थी।

लेकिन इस कहानी में थोड़ा पेच भी था। शहर के बाहरी छोरों पर श्रमिक जाति और अल्पसंख्यक लोगों के टोले थे जिनकी आजीविका मछली मारने-बेचने-सुखाने से जुड़ी थी। मछली के साथ-साथ केंकड़े-घोंघे-कछुए भी पकड़े-बेचे जाते रहे थे। ये सब उनके ख़ान-पान में भी शामिल थे। शहर में एक मुहल्ला ऐसा भी था जिसमें घर-घर कछुओं के खोल से सजावटी वस्तुओं का निर्माण पीढ़ियों से होता आ रहा था। संयोग से यह गृह उद्योग वाला टोला भी अल्पसंख्यकों का ही था। यही इस कथित धार्मिक कथा के वे घुमावदार मोड़ थे जिनके कारण सुआर्यन सेना भगवान् कच्छप महाराज में विशेष रुचि लेती आ रही थी।

भगवान कच्छप महाराज के लॉकेट-वितरण कार्यक्रमों, माननीयों के अनवरत प्रबोधनों एवं बॉलीवुड की सुपर-डुपर हिट फिल्म के बाद कच्छप बाबा केन्द्रित दर्जनों फिल्मों-सीरियल्स के अथक प्रयासों से राष्ट्र का वातावरण परिवर्तित हो रहा था। दसों दिशाओं में पुण्य प्रभा प्रवाहित होने लगी थी। राष्ट्र ने सुदूर दक्षिण में हिन्द महासागर के तट पर बाबा का एक विशालकाय मन्दिर बनाने का संकल्प लिया। इस निर्माण में सम्पूर्ण राष्ट्र

की भागीदारी हो, इसके लिए हर शहर, हर गाँव, हर घर से एक मुट्ठी चावल और एक ग्राम धातु संग्रह करना था। इसके लिए राष्ट्र की युवा शक्ति कटिबद्ध हो चुकी थी लेकिन यह कटिबद्धता उनके लिए भारी पड़ रही थी जिनकी आजीविका और खान-पान में कच्छप महाराज शामिल रहे थे।

शहरों में बाबा मन्दिर निर्माण समितियों से दोगुनी-चौगुनी संख्या में कच्छप-रक्षक संघों का गठन हो रहा था। राष्ट्र के बेरोजगार, बेकार, नशाखोरी, जुआबाज़ी, पॉकेटमारी, छिनतई, गुंडई, बलात्कार में व्यस्त युवा शक्ति की चेतना एकाएक जाग्रत हो गई। उनके अन्तर्मन के चक्षु खुल गए। युवकाई अँगड़ाई लेकर उठ खड़ी हुई और सत्यपथ पर बढ़ चली। अब और नहीं...बस और नहीं...भगवान् कच्छप महाराज पर अत्याचार और नहीं। जगह-जगह मछली-वैन, ट्रक, जीप, टोकरियों की जाँच में कच्छप रक्षक संघ के जाग्रत युवा संलग्न हो गए। दुर्घटना से सावधानी भली की तर्ज पर जाँच में कच्छप महाराज मिलें या न मिलें दुष्टों को दंडित किया जाना अपरिहार्य कर्तव्यों में सम्मिलित था। प्रथम चरण में दंड की मात्रा नियंत्रित रखी गई। यह ख़ास ध्यान रखा गया कि ऐसे हर ऐक्शन की वीडियोग्राफी की जाए और उसे सोशल मीडिया पर वायरल किया जाए। जैसी कि पूर्व से ही आशंका थी, कुछ नास्तिक टाइप सेकुलर प्रॉस्टीट्यूट्स ने इस कार्यक्रम की कटु आलोचना की। प्रिंट और इलेक्ट्रॉनिक मीडिया इनके चिल्ल-पों से भन्ना गई।

लेकिन कच्छप-रक्षक संघ का यह कार्यक्रम नियमित और विस्तृत होता चला गया। मीडिया पर आस्था बनाम संविधान की बहसें इतनी लम्बी खिंचने लगीं कि तंग आकर मीडिया ने अपनी नज़र उधर से मोड़ ली। अब ऐसे समाचार प्रथम पृष्ठ से खिसककर धीरे-धीरे चौथे-पाँचवें पृष्ठ पर पहुँच गए। चैनल्स ने सिद्धान्ततः यह स्वीकार कर लिया कि आस्था हर तर्क से परे है, इस पर क्या चर्चा करना?

प्रथम चरण की सफलता के बाद कच्छप-रक्षक संघों की वाहनों की सघन जाँच और दुष्ट-दलन की गति और मात्रा बढ़ गई। अब दंड के क्रम में कायर-कमज़ोर-जर्जर देह-मन वाले विधर्मियों के प्राण उनका साथ छोड़ने लगे। चैनल्स पर पुनः चीख-पुकार शुरू हुई। एकाध-दो माह में पुनः पूर्ववत् शान्ति पसर गई तो तीसरे चरण का शुभारम्भ हुआ, जिसमें रक्षक

संघ की युवा मंडली सन्देहास्पद घरों में घुस कर रसोई-फ्रिज में कच्छप महाराज के गोशत की तलाश करने लगी। यहाँ भी पुराना सूत्र लागू हुआ। गोशत मिले न मिले, दंड अवश्य दिया जाए ताकि सनद रहे। कछुआ-खोल का गृह उद्योग महीनों से बन्द पड़ा था। फिर भी टोले को पुराने पापों की सज़ा दी गई। अब इन नये कार्यक्रमों के क्रम में भी कायर-कमज़ोरों-जर्जर देह-मन के विधर्मियों के प्राणों ने उनका साथ छोड़ा। अब इसमें मासूम रक्षकों की क्या ग़लती? उन्होंने सारी विधर्मी-पापी देहों को पाप-मुक्त करने के लिए एक तरह से ही दंडित किया। अब चन्द देहों के प्राण ही बिदक कर छिटक लिए, तो उसमें उनका क्या क़सूर?

अब चौथे चरण में कृतज्ञ समाज को अपना आभार प्रकट करना था। समाज अपने जन-प्रतिनिधियों, माननीय विधायकों, प्रातः स्मरणीय सांसदों के नेतृत्व में आगे आया। इन रक्षक युवाओं को सम्मानित करने का दौर चल पड़ा। सम्मान-समारोहों की संख्या इतनी बढ़ गई कि फूल-मालाएँ कम पड़ने लगीं। जिन वीर सपूतों ने अनोखी वीरता का प्रदर्शन किया था यथा अकेले ही विधर्मी को कुदाल से ही काट डालने या जिन्दा जलाते वीडियो बनाने आदि-आदि का, उनकी मूर्तियाँ तक स्थापित की जाने लगीं। शायद इसे ही सतयुग का आना कहते थे।

लेकिन ख़ास बात यह थी कि इस मामले में सारे जहाँ का मौसम एकसार हो रहा था। इस मोर्चे पर हमारे पड़ोसी देशों के रिकार्ड हमसे उन्नीस नहीं, इक्कीस ही थे। वह पाक़ीज़ा ज़मीं, जन्नत-सा देश जिसके लिए सन् सैंतालीस में लाखों लोगों का क़त्ल करना पड़ा, अपनों की भी शहादतें देनी पड़ीं, करोड़ों ज़िलावतन हुए। अब जाकर वहाँ तक़रीबन जन्नत उतर ही आया था...तक़रीबन। इस ख़ुशआमदीद में ईश-निन्दा क़ानून ने बड़ा रोल निभाया था। सच कहें तो मोहतरमा जन्नत के लिए रेड कार्पेट इस क़ानून ने ही बिछाया था। अब ग़ैर-मज़हबियों को औक़ात में रखने के लिए दंगे जैसे नाटक-नौटंकियों की ज़रूरत ही नहीं रह गई थी। अब नल पर पानी भरने के लिए भी किसी ग़ैरमज़हबी ज़नाना से हुए रूटीनी झगड़े का रुख़ इस कानून के बिना पर बदला जा सकता था। उस पर ईश-निन्दा का आरोप लगाकर न केवल जेल बल्कि फाँसी की सज़ा सुनाई जा सकती थी। अगर रियासत का गवर्नर उस नापाक मोहतरमा से मिलने, उसका सच

जानने जेल जा पहुँचे, तो यह इतनी बड़ी ख़ता थी कि उसके बॉडीगार्ड को उस ख़तावार गवर्नर के क़त्ल की न केवल इजाज़त थी बल्कि पूरी क़ौम ऐसे पक्के मज़हबी नौजवाँ को अपना हीरो बनाने को बेक़रार बैठी थी। इसी सिलसिले से न केवल मज़हब की पाक़ीज़गी का इश्तहार किया जा रहा था बल्कि ग़ैर-मज़हबियों को आसानी से निपटा, जन्नत उतरने की राह आसान की जा रही थी।

सन् इकहत्तर में हमारी ही मेहनत से अवतरित होनेवाले देश का अन्दाज़े-बयाँ थोड़ा जुदा-सा था। वहाँ मज़हब के जुनूनी नौजवानों ने बाज़ाप्ता एक लिस्ट बना रखी थी। इस लिस्ट में कोई भेदभाव नहीं किया गया था। नास्तिक, सेकुलर प्रॉस्टिट्यूट, साझी तहज़ीब की वकालत करनेवाले ग़द्दार, मिली-जुली विरासत पर क़लम घसीटनेवाले देशद्रोही, उदारता-प्रगतिशीलता बघारनेवाले ब्लॉगर्स आदि-आदि, सब एक ही तराज़ू पर तौले गए थे। नफ़रत के जुनून का उफान इतना तेज़ था कि एक-एक दिन में तीन-चार निपटाये जा रहे थे। यहाँ भी अब जन्नत की राह आसाँ ही थी। दरअसल अब ख़ुद मोहतरमा जन्नत को कन्फ्यूज़ हो जाना था कि किस देश में तशरीफ़ फरमाएँ।

वास्तव में बस तीन-चार सालों में हालात धीरे-धीरे इतने भयावह हो गए थे कि वास्तविकता के सामने आते अब्बू के एकतारा की तरह हम भी लगातार काँप रहे थे।

22

शहर के आईन में ये मद भी लिक्खी जाएगी,
ज़िंदा रहना है तो क़ातिल की सिफ़ारिश चाहिए।

—हक़ीम मंज़ूर

अलस्सुबह वही रूहानी रक़्स का जलवा था। आज अब्बू-कमोल के साथ अम्मू भी शामिल हुई थीं। नानू की ग़मी और शहर के बदलते हालात अम्मू के दिलो-दिमाग़ पर थोड़ा ज़्यादा ही असर डाल रहे थे। 'मौसीक़ी-मंज़िल' की तन्हा कोठरियाँ काटने दौड़ती थीं। रातों की नींद करवटों के तले दब कर छिटक जा रही थी। शब्बो भाभी अपने 'सिस्टरहुड' की सिस्टर्स के साथ मौसीक़ी की राह पर निकल पड़ी थीं। देश-विदेश की यात्राएँ चैन नहीं लेने दे रही थीं। चैन वे चाह भी नहीं रही थीं। ग़म ग़लत करने का यह साज़ो-आवाज़ का तरीक़ा उन्हें भाने लगा था। हार कर 'मौसीक़ी-मंज़िल' की तनहाइयों को ही अम्मू और बुलबुल ने तन्हा छोड़ दिया था। उनका ज़्यादा समय अब आश्रम में ही बीतने लगा था।

उस गोल-गोल ख़ूब गतिशील घूमर नाच ने फिर अपना रूहानी असर छोड़ा था। तीनों की देह-रूह सब रुई की तरह से हल्की हो गई थी। लगा, किसी अनजाने धुनिये ने उनकी देह-मन-रूह के कपास को ख़ूब मन से धुन दिया हो। रोम-रोम से प्रफुल्लित अब्बू आज फलसफ़ियाना

मूड में थे। लफ़्ज़ ख़र्चने को बेक़रार। मुमकिन है, अम्मू की मौजूदगी का भी असर रहा हो।

अब्बू ने फ़रमाया, बरख़ुरदार, न जाने क्यों मुझे कभी-कभी किसी ख़ास लम्हे में यह लगता है कि हमारी रूह भी देह ही है, शायद कुछ ज़्यादा नाज़ुक, ज़्यादा शफ़्फ़ाफ़, ज़्यादा आज़ाद देह। और यह देह भी कुछ और नहीं, रूह ही है, केवल अपने देह धरे के दंड, काम-क्रोध-लोभ-मोह-मद के कारण मैली। देह के अस्ल बुनियाद, ये मूल तत्त्व बहुत ही नापाक, निर्मम, हिंसक और दूषित हैं। दिक़्क़त यह हैं कि देह की इस मैल को कोई स्नान, कोई साबुन साफ़ नहीं कर सकता। मेरी और मेरे गुरुओं-मुर्शिदों की समझ में इसे साफ़ करने का एक ही उपाय है कि मुहब्बत की चाशनी में इसे भरपूर डुबोया जाए। जब उस चाशनी में एकसार लिपट जाए तो अन्दर के रहगुज़र पर उसे हौले-हौले उतारा जाए। उस रहगुज़र पर जिसके आख़िरी छोर रूह की ओखली मुन्तज़िर है। उसी ओखली में देह के अस्ल बुनियादों, काम-क्रोध-लोभ-मोह-मद की मूसल से कुटाई हो ताकि इनसे छुटकारा मिले।

अब्बू के अल्फ़ाज़ थोड़ा ठिठक गए। लगा, भीतर डूब कर कुछ खोज रहे हों। अम्मू ने पानी भरा गिलास बढ़ाया। पानी पीकर उन्होंने पलकें बन्द कर लीं। चन्द लम्हों के बाद फिर मुख़ातिब हुए, न जाने क्यूँ मुझे लगता है कि हमारे पूर्वजों ने जिस धर्म-मज़हब को मूसल बनाया था वह अब चूक गया है। वह अपनी पाक़ीज़गी खो बैठा है। उसकी सृजनशीलता बाँझ हो गई है। वह दशकों से सच्चा पीर-फ़क़ीर-मुर्शिद पैदा नहीं कर पा रहा...कहाँ हमारे समय में कोई गौतम...कोई गोरख...कोई कबीर पैदा हो रहे हैं।...न कोई बड़ा फ़िलॉस्फ़र...न ऊँचा फ़नकार...न बड़ो बाबा जैसा मौसीक़ीकार...। दरअसल मज़हब की नदी की धार नफ़रत के चट्टानों में फँसकर बहना भूल गई है। यही वह सबब है जिसके कारण उसकी चमक गुम गई है और बंधे हुए पानी की तरह सड़ाँध आने लगी है।

इसीलिए मुझे लगता है कि रूह की ओखल में देह की मैल को धोने के लिए मौसीक़ी को...मौसीक़ी ही क्यों, किसी भी फ़न को...क्रिएटिविटी को...पसीने में नहाई हुई मेहनत को मूसल बनाया जाए। तभी इनसानियत के बीमार मन, घुन खाई देह और हताश रूह को ताज़ा हवा मिल पाएगी।

नहीं तो यह बेमतलब की नफ़रत और हिंसा की आग में ख़ुद को ही जला कर ख़ात्मे के कगार पर पहुँचने ही वाला है।

अब्बू के सत्तर साल के तजुर्बे और रूह की पाकीज़गी ने बजा फ़रमाया था। थोड़ा कटु, कड़वा, किन्तु तपा हुआ सच। पूरे पहर अब्बू के अल्फ़ाज़ ही दिलो-दिमाग़ में गूँजते रहे। रियाज़ से लेकर बच्चों की मौसीक़ी की तालीम तक मन उन्हीं की तासीर में डूबा रहा। किन्तु नाश्ते के वक़्त अम्मू की उदासी और फ़िक्रमन्दी ने सीधे खुरदरी ज़मीन पर उतार दिया। पुणे से ख़बर थी कि डॉ. मांजरेकर और नानू की क़त्ल की जाँच में स्टेट पुलिस आगे ही नहीं बढ़ पा रही। पिछले छह-आठ महीने से एक भी गिरफ़्तारी नहीं...कोई चार्जशीट तक नहीं। मांजरेकर साहब के संगी-साथी-शागिर्द, उनके संगठन के लोगों ने स्पेशल इन्वेस्टिगेशन टीम बनाने के लिए मुम्बई हाईकोर्ट में रिट दाख़िल किया था, किन्तु वहाँ से कुछ हासिल नहीं हुआ। अब वे सुप्रीम कोर्ट में अपील करने जानेवाले हैं। हमें भी उसमें शामिल होने को न्योता है ताकि नानू का मामला कमज़ोर न पड़े।

तय हुआ कि वीरभूम से कमोल के बाबा को बुलाया जाए। आश्रम-बुलबुल की ज़िम्मेवारी मयंक परिवार और कुछ सीनियर बच्चे-बच्चियों को सौंप कर सभी लोग दिल्ली चलें। संगी-समधी मदन बाउल को दिल्ली में एक अच्छा वकील तय करने को कह दिया गया था। सुप्रीम कोर्ट ने दो-चार सुनवाइयों के बाद कर्नाटक-महाराष्ट्र में पिछले कुछ वर्षों में हुए ऐक्टिविस्टों-लेखकों-विचारकों-पत्रकारों की हत्याओं की जाँच के लिए बनी हुई विशेष जाँच दल को ही डॉ. मांजरेकर और नानू के क़त्ल की जाँच की ज़िम्मेवारी सौंप दी। यह एक बड़ी उपलब्धि थी। पहली बार क़ानून ने संजीदगी से नानू के क़त्ल को विशेष जाँच के क़ाबिल माना था।

अब तक तो अम्मू-अब्बू-कमोल के दरख़्वास्तों-अपीलों का कोई असर न शहर के कलक्टर, न रियासत के मुख्यमंत्री और न ह्यूमन राइट कमीशन के चेयरमैन पर पड़ते देखा था। बिना नाग़ा लगातार पहुँचाये गए उन दरख़्वास्तों से स्टेट पुलिस के कानों में जूँ तक नहीं रेंगी थीं। वह हिली तक नहीं। आला हाकिम मान कर चल रहे थे कि वारदात की जगह महाराष्ट्र में है तो वहाँ की पुलिस तो देख ही रही होगी। उस जाँच में बेमलतब टाँग क्यों अड़ाई जाए? जिनके परिवार में हादसा हुआ है उनकी तो ड्यूटी है कि

वे ऐसे दरख़्वास्त लगाएँ। वे क़ानून की बारीक़ियाँ तो जानते नहीं, भावुक लोग हैं, रोएँगे और रोना सुनाएँगे भी। रुलाई सुन लेनी है ताकि अगला ज़्यादा दुखी न हो। लेकिन जाँच तो महाराष्ट्र पुलिस ही करेगी। ऐसा नहीं था कि स्टेट पुलिस के इस मिज़ाज को अम्मू-अब्बू समझ नहीं रहे थे। लेकिन अभी तक अँधेरे में कोई राह नहीं सूझ रही थी। अब सुप्रीम कोर्ट में यह पहली बार लगा कि घने अँधेरे में कोई रोशनी कौंधी हो।

कमोल ने इस 'स्पेशल इन्वेस्टिगेशन टीम' के पिछले वर्षों में की गई जाँच की तफ़्तीश शुरू की। पहले से सुपुर्द हत्याओं के मामले में इस टीम ने क्या हासिल किया है? पुरानी पत्र-पत्रिकाओं के रिपोर्ताज़-आलेख, गूगल का खजाना और कोल्हापुर-पुणे-बैंगलुरू-मुम्बई के साथियों की सूचनाओं ने दिल्ली में मिली ख़ुशी की रोशनी थोड़ी मद्धम कर दी। इस विशेष जाँच दल ने गिरफ़्तारियाँ तो की थीं। उन हत्याओं में इस्तेमाल मोटरसाइकिल, बन्दूक़ और लगभग सोलह-सत्रह सौ सिम कार्ड, सी.डी. दो दर्जन के लगभग, सत्रह पासपोर्ट आदि की ज़ब्ती भी एक बड़ी उपलब्धि मानी जा रही थी। किन्तु इन वारदातों को अंजाम देने की प्लानिंग बड़ी ज़बरदस्त थी। हर वारदात में आठ से दस टीमों ने अपनी-अपनी भूमिका निभाई थी, जिनके बीच की कड़ियाँ अभी तक ग़ायब थीं। बन्दूक़ चलाने की ट्रेनिंग देनेवाली एक अलग टीम थी। इस टीम ने अपने धर्म की नुक्ताचीनी करनेवालों को सबक़ सिखाने को बेक़रार लगभग पन्द्रह हज़ार जुनूनी युवाओं को पिछले दो-तीन वर्षों में ट्रेनिंग दी। किन्तु टार्गेट तय करना किसी दूसरी टीम के ज़िम्मे था। टार्गेट की दिन-रात-महीनों रेकी करना तीसरी टीम का काम था। शूटर्स तय करना चौथी टीम की ज़िम्मेदारी, असलहा पाँचवी टीम के हाथों, बाइक और वारदात वाले शहर से बाहर निकालने की ज़िम्मेवारी छठी टीम के कन्धों पर। रेकी करनेवालों के लिए किराये के मकान की व्यवस्था सातवीं टीम और शूटर्स के लिए ठहरने की व्यवस्था आठवीं टीम के ज़िम्मे। इन टीमों के लोगों में आपस में न कोई जान-पहचान थी और न कोई सूचना साझी की गई थी। सारी टीमों ने अलग-अलग अपने काम को बख़ूबी अंजाम दिया था। मोबाइल का उपयोग भी नहीं के बराबर किया गया था। गिरफ़्तार लोगों में एक डॉक्टर, एक आई.टी. प्रोफेशनल से लेकर छोटे शहर-क़स्बे के छिनतई करनेवाले तीन छोकरों और दो हार्ड

कोर क्रिमिनल तक शामिल थे। कोई तालमेल बैठ ही नहीं रहा था। इसलिए पहेली सुलझ नहीं पा रही थी। गोपनीयता इतनी ज़्यादा बरती गई थी कि इन गिरफ़्तार आरोपियों के घर के लोगों को भी नहीं मालूम था कि ये किस काम में लगे हुए थे।

मतलब कड़ियाँ अभी पूरी तरह उलझी थीं। एस.आई.टी. को शक सुआर्यन जागरण सेना पर तो था, किन्तु कोई ठोस प्रमाण अभी तक हासिल नहीं हो सका था। मास्टर माइन्ड अभी तक सात परदों के भीतर आराम से बैठा मुस्कुरा रहा था, अपनी लिस्ट के अनुसार नया टार्गेट तय करता।

23

कैसे आ सकती है ऐसी दिलनशीं दुनिया को मौत,
कौन कहता है कि ये सब कुछ फ़ना हो जाएगा।

—अहमद मुश्ताक

कमोल की तफ़्तीश से कोर्ट में मिली चन्द लम्हों की ख़ुशी बिला गई। 'विशेष जाँच दल' की कछुआ-गति और आधे-अधूरे नतीजों की हक़ीक़त से उम्मीदों पर पाला सा पड़ गया। सच कहें तो नानू की ग़मी के बाद उदासी रुख़सत ही नहीं हो रही थी। एक अच्छी, तो चार बुरी ख़बरें उदासी बढ़ाने आ जातीं। अब्बू और कमोल के बाबा के संगी-सँगाती पड़ोसी देशों में भी थे। उनमें से कुछ ने तो बड़ो नानू-नानू के क़दमों में साथ-साथ तालीम पाई थी। कुछ से केन्दुली के जयदेव मेले, शान्ति निकेतन के पौष मेले या ख़्वाजा निज़ामुद्दीन औलिया के उर्स में भेंट हुई, दोस्ती हुई और भाईचारे में बदल गई। फ़ितरतन अब्बू-बाबा के हमराही-हमरंग साथी भी इन्हीं की तरह क़ैद-तअय्युन की हदों को तोड़नेवाले ठहरे। ग़ैर-मज़हबी, काफ़िर जैसे लफ़्ज़ों और उनकी तासीर से दूर साझी-तहज़ीब, साझी-रवायतों के पैरोकार, सबों की ईमाँ की पाकीज़गी के तलबगार। वे ठीक ही फ़रमाते थे कि फूल वही, चमन वही, बस फ़र्क़ हमारी नज़रों का है। हम अगर व्यक्ति की सीमाओं, हुदूदे-ज़ात से उठकर, बाहर निकल कर देखें, तो न

कोई ग़ैर नज़र आएगा और न कोई रक़ीब। लेकिन बाहर हवा बदली हुई थी। मंज़र ख़ुशनुमा नहीं, रंजीदा हो गए थे। किन निगाहों से खंजर बरसेंगे, कहा नहीं जा सकता था। नतीजतन कहीं से किसी की शहादत की ख़बर सहमी हुई चुपके से आती, सहमी साँझ को और भी सहमा जाती थी। सूफ़ी संतों, बाउल फ़क़ीरों, मौसीक़ीकारों पर काली नज़रें कुछ ज़्यादा ही नेमतें बरसा रही थीं। पहले पूरब के बंगदेश से कमोल के बाबा-अब्बू के अज़ीज़ हमारे प्यारे चाचू ढाका की राजशाही यूनिवर्सिटी के बाउल प्रोफेसर साहब के शहादत की ख़बर आई। अभी ग़म की शामों ने अपने आँसू ठीक से पोंछे भी नहीं थे कि मैमनसिंह के सूफ़ीसंत, बाबा-अब्बू के जिगरी दोस्त का क़त्ल हो गया। फिर कुछ ही दिनों के बाद पश्चिम के पाक देश से बहुत ही ऊँचे सूफ़ी गायक की शहादत की काली ख़बर रुदाली औरतों की तरह अब्बू की कोठरी में स्यापा करने लगी।

आजकल अब्बू की आँखें डबडबाये हुए आकाश की तरह हो गई थीं, जो बरसती भी नहीं थीं और ख़ुश्क भी नहीं होती थीं। लगता है, मन के चूल्हे में ग़म की गीली लकड़ियाँ सुलगती कम और धुआँ ज़्यादा देती थीं। अब्बू के लफ़्ज़ों में भी उस धुएँ की कसक होती, बरख़ुरदार! लगता है हमारे संगी-साथी, हमारे अज़ीज़, घरों की गोरैया हो गए हैं। अब हमारा चहचहाना लोगों को नहीं भाता। हर कोई ताली बजा कर उन्हें भगाना चाहता है। एक-एक कर सब गुम होते जा रहे हैं। लेकिन हरेक के गुम होते इस कायनात-झील की लहरें काँपती हैं और उनमें से एक लहर मेरी रातों को कँपकँपाती मुझ तक पहुँचती है। फिर मेरी रूह और मेरा इकतारा काँपते रहते हैं। हो सकता है कि उस गोरैया ने अपनी सारी चहचहाहटें ख़र्च कर दी हों, सारे गान गा लिए हों। फिर भी किसी दरख़्त को उसे आसरा तो देना था। यूँ सैयादों के भरोसे तो नहीं छोड़ना था। ऐसा क्या हुआ कि हर दरख़्त ने अपनी शाख़ें समेट लीं, सबों की दीद की रोशनियाँ राख हो गईं। सड़क के दोनों ओर के घरों के दरवाज़े-खिड़कियाँ-रोशनदान सब बन्द हो गए और हमारे अज़ीज़ की अपनी ही पुकार उनके पास लौटकर आती रही...आती रही और सैयाद मुस्कुराता रहा।

बरख़ुरदार! यह भी सही है कि भादो की भीगी रात की तरह मौत की कोई परछाईं नहीं होती। या फिर वह हमारी परछाईं की तरह हमारे

संग-संग चलती रहती है और हम उसे कभी लाँघ नहीं पाते। लेकिन वह जब चाहती है, हमें अपने आगोश में ले लेती है। तब हमारी डूबती नब्ज़ों में हमारे हर दर्द को नींद आने लगती है। जिस्म इच्छाओं से लदी नाव की तरह गहरे समुद्र की तली में औंधे मुँह रेत में धँसता जाता है। तब भी एक इच्छा सतह पर तैरती रहती है। जिसे रवि ठाकुर ने यूँ बयाँ किया कि मोरिते चाही ना आमी सुन्दर भुवने (मैं अभी सुन्दर सुघड़ भुवन को छोड़ मरना नहीं चाहता)। किसी दूसरे शायर ने फुसफुसाया कि थोड़ी बारिश हो जाए, तो चलूँ। थोड़ी धूप खिल जाए, तो चलूँ। थोड़ी तुतलाहट मिल जाए, तो चलूँ। किन्तु, ऐसी नन्ही-मुन्नी इच्छा के तिरते रहने से शायद कहीं कोई फ़र्क़ नहीं पड़ता, जिस्म उस अतल तल की रेत में डूबता चला जाता है और रूहें साँसें लेने लगती हैं।

अभी अब्बू के लफ़्ज़ों ने झरना बन्द नहीं किया था। मन के अन्दर का शिउली गाछ बीती रात फूलों से ज़्यादा ही लद गया था, जो अलस्सुबह टपक-टपक कर उनके ही क़दमों का बोसा लेना चाह रहा था बरख़ुरदार! हालाँकि हमारे बुज़ुर्गों, मुर्शिदों-गुरुओं और सूफ़ी-सन्तों ने इस मौत के तसव्वुर को बहुत ही ख़ूबसूरती से सजाया है। इनके यहाँ मौत से एक बेतकल्लुफ़ी है। उससे ज़िन्दगी से भी ज़्यादा लगाव-दुलार है क्योंकि उसके कारण ही वह पर्दा हट जाता है जो ख़ुदी और ख़ुदा के बीच पड़ा हुआ है। रूमी तो साफ़-साफ़ कहते हैं कि मुझे क़ब्र के सुपुर्द करते हुए मुझसे विदा-विदा नहीं कहना क्योंकि वह क़ब्र तो सारी जन्नतों और मेरे बीच बस एक आख़िरी पर्दा है। वे फिर फ़रमाते हैं कि अगर तुमने मेरा अन्दर जाना देखा है, तो बाहर निकलना भी देखोगे। अस्त होने से सूरज या चन्दा को भला क्या हानि होती है? एक दूसरे शायर फ़रमाते हैं कि जिस मिट्टी में पले-बढ़े, बड़े हुए, उस मिट्टी से परहेज़ कैसा?

हमारे बुज़ुर्गों ने सच ही फ़रमाया है। हमें उनके लफ़्ज़ों पर कोई शक नहीं है। किन्तु हर ग़मी से कायनात-झील की लहरें, हमारी रातें, हमारे मन-प्राण और हमारा इकतारा काँपता क्यों रहता है? हमारे सीने के भीतर खोखला-सा क्यूँ लगता रहता है? ग़मी की, क़त्ल की हर ख़बर उस खोखलेपन को और गहरा क्यों कर देती है? एक जलन-सी क्यूँ महसूस होती रहती है, सीने में भी और आँखों में भी? लगता है, हमारे अज़ीज़

अपने में ही नमक की तरह घुल गए और वह सारा नमक हमारे सीने, हमारी पलकों में समा गया है।...नश्वरता हवा में उड़ती रहती है।...नदी किनारे बाल बिखराये खड़ी एक स्त्री अक्सर दिखती है, जो हमारी नींदों को आख़िरी नींद का रियाज़ करवाती रहती है। छाती धड़कती रहती है, डर लगता रहता है। पर कहीं से कोई भी हाथ बढ़ाता नहीं दिखता। लगता है कहीं कोई नहीं है। नक्षत्रों, सौरमंडलों, आकाश-गंगाओं में भी कहीं कोई नहीं है। सब अपनी-अपनी आग में जल रहे हैं। हमारी आग के लिए किसी के पास एक चुल्लू जल भी नहीं बचा है।

ऐसे भयावह समय में मेरी आरज़ू है कि मेरी आँखों, मेरे सीने में पानी बचा रहे। जहाँ मेरे अज़ीज़, मेरे हमदम, हमनवाँ, हमरंगी, हमनशीं पनाह पा सकें। वो नहीं तो उनकी छवि फूल की पंखुड़ियों-सी वहाँ तिरती रहे। उनके होने की ख़ुशबू मेरे चारों तरफ़ छाई रहे। उनके साथ-साथ उनकी थोड़ी-सी मौसीक़ी, थोड़ी-सी गुफ़्तगू, थोड़ी खिलखिलाहट, थोड़ी-सी बारिश, थोड़ी-सी धूप, थोड़ी-सी तितलियों की रवानगी भी बची रहे। इस बहाने वे नश्वरता की दहलीज लाँघ जाएँ। जब तक मेरा यह नाचीज़ जिस्म है, सीने में साँसें हैं, आँखों में आँसू हैं मेरी यह नन्हीं-सी इच्छा तिरती रहे।

24

निगह की मंज़िले-मकसूद मेहर-ओ-माह नहीं,
ये जल्वागाह के परदे हैं, जल्वागाह नहीं॥
(मेहर-ओ-माह: सूरज-चाँद। जल्वागाह: दर्शनस्थली)

—मज़ाज लखनवी

बांग्लादेश के अब्बू-बाबा के संगी-साथी अपने देश में चल रही नफ़रत और दरिंदगी के कार्य-व्यापार से बहुत दुखी-बहुत फ़िक्रमंद थे। इसके प्रतिकार, प्रतिरोध में कुछ सकारात्मक करना चाह रहे थे। इसी सिलसिले में सबकी सहमति से वार्षिक शास्त्रीय महोत्सव की शुरुआत हुई थी। बांग्लादेश चैतन्य महाप्रभु, लालन शाह फ़क़ीर, बड़ो बाबा अलाउद्दीन ख़ान, बड़ो नानू महताबुद्दीन ख़ान, उस्ताद विलायत ख़ाँ, पंडित रविशंकर, पंडित निखिल बनर्जी आदि-आदि महान संतों-फ़क़ीरों, संगीतज्ञों की जन्म-कर्म भूमि है। इसके सांस्कृतिक स्वरूप को गढ़ने में संतों, सूफ़ियों और बाउलों के साथ-साथ अवनीन्द्रनाथ टैगोर, रवीन्द्र नाथ टैगोर, नज़रूल इस्लाम जैसों ने महत्त्वपूर्ण भूमिका निभाई है। हमारी साझी संस्कृति, साझा इतिहास, साझे धरोहरों की यादें ताज़ा हों। दोनों देशों की अड़तालीस सौ किलोमीटर की साझी सीमा, एक जैसी हवा, एक जैसा जल, धान की धानी चुनर का एक जैसा गगन तक विस्तार, इलिश माछ और रशोगोल्ला, सैकड़ों सालों का

साझा साहित्य, रोवीन्द्र संगीत और नाच...एक अनन्त...अन्तहीन सिलसिला जिसको फिर से जीने...महसूसने की ललक फिर से जगे। सात दिनों तक... पचपन घंटे शास्त्रीय संगीत-गायन सुनने-महसूसने के बाद आत्मा पर पड़ी हुई धूल थोड़ी तो साफ़ होगी। इस विशाल-आत्मीय आयोजन के पीछे का यही मर्म...यही सूत्र...यही सार।

नई पीढ़ी हमारे समय की संगीत-नृत्य की महान विभूतियों को देखे-सुने। उन्हें महसूस करे। फिर ख़ुद ही अपना नज़रिया बनाए। ये जो कुफ्र और ईमाँ के बीच रोज़-रोज़ नई-नई दीवारें खड़ी कर रहे हैं। ख़ुद ही फ़रियादी और ख़ुद ही मुंसिफ़ बनकर रोज़ सज़ा मुकर्रर कर रहे हैं। दरिंदगी के रस्ते मज़हब की पाकीज़गी पाने की जहालत में फँसे हैं और अपने जाहिलपने पर जिन्हें बेहिसाब ग़ुरूर है। उनकी भी दीद को इस महोत्सव के जानिब में शायद थोड़ी रोशनी का दीदार हो।

हर वर्ष की तरह बड़ो नानू की विरासत को भी न्योता आया था। अब तक नानू उस्ताद अय्यूब ख़ान और अम्मू विदुषी रागेश्वरी देवी की भागीदारी होती रही थी। नानू तो अब रहे नहीं। अम्मू का रियाज़ भी छूटा हुआ। अब्बू और कमोल तो संकल्पबद्ध कि इस परिवार की बेटियों को ही नुमाइंदगी करनी चाहिए। वे ही सच्ची वारिस, उनकी ही विरासत इसलिए उन्हें ही सँभालनी है। मान-सम्मान-अभिमान का हक़ भी उन्हीं का। अपनी तपस्या अठारह-अठारह घंटे के रियाज़ से अम्मू ने अपने को साबित भी किया था। शब्बो भाभी उसी रास्ते पर थीं। बहरहाल, ढाके वाले आयोजन में तो इस साल उनके 'सिस्टरहुड' को अलग से न्योता मिला था। इसीलिए अब सवाल यह था कि परिवार से ढाका में इस ख़ानदान की नुमाइंदगी कौन करे?

अब्बू और कमोल के साथ दिक़्क़त यह थी कि उनके जोगिया और बाउलपने के संस्कार को मंच-प्रदर्शन, तालियाँ, वाहवाही, फूल-माला, तेज़ रोशनी, लोगों की भीड़, सफ़ेद शफ़्फ़ाफ़ भद्रोजन, जँचते नहीं थे। ग्रीन रूम की कानाफूसियाँ, टाँग खिंचाई, दूसरे के गायन में कमी निकालने के आनन्द में मदमाते दिग्गज, पैसे का मोलभाव, भुगतान की किचकिच, शराब-कबाब का ख़ानपान जैसी चीज़ों से भी उनकी साँसें घुटने लगतीं। उनके मन का जोगी और बाउल उनके मानस को समय के अनुरूप ढाल नहीं सका था।

उन्हें अपने में रहना, डूब कर रियाज़ करना, ख़ूब मन से तालीम देना... इसी में आनन्द आता था। वैसे भी बाउल के जीवन का सीधा-सा सिद्धान्त था 'सहज हो, सरल हो, मानुष धारे, मानुष हो।' इनके आदर्श दरबारी मियाँ तानसेन नहीं, झोंपड़ी वाले स्वामी हरिदास थे।

अब्बू और कमोल का मंच पर प्रदर्शन न करने के मौन संकल्प का एक और भी कारण था जिसका ज़िक्र दोनों ने कभी किसी के सामने नहीं किया। इधर कालिन्दी से जब-जब भेंट हुई थी, उसने घुमा-फिराकर यह सवाल ज़रूर ही पूछा था। कमोल ने हमेशा हँसकर टाल दिया या बात बदल दी। दरअसल कई बातें समझाई नहीं जा सकतीं, बस दिल की गहराई से महसूस की जा सकती हैं।

हुआ कुछ यूँ था कि इस ख़ानदान की सबसे गुणवन्त, नैसर्गिक प्रतिभा की धनी, माँ शारदा स्वरूपा बेटी की ज़िन्दगी में उनके मौसीक़ीकार ख़ाविन्द ने अँधेरा भर दिया था। उनकी प्रतिभा और लोकप्रियता की आँच ने उनमें इतनी ईर्ष्या जगा दी कि अपनी पत्नी की सार्वजनिक जीवन से स्वेच्छा से किए गए त्याग से भी न बुझ सकी। आख़िर अपने इकलौते बेटे की असामयिक मृत्यु से जाकर ठंडी हुई। अब उसके बाद भी उनकी आग ठंडी हुई थी कि नहीं कौन जाने! यह सब पूछने का कौन दुस्साहस करता? अब तो सब मरहूम हो गए। इन सब बातों की चर्चा करने से भी मन ख़राब होने लगता था।

बड़ो नानू की बिटिया थीं, शारदा स्वरूपा विदुषी वागेश्वरी देवी। जन्मजात प्रतिभा की धनी। बड़ो नानू बेटे अय्यूब और अन्य शार्गिदों के साथ उन्हें भी सितार की ही तालीम दे रहे थे। लेकिन अद्भुत मेधा देख सबसे कठिन वाद्य सुर-बहार सिखाने लगे। इसी बीच देश-विदेश में अपने नृत्य और नृत्य मंडली से बहुत प्रतिष्ठा पानेवाले पंडित जटाशंकर अपने छोटे भाई शिवेन्द्र शंकर को बड़ो नानू के यहाँ तालीम के लिए छोड़ गए। लेकिन कुछ ही समय बाद विदुषी वागेश्वरी के बारे में सुन-जान कर अपने छोटे के लिए उनका हाथ माँग लिया। प्रतिभा-मेधा के हिसाब से दोनों में कोई मेल नहीं था। शारदा स्वरूपा वागेश्वरी अगर ख़ानदान की मौसीक़ी की रवायत को अपने अन्दर समेटने में सौ प्रतिशत सफल थी तो शागिर्द चालीस प्रतिशत से आगे नहीं बढ़ पा रहे थे। बड़ो नानू के तालीम की

चाँदनी तो एक जैसी ही बरस रही थी। सबों पर एक जैसी रोशनी बिखेरती हुई। अब सामनेवाले के दिल में इसे समेटने के लिए कितनी ललक है, कितनी ख़ाली जगह है, उस पर निर्भर करता था कि वह उस चाँदनी के अमृत को कितना समेट पाता है।

बड़ो नानू देख रहे थे कि शिवेन्द्र शंकर चालीस प्रतिशत से ज़्यादा नहीं बढ़ पा रहा। किन्तु अपने अज़ीज़ दोस्त के आग्रह और शिवेन्द्र के कैशोर्य वाले मुख के भोलेपन से बड़े नानू ठगे गए। इनका भविष्य बाँच न पाये। एक जीनियस और एक औसत कलाकार की कैसे निभेगी, इस नज़रिये से सोच ही नहीं पाए। यह बड़ी ग़लती हो गई। औसत प्रतिभा, किन्तु मर्द, उसका अहंकार, कमतरी के एहसास से उपजी कुंठा, क्या इनका तनाव बेटी झेल पाएगी? इतनी दुनिया देखी थी, धूप-हवा-पानी झेला था, किन्तु अपनी दुलारी, लख़्ते-जिगर के मामले में धोखा खा गए। तालीम पूरी होने तक सब अच्छा रहा। किन्तु जैसे ही सार्वजनिक जीवन में इस जोड़ी ने प्रवेश किया, नज़ारे बदलने लगे। पंडित जी सितार के सितारे थे और विदुषी वागेश्वरी सुर-बहार की, सो यहाँ तो कोई प्रतियोगिता-प्रतिस्पर्धा वाली बात नहीं थी। किन्तु मंच पर प्रदर्शन के बाद नज़ारे बदल जाते। वे लम्हे पंडित शिवेन्द्र शंकर के लिए शर्मिन्दगी लेकर आते। सारे श्रोता वागेश्वरी देवी को घेर लेते। उनसे बातचीत, उनकी तारीफ़, उनके ऑटोग्राफ्स। पंडित जी पास में खड़े झेंपते रहते। पत्रकारों को भी उनका ही इन्टरव्यू चाहिए होता, उनके ही फोटोग्राफ्स। कई बार तो ऑटोग्राफ़-फोटोग्राफ़ वाली भीड़ उन्हें ही अपनी ही पत्नी से धीरे-धीरे ठेल कर दूर कर देती। उन लम्हों में उन्हें लगता कि धरती फट जाती और उसमें वे समा जाते।

इस कमतरी के एहसास की आँच दाम्पत्य के दामन तक पहुँचने लगी, तो विदुषी वागेश्वरी देवी ने सार्वजनिक जीवन से संन्यास ही ले लिया। फिर लौटकर कभी मंच पर तो क्या, व्यक्तिगत आग्रह पर भी अपने फ़न का प्रदर्शन नहीं किया। अपने को बाहर की दुनिया से पूरी तरह काट लिया। अपने फ़्लैट में क़ैद, वे फिर अगले पचास सालों तक उसी शिद्दत और लगन से गुरुमाता बनकर शागिर्दों को तालीम देती रहीं। किन्तु सितार-वादन में हासिल होते ऊँचे से ऊँचे मुकाम से भी पंडित जी की कमतरी का एहसास कम नहीं हुआ। धागे में गाँठ पड़ गई, सो उनकी भटकन बढ़ती

गई। उनके जीवन में औरतें आती रहीं-जाती रहीं। नतीजतन गुरुमाता ने उनसे तलाक़ ले लिया। किन्तु एकलौते बेटे सोमेन्द्र को कठोर अनुशासन में रखकर सितार का रियाज़ करवाना शुरू किया। अपनी माँ के सुघड़ हाथों से तराशे जाने से सोमेन्द्र एक नायाब हीरे में बदल रहा था। दशकों का रियाज़ उसे अपने नानू और मामू का सच्चा वारिस साबित करनेवाला था। अपने मामू के साथ कुछ प्रोग्राम्स में शामिल भी हुआ। सितार की उसकी तैयारी लोगों को पसन्द आई थी। उसके लम्बे आलाप, ख़ूबसूरत मीड, सप्ततान पर उसकी पकड़ ने उसके प्रशंसक बनाए।

उन्हीं दिनों पंडित शिव शंकर अमेरिका से मुम्बई आए हुए थे। रिकार्डिंग स्टूडियो में सितार की एक गत सुनी। उसके अनोखेपन ने उन्हें चौकाया। जब उन्हें मालूम चला कि यह उनका ही बेटा सोमेन्द्र है, तो एक पल के लिए ख़ुशियों से झूम उठे, किन्तु दूसरे ही पल लगा कि हो न हो सितार में उनकी शोहरत को चुनौती देने के लिए उसकी माँ उसे तैयार कर रही है। अपनी छवि के प्रति अत्यंत सजग पंडित जी को अपने ही बेटे से जलन होने लगी। बाप ने बेटे को फुसलाया। अमेरिका की रंगीनियों के चित्र खींचे। यहाँ एक छोटे से फ़्लैट में माँ के कठोर अनुशासन से ऊबे बेटे ने विद्रोह कर दिया। माँ समझाती रह गई कि कम-से-कम छह महीने और मेहनत कर अपनी तालीम पूरी कर ले, किन्तु उसे आज़ादी और पिता का ग्लैमर चुम्बक की तरह खींच रहा था। और यह गुरुमाता की ज़िन्दगी का दूसरा बड़ा हादसा साबित हुआ। अमेरिका में पिता ने धीरे-धीरे उसे बेसहारा छोड़ दिया। अमेरिकन पत्नी और अपने बच्चों की परवरिश करने को मजबूर सोमेन्द्र मौसीक़ी छोड़ छोटी-मोटी नौकरी करने लगा।

बीस वर्ष बाद पिता के साथ एक प्रोग्राम में भारत लौटा। माँ से मिलने आया, फिर से सीखने की बात भी की। किन्तु पुणे के उस कार्यक्रम में कुछ गड़बड़ हुई। उसके माइक के साथ कुछ छेड़छाड़ की गई थी। फिर यह ज़ोर-शोर से प्रचारित किया गया कि सोमू में वह बात नहीं रही, सितार के सुर उसके हाथों से फिसल गए हैं। नतीजतन डिप्रेशन में वह फिर अमेरिका लौट गया और कुछ ही माह बाद निमोनिया से उसके मरने की ख़बर आई।

बहरहाल, विदुषी वागेश्वरी देवी के जीवन की त्रासदी ने भी पहले अब्बू, उसके बाद कमोल को ख़ुद ही मंच से दूर रहने को प्रेरित किया।

अब ऐसा भी ग्लैमर और उसका नशा क्या कि इनसान अपनी पत्नी, अपने बेटे से जलन महसूस करे! उनकी ज़िन्दगी तबाह कर दे! इससे तो अच्छा है कि इस मौसीक़ी के बाज़ार, चमक-दमक, देश-विदेश की यात्राओं, तालियों की गूँजों, रुपयों-पैसों के नशे से जितना दूर रहा जाए, उतना ही सहज-सरल-मानुष होना आसान।

किन्तु अभी सवाल ढाका से आए संगियों के न्योते का था। अभी सब बड़े नानू-नानू, फूफी विदुषी वागेश्वरी देवी की तस्वीरों के नीचे बैठे सोच में डूबे थे। अम्मू शान्त होकर कमोल-अब्बू की बातें सुनती रहीं। फिर आँखें बंद कर बहुत देर गुनती रहीं। अन्त में यह तय हुआ कि ढाका के महोत्सव के पीछे का मक़सद बहुत ही पाक है। आयोजक अपने ही घराने के लोग हैं। अतः अब्बू और कमोल को वहाँ जाना ही चाहिए। अपनी गायकी से अपने शहीद-मरहूम साथियों को अपनी अक़ीदत-अपनी श्रद्धांजलि देनी चाहिए। साझी तहज़ीब और रवायत के उनके उसूलों को, जिनके लिए उनका क़त्ल हुआ, अपनी मौजूदगी से मज़बूती देनी ही चाहिए।

25

तोड़ डाली मैंने जब क़ैद-तअय्युन की हदें,
मेरी नज़रों में बराबर कुफ़्रो-ईमां हो गया।
(क़ैद-तअय्युन: हठबंदिता का बंधन)

—हसरत मोहानी

अन्त में यह तय हुआ था कि आश्रम मयंक परिवार को सौंप, सभी ढाका चलें। बुलबुल को भी अपनी मम्मी से भेंट हुए दस दिनों से ज़्यादा हो गए हैं, वहाँ कुछ दिनों तक साथ रह लेगी। अम्मू को इसलिए साथ में ले लिया गया कि अकेले ज़्यादा फ़िक्रमंद रहेंगी, मन घबड़ाता रहेगा। बुरे ख़्वाब आते रहेंगे। रातों में जागी रहेंगी और फिर दिन भर तबीयत ख़राब रहेगी। डिप्रेशन भी बढ़ जाएगा। अगर दवा समय पर लेना भूलीं तो और भी परेशानियाँ। कमोल और बुलबुल ने मिलकर अकेले रहने की परेशानियों की इतनी लम्बी सूची पढ़नी शुरू की कि उन्होंने घबड़ाकर हाँ बोल दिया। अब्बू को भी लग रहा था कि लगातार किन्हीं न किन्हीं कारणों से मन के दुखी होने और घर का माहौल भी सोगवार रहने का बुरा असर अम्मू की सेहत पर पड़ रहा था। धीरे-धीरे कई छोटी-बड़ी बीमारियों के लक्षण उभरने लगे थे। ढाका चलेंगी तो मन बदलेगा। माहौल बदलेगा। दर्जनों हममुर्शीद-हमरंगी संगी-साथियों से मिलने से मन हल्का होगा। कुछ दिल

के काफ़ी क़रीब रहनेवाले सगे भाई-बहन जैसे सहपाठियों से बरसों बाद भेंट होने की भी उम्मीद थी। ऐसे अपनों को भर नज़र निहारने और हुलस कर सीने लगने से ही आधे ग़म दूर हो जाते हैं। फिर बाग़ में साथ-साथ चहचहानेवाली चिड़ियों की तरह बेफ़िकर गुफ़्तगू के लुत्फ़ के आगे ग़म क्या और ग़म की आँधियाँ क्या?

नवम्बर के शुरुआती दिन थे। गुलाबी ठंड ढाका को सिहराने लगी थी। संगीत महोत्सव रात के पहले पहर से शबनम से भीगे चौथे पहर तक गुलज़ार रहता। इसकी ख़ासियत यह थी कि हर तबक़े के सामइन हज़ारों की संख्या में जुट कर एक मेले, एक त्योहार की शक्ल दे देते। हाँ! आगे के सोफ़ों पर अपर मिडिल-एलीट क्लास क़ाबिज़ था। लेकिन ठंड की सिहरन से बांग्ला तहज़ीब की पेशानी पर कोई बल नहीं पड़ा था। शफ़्फ़ाफ़ धोती-पैजामा-बूटेदार रंगीन मलमली-रेशमी कुर्ते और तसर-मलबरी-मूँगा-ऐरी-कोषा-ढाकाई तसर (सिल्क) और ताँत की साड़ियाँ मानो शरद ऋतु को ठेंगा दिखा रही हों। हालाँकि पशमीना की चादरें, ऊनी शाल कन्धों पर यूँ ही लटका लिए गए थे कि शरद को यह लगे कि उसका भी लिहाज़ रखा जा रहा है। पानी के साथ चाय-कॉफ़ी के थर्मस और स्नैक्स-सन्देश के डब्बे भी साथ-साथ आए थे। हालाँकि ढेर सारे स्टॉल रात भर श्रोताओं को तरोताज़ा रखने की भरदम कोशिश कर रहे थे।

पूरा ढाका उठकर चला आया था। नमोस्कार...और अस्सलाम वालेकुम...केमोन आछेन...की अनुगूँज हर पल यह एहसास दिला रही थी कि एटा बांग्लार माटी...शस्य श्यामला...सुहासिनी...सुमधुरभाषिणी... भूमि...रशोगोल्ले की मिठास और बोली-बानी की मिठास में अन्तर करना मुश्किल कि कौन ज़्यादा मीठा। यहीं जॉल (पानी) और चाय-कॉफ़ी खाई जाती थी, वह भी मीठे सन्देश के साथ। यह आमार-तोमार-सोनार बांग्ला था मन-प्राणों में भालो-बासी, भालो-बासी फुसफुसाता हुआ। जहाँ की सुहासिनी...सुमधुरवासिनी बंग महिलाओं को अपने आकर्ण नयनों और घुटनों से भी नीचे तक झूलती घुँघराली काली अलकों पर थोड़ा ज़्यादा ही अभिमान था। ऐसे मीनाक्षी जलज नयन जिनके बतियाने, बहकाने, भटकाने और डसने की काबिलियत पर यहाँ का हर शायर-कवि-गल्पकार युगों-युगों से न्योछावर था। स्त्री-शक्ति प्रवर देस-प्रदेश है यह सम्पूर्ण बोंग भूमि।

बोधिसत्व की शक्ति वज्रधातेश्वरी, लोकना, ममकई, पन्डारा, तारा से लेकर शाक्त परम्परा की उग्रतारा, छिन्नमस्तिका, भद्रकाली, जयन्ती आदि-आदि न जाने कितने शक्तिपीठ चहुँओर व्यापे हुए। तारापीठ, नलहाटी, इटखोरी, रजरप्पा, दक्षिणेश्वर से लेकर यहाँ चटगाँव, खुलना, सिलहट तक हर कहीं कोई-न-कोई शक्ति विराजमान।

हमारे पाँच पुरुष नद—सिन्धु, व्यास, सोन, दामोदर और सबसे विशाल-अगाध-असीम हिमवान का सबसे दुलारा बेटा ब्रह्मपुत्र। कई-कई देशों को सींचनेवाला, यह महानद यारलंग सांगपो-सियांग-लोहित-ब्रह्मपुत्र जैसे ही इस स्त्री-शक्ति प्रवर देश-प्रदेश में पैर धरता अपना जेंडर बदलने को मजबूर हो, महानद से नदी बन कहलाता है जमुना-पद्मा-मेघना...।

बहरहाल अभी मौसीक़ी और मौसीक़ीकारों की बातें-गल्प-गप्प ही दसों दिशाओं और बीसों पवन पर छाया था। शब्बो भाभी के 'सिस्टरहुड' को दूसरी रात, कमोल को तीसरी रात और अब्बू और बाबा को चौथी-पाँचवी रात को अपनी प्रस्तुति देनी थी। हमारे समय के श्रेष्ठतम संगीतकारों की उपस्थिति ने उस महोत्सव को एक अलंघ्य ऊँचाई और रूहानी आकर्षण से भर दिया था। भारत-बांग्लादेश और पाकिस्तान के सारे दिग्गज मौसीक़ीकारों-फ़नकारों की एक साथ मौजूदगी, मानो चाँद-तारों से सजा आसमान ही धरती पर उतर आया हो। ढाका के संगीत-रसिक श्रोता भी सुसंस्कृति की छाप छोड़ने को बेक़रार थे। राग-रागिनियों की उनकी बारीक़ समझ, वरिष्ठ संगीतकारों के लिए खड़े होकर करतल ध्वनि से उन्हें सम्मान देने का बेजोड़ अन्दाज़, पूरी रात एक तरह की ताज़गी-तन्मयता से न केवल सुनना बल्कि सही जगह पर दाद देना और सबसे बढ़कर गगन गुँजानेवाली तालियों की गड़गड़ाहट संगीतकारों को भी भाव-विह्वल कर दे रही थी।

महोत्सव में रात्रिकालीन रागों की बहार थी। संध्याकालीन राग पूरिया या पूरिया धनाश्री से शुरुआत होती। फिर रात्रि के दूसरे प्रहर में राग जोग, राग शंकर या राग हंसध्वनि की बन्दिशें समाँ बाँधतीं। तीसरे प्रहर में राग मालकौंस के सुर के पंछी पधारते। अन्तिम प्रहर राग ललित और राग सोहनी का होता। भोर की किरणें ज़्यादातर राग अभोगी या राग अभोगी कान्हड़ा के साथ पधारतीं। एक बात बहुत ही अच्छी लगी कि अधिकांश संगीतकारों ने मरहूम नानू उस्ताद अय्यूब ख़ान की बन्दिशों को तरजीह

दी। ख़ासकर राग हंसध्वनि और राग अभोगी कान्हड़ा। दक्षिण के कर्नाटक संगीत के रागों को नानू ने ही सप्रयास उत्तर भारत में लोकप्रियता दिलवाई थी। इन रागों की प्रस्तुति से मौसीक़ीकार अपने मरहूम हमसफ़र को अपनी अक़ीदतें भेंट कर रहे थे।

शब्बो भाभी की 'सिस्टरहुड' की सिस्टर्स ने भी नानू-अब्बू के बांग्लादेश के उन साथियों-दोस्तों को अपने फ़न के माध्यम से नमन किया, जिनकी साझी-संस्कृति, साझी-परम्परा की बलिवेदी कर शहादतें हुई थीं। सितार-बाँसुरी-वायलिन-तबला-पखावज की संगीत लहरियाँ पन्द्रह से बीस हज़ार श्रोताओं के तन-मन पर रिमझिम झीनी फुहारों-सी बरसती रहीं। रागों की संरचना-सौन्दर्य और संतुलन अद्‌भुत था। सातों बहनों ने अपने साज़ों की विशिष्टताओं को मिटाते हुए उन्हें एक रंग में ढाल दिया और उसी अपूर्व-रूहानी रंग में शबनम के. ख़ान का गायन भी ढल गया। असल में भिन्नता को अभिन्नता, बहुलता को एकात्मता में बदलने को साबित करने का इससे बेहतर तरीक़ा नहीं हो सकता था। सुजान श्रोताओं को मर्म पकड़ने में देर नहीं लगी। प्रस्तुति के ख़त्म होने के कुछ क्षण पहले ही सारा पंडाल खड़ा होकर तालियाँ बजा रहा था। यह 'सिस्टरहुड' को मिला अब तक का सबसे बड़ा सम्मान था।

कमोल दा जब मंच पर पहुँचा तो सामने जन-गंगा लहरा रही थी। कुछ लम्हों के लिए उनके चेहरे के रंग उड़ गए। अब्बू-अम्मू ने तुरन्त भाँप लिया। इतने बड़े मंच, इतने श्रोताओं के सामने कमोल की यह पहली प्रस्तुति थी। थोड़े सहारे की ज़रूरत ज़रूर थी। पलक झपकते सभी मंच पर। अम्मू ने तानपूरा सँभाला, अब्बू ने पखावज और बाबा मदन बाउल अपने इकतारे के साथ। अपनों की आसपास मौजूदगी भर से कमोल की साँसें स्थिर हो गईं। आँखें मूँद कर साईं लालन शाह फ़क़ीर को याद किया। उसे लगा कि वह ढाका में नहीं कुश्तिया ज़िले के बधौरा ग्राम में है, लालन फ़क़ीर के घर के सामने, जहाँ पंडित और मौलवी लालन से उनकी जाति पूछ रहे हैं...तुमने मुस्लिम माँ के हाथों भात खाया है...धर्म-भ्रष्ट...प्रायश्चित्त कोरते होबे...प्रायश्चित...टाका लागबे...टाका! माँऽ गो...प्राण बचानेवाली माँ के धरम...जनम देनेवाली माँ के धरम के मध्य पंडित और मौलवी खड़े थे... टाका-टाका...चिल्लाते।...माँ का धरम...जाति...कौन पूछता है...किसने दिया

अधिकार...टाका देकर धरम और जाति क्यों पाऊँ...प्राण बचानेवाली माँ को क्यों लजवाऊँ। धरम झूठ है...जाति झूट...झूठा मौलवी...पंडित झूठा। झूठे भद्रोजन...हाकिम झूठा। बस दुख ही सच्चा...दुखी...उत्पीड़ित मानुष सच्चा...यही मानुष...मोनेर मानुष...इन स्वप्न क्षणों के बाद कमोल का गान शुरू हुआ। अपूर्व गान...'सब लोक कय लालन कि जात संसारे...' बाउल गान की पक्के राग में प्रस्तुति एक ऐतिहासिक घटना थी। लेकिन राग के पंछी भालो कामोल की पवित्र आत्मा से अनन्त गगन की उड़ान पर थे। चुरूलिया वाला जादू फिर से जग रहा था। भोर होनेवाली थी। कमोल के सुर-पंछियों का जादू केवल पंडाल ही नहीं, समूचे वितान में छा रहा था। आसपास के छतनार गाछ-वृक्षों से तरह-तरह के पंछी पंडाल के पास की छतों-बिजली के तारों-तनी रस्सियों पर झुंड के झुंड बेआवाज़ उतरे आ रहे थे। भोर की हवा भी थम गई थी, पत्ते-लताएँ भी सरसराहट भूल, सुरों में खो गईं। वह आवाज़ थी कि पारदर्शी जलधार, जो इनसान और प्रकृति के बीच सारे परदों को काटती सबके मन-प्राण पर छाती जा रही थी! मैं और तुम के बीच का वह 'बीच' ही गुम होता जा रहा था। लोग ऐसे डूबे कि गान ख़त्म होने के बाद भी सुर-लहरियों की क्षितिज तक फैलती तरंगों में, लयकारी की ओस-सी फुहारों में भीगते रहे। यहाँ भी पंछियों के कलरव और सूरज की किरणों ने याद दिलाया कि कमोल ने गाना बन्द कर दिया है। धरम की दीवारों के कारण माँ से बिछड़ने की व्यथा लालन फ़क़ीर की दारुण पुकार सब के दिलों में हूक जगा रही थी। यह गान इस महोत्सव की अनोखी उपलब्धि बन गया था। मदन भाई और ख़ुर्शीद भाईजान ने ऐसे हीरे को कहाँ छुपा रखा था? सबसे ख़ुश तो बुलबुल। उसकी ख़ुशी का कोई ठिकाना ही न था। वह कूद-कूदकर ताली बजा रही थी...मेरे बाबा... मेरे बाबा! शब्बो भाभी की आँखें सावन-भादों हो रही थीं। उनका रोम-रोम पुकार रहा था...मेरा सोना...मेरा हीरा...मेरा बाबू...लग रहा था, अभी ही मंच पर जाएँ और बाँहों में ख़ूब जोर से भींच कर दाँतों से काट खाएँ।

लेकिन अब्बू उस्ताद ख़ुर्शीद शाह फ़क़ीर और बाबा उस्ताद मदन बाउल की प्रस्तुतियों में रोष था। एक ग़ुस्सा-एक सुलगती-धुआँती आग। मानो नानू...गुरु मरहूम अय्यूब ख़ान...डॉ. मांजरेकर...बांग्लादेश के बाउल-सूफ़ी...साझी संस्कृति के झंडाबरदार साथियों और पाकिस्तान के हमरंगी

सूफ़ी गायक की लाशें सामने पड़ी हों...सूफ़ी-अहमदिया, दरगाहों-मस्जिदों में फटते बमों और कच्छप-रक्षक सेना के हाथों क़त्ल हुए मासूमों के ख़ून की धार सामने ही बह रही हो...। इनके गान में सब शामिल हुए, गोरखनाथ से लेकर...अमीर ख़ुसरो तक...बड़ो नानू, नानू की भी बन्दिशें। अब्बू-बाबा की बेकल पुकार से खिंच कर वे सब भी मंच पर हाज़िर...।

...इतिहादेस्त मियाने मनो तो
मनो तो नेस्त मियाने मनो तो
तुम और मैं इस तरह एक हैं
कि तुम्हारे और मेरे 'बीच'
कोई 'बीच' नहीं है...
...गोरखवाणी से अन्त॥
सबद बिंदौ रे अवधू सबद निंदौ,
थांन-मांन सब धन्धा,
आतम मधै प्रामतमाँ दीसै
ज्यों जल मधे चंदा॥

पंडाल में नई किरणें अपने पंख पसार रही थीं। बाहर की झूठ-लूट-नफ़रत-दरिंदगी की जगह भीतर एक नये चन्द्रमा की चाँदनी की शीतल रोशनी जगमगा रही थी, जिसमें पिघल कर राम-रहीम एक हुए जा रहे थे, 'बीच' का 'बीच' गुम हुआ जा रहा था।

26

बात करनी मुझे मुश्किल कभी ऐसी तो न थी,
जैसी अब है तिरी महफ़िल कभी ऐसी तो न थी।

—बहादुरशाह जफ़र

महोत्सव की आख़िरी रात मुख्य रूप से क्लासिकी नृत्यों को नज़्र थी। सो आला मौसीक़ीकार-फ़नकार थोड़े सुकून से थे। किन्तु प्रिंट-इलेक्ट्रॉनिक मीडिया के पत्रकार उनके इन सुकून भरे क़ीमती लम्हों को चुराने की फ़िराक़ में मँडरा रहे थे। अब्बू-बाबा को बी.बी.सी. की रिपोर्टर रूही सिम्पसन ने घेर लिया था। बरसों बाद मिले हमजोलियों से बेतकल्लुफ़ गुफ़्तगू और हँसी-ख़ुशी का माहौल बेमतलब संजीदा हो गया। रूही ने अपना बिस्मिल्लाह ही बेचैन करते हुए किया। इस समूचे आयोजन पर ही सवाल खड़े कर दिए कि अगर मक़सद साझी-तहज़ीब, मिली-जुली रवायत को याद करना और लगातार बढ़ती कट्टरता और दरिंदगी के ख़िलाफ़ माहौल बनाने का था, तो कोई इन्टरनेशनल सेमिनार किया जा सकता था जिसमें दुनिया-भर से आला दिमाग़ों को न्योता जाता, रिसर्च बेस्ड बातें होती; कई सेकुलर देशों की मिसालें पेश की जातीं। क्या वह यूथ्स को ज़्यादा अपील नहीं करतीं?

अब्बू और बाबा मुस्कुराये। अब्बू ने बाबा को इशारा किया। बाबा ने बातें शुरू कीं, "टॉल्सटॉय ने शब्द और संगीत के असर के फ़र्क़ को समझा

था। उन्होंने लिखा है कि संगीत भावनाओं की आशुलिपि है, जो भावनाएँ शब्दों की पकड़ में मुश्किल से आती हैं, वे संगीत में सीधे अभिव्यक्त हो जाती हैं। यही संगीत की शक्ति और यही उसकी महिमा है।"

बाबा ने बात आगे बढ़ाई, "हमारी मौसीक़ी की दुनिया के बहुत ही सम्मानित उस्ताद अमीर ख़ाँ साहब ने क्या बात कही है, ग़ौर फ़रमाइए। जाति, मज़हब, सम्प्रदाय की बुनियाद पर हमारे देश को टुकड़ों में बाँट दिया गया, पर एक चीज़ वो न बाँट सके और न बाँट सकेंगे—वह है हमारा संगीत-हमारी मौसीक़ी। सात सुरों में बहनेवाली हमारे जज़्बाती एका को मज़बूत करनेवाली यह अनमोल सम्पदा हर जगह मुसल्लम है, एकदम अक्षुण्ण। क्या हिन्दुस्तान, क्या पाकिस्तान और क्या बांग्ला-देश, हर जगह के गवैये वही सुर अलापते हैं, वही राग गाते हैं और यह साबित करते हैं कि हम बुनियादी तौर पर एक ही धागे से बँधे हैं।

"मोहतरमा, इन सात दिनों ने टॉल्सटॉय साहब और हमारे बुज़ुर्ग उस्ताद की बात को सच साबित करके दिखाया है। हज़ार सालों के हमारे सम्बन्ध, ख़ान-पान, दोस्ती-यारी, नाते-रिश्तेदारियाँ, रोना-गाना किसी काग़ज़ पर खिंची रेखाएँ कैसे मिटा सकती हैं? इन पचपन घंटों में आपने सुना होगा, फ़नकार चाहे किसी देश का हो, वही राग-रागिनियाँ, वही ध्रुपद-धमाल, ख़याल-ठुमरी-टप्पा, वही किशन-कन्हैया की बाँसुरी की तान, राधारानी का मान-अभिमान, माँ शारदे-शिव-विष्णु से इक़रार और अल्लाह-मौला की बेकल पुकार, कहीं कोई फ़र्क़ नहीं। असल में हम यहीं हैं। यही इस सात दिनी मेहनत से हम साबित करना चाहते थे और हमने यह साबित किया। कोई और मीडियम, भाषण-तक़रीर, सभा-सेमिनार ये काम नहीं कर सकता था। ये बुद्धि की बातें दिमाग़ को ख़ुराक देती हैं जबकि संगीत मन-प्राणों पर असर डालता है। हमारे बुज़ुर्ग बजा फ़रमाते थे कि मौसीक़ी रूह से निकलती है और रूह को ही सुनाती है।"

न जाने रूही सिम्पसन का प्रोफेशनल दिमाग़ इस जवाब का कितना कायल हुआ? उसका अगला सवाल था कि जो इन्साँ को इन्साँ से बाँटनेवाली ज़हरीली हवा पूरी दुनिया में बह रही है, चारों ओर जो आग लगी हुई है, जिसने अफ़गानिस्तान-इराक़-सीरिया-यमन जैसे देशों को पूरी तरह से

नेस्तनाबूद कर दिया है, क्या सचमुच वह आग संगीत और संगीत के आयोजनों से बुझ पाएगी?

इस बार अब्बू मुख़ातिब हुए, "आग, आग से नहीं बुझा करती मोहतरमा। बम-बन्दूक-लाशों ने आज तक कोई मसला स्थायी तौर पर हल नहीं किया है। मज़हब और सियासत की यह जुगलबन्दी यूँ ही चलती रही, तो दो-चार देश तो क्या, पूरी इनसानी नस्ल ही ख़ात्मे के कगार पर पहुँच जाएगी। इसने हमारे दिलो-दिमाग़ पर मैल की मोटी परत चढ़ा दी है। इसे धोने के लिए एक साथ कई तरह की कोशिशें करनी होंगी, जिनमें मौसीक़ी या कोई भी फ़नकारी, क्रिएटिविटी की भी एक भूमिका होगी। मौसीक़ी यह काम करती रही है। मज़हब की दीवारें इसके सामने टिक नहीं पातीं। इसके कई सबूत हैं। मरहूम बड़े ग़ुलाम अली ख़ाँ साहब बहुत डूब कर मशहूर भजन हरि ॐ तत्सत् गाया करते थे। कहते हैं कि उनके पूर्व पुरुष उस्ताद पीर दाद ख़ाँ साहब को मौसीक़ी की देवी ने ख़ुद गायन का वरदान दिया था। बहरहाल, एक बार ख़ाँ साहब के इस भजन के गायन से कर्नाटक संगीत के मशहूर गायक पंडित जी.एन. बालासुब्रह्मण्यम् इतने भाव-विह्वल, इतने अभिभूत हुए कि उनके क़दमों में जा गिरे।

"उधर पटियाला घराने के बुज़ुर्ग उस्ताद अली बख़्श ख़ाँ साहब को दूसरे घराने के गवैयों का गान पसन्द ही नहीं आता था। उन्हें अपने घराने पर थोड़ा ज़्यादा ही ग़रूर था। एक बार पटियाले में ही दीवान साहब के यहाँ पंडित भास्करबुबा अपनी गायकी पेश कर रहे थे। उन्होंने 'फूलन के हरवा' पूरिया के ख़याल से गायन की शुरुआत की। फिर कामोद की चीज़ पेश की। अन्त में बुज़ुर्ग अलीबख़्श ख़ाँ साहब की फ़रमाइश पर दरबारी की एक बंदिश 'तू ऐसो ही करीम रहीम' पेश की। इसके बाद उस्ताद ख़ाँ साहब का झूठा ग़रूर कपूर की तरह उड़ गया और उन्होंने उठकर भास्करबुबा को गले से लगा लिया। यह है हिन्दुस्तानी मौसीक़ी की ताक़त, उसकी तासीर। जिसके प्रभाव में आते ही न कोई हिन्दू रहता है और न कोई मुसलमान। इसीलिए नफ़रत की आग बुझाने में यह बड़ी भूमिका निभाती रही है और निभा सकती है।"

"इस्लामी भाईचारे की बहुत चर्चा होती है। पैन इस्लामिज़्म भी बहसों-भाषणों-लेखों में बहुत इस्तेमाल होता है, लेकिन पश्चिम और मध्य एशिया

में तो उल्टा ही दिख रहा है। वहाँ तो एक इस्लामी देश ही दूसरे इस्लामी देश को बरबाद करने पर तुला है और अमेरिका-यूरोप की ऐसी कोशिशों को हर सम्भव मदद दे रहा है। ऐसा क्यों?" यह रूही का अगला सवाल था, जो निहायत ही सियासी था।

एकबारगी अब्बू को लगा कि टाल दिया जाए, फिर कुछ सोचकर जवाब देने का मन बनाया। "देखिए मोहतरमा! हमारे यहाँ हर कोई हिन्दू या मुसलमाँ नहीं होता। हम जोगी हैं और हमारे ये समधी और अज़ीज़ मदन साहब बाउल। हम हिन्दू भी हैं और मुसलमाँ भी या दोनों नहीं या दोनों की ख़ासियतों को समेटनेवाले...न जाने क्या। साफ़-साफ़ ख़ाँचे में हमें बाँटा नहीं जा सकता। हाँ! आज कल नफ़रत की लाठी हमें भी बाँटने की कोशिश कर रही है।

"बहरहाल, सीधे-सीधे इस्लाम और उसकी सियासत पर कुछ ख़ास कहने की स्थिति में हम नहीं हैं। लेकिन हमारे गुरु-बाबा मरहूम उस्ताद अय्यूब ख़ान साहब के अज़ीज़ दोस्त असग़र अली इंजीनियर साहब अक्सर यह कहा करते थे कि इस्लामी भाईचारा आदर्शवादियों का गढ़ा हुआ एक मिथक है। शुरुआत से ही इस्लामी समाज वर्गों और श्रेणियों में बँटा हुआ रहा है। इसमें आक़ा और ग़ुलाम भी थे, अमीर-उमरा और ग़रीब-फ़ाक़ापमस्त भी थे, अरब और ग़ैर-अरब भी, जिनके बीच तीखी आपसी दुश्मनियाँ पाई जाती थीं।

"अब देखिए! यह मज़हब आज कम-से-कम बहत्तर फ़िरकों में बँटा हुआ है। हर फ़िरका दूसरे को अपने से कमतर मज़हबी मानता है। ख़ासकर वहाबियों ने, कौन मज़हबी है कौन नहीं, इसका ठेका ले रखा है। मोहतरमा! शिया-सुन्नी देशों में लगातार बढ़ते तनाव, यज़ीदी जैसे फ़िरकों की इस्लामिक स्टेट द्वारा नस्ल तक मिटाने की कोशिश, सूफ़ी-अहमदिया दरगाहों-मस्जिदों के मलबों में...आप ही बताइए कि हम इस्लामी भाईचारे को कहाँ-कहाँ ढूँढ़ें?"

"बहरहाल! इतनी बात तो साफ़ है कि उन्नीस सौ नवासी के ईरान के इस्लामिक इंक़लाब और नौ ग्यारह के ट्विन टॉवर हादसे के बाद हालात बहुत बदल गए हैं। सियासत बहुत पेचीदा हो गई है। लेकिन इतना तो तय है कि उन्नीस सौ इक्यानवे में अफग़ानिस्तान से लेकर

इराक़-सीरिया-यमन तक इस्लामी देशों के कन्धों का ही इस्तेमाल कर झूठे-सच्चे बहानों की ओट में जितने लोगों का क़त्लेआम अमेरिकी यूरोपीय सेनाओं-हथियारों ने किया है वह अगर यूरोप में हुआ होता तो हॉलोकॉस्ट कहलाता। वहाँ के साइंटिस्ट से लेकर शायर तक छाती कूट रहे होते। मीडिया में ज़लज़ला आ जाता। लेकिन चूँकि यह एशियाई देशों में हो रहा है इसीलिए यह आतंक के ख़िलाफ़ युद्ध भर है। लगता है ढोंग की हर सीमा पार हो गई है।

"मोहतरमा! आप मुसलमानों के बीच फ़िरक़ापरस्ती को बढ़ावा देनीवाली अमेरिकी-यूरोपियन पॉलिसीज़ की बाबत कोई सवाल नहीं पूछ रही हैं? लेकिन इस मुद्दे पर तो बात होनी चाहिए।"...बोलते...बोलते अब्बू थोड़े उत्तेजित से हो गए थे। थोड़ी देर आँखें बन्द कर चुप रहे। फिर एक घूँट पानी पी हौले-हौले बोलना शुरू किया, "देखिए! दरअसल इस्लामिक आतंकवाद भी एक ख़ालिस पॉलिटकल स्लोगन है। इसे समझते सब हैं लेकिन बोलना-लिखना कोई नहीं चाहता। खाड़ी देशों के पेट्रोल कुओं पर क़ब्ज़ा और अपने देश की आर्म्स इंडस्ट्रीज का चढ़ता-उतरता ग्राफ़ अमेरिकी-यूरोपीय देशों की गल्फ़ पॉलिसीज तय करता है। इसे भी सब जानते हैं लेकिन कोई बोलना-लिखना नहीं चाहता। लेकिन अफ़ग़ानिस्तान से लेकर सीरिया-यमन तक चल रहा होलोकॉस्ट...कभी-न-कभी इनकी ज़िम्मेवारियाँ तय होंगी। जवाब तो देना होगा...आज नहीं तो कल।"

लगता है मोहतरमा रूही सिम्पसन को एक फ़क़ीरनुमा मौसीक़ीकार से ऐसे उत्तर की उम्मीद नहीं थी। कुछ लम्हों के लिए वह अब्बू का चेहरा देखती रह गईं। कुछ सोचा, फिर अगले सवाल की ओर बढ़ीं, "मेरे डैड ब्रिटिश हैं, मम्मी बंगाल से, इसीलिए बाउल तो जानती हूँ। पूरन दास बाउल और पार्वती बाउल से मिली भी हूँ। उनका इन्टरव्यू भी किया है। पूरन दास की फ्रेंच पत्नी से तो पहले से जान-पहचान रही है। किन्तु जोगियों के बारे में कुछ भी नहीं जानती। आपने कहा कि न आप मुसलमान हैं न हिन्दू। या फिर थोड़ा-थोड़ा दोनों हैं या दोनों की ख़ासियत समेटनेवाले किसी तीसरे पंथ के राही हैं। आख़िर जोगी हैं क्या?"

"हाँ! हम जोगी हैं। गुरु गोरखनाथ के चेले। कानफटा होकर हमारा ख़ानदान जोगी बना था। सैकड़ों सालों से पूर्वी उत्तर प्रदेश के ढेर सारे

मुस्लिम गाँवों ने गुरु गोरखनाथ की राह चुनी थी। गेरुआ वस्त्र, इकतारा और गोरखबानी-भरथरी गीत गाते पूरे उत्तर भारत में घूमते रहना। भिक्षाटन से पेट भरना। हमारे लिए हिन्दू-मुस्लिम का फ़र्क़ नहीं था। मन हुआ पूजा कर ली, मन हुआ नमाज़ पढ़ ली। या मन नहीं माना तो गुरु दीक्षा के अनुसार अपने भीतर ही रोशनी की तलाश में डूबे रहे। पीढ़ियों से ऐसा चलता आ रहा था। कम-से-कम हम जोगियों की मज़हबी कट्टरपन और नफ़रत से कोई जान-पहचान नहीं थी। उल्टे हम इनके ख़िलाफ़ एक ठंडी हवा के झोंके थे। ऐसी चिनगारियों को पल में बुझानेवाले। लेकिन न जाने इधर क्या हो गया है। नयी उमर के लोग हमें समझते ही नहीं। मोबाइल-यूट्यूब कि इन्टरनेट पर किन्हीं इस्लामिक स्टेट, जैशे-मुहम्मद और न जाने कौन-कौन-सी जमातों की तक़रीरें सुन-सुनकर मुसलमान लड़कों की त्योरियाँ चढ़ी रहती हैं कि हम मुसलमान होकर जोगिया रंग के कपड़े क्यों पहनते हैं? दूसरी तरफ़ कच्छप-रक्षा संघ जैसे संगठनों के लड़कों को भी हमारे गेरुआ बाने पर सख़्त एतराज़ है। ये लोग भी कई बार टोक चुके हैं। इनके हाव-भाव से लगता है कि ये बीच सड़क पर हमारे कपड़े उतार देंगे।

"ज़ाती तौर पर मेरे साथ अभी तक बुरा व्यवहार नहीं हुआ, लेकिन पिछले दस सालों में इस दोतरफ़ा मार से जोगी और जोगियों के गाँवों की सूरत बदल गई है। एक-दो जोगियों के साथ भी अगर कहीं मारपीट हो गई, तो डर पूरे गाँव में ही महामारी-सा फैल गया। गेरुआ बाना तो छोड़िए, इकतारे तक छुपा दिए गए हैं। बौद्धों के वज्रयान के आख़िरी दिनों में जब वह पंच-मकार के दलदल में गले तक धँस गया था, तो 'जाग मच्छन्दर जोगी आया' का अलख जगाते गोरख आए और समाज को फिर से जगाया। जिन जोगियों ने समाज को तन कर खड़ा होना सिखाया, नई रोशनी दी, उनके ही गले पर पैर रखकर पंथ से जबरन दूर किया जा रहा है।

"मोहतरमा! जबरदस्त लू चल रही है। कहीं कोई दरख़्त, कोई छाँह नज़र नहीं आती। ऐसी मिट्टी में जहाँ आदिकाल से सच तक पहुँचने के कई-कई रास्तों का मान रहा हो, उसे दिल से स्वीकारा गया हो, वहाँ केवल अपने 'सच' को ही 'सच' और दूसरे का 'सच' 'झूठ' समझने का

पागलपन कहाँ से आ गया? समझ में नहीं आता। कबीर ने तो फ़लसफ़ाना अन्दाज़ में नहीं, बहुत प्यार से समझाया था, 'कबीर कुआँ एक है और पनिहारी अनेक/बर्तन सबके न्यारे हैं, पानी सबमें एक।' अब सियासी समझ समझने को तैयार ही नहीं हो, तो कोई जोगी क्या करे?"

मोहतरमा रूही सिम्पसन को शायद, जो चाहिए था वह मिल चुका था। अब उन्होंने इन्टरव्यू ख़त्म करने की इजाज़त माँगी।

27

कहूँ मैं जिस से उसे होवे सुनते ही वहशत,
फिर अपना क़िस्सा-ए-वहशत कहूँ तो किस से कहूँ॥

—बहादुरशाह ज़फ़र

रूही सिम्पसन ने अब्बू-बाबा के इन्टरव्यू को अच्छी-ख़ासी तवज्जो दिलवाई। बी.बी.सी. के रेडियो और टी.वी. चैनल के साथ सोशल मीडिया पर भी यह इन्टरव्यू ख़ूब चर्चित हुआ। किन्तु अपने देश के अख़बारों ने सोशल मीडिया से इन्टरव्यू उठाया और उस हिस्से को हाईलाइट किया जिसमें देश के माहौल की आलोचना थी। किसी-किसी हिन्दी अख़बार ने कच्छप-रक्षा सेना की हरकतों वाले हिस्से को हेडलाइन में डाल कर सनसनी फैला दी। नतीजतन पूरा इन्टरव्यू विवादास्पद हो गया। मौक़ा तलाशती हुड़दंगियों की टोली को बैठे-बिठाए मन लायक़ काम मिल गया। नतीजतन 'मौसीक़ी-मंज़िल' के बाशिन्दों की एयरपोर्ट से ही काले झंडे, देशद्रोही घोषित करते बैनर्स, 'दुश्मन देश के दुलारो वापस जाओ', 'संगीत के बहाने सियासत नहीं चलेगी', जैसे नारों से जो स्वागत की शुरुआत हुई वह राजधानी में पहले से तय अब्बू-बाबा के गायन के कार्यक्रम को स्थगित करने तक लगातार चलती रही। अब्बू-बाबा-अम्मू सबने ढाका के सात दिनों में ख़ुशियों की बहुत लम्बी-चौड़ी गठरी बाँधी थी जिसमें बरसों-बरस बाद मिले हमदम-

हमनशीं-हमरंगियों के गिले-शिकवे, गाली-ग्लौज, धौल-धप्पे, गप्प-शप्प, सच्चे-झूठे वादे, आनेवाले कल की लम्बी-चौड़ी प्लानिंग, बच्चों के लिए दुआ-आशीष, तालीम के वक़्त की यादों की जुगाली, बांग्ला डिशेज के अपूर्व स्वाद, सन्देश के साथ कॉफी-चाय की मिठास और न जाने क्या-क्या अगड़म-बगड़म भरे थे। इतनी बड़ी गठरी-मोटरी लेकर जब चले तो क़दम ज़मीं पर ही नहीं पड़ रहे थे। किन्तु अपने देश की राजधानी ने उतरते उस गुब्बारे-सी फूली गठरी में सूई चुभो दी गई। ख़ुशियाँ हौले-हौले हवा में बिलाने लगीं। बची-खुची जो थीं अब शहर में आकर हवा हो गईं।

आश्रम पहुँच, अभी सभी अपना पैर-हाथ सीधा ही कर रहे थे कि मयंक घबड़ाये हुए आए। लैपटॉप को ऐसे पकड़े हुए मानो कोई ज़हरीला कीड़ा हो। उनके चेहरे से उड़ती हवाइयाँ कमरे की हवा के चेहरे पर जा बैठीं। हवा की देह थरथराहट से भर गई। अन्देशे रोशनदान से झाँकने लगे। मयंक ने लैपटॉप ऑन किया और ट्विटर के ट्विट्स दिखलाने शुरू किये। न केवल ट्विटर बल्कि फेसबुक-व्हाट्सऐप सब जगह ट्रॉलिंग की बौछार हो रही थी। ढाका संगीत महोत्सव, गेरुआ बाना के बहाने ज़हर के पीपे खोल दिए गए थे। राजधानी के देशद्रोह के बैनर्स और दुश्मन देश के दुलारे नारों की सप्रसंग व्याख्याएँ की गई थीं। अपने हिसाब से बहुत गम्भीर और राष्ट्रवादी प्रश्न खड़े किए गए थे जैसे कि अगर इस्लाम में संगीत कुफ्र है तो मुसलमान उस्ताद और ख़ान साहब इसे छोड़ क्यों नहीं देते? क्या ज़रूरत है ऐसे नापाक पेशे से जुड़ने की?

अब्बू के जोगिया वस्त्र पुनः सवालों के घेरे में थे। ट्रोलर्स के मुताबिक़ मुसलमान धोखा देने के लिए ग़ैरिक वस्त्र धारण करते हैं ताकि नासमझ ग़रीब, अनपढ़ लोगों को अपने जाल में फाँसा जा सके और उनका धर्म-परिवर्तन करवाया जा सके। यह सब यहाँ की आबादी के संतुलन को बदलने के बृहद् षड्यंत्र का हिस्सा है। ऐतिहासिक उदाहरणों से यह थ्योरी प्रमाणित करने की कोशिश की गई कि जिस प्रकार मध्यकाल में तुर्क-अफ़ग़ान-मुग़लों के समय सूफ़ी-संतों ने गीत-संगीत, धूप-धुअन, झाड़-फूँक आदि के सहारे समाज के निचले तबक़ों को इस्लाम के दायरे में लाने में बड़ी भूमिका निभाई, उसी प्रक्रिया को ये ग़ैरिक वस्त्रधारी मुसलमान जोगी आगे बढ़ा रहे हैं।

पुनः एक मौलिक प्रश्न बहुत शोध के उपरान्त प्रस्तुत किया गया था कि संगीत की 'घराना-परम्परा' मुस्लिम उस्तादों-ख़ान साहबों की वर्चस्ववादी सोच से पनपी थी ताकि न केवल घरानों पर उनका क़ब्ज़ा पीढ़ी-दर-पीढ़ी बना रहे बल्कि वे केवल मुस्लिम शागिर्दों को ही असली और गूढ़ शिक्षा दे सकें। इस पद्धति से न केवल मान-सम्मान बल्कि धन-सम्पदा की प्राप्ति भी सुनिश्चित की जा रही थी।

साझी-संस्कृति और मिलीजुली परम्परा के विरुद्ध तथा 'सुआर्यन राष्ट्र' के पक्ष में दर्जनों ट्वीट्स थे जिन्हें लाइक एवं रिट्वीट करनेवालों की संख्या लगातार बढ़ती जा रही थी। इन ट्वीट्स के साथ एक और ख़ास बात यह थी कि एक तरह के कन्टेंट के ट्वीट्स और दो सौ से ज़्यादा ट्विटर्स एक साथ ट्रीवट कर रहे थे। इन ट्विटर्स में कुछ के फॉलोअर्स की संख्या हज़ारों में थी।

'सुआर्यन राष्ट्र', जो ट्विटर, व्हाट्सऐप, फेसबुक, इन्स्टाग्राम पर वायरल हो रहा था, उसकी बानगी कुछ यूँ थी—'नेशन-स्टेट' की अवधारणा अब पूरे विश्व में स्वीकृति पा चुकी है। कोई भी राष्ट्र हो, उसकी अपनी पारम्परिक मातृभूमि-पितृभूमि में उसका अपना राज्य होना चाहिए, जो उस राष्ट्र की भावनाओं तथा आकांक्षाओं का प्रतिनिधित्व करे। दुनिया के छोटे-छोटे गुड़िये-सरीखे राष्ट्रों के भी अब अपने राज्य हो गए। परन्तु हम सुआर्यन, जो सारे संसार की आबादी का छठा हिस्सा हैं और संसार के प्राचीनतम राष्ट्र हैं, हमारा ही अपना 'नेशन-स्टेट' नहीं बन पाया है। जो लोग कहते हैं कि "सुआर्यन राष्ट्र बनाना है" वे ग़लत शब्दों का प्रयोग करते हैं, सही शब्द होंगे, "सुआर्यन राष्ट्र को अपनी स्वाधीनता प्राप्त करनी है।" स्वतंत्रता की एक नई लड़ाई छेड़नी है, सुआर्यन राष्ट्र को ग़ुलामी की ज़ंजीर तोड़कर अपने लिए सच्ची आज़ादी हासिल करनी है—यही है हमारा एकमात्र राष्ट्रीय लक्ष्य।

'साझी-संस्कृति' को लेकर भी ट्रोलर्स के महान् विचार कम आकर्षक नहीं थे, एक मिली-जुली-कम्पोजिट—'राष्ट्रीय संस्कृति' की अवधारणा भी कपोल-कल्पना की उपज है। वस्तुतः इस राष्ट्र में हमारी एक ही राष्ट्रीय संस्कृति है, जो कि 'सुआर्यन संस्कृति' है। इसी के समानान्तर हमारी धरती पर विदेशी आक्रान्ताओं तथा शासकों द्वारा छोड़ी गई संस्कृतियों के भी कुछ

टुकड़े बचे हुए हैं। विश्व के अनेक देशों में ऐसी आक्रान्ता संस्कृतियाँ अपने धब्बे छोड़ जाती हैं। उससे राष्ट्रीय संस्कृति नष्ट होकर कोई मिली-जुली संस्कृति नहीं बनती, बल्कि वह आक्रान्ता संस्कृति सदा एक शत्रु-संस्कृति या परजीवी संस्कृति मानी जाती है। राष्ट्र को निरन्तर यह प्रयास करना चाहिए कि उस शत्रु संस्कृति का यथासम्भव बहिष्कार करे एवं अपनी राष्ट्रीय संस्कृति को उससे कलुषित होने से बचाए।

विज्ञान एवं तकनीकी विकास के बाद अब विश्व में शायद एक भी देश ऐसा नहीं होगा जिसकी संस्कृति का अन्य देशों की संस्कृति के साथ कुछ आदान-प्रदान नहीं हुआ हो, और जहाँ दूसरी संस्कृतियों के कुछ अंश दृष्टिगोचर नहीं होते हों, किन्तु इससे राष्ट्रीय संस्कृति का स्वरूप नष्ट नहीं होता। हमारे देश में कुछ विधर्मियों ने हमारा शास्त्रीय संगीत सीख लिया, या विधर्मी शासकों ने कुछ भव्य इमारतें बनवाईं या सुआर्यन अपनी स्वभावगत उदार दृष्टि के कारण विधर्मी फ़क़ीरों-संतों के मज़ारों-दरगाहों पर भी माथा टेकने लगे—इसी से हमारी राष्ट्रीय संस्कृति कोई साझी-संस्कृति या मिली-जुली परम्परा नहीं बन जाती। यह धारणा सैकुलरवाद के बीमार सोच की उपज है।

कुछ ट्वीट्स थोड़े ज़्यादा ही विद्वत्तापूर्ण थे। इनमें बौद्धों, नाथ-सिद्धों, संतों को एक लाठी से हाँका गया था। उन ट्वीट्स का लब्बोलुआब यह था कि इन पंथों ने सुआर्यन सनातन धार्मिक-सामाजिक व्यवस्था के मूल स्तम्भों पर चोट कर विधर्मियों के लिए रेड कार्पेट बिछाया। इन पंथों ने हमारे अपौरुषेय धर्मग्रंथों, धर्मस्थानों, वर्णाश्रम-पुनर्जन्म-कर्मवाद-अवतारवाद जैसी मूल अवधारणाओं पर चोट की। मज़ाक़ उड़ाया। सामान्य जन के मन में उनके प्रति मान-सम्मान घटाया। ऐसी पंगडंडियाँ बना दीं जिन पर आक्रान्ताओं के लिए एक हाथ में तलवार दूसरे हाथ में मज़हबी झंडा लेकर घोड़े दौड़ाना आसान हो गया। हमारा राष्ट्र ग़ुलाम बना। हमें बार-बार लज्जित किया गया। हमारा मनोबल तोड़ने की बहुविध कोशिशें की गईं। इसके लिए ज़िम्मेवार ये 'घर के भेदी' ही थे। इन्हीं के कारण 'आन्तरिक-शत्रु' आज भी मौजूद हैं। ये और सारे सैकुलरवादी राष्ट्रदोही-धर्मद्रोही थे, हैं और रहेंगे।

मयंक के लैपटॉप के बन्द होते, उस कमरे में सन्नाटा भी सिर पकड़कर बैठ गया। राजधानी से निकलते जो राहत-सी दिखी थी वह पिछले दरवाज़े

से न जाने कब खिसक चुकी थी। अपने चेहरे से हवाइयाँ उड़ाती हवा को कँपकँपी के बाद बुख़ार चढ़ रहा था। राहत की खोज में पुतलियाँ दीवार-घड़ी की पेंडुलम-सी हो रही थीं। राहत कहीं दिख नहीं रही थी। सबों की लम्बी-लम्बी साँसों से कमरे की हवा का सर फटने-फटने को था, तभी मयंक ने ही राह सुझाई। उसने राहत के रहगुज़र का रहबर बनने का ज़िम्मा लिया। उसके अनुभव ने बताया कि ट्रोलर्स की रणनीति यह होती है कि पहले किसी मुद्दे को कन्ट्रोवर्सियल बनाया जाए। फिर सच्चे-झूठे फ़ॉलोअर्स के हज़ारों रिट्वीट्स से उसे वायरल किया जाए। फिर टी.वी. चैनल्स पर उस मुद्दे पर प्रायोजित बहसें करवाई जाएँ। उसके बाद प्रिंट मीडिया, तब सड़कों पर उस वर्चुअल लड़ाई को रियलिटी शो में बदल दिया जाए। सुआर्यन दो-तीन क़दमों की बढ़त ऑलरेडी ले चुके हैं। उस रास्ते हम जाएँगे तो पिछड़ जाएँगे। और कहीं लड़ाई को सड़क तक पहुँचाने में वे लोग सफ़ल हो गए तब हमारा पिटना और हारना तय है। इसलिए हम प्रिंट मीडिया से शुरू करेंगे। उसके बाद हमारे आर्टिकल्स चैनल्स के बहस के मुद्दे तय करेंगे, जिन्हें सोशल मीडिया पर वायरल बनाने की ज़िम्मेवारी हमारी टीम, हमारे दुनिया-भर में फैले साथियों और हमारे जैसे साझी तहज़ीब में विश्वास रखनेवाले अजाने हमसफ़रों की होगी। सुआर्यन के सवालों के जवाब में आर्टिकल्स लिखने का ज़िम्मा कमोल कबीर साहब का और एडिटर्स से कोऑर्डिनेट करने की ज़िम्मेवारी मेरी। कई एडिटर्स तो डी.पी.एस. की स्कूलिंग के समय के साथी हैं, सो दिक़्क़त नहीं होगी। मैं पहले से इन मसलों पर उनसे बातें करता रहा हूँ। वे कब से इस तरह के लेख माँगते रहे हैं। अब देर नहीं करनी है। सबों को यह रणनीति पसन्द आई। अब सुख में डूबे मछन्दर को जगाना होगा। गोरख को फिर से अलख जगाना होगा। अब्बू ने किसी का शेर बुदबुदाया, 'अपने पुरखों की विरासत को सँभालो वरना/अबकी बारिश में ये दीवार भी गिर जाएगी।'

28

ज़ब्त करता हूँ तो घुटता है क़फ़स में मेरा दम,
आह करता हूँ तो सय्याद ख़फ़ा होता है।

—कमर जलालवी

कमोल कबीर का पहला आलेख 'हिन्दुस्तानी संगीत की विकास यात्रा' शीर्षक से था। लेख कुछ बड़ा हो गया, सो किस्तों में प्रकाशित हुआ। नाद-सामवेद गान-प्रबन्ध गान से होते, हिन्दुस्तानी शास्त्रीय संगीत ध्रुपद-ख़याल गायकी-ठुमरी-टप्पा तक कैसे पहुँचा, इसका विस्तार से वर्णन।

'इस्लाम में संगीत' पर कमोल कबीर ने अपनी ओर से कोई विशेष टिप्पणी नहीं की। हरदिल अज़ीज़ मशहूर उस्तादों और रूमी जैसे सूफ़ी संत ने जो अपने एहसास ज़ाहिर किए थे उनकी बानगी भर पेश की। उस्ताद बिस्मिल्ला ख़ाँ साहब ने बड़ी सादगी से यह स्वीकार किया था कि "मुझे लगता है हमारे मज़हब में मौसीक़ी को इसलिए हराम कहा गया कि अगर इस जादू जगानेवाली कला को रोका न गया, तो एक से एक फ़नकार इसकी रागिनियों में इस कदर डूबे रहेंगे कि दोपहर, शाम वाली नमाज़ कज़ा हो जाएगी।"

लेकिन ख़ाँ साहब ने यह भी स्वीकार किया कि "यह ख़ूबसूरत चीज़ मौसीक़ी भले नाजायज़ मानी गई हो, लेकिन किसी ने छोड़ा तो नहीं।

उस्तादों-ख़ान साहबों ने मौसीक़ी में बुलन्दियों के आकाश छुए। अब, जब हराम है, तब तो यह हाल है। अगर कहीं जायज़ होती तो सारे मुस्लिम फ़नकार कहाँ से कहाँ पहुँच गए होते।"

देश-दुनिया में मशहूर सूफ़ी संत रूमी ने माना था कि मौसीक़ी आध्यात्मिक जीवन के निरन्तर विकास के लिए एक इहलौकिक छत है। यह वो दरिया है जो रोशन होते इनसानी जज़्बात की परवरिश करती है।

'मुस्लिम उस्तादों के हिन्दू शिष्य' शीर्षक आलेख में कमोल कबीर ने अतरौली-जयपुर घराने से लेकर किराना घराने-लखनऊ घराने तक की पूरी सूची ही सामने रख दी। विशेष रूप से स्वामी विवेकानन्द का उल्लेख किया, जिन्होंने अतरौली-जयपुर घराने के उस्ताद अहमद ख़ान साहब से ध्रुपद-गायन सीखा था। ग्वालियर घराने के मशहूर उस्ताद हद्दू ख़ाँ-हस्सू ख़ाँ साहबों ने ज़िन्दगी का अधिकांश हिस्सा मुख्य रूप से चार महाराष्ट्रीय ब्राह्मण शागिर्दों जोशीबुबा, दीक्षितबुबा, बाला गुरु और शंकर पंडित को ही तालीम देने में गुज़ार दिया। किराना घराना के उस्ताद अब्दुल करीम ख़ाँ साहब ने बहुत-सी बन्दिशें लिखीं और अपनी हर बन्दिश के आगे 'ॐ तत्सत् सामवेदाय नमः' लिखा करते।

इन आलेखों के वायरल होने से ख़ुद-ब-ख़ुद लोकल टी.वी. चैनल्स सक्रिय हो गए। उधर सोशल मीडिया पर भी मयंक की टीम लगी हुई थी। एक बार 'साझी-संस्कृति', 'साझी-परम्परा' के ट्वीट्स ने फॉलोअर्स का ध्यान खींचा, बस बात बन गई। मयंक के देश-विदेश में फैले साथियों की मेहनत सफल हुई। अब एक साथ लिबरल, डेमोक्रेटिक, लेफ्टिस्ट, फेमिनिस्ट, फुलेवादी, बिरसावादी, आंबेडकरवादी सबके सब इस मोर्चे पर जूझ पड़े। लोकल चैनल्स के साथ-साथ अब नेशनल चैनल्स पर भी कमोल कबीर की माँग होने लगी थी।

कमोल की बातचीत की यह ख़ासियत थी कि वह अपनी मद्धम और कोमल पिच छोड़ता नहीं था। एक ख़ास मीठे मद्धम स्वर में उसकी बातचीत भी गुनगुनाहट की तरह प्यारी लगती। उसके सुन्दर चेहरे की मुस्कुराहट बड़ी मारक थी, जो ग़ुस्से में लाल हो रहे विरोधी को भी थोड़ी देर में मुस्कुराने को विवश कर देती थी। विशेषकर उस सच्चे बाउल की पाक रूह का एक नूर उसके चारों ओर छाया-सा रहता। एक आभा मंडल-सा

बनाता हुआ। यह दर्शकों और प्रतिभागियों को सहज ही आकर्षित करता। उसकी जानकारियाँ, तर्क और इतिहास की छोटी-छोटी कहानियाँ उसकी बातों को बहुत वजनी बना देतीं।

कमोल कबीर की सहज-सरल बातें सीधे दिलों को छूती थीं। केवल न समझने की ज़िद किए सुआर्यन जागरण सेना और भगवान कच्छप-रक्षक सेना के लोगों को ही समझ में नहीं आती थीं। वह ठीक ही कहता था कि हमारे विशाल देश की जो भौगोलिक-सामाजिक बुनावट है, जो विविधता है भाषा-बोली, रहन-सहन, ख़ान-पान, पूजा पद्धतियों की, वही इसकी विशेषता है। इस विविधता को स्वीकर कर और सबको इज़्ज़त देते हुए ही हमारे पूर्वजों ने इसे आकाश की बुलन्दियों तक पहुँचाया है।

दूसरे दिन दूसरे चैनल्स पर भालो कमोल अपने देश के सबके विचारों-आध्यात्मिक राहों की इज़्ज़त करने की परम्परा को समझा रहा था कि कैसे ईसा पूर्व बौद्ध काल में भी वैदिक धर्म के अलावा कई-कई धार्मिक पंथ और दार्शनिक सक्रिय थे। उसे सबके नाम और उनके दर्शन की विशेषताएँ भी कंठस्थ थीं, तीर्थिक, आजीविक, निगण्ठ, पूरण कस्सप, पकुध कच्चायन, अजित केशकंबली, संजय बेलट्ठियपुत्र, मक्खलि गोसाल, निगण्ठ नातपुत्त, जो बाद में जैन महावीर के नाम से प्रसिद्ध हुए। स्वाभाविक है कि वैचारिक टकराहटें तो थीं, किन्तु एक-दूसरे का वजूद मिटाने की नफ़रत नहीं थी। जिस किसी शासक ने कट्टरता दिखाने की कोशिश की वह इतिहास में खलनायक की तरह दर्ज हो गया, चाहे वह पुष्यमित्र शुंग हो या शशांक, प्रतापरुद्र देव हो या अल्लाउद्दीन खिलजी या औरंगज़ेब। इन्हें इतिहास और अवाम ने कभी इज़्ज़त नहीं बख़्शी।

तीसरे चैनल्स पर कमोल बाउल दक्कन के शासक इब्राहीम आदिल शाह द्वितीय की कहानी सुना रहा था, जिन्होंने सुन्नी होते हुए भी अपने को माँ सरस्वती और गुरु गणपति का पुत्र घोषित कर रखा था। उसके ढेर सारे फ़रमान सरस्वती वन्दना से प्रारम्भ होते थे। उसने अपनी राजधानी बीजापुर का नाम माँ शारदे के नाम पर विद्यापुर रख दिया था। युद्ध कौशल के साथ शास्त्रीय संगीत में निष्णात इस बादशाह के, कहते हैं, दस हज़ार से अधिक शिष्य थे। इसने संगीत पर आधारित एक किताब 'किताब-ए-नौरस' भी लिखी।

अगले चैनल पर कमोल कबीर अवध के आख़िरी बादशाह वाज़िद अली शाह के राजधर्म निभाने की अनोखी कहानी सुना रहा था कि कैसे फैज़ाबाद के एक सुन्नी, मज़हबी उत्पाती शाह ग़ुलाम हुसैन के नेतृत्व में सैकड़ों हुड़दंगियों की एक बड़ी सशस्त्र टुकड़ी अयोध्या के हनुमानगढ़ी पर क़ब्ज़ा करने के लिए बवाल कर रही थी। उसके साथ जब करिश्माई सुन्नी मौलवी अमीर अली और उसके हज़ारों समर्थक शामिल हुए, तो इस अभियान को जिहाद का नाम दे दिया गया। बवाल बढ़ता गया। अन्त में अक्टूबर 1856 ईस्वी में बादशाह वाज़िद अली शाह ने लखनऊ से अपनी शाही सेना भेजी, स्थानीय शिया ज़मीन्दारों की सैन्य टुकड़ियाँ भी शामिल हुईं। तीन सौ से चार सौ जेहादी मारे गए, किन्तु हनुमानगढ़ी बचा ली गई।

अगले किसी नेशनल चैनल पर कमोल इब्राहीम आदिल शाह द्वितीय की सरस्वती-वन्दना गा कर सुना रहा था। बांग्ला में एक शब्द है 'गानपागला', आमि शेई गानपागला...आमि गाइबो...फिर उसकी जादुई सर्वविजयी मधु-सी मीठी आवाज़ छाने लगी..."भाषाएँ बहुतेरी हैं/किन्तु भावुक आग्रह एक है/सौभाग्यशाली वही है/जिस पर देवी सरस्वती की कृपा बरसती हो/चाहे वह ब्राह्मण हो या तुर्क/हे इब्राहीम, इस संसार को केवल ज्ञान चाहिए/शब्दों की सत्ता के बारे में, दृढ़ निश्चयी हृदय से चिन्तन करो/सबों की मदद करो।"

इसी सिलसिले में न्यूज 17 चैनल की पार्किंग में कालिन्दी से भेंट हुई। लगता है यह संयोग नहीं था, वह इन्तज़ार कर रही थी। नज़रें चुराते हुए ही सही, उसने कई सूचनाएँ कमोल से शेयर कीं। पहली बात तो यह कि जब वे लोग ढाका गए हुए थे, तो मिसेज मयंक के मम्मी-डैडी बेंगलुरू से आए थे। उसके डैडी रियल एस्टेट के बिजनेस में हैं। वे लोग सुआर्यन के दफ़्तर में गुप्ता साहब से भी मिलने आए थे। उनकी चमकती आँखों में आश्रम के पीछे झील से सटे बच्चों के खेल के मैदान में एक फाइव स्टार होटल का स्वप्न छलक रहा था। बाज़ाफ्ता आर्किटेक्चरल डिजाइनिंग के साथ उनकी पूरी तैयारी है। और न जाने शहर में किन-किन लोगों से मिले। वैसे 'मौसीक़ी-मँज़िल' का अनोखा स्थापत्य भी उन्हें बहुत पसन्द आ रहा था क्योंकि इसे होटल में तब्दील करने में ख़र्च बहुत कम आएगा।

दूसरी ज़रूरी बात यह कि आप लोगों की सुप्रीम कोर्ट में अपील से गुप्ता बहुत भड़का हुआ है। ख़ासकर जब से एस.आई.टी. के बन्दे यहाँ तक पहुँच गए हैं, उसका ग़ुस्सा और भी बढ़ गया है। वैसे उसकी भी तीन-चार बार ग्रिलिंग हो चुकी है। और आपकी जानकारी के लिए कि इस न्यूज 17 चैनल के अधिकांश शेयर सुआर्यन संगठन ने ख़रीद लिए हैं। टीम बदली जा रही है। अब शायद आपको यहाँ से याद नहीं किया जाए। और एक बात, आपके आर्टिकल्स छापनेवाले अख़बार 'डेली एक्सप्रेस' के भी साठ परसेन्ट शेयर ख़रीदने की तैयारी पूरी हो गई है।...अब आप निकलिए। किसी ने देख लिया तो मुश्किल हो जाएगी।

तभी कालिन्दी की नज़र पार्किंग के कोने के सीसीटीवी कैमरे पर पड़ी। उसके चेहरे के रंग उड़ गए। अपने को सँभालते हुए कमोल को भर नज़र देखा। हौले से उसके सर कन्धे को छुआ, मानो सलामती की दुआ कर रही हो और बढ़ गई यह कहते हुए कि मैं इन कैमरा फुटेज का कुछ करती हूँ।

एक साथ इतनी जानकारियाँ आपस में गड्डमड्ड हो रही थीं। वह पूरी तरह कन्फ्यूज हो गया था। गाड़ी में बैठ वहाँ से निकल तो गया, किन्तु उसे कुछ समझ में नहीं आ रहा था कि किन-किन से 'मौसीक़ी-मंज़िल' और 'आश्रम' को बचाना है?

कमोल कबीर और मयंक की टीम की रणनीति से सुआर्यन की योजनाएँ गड़बड़ा गई थीं। अब सोशल मीडिया के उनके ट्रोलर्स भी बैकफुट पर थे। इसलिए अब वे सीधे सड़क की लड़ाई पर आ गए। इसका काट आश्रम के पास नहीं है, उन्हें पूरा अन्दाज़ा था। दाहिने गाल पर टैटू और पीले रंग के झंडों ने आश्रम को चारों ओर से घेर लिया। फिर वही देशद्रोहियों और दुश्मन देश के दुलारों वाले नारे थोड़े ज़्यादा भद्दे, ज़्यादा गालीनुमा अन्दाज़ में। आश्रम के अन्दर से कोई सुगबुगाहट होती नहीं देख, टैटू वाली भीड़ और उत्तेजित होने लगी। साइनबोर्ड तोड़ा जाने लगा-ढेले चलाए जाने लगे। साथ में पुलिस फोर्स के साथ मजिस्ट्रेट था, जो शायद मौसीक़ी या कमोल को पसन्द करनेवाला भी था। उसने कमोल से मोबाइल पर कुछ बातें की। फिर भीड़ से थोड़ी कड़ाई से पेश आकर तोड़-फोड़ बन्द करवाई। स्थिति नियंत्रित होते ही, आश्रम का विशाल दरवाज़ा खुला। अब्बू-अम्मू-कमोल-मयंक, सीनियर बच्चे-बच्चियों

और फूल-मालाओं के साथ बाहर आए। एक-एक कर सभी को प्यार से माला पहनाई गई। बहुत इसरार से सबों को अन्दर आने को न्योता दिया गया। रियाज़ वाले हॉल में पूरी इज़्ज़त से बिठा कर शरबत-वरबत पिलाया गया। हुड़दंगी नेताओं को कुछ समझ में ही नहीं आ रहा था। ऐसे ख़ुशनुमा हालात से उनका कभी आमना-सामना ही नहीं हुआ था। जब तक कुछ समझने की स्थिति में आते, अब्बू का गान शुरू हो गया, बैजू बावरा की बन्दिश 'तुम्हीं ब्रह्मा तुम्हीं विष्णु...तुम्हीं मन्दिर, तुम्हीं दीया...तुम्हीं सोना, तुम्हीं सोनार...' यानी सब तुम ही हो। तुम्हें ही तय करना है कि अपने आप को कैसे ढालना है। कुछ बोलों और कुछ जादुई गान का असर, अधिकांश की आँखें डबडबा गई थीं। अब अब्बू एक-एक कर सब को गले लगा रहे थे। जिनके दाहिने गाल पर सचमुच का एग्जिमा था उसे थोड़ी ज़्यादा देर तक भींचे रहते, फिर मुस्कान बिखेरते दाहिने गाल का हल्का-सा स्पर्श करते, और सचमुच एग्जिमा दाग-सहित ग़ायब होता जा रहा था। गले मिलने के बाद टैटू वाले युवा वॉशरूम में जाकर रगड़-रगड़ कर नक़ली दाग़ मिटाने की कोशिश कर रहे थे। अन्त में विदाई के समय अब्बू ने प्यार से सन्देश भेजा कि गुप्ता साहब को भी बोलिए, एक बार मुझसे आकर गले मिल लें। सारे शिकवे-गिले दूर हो जाएँगे और वह एग्जिमा भी ठीक हो जाएगा।

लेकिन उल्टी पड़ती तरकीबों से बजरंग बिहारी गुप्ता की बौखलाहट अपने चरम पर पहुँच गई। उसने अब्बू के प्यार भरे सन्देश को अपनी धार्मिक आस्था पर घनघोर आघात माना। उसकी आस्था दाहिने गाल के एग्जिमा को हृदय में उठते राष्ट्रप्रेम के ज्वार का प्रतीक मानती थी। उसका दृढ़ निश्चयी विश्वास था कि ज्वार की एक लहर छलककर उसके दाहिने गाल पर आकर टिक गई है। यह उसके लिए अत्यन्त गर्व का विषय है, जिसे उस पाखंडी ख़ुर्शीद शाह ने एग्ज़िमा कहकर न केवल उसका घोर अपमान किया है बल्कि उसके राष्ट्रप्रेम, उसकी अत्यन्त पवित्र धार्मिक भावना पर कुठाराघात किया है। अगर इस क्रिया की प्रतिक्रया हुई, तो शहर बम के धमाकों से बहरा हो जाएगा और धू-धू करती आग बुझाए ना बुझेगी। इसलिए इन देशद्रोहियों-धर्मद्रोहियों को तुरन्त गिरफ़्तार किया जाए। उसके विद्वान अधिवक्ता ने आई.पी.सी. की धारा 295 ए 'धार्मिक

आस्था आहत करना', सी.आर.पी.सी. की धारा 107 एवं 151 'आपसी सौहार्द बिगाड़ने' और 'शहर की शान्ति व्यवस्था भंग होने की आशंका' के तहत एफ.आई.आर. दर्ज करवाई और ऊपर से आनेवाले दूरभाष सन्देशों के दबाव में शनिवार की शाम तक अब्बू-कमोल-मयंक की गिरफ़्तारी हो गई। यानी अब सोमवार तक ज़मानत नहीं मिल सकती थी। हवालात में ही कमोल को यह सन्देश मिला कि 'मिसेज मयंक ज़मानत के लिए घर-आश्रम के काग़ज़ात माँगेंगी।'

29

वतन की खाक मुझे एड़ियाँ रगड़ने दे,
मुझे यक़ीं है कि पानी यहीं से निकलेगा।

—सफ़दर

लगता है, सुआर्यन के ट्रोलर्स की मेहनत रंग दिखा रही थी। सड़क-चौराहे पर जहाँ-तहाँ लोगों का झुंड बैनर्स-काले झंडे के साथ मुट्ठियाँ ताने नारे लगाता दिख रहा था। 'देश के गद्दार', 'दुश्मन देश के दुलारे' और 'संगीत के बहाने सियासत नहीं चलेगी' के नारों से माहौल गरम करने की भरपूर कोशिश की जा रही थी। किसी-किसी चौराहे पर टैटू वाले नयी उम्र के लड़के इतने ग़ुस्से में दिख रहे थे मानो कोर्ट को नहीं, 'उन्हें' ही फ़ैसला करना हो, 'ऑन द स्पॉट'। अब्बू-कमोल-मयंक को पुलिस जीप से खींच कर पीटने को आतुर। भला हो पुलिस ऑफिसर और मजिस्ट्रेट साहब का कि इतनी इज़्ज़त बख़्शी कि हथकड़ियाँ या कमर में रस्सी नहीं बाँधी थी। किन्तु सिपाहियों की आँखों में नफ़रत साफ़ दिख रही थी। वे बैनर्स-नारे और लोकल न्यूज चैनल्स के प्रभाव में थे। उनकी नज़रों में इन देश के ग़द्दारों के लिए हिक़ारत और ग़ुस्सा साफ़-साफ़ झलक रहा था।

कोर्ट का माहौल तन्दूर की तरह तप रहा था। सुआर्यन और कच्छप-रक्षक सेना ने भीड़ जुटाने में पूरी मेहनत की थी। पुलिस जीप में एक

कान्स्टेबल ने अपने मोबाइल में न्यूज 17 चैनल लगा रखा था। लगता है वहाँ की टीम सचमुच पूरी बदल गई थी। उसके सुर बदले हुए थे। चैनल हूबहू बी.बी. गुप्ता की बातों को ही अलग-अलग अन्दाज़ से दुहरा रहा था। कचहरी की भीड़ जुटाने में इस चैनल की भी मेहनत रही होगी।

बहरहाल, जिस काम को चौक-चौराहे के ग़ुस्से में तमतमाते लड़के नहीं कर पाये उसे अंजाम देने में कोर्ट की भीड़ कामयाब रही। कचहरी के दरवाज़े से लेकर न्यायिक मजिस्ट्रेट के इजलास के बीच बड़ा-सा मैदान फिर सँकरा-सा गलियारा था। उसमें पहले से नारे लगाती, ग़द्दार और दुश्मन देश का ऐजेंट मानती अटी भीड़ ने भरपूर हाथ साफ़ किये। पुलिस ऑफिसर और मजिस्ट्रेट ने अब्बू को दोनों तरफ़ से घेर कर अपनी तरफ़ से बचाने की पूरी कोशिश की। फिर भी गलियारे में खड़े एक-दो वकीलों ने थप्पड़ रसीद कर ही दिये। साथ के सिपाहियों ने कमोल और मयंक के लिए कोई भी ज़हमत नहीं उठाई। नतीजतन मिनटों में ही दोनों के चेहरे लहूलुहान हो गए। तब तक उस कैम्पस में ड्यूटी कर रही पुलिस-टुकड़ी सक्रिय हो गई। दोहत्थों से बेंत भाँज कर भीड़ को तितर-बितर किया और कमोल-मयंक को इजलास तक पहुँचाया।

एक तो कोर्ट-टाइम के बाद भी जज साहब को इस मामले में पेशी का इन्तज़ार करना पड़ा था, इसलिए पहले से चिड़चिड़ाए बैठे थे। ऊपर से जब कमोल-मयंक की हालत देखी तो बुरी तरह भड़क गए। दोनों के कपड़े चिथड़े हो गए थे, होंठ-नाक से ख़ून आ रहा था। आँखें चोटों से सूज गई थीं। ग़ुस्सा स्वाभाविक था। पुलिस अफ़सर के पास पूछी गई कैफ़ियत का माकूल जवाब नहीं था। बुज़ुर्ग को बचा कर लाते, जज साहब ने भी देखा था इसीलिए वे बच गए, लेकिन कॉन्स्टेबल्स के तत्काल निलम्बन की सिफ़ारिश की। उसके बाद तीनों अभियुक्तों के बेल बॉन्ड की माँग की। लेकिन बेल बॉन्ड की न सूचना दी गई थी और न तैयारी का मौका। इसीलिए बेल बॉन्ड तो भरे नहीं गए थे। वे फिर भड़के। आदेश हुआ कि इनके घर के लोगों को ख़बर की जाए ताकि सोमवार को सबेरे दस बजे इनके बेल बॉन्ड के साथ वे हाज़िर हों। अगर सोमवार को समय पर बेल बॉन्ड दाखिल नहीं हुआ तो इस बार पुलिस अफ़सर के निलम्बन की सिफ़ारिश की जाएगी, यह कोर्ट की चेतावनी थी।

जेल ले जाने के पहले अस्पताल ले जाने की हिदायत दी गई। अगर अन्दरूनी चोट ज़्यादा हो तो अस्पताल में ही रखने का सुझाव दिया गया। आख़िरी चेतावनी मजिस्ट्रेट साहब के लिए थी कि अगर इन्हें जेल ले जाया गया, तो आज रात और कल रविवार के चौबीस घंटे जेल में इनके साथ कोई वारदात नहीं होनी चाहिए। इसकी गारंटी आप लेंगे। अगर फिर कोई मार-पीट, हाथापाई की शिकायत मिली, तो आपके ख़िलाफ़ भी कोर्ट द्वारा संज्ञान लिया जाएगा।

जेल के बड़े गेट और अन्दर के छोटे गेट के बीच की कोठरी में बैठे सिपाहियों और मुंशीगीरी में लगे उम्रक़ैद वाले क़ैदियों की आँखों में भी वही नफ़रत थी, जो गिरफ़्तार करनेवाले कान्स्टेबल्स की आँखों में थी। कोर्ट की हिदायत के मद्देनज़र क़ैदियों को समय से पहले ही बैरक में बन्द कर दिया गया था। फिर भी दरवाज़ों-खिड़कियों से झाँकती नज़रों में वही ग़ुस्सा, वही वहशी जुनून-नफ़रत साफ़-साफ़ पढ़ी जा सकती थी जो कचहरी की भीड़ की नज़रों में थी। सारे के सारे पेशेवर अपराधी, ख़ूनी-हत्यारे-बलात्कारी देश के इन तीनों ग़द्दारों-पाकिस्तानी ऐजेन्टों को सबक सिखाने को आतुर दिख रहे थे। उनकी भुजाएँ फड़क रही थीं और मूँछें फड़फड़ा रही थीं। राष्ट्रभक्ति का ज्वार सारे बैरकों में उमड़ रहा था। न केवल उमड़ रहा था, बल्कि बाहर छलकने-छलकने को था।

बहरहाल, एक सेल में इन्हें रखने का इन्तज़ाम किया गया था। हड़बड़ी में साफ़-सफ़ाई कर कम्बल-चादर बिछा दिये गए थे। लेकिन जहाँ-तहाँ कोनों में धूल दिख रही थी। दीवारों-छत की मकड़ियों की जालियाँ झालरों की तरह लटक रही थीं। अलग से खाना पकाने के लिए एक क़ैदी को ही लगाया गया था। छोटे से गैस चूल्हे पर उसने दाल चढ़ा दी थी और सब्ज़ियाँ काट रहा था। चूँकि पुराना छोटा-सा जेल था, लगता है आज़ादी के पहले का, इसीलिए सेल में कोई बाथरूम नहीं था। उन्हें बैरकों के खुलने के पहले नहाने-धोने से निपट लेना था, फिर रात में बैरकों के बन्द होने के बाद ही बाथरूम जाने का मौका मिलनेवाला था।

अब्बू के पैरों की लड़खड़ाहट वापस आ गई थी। बायाँ पैर फिर से घसीट-घसीटकर चल रहे थे। मयंक थोड़ा ज़्यादा ही डिप्रेशन में दिख रहा था। बहुत ही शॉक्ड था। ऐसे मंज़र उसने अपने जीवन में कभी देखे ही नहीं

थे। शहर के बड़े डॉक्टर का बेटा था। प्यार-दुलार में पला-बढ़ा। आई.आई.टी. का पास आउट। उसके बाद की ज़िन्दगी सिलिकॉन वैली अमेरिका में गुज़ारी थी। हालाँकि नस्लीय हिंसा वहाँ भी थी, किन्तु छिटपुट दुर्घटना जैसी। ऐसी वहशी भीड़ की भयानक हिंसा ने उसके वजूद को हिला दिया था। हॉस्पिटल में उसके मम्मी-पापा, मिसेज-बच्चे सब जुट गए थे, बुरी तरह बिलखते हुए। अब सबके आँसू उसकी पलकों-पपोटों में डबडबाते दिख रहे थे। उससे तो पानी भी नहीं पीया जा रहा था। सबसे बुरी बात उसके दिलो-दिमाग़ को यह लगी थी कि वह थोड़ा सा ब्रेक लेकर रिलैक्स होने अपने घर, अपने देश आया। कमोल से मिलकर अपनी जन्मभूमि, यतीम बच्चों के लिए कुछ सार्थक कर रहा था। जो गन्दी हवा उसके अपने प्यारे देश के माहौल को दूषित कर रही थी उसे ठीक करने की थोड़ी-सी कोशिश की थी। जब उसे ही ग़द्दार और पाकिस्तानी एजेन्ट कहा जा रहा था, तो इससे बुरी बात क्या हो सकती है। इससे अच्छा होता कि सुआर्यन वाले उसे गोली मार देते...लेकिन ग़द्दार...देशद्रोही...। मरने के सिवाय उसके दिमाग़ में कोई और बात आ ही नहीं रही थी।

अब्बू दीवार की तरफ़ चेहरा कर के ध्यान में बैठ गए थे। शायद आज के आघातों से उबरने की कोशिश कर रहे हों। कोने की तरफ़ मुँह किए मयंक लेट तो गया था, किन्तु लगता है रुलाई रोक नहीं पा रहा था। बीच-बीच में हिचकी से देह काँप जा रही थी।

कमोल अपनी चोटों के दर्द से थोड़ा परेशान तो था, किन्तु शॉक्ड नहीं था। उसे मालूम था कि एक न एक दिन यह होगा। सुआर्यन ज़मीनी लड़ाई में घसीटेंगे, जहाँ पिटना-हारना तय था। यह बात तो मयंक ने ही समझाई थी, लेकिन उसे लगा होगा कि वह इनसे दूर रह लेगा। शहर के वी.आई.पी. परिवार का है, आँच उस तक नहीं आ पायेगी। कमोल को ऐसा कोई गुमान नहीं था। वह तो ग्राम बांग्ला का छोकरा था। हर इलेक्शन में भीड़ की ऐसी हरकतें, मार-पीट, बम और चाक़ूबाज़ी देखते बड़ा हुआ था। उसे फ़र्क़ नहीं पड़ा था। ऐसे भी अपने बाबा-माँ का भालो बेटा, सच्चा बाउल, उसके लिए दुख क्या और सुख क्या? अच्छा है दो रातें एकान्त की मिली हैं, वहीं अपने प्यारे अब्बू और अभिन्नो बोन्धु के संग। इसे आनन्द में बिताना है। आनन्द महसूस करते और करवाते। बाउल के लिए महल क्या और जंगल क्या?

कमोल के चेहरे पर मुस्कान वापस आ गई थी। वह सेल का माहौल नॉर्मल करने के लिए धीरे-धीरे कुछ गुनगुनाने का मूड बना रहा था। तभी वही मजिस्ट्रेट और जेलर साहब दिखे। जेलर बाबू बांगाली थे। बहुत जोर-शोर से नोमोस्कार-नोमोस्कार हुआ। बाद में मालूम हुआ कि उनके दादू ने कुछ दिनों तक नानू अय्यूब ख़ान से मौसीक़ी सीखी थी। उनका ख़ानदान तब से नानू के इस परिवार का मुरीद था। जेलर साहब की वाणी अविराम थी,...बस एक दिन की बात है...फेर सोब...भालो...भालो...। ऐतो बड़ो...नामकरा गायक उसके जेल में...प्रोसोन्नता का कोई ठिकाना नहीं...। कल भोर से लाइब्रेरी में, वहीं ब्रेकफास्ट। लंच उनके घर से...रुई माछ...बेगुन भाजा...आलू-पोस्तो... सन्देश...सब। ख़ाली एकटा-अनुरोध...कल संध्या लाइब्रेरी हॉल में कुछ बंगाली परिवार, भद्रोजन, मित्र-बंधु जुटेगा। हर रविवार को जुटते हैं सब, परमहंस-ठाकुर का भजन-कीर्तन गाने। किन्तु कल कमोल साहब का एकटा-छोटा सा बाउल गान। हालाँकि कमोल लोगों की हा़लत, चोट-वोट देखकर दोनों बहुत शर्मिन्दा हो रहे थे।...किन्तु कमोल साहब से बार-बार एकटा...छोटा-सा... अनुरोध...। यह तो कमोल के मन की बात थी। वह भी चाह रहा था कि अब्बू और ख़ासकर मयंक थोड़ा नॉर्मल महसूस करें। जेल में भी जेल जेल जैसा नहीं लगे। ख़ासकर नफ़रत बरसाती इन क़ैदियों-सिपाहियों की नज़रों से दूर, कल समय बिताने का अवसर मिलना उसे थोड़ी और ख़ुशी दे गया। उन दोनों के जाते ही कमोल की गुनगुनाहट कमरे में तिरने लगी, 'काना बेड़ाल लोभी होये/दधि बोले कपास खेये/गलाय बेधे छटपट करे शेषे (ओ) तार प्राण बाँचे ना...।' (अन्धी बिल्ली ने लोभ में फँसकर दही के धोखे में कपास खा लिया। जो गले में फँस गया। उसके प्राण बचेंगें नहीं...)।

...गान के असर या चोट-थकान से बिना-खाये पिए मयंक को नींद आ गई। दूसरे दिन सबेरे ही बैरकों के खुलने के पहले तीनों लोग नहा-धो कर जेल की बगल में, ऑफिस के ऊपर वाले तल्ले पर लाइब्रेरी में। जेलर मोशाय के घर से बहुत दिव्य ब्रेकफास्ट पधारा। ब्रेड-आमलेट, दूध-कॉर्नफ्लेक्स, फ्रूट, जूस, सब कुछ। मयंक की भूख खुली। मन भर खाने के बाद थोड़ा नॉर्मल-सा दिखा। जेलर मोशाय और मजिस्ट्रेट के मधुर व्यवहार से उसका खोया विश्वास लौट रहा था। समझ रहा था कि भाड़े की भीड़ के अलावा उसे और लोग ग़द्दार, देशद्रोही नहीं समझ रहे थे।

दिन में मौक़ा देख कमोल ने उसके फादर इन लॉ के बारे में जानने की कोशिश की। वह थोड़ी देर तक तो चुप रहा फिर बोलना शुरू किया, तो बोलता ही गया—"आप सब लोग जब ढाका जाने की तैयारी में थे तो वैभवी ने आपको भी बताया था कि उसके मम्मी-डैड घूमने आनेवाले हैं। मैंने भी इसे यूँ ही लिया था, रूटीन रूप में। बेंगलुरू से आए इन्हें सात-आठ महीने हो चले हैं, तो मिलने की इच्छा हो रही होगी। लेकिन आने के बाद तीनों जैसे खुसुर-फुसर किया करते और मुझे देखकर एकाएक चुप हो जाते। उन तीनों के चेहरे का रंग बदल जाता, तो मुझे यह लग गया था कि मेरे ससुर साहब हमेशा की तरह किसी बिज़नेस ट्रिप पर हैं। दरअसल वह आदमी इनसान है ही नहीं, एड़ी से चोटी तक ख़ालिस बिज़नेसमैन है। उसकी एक-एक साँस प्रॉफिट-लॉस के हिसाब से चलती है। बेईमानी-जालसाज़ी उसके रग-रग में भरी हुई है। ज़मीन-जायदाद के मुकदमे लड़ना उसकी हॉबी है। इसी हॉबी को एन्जॉय करते हुए वह रियल-एस्टेट का भारी टाइकून बन गया है। करोड़ों कमाये हैं। किन्तु ताज़िन्दगी बड़े-समृद्ध किसानों को पार्टनर बना कर ग़रीब किसानों की सड़क, हाईवे के बगल वाली ज़मीनें जिस प्रकार इस शख़्स ने लूटी हैं, पैसे के साथ-साथ ग़रीबों की हाय भी ख़ूब आई है। इसके दो-दो जवान बेटे बीमारी-ऐक्सिडेन्ट में मर गए। बहू विधवा, पोते-पोतियाँ यतीम। किन्तु ऊपर वाले की बेआवाज़ लाठी का भी इस धनपशु पर कोई असर नहीं है। इसकी यह बेटी पूरी अपने डैड पर गई है। एकदम काइयाँ है। मेरी कोई लव-वव मैरेज नहीं थी। मुझे ट्रैप किया गया था। इसका मरहूम बड़ा भाई मेरा बैचमेट था। चार साल तक तो दूर से हाय-हलो तक ही रहा। कैम्पस सेलेक्शन के बाद एकाएक नज़दीकी दिखाने लगा। इसकी बहन भी प्रकट हो गई। उसी शहर में चार्टर्ड एकाउन्टेसी पढ़ रही थी। फिर बर्थ-डे पार्टियों में, कभी इस फंक्शन-कभी उस फंक्शन में खींच-खाँच कर मुझे ले जाया जाने लगा। हर कहीं वैभवी होती। दो-चार मुलाक़ातों के बाद वैभवी तो जैसे गले ही पड़ गई। दिन-रात मोबाइल पर मैसेज, चैट की कोशिश...डेटिंग...। मैं छोटे शहर का लड़का...समझ नहीं पाया...ट्रैप हो गया।

"अब लगता है कि बेंगलुरू से वैभवी हमें हेल्प करने नहीं बल्कि अपने डैड के कहने पर उनके बिज़नेस का स्कोप ही देखने आई थी। अब

मम्मी-डैड-वैभवी की तिकड़ी ने शहर में कौन-कौन से प्लॉट देखे...अपने रियल-एस्टेट कम्पनी की फ्रेन्चाइजी के लिए किस-किस से मिली, मुझे कुछ भी मालूम नहीं। हवा भी नहीं लगने दी उन तीनों ने। लेकिन...कुछ बात ज़रूर है...। मैं कोशिश करूँगा कि यह आफ़त आश्रम से टले क्योंकि इसे आश्रम गिरवी रखने में भी एक मिनट नहीं लगेगा। इसे बेंगलुरू लौटाने का हर सम्भव प्रयास करूँगा। नहीं होगा तो पहले मैं ही सिलिकॉन वैली लौट जाऊँगा। वहीं से आश्रम के लिए जो भी हो, करूँगा।"

अब कमोल के लिए शक की कोई गुंजाइश नहीं थी। जेलर साहब के चैम्बर से उसने शब्बो भाभी को कॉल कर सारी बातें बताईं। ज़मीन के काग़ज़ात लॉकर में ही रहने देने की हिदायत दी। नानू के एडवोकेट साथी श्रीवास्तव अंकल के अलावा किसी और की सलाह न मानने की भी बात समझाई। कमोल के बोलने के पहले ही शब्बो भाभी सबेरे-सबेरे ही एडवोकेट अंकल से मिलकर सब तय कर आई थीं। कमोल ने शाम के प्रोग्राम के लिए तानपूरा-सितार-तबला के लिए आश्रम के सीनियर बच्चों को भेजने को कह दिया।

मना करने के बावजूद बारह बजते, बड़े टिफिन बॉक्स के साथ शब्बो भाभी हाज़िर हो गईं। लाइब्रेरी का माहौल और तीनों को ठीक-ठाक देख उन्हें अच्छा लगा। कमोल-मयंक के चोटों के भाँति-भाँति के निशान तो अभी थे। आँखों की सूजन कम हो गई थी, किन्तु उनके ठीक नीचे काले-लाल निशान उभर आए थे। नाकें अब भी सूजी हुई थीं। होंठों के घाव सूख तो गए थे, किन्तु रंग काला पड़ गया था। उन्होंने कमोल की बाँह और पीठ की भी चोट देखीं। लाल-नीले-काले रंग-रंग के निशान, कल की काली आँधी छोड़ गई थी। दवाओं के कारण दर्द नहीं हो रहा था, किन्तु चोट तो अच्छी-ख़ासी थी। सबों का अच्छी तरह से मुआयना करने के बाद निश्चिन्तता से बैठीं, तो वैभवी पुराण का पाठ शुरू हो गया। 'कैसे कल से ही वैभवी मैडम घर-आश्रम के काग़ज़ात के लिए बेचैन किए हुए थीं। लग रहा था बिना काग़ज़ातों के ज़मानत ही नहीं होगी और तीनों को जेल में ही सड़ना होगा। इसीलिए सबेरे-सबेरे फ़ोन कर श्रीवास्तव अंकल के पास गई। ज़मानत के लिए ज़मीन के काग़ज़ात की बात सुनकर वे हँसने लगे। तब जाकर मैं निश्चिन्त हुई। किन्तु आज वैभवी मैडम फिर से सिर

पर सवार हो गईं। मैंने श्रीवास्तव अंकल का हवाला भी दिया, किन्तु वे मान ही नहीं रही थीं। उतने बड़े वकील को ही ग़लत साबित करने लगीं। अजब हिस्टेरिकल बिहेवियर था। फिर तुम्हारा फ़ोन आया, तो बातें समझ में आईं। अम्मू ने ठीक से हैंडिल किया। नाश्ता-वाश्ता करा कर प्यार से गेट तक छोड़कर आईं।'

बातों के बहाव में कमोल ने वैभवी मैडम और उनकी मम्मी-डैडी की गुप्ता साहब से हुई भेंट के बारे में भी बता दिया। आश्रम के खेल-मैदान में फाइव स्टार होटल, उसका आर्किटेक्चरल डिजाइन, 'मौसीक़ी-मंज़िल' को भी स्टार होटल में तब्दील करने की उन लोगों की चाह, सारी बातें सबके सामने आ गईं। मयंक उनके लक्षणों से वाक़िफ़ था, सो उसे कोई आश्चर्य नहीं हुआ, किन्तु अब्बू-शब्बो भाभी बुरी तरह चौंके। लेकिन ये बातें कमोल को कैसे मालूम पड़ीं? कमोल दुविधा में पड़ गया। मयंक के सामने कालिन्दी की बात बताई जाए कि नहीं बताई जाए? लेकिन शब्बो भाभी के सिक्स्थ सेन्स ने भाँप लिया। उनका मूड ही बदल गया, तो तुम छुप-छुप कर कालिन्दी से मिलते हो? नहीं, कालिन्दी तुमसे मिलती है। ग़ुस्से की पागल मक्खी उनकी नाक पर आकर बैठ गई थी। वह उसे ज़ब्त करने की कठिन कोशिश कर रही थीं किन्तु माहौल धनुष की प्रत्यंचा की तरह तन गया था। भारी बारिश के पहले वाली उमस। सब मौन थे, सिर्फ़ सन्नाटा बज रहा था। तभी जेलर साहब का पिउन खाने के तीन पैकेट्स लेकर आया। पैकेट्स के प्रिंट्स शहर के सबसे महँगे रेस्तराँ का पता बता रहे थे। सबसे ऊपर वाले पैकेट पर एक कार्ड सटा था जिस पर लिखा था 'के'। शब्बो भाभी ने कार्ड निकाला। तमतमाया चेहरा लाल भभूका हो गया। अपना टिफिन उठाया और बिना कुछ कहे तीर-सी निकल गईं।

अब सूरज कमोल दा के सिर पर तप रहा था। सारी हँसी-ख़ुशी ग़ायब हो गई। एकाएक सब वीरान-सा लगने लगा। पैकेट्स के खाने और जेलर मोशाय के घर के माछ, भाजा, आलू-पोस्तो...किसी का स्वाद पता ही नहीं चला। शाम की महफ़िल उसके काँपते सुरों के साथ सिसक रही थी, '...आमी एकटा आसोल पागोल पेलाम ना, सेइ जोन्ने आमी पागोल होलाम ना...।'

30

मन के प्रशान्त पोखर में/बिछोह का कंकर/मछलियाँ रास्ता भूल गईं/
लहरें दसों दिशाओं को कँपाने लगीं/निस्तब्ध टँगा रहा गया सूर्य/
ग़र्म हवा सूखी पत्तियों से भर गई/बेरंग तितलियाँ पन्नों में
मरी मिलीं/चिड़ियों के स्वप्न में उतरने लगा आत्मघात/
यहाँ, सीने के भीतर/फफोलों से भर गया दिल।

तीनों की जेल की वापसी से लगा, आश्रम की रुकी हुई साँसें वापस आ गई हों। घास से लेकर छतनार गाछों की हरी पत्तियों के क्लोरोफिल ने फिर से सूर्य किरणों को चूमना शुरू कर दिया था। छात्रावासों की थमी हुई हँसी वापस आ गई। हवाएँ परदों-चादरों को छेड़ती इतराती अपने होने का एहसास कराने लगीं। क्षितिज पर धूमिल चाँद खिड़कियों से झाँके जा रहा था। लताओं-वल्लरियों ने पेड़ों को दुबारा ज़ोर से भींच लिया। गौरैया रोशनदान छोड़कर बाहर जाना नहीं चाह रही थी। खेल मैदान से शोर धूल के बगूले की तरह उठकर आसमान को गुँजा रहा था। आश्रम अपनी पुरानी लय में वापस आ गया था।

अब्बू भी अपने पुराने मूड में थे। स्नान-ध्यान करके रियाज़ के लिए बैठ गए। बच्चों को शाम की तालीम के लिए जुटने की ख़बर भिजवा दी गई थी। लेकिन कमोल दा और मयंक की लय अभी तक खोई हुई थी।

खेल-मैदान के शोर में जो बात दब गई थी वह थी मयंक और मिसेज मयंक के बीच हुई। भयानक झड़प, चीख़-चिल्लाहट। अब टिशू पेपर्स से नाक-आँखों को रह-रहकर पोछतीं, वैभवी मैडम सुबक रही थीं। मयंक ने जेलर मोशाय के कम्प्यूटर से ही कई ई-मेल सिलिकॉन वैली भेजे थे। अब उसके मोबाइल के मेल पर पॉजिटिव रिस्पॉन्स मिल रहे थे। किन्तु मैडम अभी आश्रम से टसकने को तैयार नहीं थीं। लगता है, मयंक से ज़्यादा गुप्ता साहब पर विश्वास हो गया था या डैड की दुलारी धिया...डैड का एक-दो सपना पूरा करके ही लौटना चाह रही हों।

बहरहाल, जब मयंक अपना और बच्चों का एयरटिकट करवाने लैपटॉप पर बैठा, तो वे हड़बड़ाईं। अन्त में यह तय हुआ कि मयंक पहले बढ़े। वे बच्चों के संग दिसम्बर-जनवरी तक बेंगलुरू में रहेंगी। स्कूल का नया सेशन शुरू होने के पहले बच्चों को लेकर सिलिकॉन वैली आ जाएँगी। मयंक ने इस मध्य मार्ग को स्वीकार कर लिया। चलिए! इस बला ने कम-से-कम इस शहर-इस आश्रम से टलना तो स्वीकार किया।

किन्तु भालो कमोल दा की राहत—सुगिया, जो पिंजड़ा खोल, उड़ कर चिन्ता की ऊँची डाल पर जा बैठी थी, वह उतर ही नहीं रही थी। कमरे की उमस बढ़ती जा रही थी। मन स्थिर नहीं हो पा रहा था। कभी शबनम के. ख़ान की कॉलेज वाली छवि आकर हड़काती, तो कभी चुरूलिया वाली कालिन्दी आकर चहचहाती। उससे यह घुटन बर्दाश्त नहीं हो रही थी। सितार लेकर बैठा, किन्तु लय-धुन मिली नहीं। खेल-मैदान की ओर निकल गया। लगा, बच्चे बेमतलब चीख़ रहे हैं। सर फटने लगा। चिड़चिड़ाहट बढ़ने लगी। फिर लौटकर अपने कमरे में आ गया। अब्बू की तरफ़ जाने की हिम्मत नहीं हो रही थी। कल खाने के पैकेट के ऊपर चिपके 'के' वाले कार्ड ने लगा उसे भरे बाज़ार नंगा कर दिया था। जो नंगापन उससे ही सहा नहीं जा रहा हो, उसे लेकर किस मुँह से अब्बू के पास जाता। उस दिन कालिन्दी उसके साथ जब अकेली ड्राइंग रूम में बैठी ख़याली तितलियों की पकड़ा-पकड़ी खेल रही थी, अगर गुप्ता के साथ अब्बू भी कमरे में नहीं आते, तो नंगा तो उसी दिन हो जाना था। लेकिन अब जो अनहोनी होनी है, उससे कौन बचाएगा? मन की सिहरन थम नहीं रही थी और बायीं भौंह फड़कती जा रही थी। थक-हार कर उसने टी.वी. चला

दिया और साउथ की ऐक्शन मूवी देखने लगा। हीरो के एक फड़के पर सौ-सौ गुलाटियाँ खानेवाले जोकर जैसे विलेन में उसे अपना चेहरा दिखने लगा। घबड़ाकर रिमोट दूसरे चैनल की ओर बढ़ जाता। चैनल बदलते-बदलते दोपहर ढल गई। शाम होते जिसका इन्तज़ार था वह जेठ-वैशाख की लू सी पधार गई।

शब्बो भाभी ने बिना कमरे का दरवाज़ा बन्द किए, चीख़-चीख़ कर जितना कुछ सुनाया उसमें से अधिकांश बातें कमोल दा को सुनाई ही नहीं पड़ीं या सुनाई पड़ीं तो दिमाग़ तक पहुँच नहीं पाईं। न्यूरोन्स ने शायद ढोने से ही इनकार कर दिया। कुछ दिमाग़ तक पहुँचीं तो वहाँ के न्यूरोन ने उन्हें डिकोड करने की ज़हमत नहीं उठाई। लेकिन जो बातें डिकोड होकर समझ में आईं उनका लब्बोलुआब यह था कि बाउल लोग तो होते ही ऐसे हैं। मैं ही तुम्हारे भोलेपन से धोखा खा गई थी। भालो...कमोल... कहाँ का भालो...?...भलेपन का खोल ओढ़े भयानक भेड़िया...कमोल। मैं अगर पहले से जानती कि बीवी के संग-संग साधन-संगिनी रखने का भी बाउलों में चलन है, तो मैं क्या...मेरी जूती भी तुम से ब्याह नहीं करती।... साधन-संगिनी...आयँ...सुनते हैं कि बाउल जिधर भी माधुकरी...टोहोल... भिक्षाटन के लिए निकलता है उधर ही नई साधन-संगिनी को टोह लेता है। कालिन्दी के अलावा...और कितनी साधन-संगिनियाँ छुपा रखी हैं...आज ही बता दो...ताकि श्रीवास्तव अंकल को भी सब मालूम पड़े...अलग होने में आसानी रहे...तुम बाउल लोगों का क्या...पूरन दास बाउल की तरह कोई फ्रेन्च बीवी तुम्हें भी मिल जाएगी...ये वर्दमान वाले बाउल, न जाने क्या नाम है...उनकी जैसी जापानी बीवी आ जाएगी और आश्रम के बच्चों को एक नई गुरु-माता भी मिल जाएगी...तुमको कालिन्दी...किसी और के साथ...रहना हो रहो...पर मुझे और बुलबुल को अब बख़्श दो...।

तब तक अब्बू कमरे में आ गए। कमोल को लगा कि कोई चट्टान-सी ढाल आ गई, किन्तु आज शबनम के. ख़ान हर चट्टान से टकराने को सोचकर आई थी। अब्बू ने जब अपनी बेटी की पीठ पर हाथ रख उसे समझाने की कोशिश की, तो वह और भड़क गई, "आप मेरे अब्बू हैं कि अपने इस नये-नकोरे बेटे के बाप? जमाई को बेटा बना लिया...जिस दिन ड्राइंग रूम में ये दोनों अकेले रंगरेलियाँ मना रहे थे...उसकी हरकतों को

देख...डाँटने के बजाय...ढकने लगे और बहकाने लगे।...आप क्या बहका रहे थे इस नालायक़ को...कि जितना मौक़ा इंजीनियरिंग कॉलेज ने तुम्हें शब्बो के साथ समय बिताने को दिया उतना मौक़ा अगर कालिन्दी को मिला होता तो बुलबुल की अम्मा कालिन्दो ही होती...। संसार का कोई भी बाप अपनी ही बेटी का यूँ घर जलाता है क्या? आप दोनों को क्या लगता है कि मैं यहाँ नहीं रहती हूँ, तो मुझे कुछ भी पता नहीं रहता... एक-एक ख़बर मुझे मिलती रही है।...यहाँ तक कि न्यूज 17 की पार्किंग में इन दोनों के बीच जो प्रेम-व्यापार हुआ उसकी वीडियो क्लिपिंग भी मेरे मोबाइल में है।...अब्बू, आप तो बीच में मत ही बोलिए...मुझे तो आप पर भी शक है, दो-चार जोगिनें आपकी भो कहीं न कहीं ज़रूर होंगी।... सारे मर्द एक जैसे ही तो होते हैं...उनमें भी बाउल...जोगी जैसे छुट्टों के क्या कहना...मैं जा रही हूँ और आज के बाद इस गन्दे आदमी का मुँह तक नहीं देखूँगी...और आप भी अब्बू आज के बाद मुझसे बातचीत करने की कोशिश नहीं कीजिएगा। यह अपना नया बेटा आपको मुबारक हो... आज के बाद मैं आपकी बेटी नहीं...बुलबुल आपकी नातिन नहीं...वह भी अब आश्रम में पैर नहीं धरेगी।"

तूफ़ान आकर गुज़र गया। सब कुछ बर्बाद करता हुआ। कमोल को लग रहा था कि पृथ्वी क्या...पूरी सृष्टि ही हिल रही है...सारे चट्टानों में दरारें पड़ रही थीं...यहाँ से लेकर चन्द्रमा तक और उनमें से ही किसी एक में उसे समाना था। रेलवे की पटरी में फँसा हुआ था उसका पाँव... एक ट्रेन आकर गुज़र गई थी...दूसरी आनेवाली थी उसके बिखरे पुर्जों को उड़ाने...हाईवे पर ट्रकों के नीचे अपनी स्कूटी के साथ वह घिसटता जा रहा था और निर्लज्ज प्राण बाहर आ ही नहीं रहे थे।

31

मैं नहीं हूँ नग़मा-ए-जाँफ़िजा, मुझे सुन के कोई करेगा क्या।
मैं बड़े वियोग की हूँ सदा, मैं बड़े दुखों की पुकार हूँ।
(नग़मा-ए-जाँफ़िजा = आयुवर्द्धक गीत)

—बहादुर शाह जफ़र

शब्बो भाभी का ग़ुस्सा अपने कमोल को समझ में नहीं आया।...इतना ग़ुस्सा...आख़िर किस बात पर? उस साँझ ठकमकी-सी लग गई थी। कमोल और अब्बू दोनों को। ज़ुबाँ तो हिली ही नहीं...बस उस भीषोण ग़ुस्से की आँच में मन का कोना बुरी तरह झुलस गया। मुझे अपने यार की उदासी देखी नहीं जाती थी। हर शाम बिना नाग़ा उसके पास बैठने लगा। उस शापित शाम के बाद बुलबुल-अम्मू सबों ने आश्रम आना बन्द कर दिया। शायद भाभी ने ही क़सम-वसम दे दी हो।

दुख पसलियाँ तोड़ने पर आमादा था तभी कमोल दा ने उस शाम ज़ुबाँ से थोड़ा कम किन्तु डबडबाई आँखों से बहुत कुछ कहा। शायद कुछ ग़ुबार निकला हो, छाती कुछ तो हल्की हुई हो। बार-बार यही दुहरा रहा था कि आख़िर उसकी ग़लती क्या थी?...कालिन्दी का बात करना... उसकी हल्की-सी छुअन;...स्वाद का थोड़ा-सा फ़िक्र...इतना बड़ा अपराध कैसे हो गया?...हमारे और शब्बो के बीच कितना कुछ हुआ करता था

हॉस्टल के दिनों में। एक सुबास, एक अलौकिक ख़ुशबू हमारे इर्द-गिर्द तिरती रहती। हम दोनों का रियाज़ तो पूरी कायनात सुना करती। सूरज-चाँद रास्ता भूल कर हमारी खिड़की पर टिक जाते। अगर वे सारे एहसास सच्चे थे, वो ख़ुशबू, वो नूर सच्चा था तो फिर यह दूध में खटाई-सा अविश्वास हमारे बीच कहाँ से आया? हमारे दिलों के बीच मौसीक़ी ने जो कच्चे रेशम की डोर जोड़ी थी उसे बुलबुल ने, अब्बू और अम्मू ने मज़बूत ही किया था। लेकिन वह डोर एक ही झटके में टूट कैसे गई?...कालिन्दी की एक मुस्कान-एक छुअन ने ऐसा क्या कर डाला?

हर शाम हमारे बीच यही सवाल कुंडली मारे फ़न फैलाये बैठा रहता। केवल बैठा ही नहीं रहता धीरे-धीरे अपना आकार बढ़ाता हमारे बीच की सारी जगह छेक लेता। फिर आसपास की हवा भी उसी सवाल की ग़ैर-बर्दाश्त गंध से इतनी बोझिल हो जाती कि हमारा साँस लेना दूभर हो जाता।

कमोल दा को यह लग रहा था कि सारे चाँद-चाँदनी के एहसास एकतरफ़ा थे। सिर्फ़ उसका ही दिल धड़का था। सिर्फ़ उसकी ही साँसें ख़ुशबू में डूबी थीं। क्या था मेरा माने भालो कमोल का जीवन?...क्या सिर्फ़ कमोल का कोई अस्तित्व नहीं था, सब कुछ उस 'भालो' पर ही टिका था। सिर्फ़ सबकी हाँ में हाँ मिलाते रहो...रोबोट की तरह बिना पूछे हर कहा मानते रहो तो 'भालो'। ज़रा-सा निजी कुछ...ज़रा से अपने मन से...तुरन्त भालो से बदोमाश। पहले दादू-बाबा...अब शब्बो।...बस...माँ ही सब समझती थी। वह भी तो भालो बोऊ के 'भालो' से ज़िन्दगी भर तबाह रही जैसे। दोनों की ज़िन्दगी के रंग कुछ-कुछ एक जैसे धूसर, मटमैले... ग़ुलामी के काले रंगों की छाप से भरे।

आजकल कमोल सचमुच में रोबोट-सा भोर से साँझ तक आश्रम का सारा काम निपटाता रहता।...क्या करता उसे निपटाना ही था। मयंक भी नहीं...मिसेज़ मयंक भी नहीं; अब्बू ने भी अपने को अपने कमरे तक समेट लिया था। अम्मू आ नहीं रही थीं। करना तो कमोल को ही था। भले ही भीतर-भीतर रो रहा हो। आँखें सावन का डबडबाया आकाश हो रही हों। आश्रम की ज़िम्मेवारी तो उठानी ही उठानी थी। जैसे न चाहते हुए भी साँसें देह का भार उठाए रहती हैं। मैं भी ऑफिस के पहले और शाम को कमोल दा के साथ लगा रहता। जितना बन पड़ता करता। हाँ! मेरी

मिसेज़ श्रावणी ने मिसेज़ मयंक वाली ज़िम्मेवारी सँभाल ली थी। कॉलेज में एकाउन्ट्स ही पढ़ाती थी इसलिए कोचिंग का एकाउन्ट्स समझने में उसे दिक़्क़त नहीं हुई।

दिन ढलते ही मनहूस शाम हौले से हमारे साथ आ बैठती और दुख के प्याले को खारे आँसुओं से भर कर कमोल के सामने रख देती। वह उस जाम को घूँट-घूँट पीता रात का दामन भिगोता रहता। लगता है वह आजकल मन हल्का करने के लिए कुछ-कुछ डायरी में लिखने भी लगा था। कुछ अटपटा, कुछ-कुछ कविता या बड़बड़ाहट सा। कभी-कभी पढ़कर सुनाया भी करता। उस शाम फिर से उसने अपने मन को खोला। "बात यह है बोन्धु कि हर मन को चाहिए मन का ही घर। एक अपना-सा 'मनघर' जिसमें कोई किवाड़, दहलीज़-कुंडी-ताले न हों। बस खिड़कियाँ ही खिड़कियाँ हों और ढेर सारे रोशनदान भी। लगता है रास्ते में उस 'मनघर' की परछाइयाँ तो मिलीं किन्तु सच्चा-सुच्चा 'मनघर' मेरे मन को मिल न सका। अब यह मन कोई देह तो नहीं कि कहीं भी, कैसे भी रह लेगा बस भरे उदर के सहारे।...अब घरविहीन मन भटकता रहता है इस मटकी को मिट्टी में मिलाने के सौ-सौ उपाय ढूँढ़ता।...जो मेरे यायावर मन को अपने 'मनघर' में आसरा ही न दे सकी वही मेरे मन पर सवाल खड़ी करके चली गई। क्या बिडम्बना है?

"क्या इतना लम्बा साथ भी हमारे मन को मिला न सका? क्या पुरुष-स्त्री के बीच की दीवार लोहे की होती है जो रेशम की डोरियों से खींचकर किनारे नहीं की जा सकती? क्या दो दोस्त पति-पत्नी बनते ही सिर्फ़ पति-पत्नी रह जाते हैं, दोस्ती की लाश विवाह की वेदी पर ही पड़ी रह जाती है। कि सारे मंगल गान, दुआएँ, आशीर्वाद, शुभकामनाएँ दोस्त और दोस्ती के लिए ज़हर होती हैं? क्या पति-पत्नी कभी दोस्त नहीं बन पाते? क्या विवाह की गाँठ...प्रेम के धागे को चटका कर...फिर उसे जोड़ने के लिए लगाई जाती है ताकि गाँठ सदा के लिए पड़ी रहे। पति-पत्नी के बीच हाइफन की तरह एक फाँक जेंडर की...एक फाँक ईर्ष्या...एक फाँक अविश्वास...एक फाँक असुरक्षा की उस गाँठ को भारी करती रहती है। कभी-कभी इतना भारी कि दुखों के बोझ से दुहरी होकर ज़िन्दगी मौत के क़दमों में पनाह माँगने लगती है।"

लेकिन यह उसके साथ ही क्यों हो रहा है? अपने भालो कमोल के दिमाग़ी घड़ी की सूई यहीं अटक गई थी, 'क्या मंच की तेज़-रोशनियों ने शब्बो की आँखें चौंधिया दीं और हमारे बीच का अदृश्य इन्द्रधनुष दिखना बन्द हो गया? क्या तालियों की गड़गड़ाहट और रुपयों की खनखनाहटों में दबकर मेरे दिल की धड़कन कुचल गई? क्या 'सिस्टरहुड' की बढ़ती आमदनी और शोहरत हमारे बीच की फाँक को चौड़ा करती चली गई? क्या बाज़ार भेस बदलकर शब्बो को पुष्पक विमान पर ले उड़ा है और मदहोशी में उसे पता ही नहीं चल रहा?'

'सिस्टरहुड' के पी.आर.ओ. और मार्केटिंग कन्सल्टेंट के कहने पर शब्बो भाभी लगातार समझौते करती आ रही थीं। पहले पोस्टर-बैनर से उसके नाम से 'ख़ान' हटाया गया। वह केवल शबनम कबीर रह गई। फिर उसे विदुषी शबनम के., ब्रैकेट में डॉटर ऑफ पद्म विभूषण रागेश्वरी देवी लिखा जाने लगा। फोक स्टूडियो के प्रस्ताव का अम्मू ने बहुत विरोध किया। पॉप की धुन पर ठुमरी-कजरी-टप्पे गाना, अम्मू की नज़र में इससे बड़ा पाप कुछ और नहीं हो सकता था। यह तो पूरे ख़ानदान की विरासत और पीढ़ियों की इबादत को डुबोनेवाला काम था। लेकिन मार्केटिंग कन्सल्टेंट ने न जाने क्या पट्टी पढ़ाई थी कि वह नहीं मानी। अम्मू की बद्दुआओं का भय भी उसके कदम रोक नहीं सका। मार्केटिंग की मानें तो घरानों का युग बीत चुका था अब 'सिस्टरहुड' जैसे ग्रुप ही ज़िन्दा रहनेवाले और ज़िन्दा रखनेवाले थे। शब्बो भाभी को अपने पी.आर.ओ. और मार्केटिंग कन्सल्टेंट पर ख़ुदा से ज़्यादा भरोसा था। लेकिन शायद उन्हें मालूम नहीं था कि जिस प्रकार बदले माहौल में उनके नाम का 'ख़ान' बाज़ार की उड़ान में बाधा बनने लगा तो उसे ड्रॉप करने में मिनट भर की देर नहीं लगी तो कल के दिन विदुषी शबनम के. को ही ड्रॉप करने में कितनी देर लगेगी? लेकिन अभी आँखों पर सफलता की रंगीन पट्टियाँ पड़ी थीं। उन्हें अभी न कमोल दा की छटपटाहट दिख रही थी न अब्बू के अकेलेपन की घुटन और न आश्रम में धीरे-धीरे छानेवाली उदासी की कालिख। शायद मार्केटिंग कन्सल्टेंट ने ही आश्रम से सम्बन्ध तोड़ने की सलाह दी हो।

लेकिन अपने कमोल दा को उदासी-अवसाद की हालात में यह लगने लगा था कि केवल शब्बो और सिस्टरहुड को ही दोष क्यों दिया जाए,

क्या कोचिंग इन्स्टीट्यूट की शुरुआत कर आश्रम के पाक-पवित्र इलाके में उसने ख़ुद बाज़ार के लिए चुपके से दरवाज़ा नहीं खोला था? अजाने ही सही किन्तु वह बी. बी. गुप्ता के भँवरजाल में फँस तो गया ही। सोचे तो एक तरह से मयंक के उस रियल इस्टेट टायकून ससुर को मिसेज़ मयंक ने नहीं दरअसल अप्रत्यक्षतः उसने ही न्योता भिजवाया था।

दरअसल अब्बू का कोचिंग और सिस्टरहुड की गतिविधियों में दिलचस्पी नहीं लेना, अपनी आशंका ज़ाहिर कर एकाएक थोड़ा ज़्यादा गम्भीर हो जाना क्या एक संकेत नहीं था? मौन प्रतिकार का संकेत जिसे वह समझ नहीं पाया। दरअसल सबों ने मिलकर इतनी ग़लतियाँ कर दी थीं कि अब उसका कोई हल निकालना सम्भव नहीं था। कुछ ग़लतियाँ उसकी, कुछ ग़लतियाँ शब्बो की, कुछ ग़लतियाँ कालिन्दी की।...लेकिन क्या कालिन्दी ने सचमुच कोई ग़लती की थी? क्या उसे और आश्रम को आनेवाले ख़तरे से सचेत करना कोई ग़लती थी? लेकिन शब्बो को तो यही सबसे भारी ग़लती लगी थी।

कमोल दा का डिप्रेशन यह समझा रहा था कि सच बात तो यह है कि नकचढ़ी, घमंडी, ख़ानदान की शोहरत के मद में डूबी पुणे इंजीनियरिंग कॉलेज की वह मिस शबनम ख़ान ही सच थी। वह सब झूठा...ओढ़ा हुआ नहीं था बल्कि उसका भीतरी सच्चा रूप भी वही है। वह तो बस इस्तेमाल हुआ। पहले उसकी पढ़ाई की कठिनाइयों को हल करने...फिर उसकी बीमारी—मेंटल ब्लॉक को दूर करने...फिर ताज़िन्दगी उसके हर हुक्म की तामील बजानेवाले बिना रीढ़ के ख़ाविन्द के रूप में...इस्तेमाल। बस इस्तेमाल ही इस्तेमाल।

कोई दूसरी उसके ज़रख़रीद ग़ुलाम पर नज़र क्यों डाले? उसके साथ बराबरी-दोस्ती की हैसियत से बातें करके उसे ग़ुलामी का एहसास क्यों कराए? क्यों उसकी अदृश्य ज़ंजीरों की खनखनाहट उसके कानों के पास जाकर सुनाए? दरअसल स्वामिनी के ग़ुस्से का कारण यही है।

वह प्रेम...यह ब्याह सब झूठा है।...एक दिखावा...एक सोची-समझी प्लानिंग का हिस्सा। उसकी हैसियत शतरंज की बिछी बिसात पर एक पैदल सैनिक भर की थी जिसे शब्बो जब चाहे इस-उस खाने में पटकती आ रही थी।

बिडम्बना यह भी है कि उल्टे मुझ पर ही सौ-सौ आरोप लगाकर चली गई। क्या तो वह ही मेरे भोलेपन से धोखा खा गई...क्या बात है!!! जबकि मैं भेड़िया हूँ...मैं भेड़िया...साधन-संगिनियों की टोह में घूमनेवाला भेड़िया। मेरे चरित्र की धज्जियाँ उड़ा दीं...।

...मेरे...बुलबुल के बाबा के चरित्र पर शक किया। उसे क्या मालूम जिस बाप के मन में बेटियाँ बसी हों वहाँ दूसरे की छवि नहीं समा सकती। जवान होती बेटी अपने बाबा के पैरों का सौ-सौ बंधन होती है। उसे फिसलन से बचाने वाला ठोस-मज़बूत स्पीड ब्रेकर।...अब लगता है कि वह ख़ुद तो कभी मेरे 'मैं' में समा नहीं सकी अब बुलबुल को भी मुझसे दूर करना चाह रही है। सत्रह-अठारह साल साथ रहने के बाद भी जो पराई रही वह मेरी बुलबुल, मेरे दिल के टुकड़े...मन के एक हिस्से को भी ज़बरन पराया करना चाह रही है।...इससे बड़ा अत्याचार और कुछ नहीं हो सकता।

लेकिन बुलबुल बेटी भी शायद बदल गई...कितनी उम्मीद से दरवाज़े की तरफ़ निहारता रहता था कमोल दा।...और कोई आए न आए बुलबुल तो अपने बाबा के पास आएगी ही। ...नहीं ही आई।...भीषोण निष्ठुर। मेरे कन्धे-गोद में खेल कर बड़ी हुई...मेरे हृदय का हिस्सा...अपनी मम्मा का स्वभाव कैसे पा लिया? माना मम्मा ने मना किया होगा। लेकिन कौन-सा मम्मा ने चौबीसों घंटे का पहरा लगा रखा होगा? और मम्मा भी घर में... इस शहर में तीन सौ पैंसठ दिन बैठी थोड़े रहती है।...मना ही किया... लेकिन उसका अपना मन भी तो है। उसका मन नहीं किया कि चलें बाबा से मिल आएँ। झगड़ा बाबा-मम्मा का न कि बाबा-बेटी का। बाबा से बेटी कैसे अलगाई जा सकती है? ज़रूर रिश्वत दी होगी...ख़ूब महँगी-महँगी ड्रेस, नये-नये गैजेट। टैब, मोबाइल सब। फेसबुक, व्हाट्सएप,...ऑन लाइन गेम्स।...ये सब पहले से उसकी कमज़ोरी। कितनी-कितनी डाँट तो मुझसे सुनती थी। तुरन्त मुँह लटक जाता था। फिर मुझे ही मनाना पड़ता... माफ़ी माँगनी पड़ती।...आ तो जाती...यहीं बैठकर गेम खेलती रहती...मैं मना थोड़े करता...। गला रुँध गया था कमोल दा का। फिर जो ख़ामोशी हमारे बीच पसरी वह भीगी रात के साथ गहरी होती गई।

एक शाम कमोल के कमरे में पहुँचा तो वह बाथरूम में था। कुछ पढ़ने के लिए यूँ ही टेबुल पर उलट-पुलट रहा था कि उसकी डायरी दिख

गई...खुली हुई ही थी...शायद अभी...कुछ पल पहले तक लिख रहा हो। कुछ पन्ने पलटते ही शॉक्ड रह गया। कवितानुमा हर बात...पन्नों पर उकेरी हर बड़बड़ाहट ज़िन्दगी से दूर जा रही थी।...शायद सो नहीं पा रहा था... नींद आनी बन्द हो गई थी...'नींद उल्लुओं की आँखों की पुतलियाँ हो गई हैं...पलकें रात भर नहीं झपकतीं।...यादों की टहनी पर उल्टी लटकी नींद, बेताल-सी न जाने किसका इन्तज़ार करती रहती है।'

'...अनपढ़ चाँदनी कैसे पढ़े दिल की अँधेरी दीवारों पर लिखी रंजोग़म की इबारतें। प्रेम कविताओं की मोटी किताब में दबी तितली की आख़िरी हिचकी की अजानी-अजन्मी भाषा का अनुवाद भला कैसे हो?'

'...कल्पवृक्ष के फूलों-सी देह-ख़ुशबू, अनझिप पलकों के बीच तैरती आकाशगंगा, चुम्बन गुम्फित चुम्बकीय क्षण, रति की कुछ छिटपुट स्मृतियाँ... दूर धुँधलके में।...नीचे आकाश, ऊपर धरती...डोलते दो पर्वत शिखर... अचानक झरते झरने।...नहीं कुछ भी अविस्मृत न रहे...सब भुलाना... कपूर-सा हवा में गुमाना चाहता हूँ...। ये अविस्मृत क्षण...पुच्छल तारे-से कौंधते...रेंगनी के काँटे-से चुभते रहते हैं।...रति-स्मृतियाँ मैल-सी मेरी आत्मा पर पसरी हुई हैं। आत्मा को छींटकर सारे मैल धोना चाहता हूँ।'

'...लोगबाग जो चुल्लू भर पानी में डूब मरने की बातें करते हैं... दरअसल वह पानी नहीं, शार्मिन्दगी है जिसका चुल्लू भर होना काफी है मौत को गले लगाने के लिए। सच कहें तो यह हमारी कमीनगी है जो लम्बी आयु की कामना किया करती है। बस झूठी दिलासा-आशा...झाँसा दे देकर एक-एक दिन काटने की कोशिशें...कि घने अँधकार के बाद उजाला आएगा...कि हर अँधेरी रात के बाद चमकती प्रातः तो आएगी...कि हर पतझड़ का अपना एक बसंत होता है...झूठ है सब। न कोई उजाला...न कोई सुनहरी सुबह...न कोई बसंत...नहीं कोई मेरी प्रतीक्षा नहीं कर रहा।... कम-से-कम मुझे अब इन लिजलिजे इन्तज़ार के बहानों से जीने के लिए विवश तो नहीं किया जा सकता।'

मेरी तो जैसे साँसें अटक गईं। थोड़ी देर के लिए तो कुछ समझ में नहीं आया क्या करूँ?...साफ़-साफ़ स्यूसाइडल टेंडेन्सी...ये कविताएँ थीं कि स्यूसाइड नोट्स...। एकदम भागा...सीधे अब्बू के पास। सब सुनने-समझने के बाद उनकी भी आँखें डबडबा गईं। अपने किसी साइकेट्रिस्ट

दोस्त अहमद साहब को फ़ोन लगाया। समय लिया। दोपहर बाद ख़ुद लेकर गए। मैंने भी उस दिन छुट्टी ली और साथ गया। दरअसल मैं और अब्बू दोनों बेहद डरे हुए थे। डॉक्टर अंकल से मिलने के पहले तक तो हमारी हालत ख़राब थी। अंकल की मुस्कुराहट, चैम्बर में फैली रजनीगन्धा की ख़ुशबू और हौले-हौले गूँजती पंडित पन्ना लाल घोष की बाँसुरी की तान ने आधे तनाव ख़त्म कर दिये। बाकी तनाव फूल से झरते उनके प्रश्नों की फुहार ने फूँक मार कर उड़ा दिया। कमोल दा ने भी धीरे-धीरे अपना मन खोला। डॉक्टर ने कुछ दवाएँ लिखीं। कुछ सुझाव दिए। ख़ूब प्यार-पुचकार के बाद कमोल दा को गाड़ी में भेज कुछ ख़ास हिदायतें हमें दीं। हालात ठीक नहीं हैं...कम-से-कम साल-भर दवा खानी होगी। उससे ज़्यादा ज़रूरी है कि तुम अपने भोर वाले रियाज़...इबादत... रूहानी नाच में इसे धीरे-धीरे शामिल करो। भाईजान! कभी तुमने ही तो मेरी से राग शिवरंजनी, राग विहाग, मधुवन्ती, राग भैरवी और सोहनी से भेंट करवाई थी। सचमुच उदासी-डिप्रेशन में राग शिवरंजनी, विहाग और मधुवन्ती बहुत लाभकारी हैं और अनिद्रा दूर भगाने में राग भैरवी और सोहनी का तो जवाब नहीं। दवा से ज़्यादा असर उनका ही होगा...डॉक्टर अंकल अब्बू से मुख़ातिब थे। मेरे लिए उनकी सलाह थी कि तुम कुछ दिनों के लिए अपनी मिसेज के साथ आश्रम में ही शिफ़्ट कर जाओ। दवा का समय पर खाना और बिना नागा खाना बहुत ज़रूरी है। दवाओं से नींद तो आएगी फिर भी रात में एक-दो बार यह चेक करना है कि वह सोया है कि नहीं...उठकर कहीं भटक तो नहीं रहा...। बस पहले एक महीना ठीक से दवाएँ खाए और ख़ूब नींद-भर सोये तो डरनेवाली कोई बात नहीं रहेगी।

डॉक्टर अंकल की एक-एक बात का हमने ख़याल रखा। मैं और श्रावणी बच्चों के साथ आश्रम में शिफ़्ट हो गए। ठीक कमोल दा के बगल वाले कमरे में। रात में एक-दो बार जागकर ज़रूर झाँक आता। दवा समय पर खिलाने की ज़िम्मेवारी श्रावणी के ज़िम्मे। अब्बू रोज़ ख़ूब भोर में साढ़े तीन-पौने चार तक जगाकर अपने साथ ले जाने आते। कभी सचमुच की नींद...कभी झूठमूठ की नींद के बहाने कर कमोल दा, अब्बू के संग रूहानी नाच से बचने की कोशिश कर रहा था।

उस अलस्सुबह साढ़े तीन बजे अब्बू की कातर पुकार ने ही मुझे जगाया। कमोल अपने बिछावन पर नहीं है और उसकी स्कूटी भी नहीं दिख रही। बिना ज़्यादा वक़्त गँवाए श्रावणी ने कार निकाली। मिनटों में हम सड़क पर, किन्तु जाएँ किधर? चौराहे के चारों ओर सन्नाटा था। तभी मुझे याद आया कि सपने में ट्रक के नीचे स्कूटी के साथ घिसटते चले जाने की बात एक बार कही थी कमोल दा ने। हम सीधे बाईपास की ओर बढ़ चले। थोड़ी देर बाद ही वह सत्तर-अस्सी की स्पीड में स्कूटी उड़ाता दिखा। बाईपास कुछ सौ मीटर पर ही रह गया था जहाँ से साँय-साँय करता ट्रकों का काफिला सड़क को रौंदता आँधी की तरह भागता दिख रहा था। श्रावणी ने भी सौ-एक सौ बीस की स्पीड पकड़ ली कि बाईपास में घुसने के पहले ही हर हाल में रोकना है। तभी न जाने क्या हुआ कमोल दा ने किनारे कर स्कूटी रोक ली। मोबाइल पर किसी से बातें करने लगा। जान में जान आई। कार रोककर दौड़कर उस तक पहुँचे...शिउड़ी-वीरभूम से माँ थीं...विस्तार से हालचाल पूछती...आँखों से आँसू बरसाता कमोल दा बस हाँ-हूँ किए जा रहा था।

32

ये ग़मो-निशात की बहस क्या,
कभी देख आके फ़िराक़ को,
उसी ज़िन्दगी की तुझे क़सम,
कि जो दर्द भी है, दवा भी है

—फ़िराक़ गोरखपुरी

डॉक्टर अंकल ने दवाइयों का डोज़ बढ़ा दिया। अब नींद ही नींद थी, पलकों-पुतलियों पर क़ाबिज़, कमोल दा के रोम-रोम में पैवस्त। वह चौबीस घंटों में पन्द्रह-सोलह घंटे सोया रहता, एक नवजात शिशु सा। एक तरह से तो नवजात ही था। इस बार माँ ने नहीं माँ के फ़ोन कॉल ने नया जन्म दिया। उस रात घबड़ाहट में अब्बू ने अपने संगी...अपने समधी...बाबा मदन बाउल को फ़ोन लगाया। माँ बिना ज़्यादा पूछपाछ किए सब कुछ समझ गईं और तुरन्त अपने छेले को टेरा। पुकार सुनते स्कूटी रुक गई और अनहोनी टल गई। नया जन्म...नवजात...कमोल दा सारी दुश्चिन्ताओं से मुक्त अपनी मासूमियत में डूबा...कभी नींद में ही काँपता...कभी मुस्कुराता बेफ़िक्र सोया रहता। किन्तु ख़बर सुन दौड़ी-भागी आईं अम्मू-माँ-बुलबुल और मदन बाबा-अब्बू...हम सबकी हँसी गुम थी। डबडबायी आँखें कमोल दा को ताकती रहतीं।

लेकिन जितनी देर वह जगा रहता कोशिश यह रहती कि माहौल एकदम ख़ुशनुमा रहे। गप्पें...चुटकुले...हँसी...ठहाके...कभी-कभी धौल-धप्पे भी। चार्ली चैप्लिन-किशोर कुमार-हृषिकेश मुखर्जी की कॉमेडी फिल्में और चाँद-चाँदनी सी भरी पुरानी यादें बार-बार दुहराई जा रही थीं, किसी गान के मुखड़े की तरह। किसी ने न कुछ पूछा न जानने की कोशिश की। कमोल दा की भावुक माँ और भोली बुलबुल ने भी नहीं। क्यों मुरझा रहे घाव की पपड़ी उखाड़ना...फिर से वह ताज़ा होगा...ख़ून रिसेगा...दर्द छिलकेगा...तकलीफ़ सबको होगी। सब अतीत हो जाए...राख बन उड़ जाए...चेतन-अवचेतन सब रोशन हो...दुख-चिन्ता-अवसाद की छाया भी शेष न रहे...सबकी यही दुआ—यही कोशिश...डॉक्टर अंकल से लेकर बुलबुल तक की।

कमोल दा की बीमारी ने हमारी ज़िम्मेवारी बढ़ा दी थी। आश्रम की सारी गतिविधियाँ मेरे कन्धों पर और कोचिंग श्रावणी के। वह जिस कॉलेज में कॉन्ट्रैक्चुअल लेक्चरर थी वहाँ हर चार माह बाद दो-तीन माह के लिए घर पर बैठना होता था। ख़ैरियत यह कि उस वक़्त श्रावणी का वही ऑफ पीरियड शुरू ही होनेवाला था सो विशेष परेशानी नहीं हुई।

धीरे-धीरे सब पटरी पर आने लगा था। सिवाय शब्बो भाभी के। उन्हें अभी तक यहाँ आकर झाँकने तक की फ़ुर्सत नहीं मिली थी। कभी अम्मू-कभी बुलबुल उनकी व्यस्तताओं की फ़ेहरिस्त सुनाती रहतीं। आज यहाँ... कल वहाँ...देश...विदेश...'सिस्टरहुड' के प्रोग्राम्स...रातें फ्लाइट्स में ही कट रही थीं। झुकी हुई नज़रें...दबी-दबी आवाज़ें कितना समझातीं...किन्हें समझाती? केवल माँ होने...बेटी होने का धर्म निभा रही थीं। उनके अलावा सभी के मन में यह सवाल कौंधता रहता कि अगर कमोल दा को कुछ हो-हवा जाता...तब भी वे ऐसे ही लन्दन-पेरिस उड़ती फिरतीं या झाँकने आतीं...तो फिर अभी क्यों नहीं? इस अनकहे सवाल का जवाब किसी के पास नहीं था। शायद शब्बो भाभी या उनके 'सिस्टरहुड' के मार्केटिंग कन्सल्टेंट के पास हो।

उधर अख़बार और चैनल्स सुआर्यन और कच्छप रक्षक सेना के नित नवीन कारनामों से सनसना रहे थे। सनसनाहट भरी रिपोर्टिंग्स इनकी दिन दुगनी और रात चौगुनी गतिशीलता का प्रशस्तिगान करती लगतीं। बरसों-

बरस की मेहनत से माहौल बदला हुआ था। इतिहास में दर्ज हो चुकी रात के अँधेरों में नहीं बीच दोपहर में इनके जुलूस निकलते। अख़बारों और चैनल्स में दमकनेवाले सारे चमकीले चेहरे उनकी अगुवाई करते। प्रतिष्ठित पत्रकार, विचारक, जगमगाते कविगण, प्रकांड आलोचक, रिटायर्ड नौकरशाह, रिटायर्ड न्यायाधीश...माननीय मंत्री...उद्योगपति... विद्वान किसी को अब झिझक नहीं थी। सबके सब बजरंग बिहारी गुप्ता के साथ कदम से कदम मिलाते...दाहिने गाल पर टैटू चमकाते गौरवान्वित महसूस कर रहे थे।

बीच-बीच में स्पेशल टास्क फोर्स और सी.बी.आई. नींद से जागती। दो-चार गिरफ़्तारियाँ होतीं। उनके इन्टेरॅगेशन की ख़बरें चार-छह दिन छाई रहतीं। लगता कि सारा रहस्य इस बार खुलने ही वाला है। फिर महीने-दो महीने के लिए सब शान्त हो जाता। इस बार फिर से एक नई ख़बर दसों दिशाओं को गुँजायमान कर रही थी कि सी.बी.आई. न जाने किस प्राधिकार से न जाने कौन-सा एक ख़ास अधिकार चाह रही है ताकि मांजरेकर साहब और नानू की हत्या में इस्तेमाल हुए हथियार को न जाने किस समुद्र के किस हिस्से में गोताख़ोरों की सहायता से तलाश सके। दो-चार दिनों तक यह ख़बर हेड लाइन बनी रही। फिर गोताख़ोरों के साथ गुड़ुप हो गई।

यहाँ बड़ो नानू उस्ताद महताबुद्दीन ख़ान संगीत आश्रम में बच्चों की खिलखिलाहट, चिड़ियों की चहचहाट और तितलियों की फूलों के साथ आँखमिचौली बदलते मौसम की अगवाई कर रही थीं। अब्बू की भोर वाले रियाज़ और रूहानी नाच में कमोल दा ख़ुद ही शामिल होने लगा था। राग शिवरंजनी-विहाग-मधुवन्ती तो सोने में सुगंध की तरह उसके वजूद पर छाये जा रही थीं। दादा की अनिद्रा-चिन्ता-अवसाद मिट्टी की सूखी पपड़ी की तरह झरते जा रहे थे। किन्तु कोचिंग को सँभालने में ख़ब्तुल-हवास हुई श्रावणी के तनाव का ग्राफ़ बढ़ता जा रहा था। उसका मानना था कि पेरेंट्स मीट के दिनों में बच्चों के अभिभावकों के साथ शहर के बिल्डर्स भी आश्रम का चक्कर लगाया करते हैं। इस बार तो अपने अपार्टमेंट के बिल्डर चौधरी जी पर नज़र पड़ी। पूछने पर घबड़ा गए और किसी भतीजे के बारे में बताने लगे कि यहीं कोचिंग करता है। उसी के पापा के साथ आए हैं। किन्तु उस भतीजे का नाम और सेक्शन नहीं बता पाये। हाल ही

में कुछ सीनियर बच्चों ने तो कॉलेज से लौटते वक़्त बिल्डर्स लेन के पास गुप्ता जी की कार में मिसेज मयंक...वैभवी मैडम को भी देखा था।

लेकिन आश्रम में हमारे अलावा किसी और को इन बातों की चिन्ता नहीं थी। अम्मू-अब्बू-बाबा सभी अभी केवल और केवल कमोल दा के बारे में सोचना चाह रहे थे। बाबा मदन बाउल न जाने कब कमोल से इतना बतियाये हों। हो सकता है जब बहुत छोटा हो।...गोद में खेलता हो...तब दुलराते-बतियाते रहे हों। होश सँभालते तो भालो कमोल ने केवल और केवल उनके आदेश ही सुने थे। लेकिन अब...हमेशा बतियाने के मूड में रहते।...बातें...कुछ आपबीती...कुछ जगबीती...कुछ बाउल दर्शन...कुछ स्व दर्शन।

बाबा कमोल दा को समझाते रहते कि अच्छा और बुरा का भाव मन में नहीं रखना चाहिए। अच्छा और बुरा कुछ नहीं होता। वे घटनाएँ होती हैं जो अच्छी-बुरी होती हैं। हर व्यक्ति के जीवन में दुख आता है। लेकिन इसके बहाने हम सबको ज़िन्दगी के ज़रूरी पाठ सीखने चाहिए। उसे गाँठ में बाँध अनावश्यक चिन्ता-तनाव के दुष्चक्र में नहीं फँसना चाहिए। अपने इस छोटे से दुख से उबरो खोका! नज़र उठाकर देखो...तुम्हारे आस-पास... देश में...बाहर हज़ारों-लाखों लोग आधी रोटी खाकर बस ज़िन्दगी किसी तरह जीने भर के लिए रात-दिन ज़द्दोजहद कर रहे हैं। फिर भी ज़िन्दगी उनके हाथों रेत की माफ़िक़ फिसली जा रही है। उनके दुखों को अपना बना कर देखो। उनके हिस्से की रोटी...उनके हिस्से की धरती और आसमान... उनकी साँसें आख़िर कौन चुरा रहा है...उसकी तफ़्तीश करो...डूबो। देखो खोका! कैसे दिन आए हैं कि किसी को भी कहीं भी घेरकर मार दिया जाता है...कहीं कोई ख़ून का निशान नहीं...कहीं कोई चिह्न नहीं...कहीं कोई हत्यारा नहीं...मानो वे हवा से आए थे और हवा बन गए। वे बुदबुदे थे मिट्टी के और मिट्टी बन गए। मानो वे पोंछ दिए गए हों धरती से... जैसे तुम्हारे नानू जैसे मांजरेकर साहब जैसे...। अपना 'स्व', अपना 'अहम्' उस पर पड़ी खरोंच को भूलकर आगे तो बढ़ो। यह तुम्हारा नन्हा सा दुख, यह कुहरे-सा अवसाद इसे ग़ायब होते देर नहीं लगेगी।

बाबा की बातें राग शिवरंजनी से कम असरदार नहीं थीं। लेकिन माँ को इन गहरी बातों से बहुत मतलब नहीं था। वह बस अपने कमोल को

दुलारते रहना चाहती थीं। उसके बड़े-बड़े घुँघराले बालों में रच-रच कर तेल लगा कंघी करती रहतीं। कभी-कभी भोर की मीठी धूप में लिटा कर पूरी देह में मालिश किया करतीं। बुलबुल ने भी बड़ी ज़िम्मेदारी सँभाल ली थी। समय पर अपने बाबा को दवा खिलाने, उन्हें सँभालने की ज़िम्मेदारी। रात में भी अपने बाबा को पकड़कर सोती। बाबा फिर कहीं...।

उस सुरमई सुन्दर शाम अम्मू सूरदास का भ्रमरगीत गुनगुनातीं कमोल को स्त्री मन का रहस्य समझा रही थीं।...उधौ मन नाहीं दस-बीस...। मन तो दस-बीस है नहीं, अब जिसने अपने इकलौते मन को तुम्हारे हवाले कर दिया वह प्रतिदान में तुम्हारा पूरा का पूरा मन चाहेगा। मन कोई मन्दिर का प्रसाद...गुरुद्वारे का भोग नहीं कि मिल-बाँटकर खाया जाए। स्त्री को अपने माशूक़ का पूरा का पूरा मन चाहिए होता है। तनिक भी बाँट-बँटवारा नहीं...। जो तुझे जितनी शिद्दत से चाहेगी...वह उतनी ही शिद्दत से तुम्हें चारों ओर से घेरकर रखना चाहेगी। हालाँकि सोचिए तो यह सही नहीं है। हरएक को अपना स्पेस चाहिए...ख़ुद की ख़ास जगह...जहाँ वह खुलकर साँसें ले सके...लेकिन न चाहते हुए भी सच यही है कि स्त्री मोनोपोली चाहती है और पुरुष...वह तो पैदाइशी फ्यूडल...स्त्री को अपनी प्रॉपर्टी समझनेवाला मालिक-भगवान।

हम स्त्रियों ने अपनी मुहब्बत...अपने माशूक़ पर अपना पूरा हक़-पूरा हक़ूक़ बनाए रखने की चाहत में भ्रमरगीत की गोपियों के समय से ही बहुत सारे इल्म...बहुत सारी करामातें विकसित की हैं। हम अपने कृष्ण की कुब्जा को सौ कोस दूर से भी सूँघ लेती हैं और लानत-मलामत की कोई हद नहीं छोड़तीं...यही सच है...हम स्त्रियों की जेनटिक कमज़ोरी...।

...लेकिन लानत-मलामत का डोज़ भी माशूक़ की बेवफ़ाई की हिसाब से कम-ज़्यादा तो होगा।...शब्बो का रिएक्शन...एकदम अतिरेक-एक्स्ट्रीम था।...अम्मू का मोनोलॉग...कमोल दा को समझाते-समझाते ख़ुद को समझाने लगा था। कहाँ भ्रमरगीत-गोपियाँ-कृष्ण और कुब्जा। वह सब भूल बस कमोल की अम्मू बन सोचने और बड़बड़ाने लगी थीं...नहीं करनी चाहिए था इतनी बेइज़्ज़ती...अपने कमोल की...भालो कमोल की...जिसने एक तरह से उसकी मौसीक़ी को दूसरा जन्म दिया...।...एक तरह से उसे ही नई ज़िन्दगी दी...उस पर लांछन लगाते...चिल्लाते एक बार भी उसकी रूह

नहीं काँपी...ज़ुबान नहीं लड़खड़ाई।...न यह मेरी बेटी शब्बो नहीं है... यह कोई और है...म्यूज़िक मार्केट की सुपर स्टार विदुषी शबनम...। इस स्टार, सुपर स्टार को मेरे संस्कारों और मेरे बेटे कमोल की बेइज़्ज़ती करने का हक़ नहीं...।...कोई हक़ नहीं...बड़बड़ाती अम्मू...धीरे-धीरे मौन हो गईं। तभी सन्नाटे से घबड़ाकर बुलबुल ने टी.वी. ऑन कर दिया। म्यूज़िक चैनल पर 'सिस्टरहुड' की सिस्टर्स जलवा अफ़रोज़ थीं। फ्यूज़न म्यूज़िक पर विदुषी शबनम के टप्पे गा रही थीं।

33

पत्थर डूबे तो आवाज़ होती है
आज आदमी इस दुनिया में
बेआवाज़ डूब जाता है

—अरुण कमल

ज़ोर-ज़ोर से किवाड़ की सांकल बजने से नींद खुली। अभी तो खिड़की के बाहर अँधेरा ही था। मोबाइल में देखा तो सबेरे के पौने चार बजे थे। अब इतने सबेरे...क्या हो गया? फिर मन धड़का...क्या कमोल दा...फिर से...। जल्दी से सिटकनी खोली सामने गार्ड खड़ा था। थोड़ी-सी झल्लाहट हुई। मालूम हुआ कालिन्दी मैडम आई हैं। साथ में एक और मोहतरमा हैं बुर्के में। दोनों अब्बू से मिलना चाह रही हैं। कमोल दा मिले नहीं। कमरा बाहर से बन्द था। सो मुझे उठाना पड़ा।

अभी तो अब्बू, बाबा, अम्मू, कमोल दा सभी रियाज़ में डूबे होंगे। उसमें ख़लल डालना मुनासिब नहीं था। थोड़ा इन्तज़ार करने की ग़रज़ से मैंने चाय-कॉफ़ी की पेशकश की किन्तु उन दोनों को पौ फटने से पहले लौटना था। मन मार कर अब्बू के रियाज़तगाह में गया। कालिन्दी का नाम सुनते अम्मू और कमोल दा का चेहरा उतर गया। बुलबुल तमतमाने लगी। लेकिन अब्बू और बाबा शान्त रहे और उनकी निगाहें ख़ैरमक़्दम को तैयार लगीं।

दोनों बहुत हड़बड़ी में थीं। बातचीत शुरू हुई। मालूम हुआ बुर्क़े वाली मोहतरमा नीलोफ़र परवीन भी कालिन्दी मैडम के साथ ही बैंक में काम करती हैं। बमुश्किल बीस-पच्चीस मिनट वे रुकी होंगी। लेकिन इतनी जानकारियाँ, इतनी सूचनाएँ कि उन्हें समझने-महसूसने में हमें घंटों लगनेवाले थे। वैसे भी मयंक के जाने और कमोल दा की तबियत ख़राब रहने के कारण सोशल मीडिया की गतिविधियों से हम कट से गए थे। हाँ! बिल्डरों के आश्रम में आमदोरफ़्त और शहर में वैभवी मैडम की मौजूदगी से हम वाकिफ़ थे किन्तु मामला इतना गम्भीर होगा इसका अन्दाज़ा नहीं था।

आँधी बनकर आईं और तूफ़ान-सी लौटीं दोनों मैडम की बातों का लब्बोलुआब यही था कि बड़ो नानू महताबुद्दीन ख़ान के घराने पर लगा ग्रहण अभी और गहरानेवाला है। शहर में न केवल वैभवी मैम बल्कि उनके डैडी भी लम्बे समय तक मौजूद रहे थे। 'मौसीक़ी-मंज़िल' की आर्किटेक्चरल डिज़ाइन और आश्रम का नदी किनारे का खेल मैदान उन्हें हिसाब से ज़्यादा भा गया था। कुछ-कुछ पहली नज़र वाली मुहब्बत जैसा मामला, यह तो पता था। मयंक ने पहले भी बताया था। किन्तु हर हाल में हासिल करने की ज़िद थी और इसके लिए शतरंज की बिसात बिछाई गई थी। यह नई जानकारी थी। रियल-एस्टेट टाइकून डैडी साहब के वकीलों ने बड़ी मेहनत से यह ख़बर निकाली थी कि 'मौसीक़ी-मंज़िल' की ज़मीन बड़ो नानू को दान में मिली थी। इस रियासत के राजा साहब जन्नतनशीं जूदेव जी ने तब गुरुदक्षिणा में दी थी। इस ख़बर के बाद डैडी साहब कई-कई मोर्चों पर एक साथ सक्रिय हुए थे। रेवन्यू मिनिस्टर को समझाया गया कि राजा साहब की सीलिंग से ज़्यादा ज़मीन में 'मौसीक़ी-मंज़िल' की ज़मीन को दिखला कर उसे क़ब्ज़े में ले लिया जाए। अभी मिनिस्टर साहब बात ठीक से समझे भी नहीं थे कि दूसरी माँग पेश कर दी गई कि नदी के किनारे ग्रीन एरिया वाली ज़मीन और आश्रम के खेल मैदान की लगभग दस एकड़ ज़मीन निन्यानवे वर्ष की लीज पर दी जाए ताकि एक फाइव स्टार होटल खड़ा किया जा सके। मंत्री महोदय को इसके बदले बेंगलुरू के पॉश एरिया में एक फ्लैट और होटल बिजनेस में बीस प्रतिशत की पार्टनरशिप का ऑफर दिया गया था। अपने ऑफर्स को डैडी जी ओवर एस्टीमेट कर रहे थे और ओवर कॉन्फ़िडेन्ट हो यह मानकर चल

रहे थे कि मिनिस्टर साहब के लिए ना बोलने का कोई मौक़ा ही नहीं था। किन्तु जिस ख़ानदान में दो-दो पद्म विभूषण हों, अन्तरराष्ट्रीय ख्याति के कई-कई मौसीक़ीकार हों, वक़्त पड़ने पर राज्यपाल-राष्ट्रपति आवास तक जो पहुँच सकते हों, उनकी प्रॉपर्टी में हाथ लगाना मंत्री महोदय को कुछ अच्छा नहीं लग रहा था। कोई नये पॉलिटिशियन तो थे नहीं। बिज़नेस और राजनीति में ही बाल सफ़ेद किए थे। उन्हें ख़ूब मालूम था कि ऐसे-ऐसे टाइकून आते-जाते रहेंगे लेकिन उन्हें तो राजनीति यहीं इसी मिट्टी में करनी है। लेकिन...फिर भी...अब सीधे-सीधे ना कह दें तो राजनीतिज्ञ किस बात के? लेकिन डैडी साहब भाँप गए कि दाल यहाँ गलनेवाली नहीं। किन्तु वे भी हार माननेवालों में से नहीं थे। वकीलों की एक टीम राजा साहब के वारिस को ढूँढ़ने कोलकाता की ओर निकल गई। इधर डैडी साहब ने टूरिज्म मिनिस्टर को अपने शीशे में उतारने की कोशिश में लग गए। बड़े-बड़े सब्ज़बाग़ दिखाए गए। होटल बिजनेस की पार्टनरशिप बीस से तीस प्रतिशत कर दी गई। बेंगलुरू में एक के बदले तीन फ्लैट्स। लेकिन यहाँ भी वही टालमटोल का रवैया।

डैडी साहब के लिए राहत की बात थी कि सुआर्यन सेना और बी.बी. गुप्ता हर क़दम पर उनके साथ थे। उनके सपनों को ज़मीन पर उतारने को कटिबद्ध। इस बार डैडी साहब ने भी ख़ूब दिल खोलकर डोनेशन्स दिए। नतीजन दुगुने जोश के साथ फिर से सुआर्यन-ट्रोल्स सोशल मीडिया पर एक्टिव हो गए थे। पुराने आरोप नये-नये पैकेज में ज़्यादा घृणा, ज़्यादा ज़हर के साथ परोसे जा रहे थे। वही मुसलमान गायकों के हिन्दू नाम, उनकी भजन गायकी, अब्बू का गेरुआ बाना फिर से टार्गेट थे। ट्विटर, व्हाट्सएप, फेसबुक, इन्सटाग्राम फिर से बजबजाने लगे। लेकिन इस बार मामला सुआर्यन तक नहीं थमा था। वैभवी मैडम ने दीनदारी की नुमाइश करनेवाली चन्द इस्लामी अंजुमनों-तंजीमों तक डोनेशन्स के मोटे-मोटे लिफ़ाफ़े भिजवाये थे। नतीजन मुकम्मल मौसीक़ी के ही ख़िलाफ़ शरीअत का वास्ता दे-देकर वहाँ से जंग के बिगुल फूँके जा रहे थे। ख़ासकर यही सब बताने नीलोफ़र मैम पधारी थीं। उनके मोबाइल में देवर के व्हाट्सएप से फॉरवर्डेड मैसेज थे, वे भी इस घराने के बारे में उतने ही ज़हरीले-ज़हरआमेज़ जितने सुआर्यन के। हाँ! अन्दाज़े बयाँ अलग था।

नीलोफ़र मैम की डबडबाई आँखें और भर्राई आवाज़ यह बतलाने की कोशिश कर रही थी कि हालात ने उन जैसों को ऐसे मुकाम पर पहुँचा दिया है जिसके एक ओर कुआँ तो दूसरी ओर खाई है, "एक तरफ़ अजब तरह का माहौल बनाने की कोशिश की जा रही है जहाँ हमारा वजूद ही गुनाह मान लिया गया है। हमारे घर बच्चा जन्म ले तो भी वह गुनाह क्योंकि इससे देश का जनसंख्या-संतुलन गड़बड़ा रहा है। अगर वह पढ़-लिखकर समझदारी की बातें करने लगे, कुछ अलग हट कर बोले-लिखे तो वह अलगाववादी। हमारा खाना-पीना तो पहले से ही गुनाह घोषित है क्योंकि हम हमेशा, तीनों वक़्त कच्छप महाराज का बड़ा गोश्त ही तो खाते हैं। हमारा निकाह भी सामाजिक बुराई क्योंकि वह तीन तलाक़ में बदलेगा ही बदलेगा और ऊपर से हलाला जैसी गन्दगी...। हमारा मरना भी एक क़ुसूर क्योंकि हमें दफ़नाने में देश की बेशक़ीमती ज़मीन बरबाद हो रही।

"दूसरी ओर हमारे लोग ज़्यादा ही दीनी...ज़्यादा ही मज़हबी बनने की कोशिश में लगे हैं। बात-बात पर शरीअत का वास्ता दिया जा रहा है। दीन के नाम पर हिन्दुस्तानी तहज़ीब, रस्मो-रिवाज को छोड़ने का दबाव बनाया जा रहा। शादी-ब्याह की पुरानी रस्में, गाना-बजाना, नौशे का परिछन...सब धीरे-धीरे बन्द होता जा रहा है। हमारी पूरी कोशिश रहती है कि ईद-बक़रीद पर सब हमारे घर पर आएँ, गले मिलें, मुबारकबाद दें। लेकिन हम होली तो छोड़िए, दीवाली में भी उन दोस्तों के घर जाना टालने लगे हैं कि दीन के ठेकेदार क्या कहेंगे? ज़्यादा मन हुआ तो फेसबुक पर किन्हीं अज़ीमुश्शान शायर की होली-दीवाली की नज़्म डाल दी। हो गई फॉर्मेलिटी पूरी।

"आजकल हमारे लड़कों को थोड़ी ज़्यादा ही फ़िक्र हो रही है कि शबनम ने अपने नाम से 'ख़ान' क्यों हटाया? अम्मू का नाम रागेश्वरी देवी क्यों है? अब्बू गेरुआ बाना क्यों पहनते हैं? कमोल ने शबनम से निकाह पढ़ा था कि शादी की थी? अगर निकाह पढ़ा था तो ख़ुद दीन के साये में आया कि नहीं आया? यही बातें सोशल मीडिया, उर्दू अख़बारों के एडिटोरियल्स, चौक-चौराहे से लेकर दस्तरख़्वान तक गूँज रही हैं। अब अल्लाह ही जाने कि आगे क्या हो। वैभवी मैम ने शतरंज की बिसात पर न जाने क्या चालें तय की हैं। यह तो वही जानें और उनके डैडी साहब

जानें। हमारी तो यही इल्तिजा है कि आप लोग थोड़ी सावधानी बरतें। अब्बू साहब घूमना-फिरना थोड़े दिनों के लिए बन्द कर दें तो बेहतर। मन्दिर और मस्ज़िद की ओर आने की तो सोचें भी नहीं।"

नीलोफ़र मैम चुप हुईं तो कालिन्दी मैडम शुरू हुईं। इस बार वे अम्मू की ओर मुख़ातिब थीं। उनकी गुज़ारिश थी कि शब्बो भाभी को यह ख़बर दी जाए कि प्रोग्राम्स के बाद इन्टरव्यू देने से बचें। उनका ग़ुस्सा उनकी सबसे बड़ी कमज़ोरी है। इन्टरव्यू लेने के बहाने उन्हें प्रोवोक करने की प्लानिंग है ताकि वे ग़ुस्से में कुछ ऐसा-वैसा बोल दें जिसे कन्ट्रोवर्सियल बनाकर पहले वायरल बनाया जाए। फिर जुलूस-रैलियों से ऐसा माहौल बनाया जाए कि 'सिस्टरहुड' से उन्हें ड्रॉप करवाया जा सके। ख़ानदान की आमदनी का बड़ा स्रोत बन्द हो।

और कमोल तो सोशल मीडिया पर पूरी तरह मेंटल...पागल घोषित हैं...सुसाइडल प्रवृत्ति से भरे हुए। ख़ुद को ख़त्म करने को उतारू। भूल से भी अकेले स्कूटी या कार लेकर नहीं निकलें...माँ गो...काली माँ...वरना कोई-न-कोई भारी गाड़ी अपना खेल कर जाएगी।

दोनों मोहतरमा तो अपने दिलो-दिमाग़ को हल्का कर निकल गईं किन्तु उसके बाद हमारे दिलो-दिमाग़ में जो गर्दो-ग़ुबार उठा वह बैठने का नाम नहीं ले रहा था। सच कहें तो हमारे होशो-हवास गुम थे। पानी का घूँट भी गले के नीचे नहीं उतर रहा था। घंटों यूँ ही बदहवासी-बेज़ारी में गुज़रे फिर सबों ने यहाँ-वहाँ फ़ोन लगाना शुरू किया। दोपहर में कलक्टर-एस. पी. से भेंट की गई।

मेहनत रंग लाई। तीन-चार दिनों के बाद ही पुलिस फोर्स की एक टुकड़ी आश्रम के मेन गेट के पास वाले कमरे में आ डटी। पुलिस थाने का आउटपोस्ट ही खोल दिया गया। 'मौसीक़ी-मंज़िल' भी थाने की गश्ती सूची में शामिल कर लिया गया था। शब्बो भाभी को पुलिस महकमे ने एक बॉडीगार्ड मुहैया करवा दिया था। यहाँ तक कि हम सब भी कभी बाहर निकलते तो सादी वर्दी में एक-दो पुलिस वाले हम पर नज़र रखते। दूरदर्शन ने कमोल दा का बाउल गान का प्रोग्राम रखा और उसका ख़ूब प्रचार भी किया। कुछ पत्र-पत्रिकाओं ने फिर से उसके आलेखों को छापना शुरू किया। इसी बीच फिर स्पेशल टास्क फोर्स नींद से जागी और इस

बार गुप्ता के दो सहयोगियों को गिरफ़्तार कर पुणे ले गई। इन सब बातों का असर यह पड़ा कि सुआर्यन और दीनी दोनों ट्रोल्स थोड़े शान्त हो गए।

तनाव के दिनों में शहर में एक तरह से अकेले पड़ जाने पर अब्बू और बाबा ने गहराई से यह समझा और समझाया कि शास्त्रीय संगीत की संगत ने एक अलग तरह के अहम् भाव से हमें भर दिया है। हम औरों से थोड़ा अलग, थोड़ा विशिष्ट मानने की ग्रंथियों से भरे हैं। आख़िर हमने कब औरों से जुड़ने की कोशिश की। कब किन्हीं मज़दूरों की आम सभा में उनके सुर में सुर मिला कर गाया। कब किसानों-छात्रों के जुलूस का हिस्सा बने। कभी भी किसी भी समूह के साथ न जुड़े, न उनकी तकलीफ़ों में भागीदारी निभाई, न उनके ख़ून-पसीनों के साथ हमारे ख़ून-पसीने बहे। इसीलिए आज ज़रूरत के समय हमारे साथ कोई खड़ा नहीं।

बात बिलकुल सही थी। बिना देर किए इस पर अमल करने की ज़रूरत थी। आश्रम के सीनियर बच्चों के बैंड को इशारा किया गया और उन्होंने अपने रास्ते तलाशने शुरू किए। वक़्त बीतते पहले शहर...फिर राज्य... साल के अन्त तक देश-भर की हर वाजिब लड़ाई के मोर्चे पर तनी हुई मुट्ठियों के संग-साथ आश्रम के बच्चों की गायन मंडली रहने लगी। बाद में विशेष अवसरों पर कमोल दा और शब्बो भाभी की भी पुकार होने लगी...जिसकी इज़्ज़त वे रखते।

हाँ! यह सही था कि शब्बो भाभी बदल रही थीं। कालिन्दी मैडम की ख़बर की सचाई ने उनके अहम् को, मन की गाँठों को पिघला दिया था। उतरी हुई ख़ुमारी और ग़लती के एहसास ने उनमें बदलाव की शुरुआत तो की थी किन्तु उनके बेमतलब के ग़ुस्से ने कमोल दा पर जो आफ़त बरपाई थी, ठेलकर जिस तरह मौत के मुक़ाम पर पहुँचाया था वह शर्मिन्दगी हटाये न हट रही थी। कमोल दा की ओर से इस बदलाव की अनदेखी भी स्वाभाविक ही थी। नेह का कच्चा धागा इतनी जगह से टूट गया था कि गाँठ लगाना भी कठिन। आख़िर कितनी गाँठें लगाई जाएँ? लेकिन बुलबुल अपनी ओर से कोकून से रेशम कातने में कोई कोताही नहीं बरत रही थी। उसकी कोशिश थी कि कात-कात कर रेशम के कच्चे धागों की ढेर लगाई जाए। उन ढेरों में से कोई तो एक धागा होगा जो उसके परिवार को फिर से कभी तो बाँध पायेगा।

लगा सब ठीक हो रहा है। हँसी और ख़ुशी दोनों सहेलियाँ गप्प करती मेले में कहीं भटक गई थीं। वो रास्ता पूछती वापस आ गई हैं। रंजोग़म जो न जाने कब से आलथी-पालथी मार पसर कर हमारे आँगन में बैठा था और सूप में हमें ही फटके जा रहा था। दोनों सहेलियों की खिलखिलाहट सुन चौंक कर उठा और कपड़े झाड़ता कहीं आसपास घूमने निकल गया। तब हमें कहाँ पता था कि काल हमारे वजूद के पेड़ पर बैठे सुग्गे सा हमारे होने को कुतरता रहता है। 'होने' और 'न होने' के बीच सरक कर निकलते काल की कोई आहट भी नहीं आती।

अब ईद के दिन अब्बू सुबह-सबेरे नहा-धोकर अपना नया जोगिया बाना पहन कर बड़ी मस्ज़िद की ओर चले। किसी को कोई आशंका नहीं हुई। चहुँओर ख़ुशी का माहौल, हर एक से गले मिलने, मीठी सेवइयाँ खाने-खिलाने का त्योहार। आज के दिन गिले-शिकवे सब बालू की भीत की तरह ढह जाते हैं। बुरे ख़यालात हवा हो जाते हैं। दुश्मनियाँ गुम जाती हैं। आज के दिन बुरा क्या सोचना? केवल यह लग रहा था कि एक तो साठ-बासठ की उम्र, ऊपर से स्टील प्लेट लगे पैर, ऐसे में बड़ी मस्ज़िद की एक सौ अट्ठावन सीढ़ियाँ कैसे चढ़ पाएँगे? आश्रम के कुछ सीनियर बच्चे नये-नये कपड़े पहन संग-साथ जाने को तैयार बैठे थे। वे कन्धे पर बैठाकर अब्बू को सीढ़ियाँ चढ़ाने को तैयार थे। किन्तु वे मानें तब तो। वे तो हर बीस सीढ़ियों के बाद दो-तीन मिनट सुस्ताते, साँसें थिर करते फिर चढ़ना शुरू करते। आख़िर उन्होंने थोड़ी थकान के साथ ही सही मंज़िल पा ही ली। लेकिन सुस्ता कर जैसे ही मस्ज़िद के दरवाज़े की ओर बढ़े कि पन्द्रह-बीस नौजवानों के एक हुजूम ने उन्हें घेर लिया। वे अब्बू के जोगिया बाने को देख अजब पागल-सा हो रहे थे। साथ के बच्चों ने अब्बू को छेंककर निकालने की कोशिश की तो दूसरे हुजूम ने उन्हें ही खींच लिया और घसीटते दूसरी तरफ़ ले गए। तब तक जोगिया बाने को फाड़ने के जुनून में अन्जाने में या जान-बूझकर अब्बू को ज़ोर का धक्का लगा। देखते-देखते अब्बू की देह लुढ़कती सीढ़ियों के नीचे पहुँच गई। अपने ही ख़ून में डूबी अब बस देह ही थी अब्बू नहीं थे। अब्बू के 'होने' से 'न होने' के द्वार के पार ओझल होने से पहले थामनेवाली कोई पुकार नहीं थी। लड़खड़ाते पैरों को सीढ़ियों पर कोई दूसरा सहारा नहीं था। रक्त के उस

दुपहरिया अँधेरे में सीढ़ियों के पत्थरों की चीख, घासों का हाथ बनकर न सँभाल पाने की कातर पुकार अनसुनी रह गई। अब्बू अब नहीं थे। रक्त में डूबी हुई मिट्टी के बुदबुदे थे। स्मृतियाँ थीं उनकी अनुपस्थिति के लम्बे-अंधियारे गलियारे में चींटियों की अन्तहीन क़तारों की तरह। हमारे हृदय के अँधेरे आकाश में दूर से आती इकतारे की आवाज़ थी। हमारी छाती को अन्दर से मसलता अकथ दुख था। रुलाई थी। आवाज़...बेआवाज़... गूंगी रुलाई...।

34

बीच के किसी स्टेशन पर/दोने में पूड़ी-साग खाते हुए/आप छिपाते हैं अपना रोना/
जो अचानक शुरू होने लगता है/पेट की मरोड़ की तरह/
और फिर छिपा कर फेंक देते हैं कहीं कोने में/
अपना दोना/सोचते हैं; मुझे एक स्त्री ने जन्म दिया था/
मैं यों ही दरवाज़े से निकलकर नहीं चला आया था।

—असद ज़ैदी

अब्बू के साथ हुए हादसे...कि हत्या...जो भी हो...के बाद के लम्हों-घड़ी को अगर तीन लफ़्ज़ों में बयाँ करना हो तो वे लफ़्ज़ थे; दुख, ग़ुस्सा और हताशा। इन्हीं तीन लफ़्ज़ों में केवल मैं नहीं बल्कि पूरे आश्रम और 'मौसिक़ी-मंज़िल' का हरेक शख़्स डूब-उतरा रहा था।

सच कहें तो हम बदहवास थे। अच्छा-बुरा कुछ पता नहीं लग रहा था। दिलो-दिमाग़ में एक सन्नाटा भाँय-भाँय कर रहा था। कोई बात, कोई वाक़या, कोई याद कुछ भी वहाँ नहीं था। लोग-बाग आ-जा रहे थे। हाँ! मिट्टी ले जाने की तैयारी हो रही है बस इतना ही...बाकी कुछ दिख भी नहीं रहा था। लग रहा था कि अब्बू नहीं हम सबों को उन सीढ़ियों से ठेला गया था और दिमाग़ में चोट लगी थी...या कोई बड़ा पत्थर ही सिर पर आन गिरा हो। कभी लगता कि किसी सूखे कुएँ में हम गिर पड़े हों और

उसका मुँह ही बन्द कर दिया गया हो। एकाएक सबके सब ख़ामोश हो गए थे। कमोल दा मुट्ठी भर-भर कर अपनी दवाएँ खा रहा था कि उस पर फिर से दौरे न पड़ने शुरू हो जाएँ।...वह शहर ही था जिसने अब्बू के जनाज़े की तैयारी की। वह शहर ही था जिसने अब्बू को मिट्टी दी। वह शहर ही था जिसने अपने ईद को मुहर्रम में बदलकर भी हमारे मुश्किल वक़्त में हमारे साथ खड़ा रहना कुबूल किया।

मौत से मुलाक़ात के ठीक पहले के लम्हों में इनसान को क्या कोई याद आती है, हाँ! तो क्या? अब्बू को सीढ़ियों के पत्थरों से टकराते-गिरते वक़्त...आख़िरी लम्हों में क्या-क्या याद आया होगा? क्या पूर्वी उत्तर प्रदेश का अपना गाँव...धान के हरे...सुनहरे खेत...मछलियों से भरी नदी...अब्बा सिकन्दर शाह...अपनी अम्मी...इकतारा...लड़कपन के संगी-साथी...। क्या वह संगीत-सभा भी याद आई होगी जिसमें ख़ुद गुरु गोरखनाथ उनके गायन को सुनने पधारे...जिसके रसधार में अम्मू ऐसी डूबीं कि कभी उपराई ही नहीं...क्या कठिनतम रागिनी की कोई लय...क्या रूहानी नाच की कोई मुद्रा...कोई गति...यह सब कुछ...कि कुछ भी नहीं...।

दुख और निराशा के उन घड़ियों...दिनों में यह शिद्दत से महसूस होना शुरू हुआ कि दरअसल हम एक यातना-शिविर में रह रहे थे...और हमारी मौत की सज़ा पहले से तय थी।...किसे गोली मारनी है...किसे सीढ़ियों से धकेलना है...किसे बीच चौराहे पर घेर कर दिनदहाड़े ज़िबह करना है...किसे हाथ बाँध पेड़ से लटका फाँसी देनी है, सब पहले से तय। बस फन्दा कसने और नक़ाब पहनाने के बीच का जो अन्तराल है उतना ही वक़्त हमारे लिए शेष था।

हमारी डूबती धड़कन और बढ़ती हताशा बार-बार याद दिलाती थी कि हम किसी वक़्त में नहीं बल्कि यातना-शिविर में थे या यातना-शिविर ही वक़्त में तब्दील हो गया था। और वक़्त ऐसा था कि हमें रोज़ मातम करने थे। कल नानू का मातम कर रहे थे। फिर अब्बू का मातम।...उसके बाद घराने के किसी और का...। हमें मातम करने के अच्छे तरीक़े ईजाद करने थे। जो कुछ बचा है उसे बहुत सहेज कर रखना था। इस घराने की सारी निशानियाँ। सारे बेशक़ीमती साज़। बड़ो नानू, नानू, अब्बू, अम्मू सबके अनूठे गायन। इनके ईजाद किए ढेर सारी राग-रागिनियाँ...। म्यूज़िक

नोट्स। कमोल दा...शब्बो भाभी को म्यूज़िक स्टूडियो खोलने में अब देर नहीं करनी चाहिए। वरना सारी विरासत लूट जाएगी।

शोक-दुख और हताशा के इस भारी अँधेरे वक़्त में भी अम्मू और माँ को देखकर संवेदी ऊतकें फिर से साँसें लेने लगती थीं। अजब है औरतों-माताओं-अम्मुओं के पास सोग करने-मातम मनाने या रोने-बिलखने के लिए भी ठीक से अवकाश नहीं। उन्हें देह का भार ढो-ढोकर ही सही सबका ख़याल रखना था...जनाज़े में शामिल होनेवालों...जानेवालों...लौटनेवालों... सबों का...। इन्हें देखकर यह लगता था कि मातम-दुख-सोग को भी गूंधा-बेला जा सकता है, सेंका जा सकता है, ठंडा और गर्म किया जा सकता है। न जाने क्यों इन्हें इस हालात में खटता देख 'यातना-शिविर' हौले-हौले 'राहत-शिविर' में तब्दील होता नज़र आता था।

सोग-मातम के तीन दिन घिसट-घिसटकर गुज़र रहे थे किन्तु हताशा-निराशा-अविश्वास की भावनाएँ टलने को तैयार नहीं, वे थिर होकर बैठ गई थीं। हिलती ही नहीं। बन्द कुएँ के मुँह पर पड़ा पत्थर भी नहीं हिल रहा। हमारे अन्दर कोई बैठकर फुसफुसा रहा था कि 'अब कुछ नहीं हो सकता...।' थोड़ा-सा साहस...अम्मू...माँ को देख थोड़ी-सी हिम्मत बटोरने की कोशिश अभी शुरू ही होती कि फिर कोई फुसफुसाता कि 'इससे क्या होगा'...'अब कोई फ़ायदा नहीं'...'सब बेकार है'...'इसका कोई मतलब नहीं...।' लगता है कमोल दा की तरह मुझे भी अवसाद के दौरे पड़ने लगे थे।

तीन दिन सोग के, तीन दिन मातम के...विलाप के...आँसू और हिचकियों के तीन दिन बीत गए थे। उसके बाद चौथा दिन था, चहारुम का दिन। उस दिन पाक क़ुरान शरीफ़ का पाठ होना था। अब्बू के संगी-साथियों को गुरु गोरखनाथ को याद करना...टेरना...उनके पद गाने थे। फ़कीरों-ग़रीबों को खाना खिलाया जाना था...कपड़े-लत्ते दान देने थे। उस रात बड़ो नानू के घराने के सारे मौसीक़ीकार अपने हमदम-हमनवा-हमज़बाँ-हमनफ़स-हमनशीं को अपनी मौसीक़ी-अपने साज़ से ख़ास अन्दाज़ में विदाई देनेवाले थे। पत्थरों को भी आँसुओं से भिगोनेवाला वह मंज़र सदियों को याद रहनेवाला था। यह इस घराने की ख़ास रवायत थी जो हर हाल में निभानी थी...जारी रखनी थी।

उस दिन सूरज उगने के पहरों पहले फिर से अम्मू ने अपना तानपूरा उठाया था। राग जोगिया में ख़याल...बोल एकदम नये थे...'तुम्हारे और हमारे बीच काया का जंजाल है...उल्काएँ टूट रहीं थी...घने जंगलों में आग धधक रही थी...थम चुका था बिल्लियों का रोना..., हमें पता ही न चला...तुम्हारे जाने की बेला इतने चुपके से आई...हमें पता ही न चला... सूखी लकड़ियाँ भीतर से गीली होने लगी थीं...खारा होने लगा था कुएँ का पानी...बन्द हो गई थी चिड़ियों की चहचहाहट तुम्हारे जाने की बेला इतने चुपके से आई...हमें पता ही न चला...तुम्हारे और हमारे बीच काया का जंजाल है।'

...गायन था कि विलाप...आलाप था कि मातम...जो भी था...धड़कता हुआ जीवन था...संवेदी ऊतकों की साँसें तेज़ हो गई थीं...ठूंठ पर नन्हे रोयें जैसी पत्तियाँ प्रकट हो रही थीं...धीमे-धीमे झरने का पानी पत्थरों को काट रहा था।

चहारुम के तीसरे पहर, सब कुछ ठीक चल रहा था। फ़क़ीरों-मुफ़लिसों, ग़रीबों की पंगत बैठ रही थी...उठ रही थी। ख़ूब शौक से जीम कर कपड़े-लत्ते-रुपये लेकर दुआ देती विदा हो रही थी। लोगों की चहल-पहल, खाने की ख़ुशबू, दुआओं की महक सब मिलकर सोग-दुख-मातम की ज़ंजीरें खोल विदा कर रहे थे। माहौल हल्का हो रहा था। तभी व्यवस्था में लगे आश्रम के सीनियर बच्चों के चेहरे पर हवाइयाँ उड़ने लगीं। व्हाट्सएप मैसेज वायरल हो रहा था कि 'मौसीक़ी-मंज़िल' में फ़क़ीरों-मुफ़लिसों के खाने के लिए कच्छप महाराज का गोश्त पका है। पकते गोश्त की एक फेक तस्वीर भी लगाई गई थी। दो घंटे से यह ख़बर वायरल थी यानी कि सुआर्यन और कच्छप रक्षक वाले बवाल काटने को पूरी तरह तैयार थे। बलवाई कभी भी आ सकते थे। हमें असमंजस में देख शब्बो भाभी ने कमान सँभाल ली। बच्चों को लेकर अन्दर के कमरे में चली गईं। इस बार मोर्चा लेना था। एक साथ सैकड़ों मोबाइल्स घनघनाये। दर्जनों मोटर साइकिलें-गाड़ियाँ दौड़ीं। हर संगी-साथी को ख़बर हो। सुआर्यन को छोड़ पूरे शहर को ख़बर हो। सारे छात्रावास, हॉस्टल, मठ-मठिया-मदरसे में रहनेवाले साथियों को, आसपास के गाँव से कॉलेज जानेवाले संगियों, उनके अभिभावकों को, मज़दूर कॉलोनियों के हमसफ़रों को...सबको। यह शहर

को तय करना था कि हिन्दुस्तानी मौसीक़ी और तहज़ीब की जीती-जागती मूर्ति 'मौसीक़ी-मंज़िल' को रहना है या आज के बवाल में ज़मींदोज़ हो जाना है। अबकी बार आर या पार का मूड...।

हुआ वही जो आश्रम के सीनियर बच्चों, शब्बो भाभी और 'मौसीक़ी-मंज़िल' के मुरीदों-चाहनेवालों ने तय किया। आसपास का सारा गाँव और पूरा शहर हर चौक-चौराहे पर सुआर्यन और कच्छप सेना के बलवाइयों को सबक सिखाने को तैयार बैठा था। टैटू वाले बलवाइयों की टुकड़ी ने जैसे ही 'मौसीक़ी-मंज़िल' पर पेट्रोल बम फेंककर शुरुआत की बस पिटाई शुरू हो गई। पूरे शहर में हर गली-मुहल्ले-चौक-चौराहे पर उनकी पिटाई हुई। ऐसी दमदार पिटाई कि पीढ़ियाँ याद रखेंगी। डिक्की से बम निकालने, कट्टे से फ़ायर करने के पहले ही लाठी-हॉकी स्टिक्स की मार से हाथ बेकाम हो गए। सारे बम-कारतूस रखे रह गए। घंटे भर में तो सुआर्यन सेना की कमर ही तोड़ दी गई...।

जो भी हुआ ठीक ही हुआ। किन्तु मौसीक़ी से हमदम को विदाई देने की रस्म अधूरी रह गई। बाबा ने साथियों से क़सम ली कि चहारुम नहीं तो चहल्लुम के दिन यह रस्म पूरी की जाए। इस बार उनके ठौर पर... उनके रोबिन ठाकुर संगीत महाविद्यालय में इन्तज़ाम होगा। अभी काफ़ी वक़्त है इसलिए घराने के सारे शागिर्दों-मुरीदों को न्योता जाए चाहे वे ढाका-कुश्तिया में हों या लाहौर-इस्लामाबाद में, सबको बुलाया जाए। सबने ख़ुशी-ख़ुशी हामी भरी।...वीरभूम में मिलना तय हुआ...बाउलों की भूमि की मीठी पुकार की अनसुनी कौन कर सकता था।

35

क़ातिल की यह दलील मुंसिफ़ ने मान ली,
मक़तूल ख़ुद गिरा था ख़ंजर की नोक पर।

चहारुम के दूसरे दिन कमोल दा के बाबा और माँ शिउड़ी-वीरभूम के लिए निकल गए। इधर बाबा और माँ का आश्रम में बार-बार आना हुआ। कमोल दा की तबियत...हालात ही कुछ ऐसे थे। माँ की इच्छा थी कि कमोल को ही शिउड़ी ले चलें। शिउड़ी, कभी गाँव धूरिशा कभी मामाघर चुरूलिया घूमेगा-फिरेगा। बचपन के यार-दोस्तों के साथ, चचेरे-ममेरे भाई-बहनों के साथ गप्प-शप्प करेगा, मन बदलेगा। तबियत ठीक हो जाएगी। लेकिन डॉक्टर यहाँ, दवा-दारू यहाँ, बुलबुल भी यहाँ। माँ की इच्छा थी कि बुलबुल भी साथ चलती किन्तु वह अपनी पढ़ाई, अपना स्कूल...छोड़ नहीं सकती थी। यहाँ अब्बू भी तो...बाबा से जरा भी उन्नीस नहीं...कमोल से ज़्यादा ही दुलार-प्यार करनेवाले। इसीलिए बाबा-माँ का ही बार-बार आना हुआ। अच्छा ही हुआ माँ और अम्मू को निश्चिंत हो सुख-दुख बतियाने का मौका मिला। धीरे-धीरे दोनों के बीच की औपचारिकता धुल गई। दुख ने, आफ़त-विपत ने दोनों को बहनापे की डोर से बाँध दिया। माँ-बाबा को पोती के साथ खेलने-खिलाने का सुख भी तो यहीं मिला...मन भर मिला।

बुलबुल छुट्टियों में अपने बाबा-मम्मा संग दादूबाड़ी शिउड़ी आती तो थी किन्तु दो-चार दिनों से ज़्यादा कहाँ रुक पाती थी। पहले उसकी मम्मा को दिक़्क़त...कमोड नहीं...ए.सी. नहीं...यह नहीं...वह नहीं। बाद में ट्यूशन...कोचिंग...पढ़ाई बाधा बनते रहे। उन छुट्टियों के दो-चार दिनों में दादी ठीक से पोती को निहार भी नहीं पाती थीं। घुँघराले बालों में ख़ूब-ख़ूब तेल लगा, कंघी से सँवारने का सुख तो दादी को यहीं मिला। अपने हाथों से राँध-राँध कर रसोई, ठेठ बोंग भोजन... भात-माछ झोल, रुई माछ, दोईमाछ, भापा इलिश, डाबचिंगरी,...बैगुन भाजा, सुक्तो, आलू-पोस्तो, चरचरी, कलाई दाल, नारियल-गुड़ वाला पीठा, पाटिशाप्ता और न जाने क्या-क्या...। सामने बैठकर आग्रह कर-करके खिलाने का सुख...बेटा कमोल, पोती बुलबुल, उसके नाना-नानी, काकू-काकी सबों को। पकाने-खिलाने में माँ कभी थकती ही नहीं थीं। पकवान की प्रशंसा उनके चेहरे की चमक को सौ-सौ गुना बढ़ा देती थी। ख़ासकर पोती ने जो परसन में कुछ माँग लिया तो दादी की फुरती देखते बनती थी। रेल में बैठे-बैठे माँ के मन में सारी छवियाँ एक-एक कर आ-जा रही थीं।

लेकिन शब्बो बोधु (बहू) माँ के मन में शुरू से एक खटके की तरह रही। मन के आईने में पड़ा हुआ एक बाल। माँ के मन में तो ख़ूब ढूँढ़कर अपनी पसन्द की बोधु लाने की इच्छा थी। एकदम दुर्गा जैसी... ठेठ बंगालन, आकर्ण आँखें और ऐड़ी तक घुँघराले काले बालों वाली। पान के पत्तों के पीछे छुपता-दिखता पूर्णिमा की चाँद-चाँदनी सा उस बोधु का मुखड़ा। माँगटीके के ऊपर मुकुट, ललाट पर चन्दन-कुमकुम की सजावट, बड़ी-सी लाल बिन्दी पर नन्ही-सी टिकुली, आँखों को कानों से जोड़ती काजल की धार, नाक में मोती लड़ी वाली नथुनी, कानों में बड़े-बड़े झुमके, गले में पहले स्पर्श करता सिक, पट्टीदार फिर लम्बा-सा सीताहार, लाल डिजाइनदार सोने की जरी से भारी बनारसी साड़ी, बाजूबन्द, कलाई में मीनारवाला, मांताशा-कंगन, शांखा, पोला, लोहाबांधानो, उँगलियों से कलाई तक रत्नोचुर, पैरों में छमछम करती पायल, पैरों और हथेलियों में आलता। ताज़ा आलता तलवों की छाप छोड़ता जैसे कमल की पंखुड़ियाँ...पंखुड़ियाँ ही पंखुड़ियाँ...आंगन कि

कमल फूल का पोखर।...पीछे-पीछे ससुरबाड़ी से आए सिर पर टोपोर, गले में सोने की सिकड़ी धारे, शुद्ध तुषार की धोती-कुर्ता में सोना बेटा कमोल... ।...ससुरबाड़ी से इकलौते बेटे के लिए टोपोर आए...यह सपना ही रहा गया।...कहते हैं भगवान शिव ने पहली बार धरा था टोपोर...वही पावन-पवित्र टोपोर मेरा बेटा धर न सका...हाय!

यही तो छोटा-सा सपना था। मन के कोने में कहीं दबा-सोया सपना अभी भी कभी-कभी आह बनकर आँखें डबडबाया करता। इच्छा तो यही थी कि पाँच भाभियों में से ही किन्हीं की भतीजी...जो उनके सपनों की बोधु जैसी ही कुछ-कुछ हो। कालिन्दी ही बाद में माँ को धीरे-धीरे भाने लगी थी...कितना तो इन्तज़ार किया भालो मेये ने कमोल का। यह शब्बो...ठीक-ठीक कहा जाए तो ज़बरदस्ती उनके गौ जैसे बेटे के गले पड़ गई। अब संयोग यह कि कमोल-बाबा के गुरु-भाई की बेटी और गुरु जी की पोती...ये तो एकदम लहालोट। कहाँ उठाएँ, कहाँ बैठाएँ। घर स्वामी का...स्वामी ही बोधु को हथेली पर लिए हुए घूम रहे तो माँ बेचारी क्या करती?

लेकिन शब्बो ने अपनी ओर से शायद ही कोई कोशिश की हो कि कमोल-माँ, अपनी सासू-माँ के संग बैठना है...यूँ ही गप्प-शप्प करनी है। ससुराल...ससुराल के नाते-रिश्ते को समझना है।...गाँव के घर धूरिशा भी जाना है।...गोतिया-सम्बन्धियों से जान-पहचान करनी है...कभी नहीं। वह तो अपने को भद्रोलोक...हम लोगों को निम्नोवोर्ण समझती रही। ग्राम्य बांग्ला लोग...इनसे क्या मिलना...क्या बतियाना...? सत्रह-अठारह साल शादी के हो गए...सत्रह-अठारह बार भी शिउड़ी नहीं आई होगी। शुरू-शुरू में थोड़ा आना-जाना हुआ। वह भी सात-आठ बार से ज़्यादा क्या आई होगी। अब चूँकि बुलबुल गोद में थी या बहुत छोटी थी...बुलबुल के बाबा उसका ख़याल रख नहीं सकते थे सो मजबूरी में।...ठीक-ठीक कहें तो अपनी बेटी के लिए संग-साथ आ गई। अब तो और भी दूर। अपने घर के लिए। बुलबुल—कमोल के लिए ही समय नहीं...तो कहाँ सास...कहाँ ससुर...।

कमोल...अपना भालो कमोल भी अपनी शादी से बहुत ख़ुश रहा...ऐसा तो माँ को कभी नहीं लगा। अब शादी हो गई...तो निभाना ही था। उसके दादू ने, बाबा ने बचपन से ऐसे ही ढाला था कि 'ना' उसके मुँह से निकलता ही नहीं था। अपनी माँ की देह का हिस्सा...रक्तो-माँस...उससे अलग कहाँ...उसका सुख-दुख तुरन्त महसूस होता था माँ को। हॉस्टल में कभी भी सर्दी-खाँसी, बुख़ार होता तो माँ को आभास हो जाता कि बेटे को कुछ हुआ है।...तुरन्त फ़ोन करके मन के खटका के बारे में पता करती और हमेशा पाया कि उसके मन का अन्देशा सही था। जिस दिन से शब्बो उल्टा-सीधा बोल कर गई थी कमोल के साथ-साथ माँ भी बेचैन हो गई थी। लेकिन इस बार माँ को ठीक-ठीक समझ में नहीं आ रहा था कि उसके छेले के साथ हुआ क्या है? लेकिन किसी काम में मन नहीं लग रहा था...न पूजा-पाठ में...न भोजन राँधने में। उस रात जब कमोल स्कूटी लेकर निकला तो माँ की भी नींद झटके से खुल गई, बेचैनी कुछ ज़्यादा ही होने लगी थी...लगा कि साँस लेने में कठिनाई हो रही है...छाती पर भारी पत्थर-सा...बहुत ही पसीना...बार-बार छेले का ख़याल...लगा कमोल-बाबा को उठाए...तब तक फ़ोन ही आ गया...।

रेल की खिड़की से दिखती-भागती छवियों के साथ-साथ माँ की यादों की छवियाँ भी दौड़ती-भागती आ-जा रही थीं। सामने की सीट पर बैठे कमोल-बाबा न जाने क्या सोच रहे हों? तनिक देर के लिए माँ ने नज़र उठाकर बाबा को देखा। उन्हें भी अपने में मगन देख फिर से अपनी यादों में गुम हो गई।

बाबा अपनी ही धुन में डूबे थे। पॉकेट में वह सूची कसमसा रही थी जो अपने गुरु भाइयों के संग मिल-बैठकर ख़ूब सोच समझकर बनाई थी। बड़ो नानू के घराने का कोई भी हमउम्र-सीनियर-जूनियर मौसीक़ीकार नहीं छूटे...इसका ख़ास ख़याल रखा गया था। साथ ही बाबा के विशेष आग्रह से बुज़ुर्ग सूफ़ी गायकों और बाउल गायकों के नाम जोड़े गए थे। बाबा बार-बार पॉकेट में पड़ी उस सूची को छूते...ख़ूब पुलकित होते। सबको बुलाना है। आश्रम से सबको फ़ोन किया गया था बाबा ने ख़ुद ही सबको न्योता दिया था...। अम्मू ने भी अपनो दुखी...भर्राई आवाज़ में एक-एक कर सबों से बातें की थी। ई-मेल में विस्तार से शिउड़ी और रोबिन ठाकुर

संगीत महाविद्यालय का पता भेजा गया था। अब तो शिउड़ी, बोलपुर, तारापीठ में ढेर सारे होटल हो गए थे। ठहरने-ठहराने की कोई दिक़्क़त नहीं थी। ख़ुर्शीद भाई...भाई से भी बढ़कर...पचास सालों से भी ज़्यादा का साथ...उनकी शहादत को सलाम करने संगी-साथी आएं तो। सबों का स्वागत होगा। वीरभूम की मिट्‌टी स्वागत को तैयार थी।

कितने छोटे-छोटे थे वे दोनों। तेरह-चौदह से ज़्यादा की क्या उम्र रही होगी जब गाना सिखाने बड़ो उस्ताद महताबुद्‌दीन ख़ाँ साहब लेकर आए थे। इस अनजान जगह...अनजान बड़े-बड़े लोगों के बीच हमी दोनों एक-दूसरे से सहारा थे। शुरू-शुरू के दिनों में एक-दूसरे का मुँह देखकर रोना रोकते। माँ-बाबा की कितनी-कितनी याद आती थी...ठीक-ठीक ख़ुर्शीद का भी यही हाल। रुलाई दबाये-दबाये बर्दाश्त नहीं होती तो रातों में साथ-साथ रोते और साथ में ही एक-दूसरे को चुप भी कराते रहते।

उस वक़्त कितने मासूम...कितने अनजाने थे हम दोनों। बड़ो उस्ताद साहब ने कितनी बड़ी दुनिया...कितना बड़ा आकाश हमें सौंपा था यह हमें कहाँ पता था? हमारे अजाने एक अद्‌भुत नियामत, अनोखा वरदान हमारी झोली में आ गिरा था। उस वक़्त इसका अन्दाज़ा भी हमें नहीं था। कहाँ तो घराने के बड़े नामी-गिरामी उस्तादों की कोशिश यह रहती कि ख़ानदान के बाहर के किसी को शागिर्द ही न बनाया जाए। किन्हीं कारणों से किसी ने गंडा बँधवा ही लिया तो उसे इतना परेशान किया जाए...इतनी सेवा ली जाए कि ख़ुद ही घबड़ाकर भाग जाए। अगर तब भी नहीं भागा तो दस-बीस सालों में थोड़ा-बहुत कुछ इतना भर सिखा दिया जाए कि अपना-अपने परिवार का इज़्ज़त के साथ पेट भर सके ताकि उस्ताद का नाम ख़राब नहीं हो।

उन्होंने अनगिनत बार अपनी कहानी सुनाई थी कि कैसे बड़ो बाबा अल्लाउद्‌दीन ख़ाँ जो उन दिनों आलम के नाम से जाने जाते थे और वे यानी महताब दोनों को रामपुर दरबार के मशहूर बीनकार वज़ीर ख़ाँ का शागिर्द बनने की धुन सवार हुई। ख़ाँ साहब तानसेन की पुत्री सरस्वती के वंशज थे। उन दिनों रामपुर में उनके नीचे पाँच सौ गवैये, साज़िन्दे और नृत्यकार रहा करते। आलम-महताब ने वज़ीर ख़ाँ तक पहुँचने की कोशिशें कीं लेकिन हर बार उन्हें नाकामयाबी का मुँह देखना पड़ा। आख़िर छह

माह बाद हार-थककर दोनों ने कैसे अफ़ीम खाकर ख़ुदकुशी की ठानी... कैसे राजा साहब के बग्घी के सामने गए गिरफ़्तारी हुई...फिर राजा साहब ने उनकी कहानी सुनने के बाद वज़ीर ख़ाँ साहब को उन्हें शागिर्द बनाने का हुकुम दिया। यह सब एक लम्बी कहानी थी जिसे बड़ो उस्ताद साहब बहुत रस ले लेकर सुनाते। इस कहानी का लब्बोलुआब यह कि उस्ताद वज़ीर ख़ाँ ने राजा साहब के दबाव में दोनों को गंडा तो बाँध दिया किन्तु सिखाने की इच्छा तनिक भी नहीं थी। वे रियाज़ के समय अपने बेटे को तो सामने बैठाते किन्तु दोनों शागिर्दों को दरवाज़े के पास जूते खोलने की जगह पर बैठाते। दोनों महीनों यूँ ही ज़लील होते रहे। आख़िर दोनों के जुनून और क़ाबिलियत से हार कर उस्ताद ने अपने धरम का पालन शुरू किया।

बड़ो उस्ताद साहब इस घटना को बहुत ही ग़ैर संजीदगी से सुनाते। यह उस वक़्त की बहुत ही आम रवायत थी। लेकिन बड़ो बाबा अल्लाउद्दीन ख़ान साहब ने इस रवायत को ही उलट दिया। उन्होंने अपने बेटे-बेटियों के अलावा, सैकड़ों की संख्या में शागिर्द बनाए और शागिर्द बनाते वक़्त केवल लगन और क़ाबिलियत देखी, मज़हब...जाति...घर-ख़ानदान कुछ भी जानने की कोशिश नहीं की। बड़ो उस्ताद महताबुद्दीन साहब तो अपने बड़े भाईजान से भी दो क़दम आगे। बेख़ुदी के आलम में यहाँ-वहाँ भटकते... दूर गाँव-देहातों से...लोक संगीत में डूबे ग़रीब परिवारों के घरों के बच्चों को शागिर्द बनाकर ले आते। यह लोक और शास्त्रीयता का मेल कराने का उनका ईजाद किया हुआ अनोखा तरीक़ा था। इसी सिलसिले में ही तो ख़ुर्शीद भाईजान और वे ख़ुद उनके साये में आ खड़े हुए थे। मतलब कि बड़ो बाबा और बड़ो उस्ताद साहब दोनों ने मिलकर घरानेदारी की नफ़ासत के पर्दे में छुपी बैठी परले दर्जे की ख़ुदग़र्जी की सारी हेकड़ी निकाल दी। उसके बाद घराने केवल बेटों-भतीजों तक सिमटे नहीं रह सके। बदलते-बदलते आज हालात ये हैं कि आप कोई भी हों, आपका पेशा कुछ भी हो बस आप में मौसीक़ी सीखने की सच्ची चाह होनी चाहिए फिर कोई उस्ताद आपको मना नहीं कर सकता।

रेल की तेज़ गति जैसी ही बाबा के ज़ेहन में भी यादें आ-जा रही थीं। वैसे पुराने ज़माने के इन संगीत घरानों की कई ख़ूबियाँ भी थीं। गोपाल नायक और अमीर ख़ुसरो के ज़माने के भो पहले की राग-रागिनियाँ अपनी

सारी पाकीज़गी और शुद्धता के साथ आज भी हमारे बीच मौजूद हैं तो राजाओं और बादशाहों के दरबारों के बाद यही वे घराने हैं जिन्होंने उन्हें दिलों में समो कर, रोम-रोम में पैवस्त कर उन्हें बचाया। एक तरह से लुप्त हो चुके मन्दिरों-मठों के ध्रुपद गायन को डागर बन्धुओं के घराने ने ही छाती से लगा संजोकर रखा। लेकिन उस ज़माने की एक बुराई यह भी थी कि भले ख़ानदान की महिलाएं गायन के पेशे में नहीं आती थीं। माहौल ही कुछ ऐसा ही बनाकर रखा गया था। ख़ुदा जन्नत बख़्शें लखनऊ-आगरा-बनारस-गया-पटना-दरभंगा की बाई जी लोगों को जिन्होंने अपने जानो-जिगर में ठुमरी-दादरा-कजरी-होरी-टप्पा-ग़ज़ल को बसाकर रखा। हुस्नाबाई, विद्याधरी, राजेश्वरी, ग़फ़ूरजान, मुन्नाजान, सरस्वती बाई जैसे दर्जनों नाम ऐसे हैं जो आज भी रसिकों की ज़ुबाँ पर हैं। जद्दनबाई, रसूलन, सिद्धेश्वरी और अख़्तरी बाई ने मिलकर समय और समाज को बहुत कुछ बदला। आज़ादी के बाद के नये दौर में केसरबाई केरकर, मोगूबाई कुर्डीकर और हीराबाई बड़ोदेकर ने महिलाओं के हक़ में मुकम्मल बदलाव लाने में कामयाबी पाई। वह विदुषी हीराबाई बड़ोदेकर ही थीं जिन्हें आज़ादी की पहली-पहली सुबह को पंडित ओंकारनाथ ठाकुर के साथ सरदार वल्लभ भाई पटेल ने वन्दे मातरम् गाने के लिए याद किया। 15 अगस्त, 1947 को सुबह छह बजे आकाशवाणी मुम्बई से पंडित ठाकुर और दिल्ली आकाशवाणी से विदुषी बड़ोदेकर ने अपनी तराशी-पकी स्वरलहरियों से सारी धरती, सारा आकाश, समस्त ग्रहों-उपग्रहों, आकाशगंगाओं को अपनी सुजलां, सुफलां, मलयज शीतलाम् वाली शस्य, श्यामल भारत माता के दिव्य-भव्य स्वरूप का दर्शन कराया।...और अपनी माँ को भी आश्वस्त किया...के कहे मा तुमि अबले...। अद्भुत क्षण...याद कर आज भी रोंगटे खड़े हो जाते हैं।

बाबा अपनी सोच से बाहर आए। खिड़की से बाहर भागते खेतों-जंगलों, नदियों-नालों को देखा। नज़रें जुड़ा गईं। सामने कमोल-माँ को नज़र भरकर देखा। वे बैठी-बैठी अब सो रही थीं। ध्यान अब कमोल-शब्बो की अम्मू... रागेश्वरी देवी...उनकी उपलब्धियों की ओर गया। यह सब हीराबाई बड़ोदेकर जैसी विदुषियों के बनाए रास्ते के कारण ही सम्भव हुआ। आज़ादी की उस हज़ारों सूर्य वाली सुबह को किराना घराने के उस्ताद अब्दुल करीम ख़ान

और ताराबाई माने की सुपुत्री विदुषी बड़ोदेकर ने भारत माता के साथ-साथ महिला मौसीक़ीकारों का परचम भी लहराया था।

बाबा सोच रहे थे कि नये समय ने अगर कई तरह की आज़ादी और ख़ुशियाँ दीं तो नयी क़िस्म की तकलीफ़ें-दुख भी दिए हैं। घराने और घरानों के बुज़ुर्ग उस्तादों के प्रभाव घटने के साथ-साथ मौसीक़ीकारों के बीच की 'बिरादरी' वाली भावना-एहसास भी कमज़ोर पड़ा है। एक साथ उठने-बैठने, दुख-सुख बाँटने का सिलसिला ख़त्म-सा हो चला है। कोई इस बाबत ढंग से सोच भी नहीं रहा। शायद इस बार सब शिउड़ी में जमा हों तो कुछ सोचा जाए...एक संगठन बनाया जाए ताकि संकट के समय सब एक-दूसरे के साथ खड़े हो सकें। कोई अपने को नितान्त अकेला महसूस नहीं करे...जैसा कि 'मौसीक़ी-मंज़िल' इन दिनों महसूस करती रही है...।

बाबा पिछले दो दशकों से नयेपन की आँधी के साथ मौसीक़ी की दुनिया में मशीनों की बढ़ती आमद से दुखी और चिन्तित रहे हैं।...लेकिन उनकी चिन्ता से कोई फ़र्क़ तो पड़ नहीं रहा है। संगीत के कार्यक्रमों के दौरान मंच पर मशीनों का प्रयोग बढ़ता जा रहा है। मौसीक़ीकार पर मशीन हावी होती नज़र आ रही है...कोई संतुलन होता भी नहीं दिखता।

यह ठीक है कि हमारे शुरुआती दिनों और गुरु उस्ताद अय्यूब ख़ान-बड़ो उस्ताद महताबुद्दीन ख़ान के समय में शास्त्रीय संगीत की प्रस्तुतियाँ ज़्यादा से ज़्यादा सौ-डेढ़ सौ श्रोताओं की महफ़िलों, जलसों में हुआ करती थीं। आज विशालकाय सभागारों में पाँच सौ से लेकर हज़ारों श्रोताओं के सामने प्रोग्राम्स होते हैं। सो माइक्रोफ़ोन और एम्प्लिफ़िकेशन बिना कोई मौसीक़ीकार गाने-बजाने को तैयार नहीं जो स्वाभाविक है। अब गायकों का गला ही माइक के लिए तैयार किया जा रहा है। गायकों के बीच अब खुली-ज़ोरदार आवाज़ें कम और माइक का सहारा लेकर गूँजनेवाली आवाज़ें ज़्यादा प्रचलित हैं। वादक भी अपने साज़ों के लिए अलग-अलग प्रोसेसर का उपयोग करने लगे हैं। किसी मशीन से साज़ की मूल ध्वनि को बदला जा सकता है तो किसी से उसकी गूँज बढ़ाई जा सकती है। बहरहाल एम्प्लिफ़िकेशन के इस नये डिजिटल दौर में मौसीक़ी के प्रोग्राम्स में अक्सर डेसिबल युद्ध का नज़ारा दिखने लगा है। रॉक संगीत के ऊँचे वॉल्यूम ने शास्त्रीय संगीत में घुसपैठ बना ली है, इससे ज़्यादा

तकलीफ़देह बात और कुछ नहीं हो सकती। रूह से रूह तक उतरनेवाली हिन्दुस्तानी मौसीक़ी, जो कभी इबादत हुआ करती थी अब डेसिबल युद्ध की रणभूमि में तब्दील होती जा रही है। रोने-सिर पीटने के अलावा कुछ तो किया जाना चाहिए।

गुरु भाइयों-बहनों के शिउड़ी-जुटान में इस पहलू पर भी बात करनी है। साज़ों की मूल मिठास...राग-रागिनियों की पाकीज़गी बचाने की कोशिशें हम नहीं करेंगे तो कौन करेगा? सबसे ज़्यादा दुर्गति तो बाउल संगीत की हुई है। उसमें और पॉप म्यूज़िक में फ़र्क़ ही मिटा दिया गया है।...नहीं चलेगा। हम सब मिलकर इस हालत को बदलेंगे...। केन्दुली-मोनेर मानुष अखाड़ा का एकतारा, कुश्तिया ज़िले के दोतारा, खोमोक, आनन्द लहरी, गबगुबी...सबको फिर से जगना होगा, जगाना होगा। उनकी मिठास संजोने की कोशिश करनी ही करनी होगी। इसी बार ही इनकी रिकार्डिंग की व्यवस्था की जाए।...न जाने कब कमोल-शब्बो का रिकार्डिंग स्टूडियो खड़ा होगा? तब तक सब नष्ट-विनष्ट हो जाएगा। सब छिन्न-भिन्न।... फिर से हिन्दुस्तानी मौसीक़ी...बाउल...सूफ़ी गान की भीतर से स्वयं फूटकर बहनेवाली रवायत को ज़िन्दा नहीं किया जा सका...सबके लिए तो सम्भव नहीं लेकिन कुछ को तो उस मानसिक अवस्था...मनःस्थिति तक पहुँचाने की कोशिश...मन के भीतर मोनेर मानुष ढूँढ़ने की राह पर नहीं लाया जा सका...मौसीक़ी को इबादत में ढालने की तज्वीज़ नहीं सिखाई जा सकी तो हम सबका, इस घराने का, 'मौसीक़ी-मंज़िल' के होने...भाईजान उस्ताद ख़ुर्शीद शाह जोगी की शहादत का कोई मतलब ही नहीं। लगेगा यह ज़िन्दगी यूँ ही बेमतलब निकल गई।

बाबा की यादें यहाँ से वहाँ, वहाँ से यहाँ भटका रही थीं। क्षणों में जीवन भर की यात्रा के सुख-दुख, हँसी-ख़ुशी सिनेमा के सीन की तरह आ-जा रहे थे। रेल भी अपनी गति से भागी जा रही थी। उनका स्टेशन भी नज़दीक आ रहा था। तभी बोगी में कुछ गड़बड़ी का एहसास हुआ... कुछ रोने-बिलखने, गिड़गिड़ाने-चीख़ने की आवाज़ें सुनाई दी। बाबा अपने ख़याली आकाश से धरती पर उतर आए। कमोल-माँ अभी भी सो रही थीं। बोगी के अधिकांश यात्री कान में इयरफ़ोन लगाये अपने मोबाइल-लैपटॉप पर या तो फिल्म देख रहे थे या गेम खेलने में भिड़े थे। कुछ औंघ रहे

थे...सो रहे थे। जो जगे भी थे वे भी उस रोने-चिल्लाने की तरजीह नहीं दे रहे थे। विचित्र बात थी। बाबा उठे और उन आवाज़ों की ओर बढ़े।

सामने ग़ज़ब दृश्य था। तीन दाढ़ी-टोपी वाले अठारह-उन्नीस साल के दुबले-पतले लड़कों को दस-बारह तगड़े नौजवान घेरे हुए अजब व्यवहार कर रहे थे। कोई उनकी टोपियाँ उछाल रहा था...कोई उनकी दाढ़ियों में उँगली फिराने के बहाने उन्हें नोच दे रहा था...उनकी आँखों पर पट्टी बाँध...किसने पहले थप्पड़ मारा पहचानो खेल के बहाने उनकी बुरी तरह पिटाई शुरू कर दी गई थी। सबसे कमज़ोर लड़के की नाक-कान से ख़ून बहने लगा था, लेकिन ज़ालिम रुकने का नाम नहीं ले रहे थे। बाबा ने डपटने...रोकने की कोशिश की तो इन्हीं पर पिल पड़े। लगे हड़काने, "...ओ बूढ़ो बाबा निजेर जाएगाये गिये बोसे जान" (ओए बूढ़े बाबा अपनी जगह पर जाकर बैठ जाओ।)

...निजेर चरखाए तेल दीन।

(अपने काम से काम रखो)

...ओन्येर काजे माथा गोलाबेन ना।

(दूसरे के काम में टाँग नहीं अड़ाना चाहिए।)

...एई लाइने ट्रेन थेके पोड़े प्रायाई लोके मारा जाए...।

(इस लाइन में ट्रेन से गिरकर अक्सर लोग मरते रहते हैं।)

...आपनी कैनो निजेर नाम लेखाते चान।

(उनमें अपना नाम क्यों लिखवाना चाहते हैं।)

...सुनते पाच्छेन ना? जान...।

(सुनाई नहीं पड़ रहा? जाओ।)

बाबा ने दायें-बायें देखा। लोग नज़रें चुरा रहे थे। तब तक माँ पीछे-पीछे पहुँच गईं। अब वे गुंडे माँ को समझा रहे थे—

"...मासी माँ, एनाके निये जान। इनी हीरोगिरि देखाच्छेन...।

(माता जी इन्हें ले जाइये। इनको हीरोपंथी सूझ रही है।)

...आमी निजेर धरमो, निजेर राष्ट्रेर इतिहासेर उपर लागा दाग मेटाबार चेष्टा कोरछि आर तोमरा मोनुषत्वो सीखाच्छो...।

(हम अपने धर्म, अपने राष्ट्र के इतिहास पर लगे धब्बों को धोने की कोशिश कर रहे हैं और इन्हें इनसानियत सूझ रही है।)

...आमार ऐ रोकोम सेक्युलर लोकेदेर घेन्ना लागे।

(हमें ऐसे सेक्युलर लोगों से चिढ़ है।)

...एना के तड़ातड़ी निये जान। आमार मूड ख़राब होले आमी किन्तु कारूर नोई...।

(इन्हें जल्दी ले जाइए। नहीं तो हमारा मूड ख़राब हुआ तो ठीक नहीं होगा।)

माँ उन सबकी धमकियों...विडाल जैसी आँखों...भाव-भंगिमा से डर गईं। बाबा को खींच अपनी सीट पर ले आईं। बाबा ने तब तक मोबाइल से कुछ तस्वीरें लेकर दो मिनट का वीडियो बना लिया था। उन्हें तुरत-फुरत रेलवे पुलिस फोर्स के नम्बर पर भेजा। वे अपनी सीट पर बैठ तो गए थे किन्तु चैन नहीं मिल रहा था। अगला ही स्टेशन शिउड़ी था। अपने शागिर्दों को भी मैसेज भेजने लगे...कुछ तो करना चाहिए...कुछ तो करना होगा...। लेकिन मनुष्य इतना क्रूर...इतना नृशंस...उन्हें मशहूर प्राइमेटोलॉजिस्ट जेन गुडऑल की पंक्ति याद आ रही थी, 'ह्यूमन आर द ओनली एनिमल कैपेबल ऑफ बीइंग क्रूएल।'

36

यह अभिषेक का समय है/जीने के धूल-धक्कड़/
मैल-कलुष को तजने का/समय/समय हवा की तरह हलके होने का/
जो कुछ किया-धरा/उसे ज्यों का त्यों/उतारने का/समय

—अशोक वाजपेयी

स्टेशन पर पुलिस फ़ोर्स भी थी और म्यूज़िक कॉलेज के लड़के भी। लफ़ंगे तो पीछे के दरवाज़े से उल्टी दिशा में उतरकर भाग निकले। घायल तीनों बच्चों की हालत अच्छी नहीं थी। किसी की पसली में गहरी चोट थी तो किसी के नाक की हड्डी टूटी थी। बाबा ने उन तीनों बच्चों का इलाज करवाया। बाज़ाब्ता मेडिकल सर्टिफिकेट लगाकर रेलवे थाना में प्राथमिकी दर्ज करवाई। घायल बच्चों का बयान भी दर्ज करवाया। लेकिन उन चोटिल बच्चों के घर एक स्टेशन आगे के गाँव में थे और वे रेल तो क्या प्लेटफार्म पर भी पैर रखने से डर रहे थे। आख़िर बाबा ने भाड़े पर एक टैक्सी की। अपने दो लड़कों के संग उन बच्चों को भिजवाया तब जाके अपने घर गए।

शिउड़ी पहुँचकर भी बिना घर गए, बिना कुछ खाये-पिए ख़ब्तुल हवास हो तीन-चार घंटे यहाँ से वहाँ दौड़-भाग करते बाबा को देख माँ एकदम खीझ गईं। थाने के कोने में उस टूटी बेंच पर कब तक बैठी रहतीं।

वैसे भी जो थाने में आता वह अजीब निगाहों से देखता। ऊब कर रिक्शा पकड़ा और सामान के साथ ख़ुद ही घर आ गईं। आख़िर भात-माछ भी तो उन्हें ही राँधना था। घर में कौन बोऊ (बहू) बैठी थी जो राँध-परसकर खिलाती। हफ़्तों से बन्द घर-दुआर की गन्दगी, झोल-जाल से अलग दुर्गति... सब साफ़-सफ़ाई भी उन्हें ही करनी थी। घर भी इतना बड़ा-विशाल, एक छोटी-मोटी हवेली की तरह खड़ा कर दिया था। अब कमोल-बाबा को खंचिया भर पुण्य बटोरना है तो अपने चेलों-चपाटों संग बटोरते रहें। वैसे भी घर आकर भी क्या मदद करते? उल्टे हर घंटा-आध घंटा पर चा-चा (चाय-चाय) चिल्लाकर काम ही बढ़ाते।

न जाने क्यों आज हमारे मन में यह खटका हो रहा है कि बाबा ने उस दिन जो प्राथमिकी दर्ज करवाई...ठीक तो किया ही...यही किया जाना चाहिए था...लेकिन...फिर भी ऐसा लग रहा है कि वह प्राथमिकी ही कमोल दा के लिए काल हो गई।...ठीक-ठीक तो नहीं कहा जा सकता कि यही हुआ होगा...किन्तु एक आशंका बादुर की तरह मन में फड़फड़ाती रहती है।

बहरहाल, उस दिन खा-पीकर जब बाबा तख़्त पर लेटे तो उनका मन बहुत बेचैन था। यह कैसा समय अपने देश में भी आ गया कि कुछ लोगों को इनसान का दर्जा ही नहीं दिया जा रहा है। मानो वे कुछ कमतर प्राणी हों, जिन्हें मारने-पीटने में कोई हर्ज़ नहीं हो। मारने-पीटने, जान तक ले लेनेवाले लोग छाती चौड़ी कर निकल लेते मानो किसी क़ानूनी काम को अंजाम दिया हो। दर्शकों की भीड़ भी इन्हें फिल्मी हीरो की तरह देखती रहती। एक शाम ख़ुर्शीद भाई के डॉक्टर दोस्त अहमद साहब के यहाँ इस पर बहुत विस्तार से बातें हुई थीं। अब चूँकि भगवान कच्छप महाराज भी राष्ट्र की पवित्रता की अवधारणा से जुड़े हुए हैं इसलिए उन्हें लेकर क़ानून हाथ में लेनेवालों में भी एक गौरव का भाव होता है। कोई अपराधबोध नहीं क्योंकि लिंचिंग करनेवाले यह मान रहे हैं कि वे सब लोग राष्ट्र के लिए एक महत्त्वपूर्ण धार्मिक कार्य को अंजाम दे रहे हैं।

उस शाम डॉक्टर अहमद ने न्यूरोलॉजी की ऑटोटॉमी थ्योरी समझाई कि शरीर के किसी अंग का कोई तंत्रिका-तंत्र क्षतिग्रस्त होने के बाद जब दिमाग़ को सिग्नल भेजना बन्द कर देता है, तब दिमाग़ भी उस अंग को अपना हिस्सा मानना छोड़ देता है। वह मानने लगता है कि वह कोई बाहरी

वस्तु है तब सेल्फ़-म्यूटिलेशन की प्रक्रिया शुरू होती है यानी अंग अपने को ही विकृत और नष्ट करने लगता है।

डॉक्टर ने इसके बाद इस ऑटोटॉमी और सेल्फ म्यूटिलेशन को नेशन-बॉडी सन्दर्भ में समझाया। हालाँकि सच यह है कि नेशन-बॉडी के किसी अंग की कोई तंत्रिका क्षतिग्रस्त नहीं हुई है। किन्तु समुदाय विशेष से जातीय-आर्थिक असुरक्षा के सिद्धान्त गढ़े गए। बरसों से इन वर्चुअल ख़तरों के बारे में दुहरा-दुहरा कर नेशन-बॉडी के दिमाग़ को इतना अनुकूलित कर दिया गया कि ख़तरे से बचाव में नेशन-बॉडी ने उस अंग विशेष को अपना मानने से इनकार कर दिया है। उसके बाद लिंचिंग के माध्यम से सेल्फ़-म्यूटिलेशन की प्रक्रिया की भी शुरुआत हो गई है। ऐसी आत्मघाती प्रक्रिया कि अगर इसे अभी ही नहीं रोका गया तो सचमुच हमारी नेशन-बॉडी रोगग्रस्त हो जाएगी।...यह सब सोचते-सोचते बाबा को झपकी आ गई।

एक-डेढ़ घंटे से कम क्या सोये होंगे। शाम ढलने को आई थी। जगे तो माथा भारी था। चा-भाजा-सोन्देश सब खाने के बाद भी मूड उखड़ा हुआ ही था। लुंगी पर कुर्ता डाल स्लीपर पहन चौक तक निकल लिये। ताम्बूल खाने के बहाने कुछ गप्प-शप्प होगी। मन बहलेगा। ताम्बूल दुकान पर क़रीब घंटा भर देश-दुनिया गपियाने के बाद सचमुच मन सेमल की रुई हो गया। लेकिन जैसे ही पैसा देने के लिए कुर्ते के जेब में हाथ डाला तो मानो झटका-सा लगा। वहाँ शिउड़ी-जुटान की सूची खड़खड़ाई। मानो भूल जाने का उलाहना दे रही हो। उसके बाद बाबा एकदम तेज़ी में आ गए। एस.टी.डी. बूथ से कॉलेज हॉस्टल के फाइनल इयर के बच्चों से बात की। तुरन्त सबों को घर पर बुलाया। घर की छत पर दरी बिछा काग़ज़-पत्तर लेकर बैठ गए।

बच्चे-बच्चियों के पहुँचते ही शिउड़ी-जुटान की तैयारी की कमेटियाँ, सब-कमेटियाँ बननी शुरू हो गईं। एक रजिस्टर में सबकुछ ख़ूब सोच-विचारकर दर्ज किया जाने लगा। स्टेशन पर स्वागत करनेवाली टीम में कौन-कौन होगा? स्टेशन मास्टर को पहले से चिट्ठी प्रिन्सिपल साहब के पैड पर भिजवानी होगी। भोजन-व्यवस्था, ठहराव, निमंत्रण-पत्र का मज़मून-डिज़ाइन। दो-तीन घंटे में प्रोग्राम की मोटा-मोटी रूपरेखा बन गई। बाबा ख़ूब संतुष्ट...बच्चों को विदा कर; खा-पीकर ख़ूब निश्चिन्त होकर सोए।

बाबा नींद में शिउड़ी-जुटान के कार्यक्रम में थे। दक्षिण एशिया के सभी दिग्गज संगीतकारों की उपस्थिति मंच को स्वर्ग-सी दिव्य आभा से आभूषित कर रही थी। वीणा, रुद्रवीणा, सुरबहार, सितार, सन्तूर, सरोद, घटम, मृदंग, तबला, वेणु, वायलिन, जलतरंग आदि-आदि सारे वाद्यों के वरिष्ठ वादक एवम् वरिष्ठतम् गायकों की एक झलक देख श्रोताओं के आनन्द का ठिकाना न था। मंगल भाव से मरहूम ख़ुर्शीद भाईजान को याद करता...सलाम भेजता संगीत दसों दिशाओं में गूँज रहा था। हमारे बीच के सारे अवरोधों-सीमाओं, घृणा-हिंसा के पहाड़ों को ढाहता हमारी मनुष्यता को टोह मारकर जगानेवाला संगीत समुद्र की उत्ताल लहरों की तरह भिगोये जा रहा था। बाबा को अपने गुरु भाइयों-बहनों के कंठों की मिठास में न जाने क्या-क्या घुला लग रहा था...भोर की ओस, पूर्णिमा की चाँदनी, वन केवड़े की सुगन्ध, घने जंगल में टपका मधु कि तितलियों ने बटोर-बटोर कर जो जमा किए फूलों के वे सारे रस या सबके सब एक साथ।

इन श्रेष्ठ संगीतकारों को सुनने शिउड़ी में दूर-दूर से पधारे रसिक श्रोता आधी ख़ुदी-आधी बेख़ुदी में डूब-उतरा रहे थे। ये सभी दिव्य संगीत में डूबकर आधी नींद में थे और आधे जागरण में...। वहाँ आधा स्वप्न था और आधा यथार्थ। स्वर लहरियाँ दिल में लगातार टोहके लगा रही थीं जिससे उठती हूक समूचे वजूद को ही कहीं अज्ञात की ओर...अनादि-अनन्त की ओर उठाकर ले जा रही थी। सच्चे सुर मन की गिरहों को खोलते दिमाग़ में बैठे पशुओं को सुलाते उन्हें चेतन से अवचेतन...अचेतन में गुमाते जा रहे थे। अन्तर में बिजली की तरह कौंधने का एहसास संगीतकारों के हृदय से होता रसिकों के हृदय में समाता जा रहा था। थमे-थमे से लम्हों में कुहरे-सा छाया स्वर-सुर-लय कहीं बहुत भीतर काँपता शेष रह जा रहा था...मंगल कामनाओं की तरह...आरती के दिये की लौ की तरह...।... मधुर-मदिर स्वप्न में खोते बाबा नींद के अतल-जल में डूबते चले गए।... भोर वाली मीठी-नशीली नींद में।

बाबा और उनकी टीम 'शिउड़ी-जुटान' में रात-दिन इतनी डूबी कि लगा दिन-हफ़्ते सभी पलक झपकते बीत रहे हों। रोज़ सबेरे उत्फुल्ल असीम ऊर्जा से भरा एक इन्द्रधनुष उगता और देखते-देखते गुम हो जाता।

वैसे बाबा और उनकी टीम के पास समय भी कहाँ था? तीस-पैंतीस दिनों में ही तो सारी व्यवस्थाएँ करनी थीं। वह तो भला हो प्राचार्य और कॉलेज प्रबन्धन के सज्जनों का जिन्होंने बाबा की योजना अपनी मान ली थी। वैसे सारे पत्राचार, बैनर्स, पोस्टर्स में नाम तो प्राचार्य और कार्यकारिणी के चेयरमैन का ही जा रहा था। पहले ही हफ़्ते कॉलेज प्रबन्धन के लोग और प्राचार्य ज़िला कलक्टर से मिल आए थे और उन्होंने भी ख़ुशी-ख़ुशी स्वागत समिति की अध्यक्षता स्वीकार की थी। बस अब यह लग रहा था कि बाबा का सपना पूरे कॉलेज, पूरे शहर का सपना हो गया हो। हर चौक-चौराहे, चाय-पान दुकान पर 'शिउड़ी-जुटान' की चर्चा छाई हुई थी। सब कुछ कमोल की माँ के शब्दों में कहें तो शुभो-शुभो ही हो रहा था कि अचानक अघट घटने लगा।

अतिथियों से अन्तिम स्वीकृति और टिकट आदि की व्यवस्था के लिए बच्चे फ़ोन कर रहे थे। देश के सारे कोनों में तो कॉलेज के फ़ोन से बात हो गई किन्तु उसमें आई.एस.डी. की सुविधा नहीं थी। सो बच्चों ने बाज़ार के बूथ से एक-एक कर ढाका-कुश्तिया-राजशाही फिर लाहौर-इस्लामाबाद के अतिथियों से बातें की। न जाने सुननेवालों ने क्या समझा... अगले को क्या समझाया। शहर का मौसम अचानक बदल गया, इतनी गर्मी की लगा एकाएक लू चलने लगी हो।

दूसरे ही दिन संगीत महाविद्यालय के परिसर में राष्ट्रवादी छात्र संघ का बैनर लहराते दर्जनों बाहरी लड़के जबरन घुस आए। पहले प्राचार्य को ज्ञापन दिया, फिर नारों से कॉलेज की दीवारों को हिलाने लगे। वे किसी भी हाल में पाकिस्तानी संगीतकारों को शिउली में बर्दाश्त करने को तैयार नहीं थे। उन्हें गुरु भाई-बहन जैसे रिश्तों, एक ही राग-रागिनियों, एक ही लय-सुर में डूबती-उतराती उन सबों की एक सी ज़िन्दगी, राम-कृष्ण को टेरते उनके भजनों, ख़ुर्शीद भाईजान की शहादत...उनका चालीसवाँ...किसी बात से कोई मतलब नहीं था। बस पाकिस्तानी नहीं चाहिए। पाकिस्तान दुश्मन देश है तो वहाँ के लोग हमारे भाई-बहन कैसे हो सकते हैं...वे बस हमारे दुश्मन हैं...दुश्मन रहेंगे। चाहे वे कलाकार हों, संगीतकार हों या कोई हों।...इन सबसे उनके संगठन का कोई मतलब नहीं था। वे बस यह जान रहे थे कि अगर पाकिस्तान से आए एक भी कलाकार ने शिउड़ी

में क़दम रखा तो यह 'शिउड़ी-जुटान' तो नहीं हो सकेगा...हाँ! दो-चार अर्थियाँ-जनाज़े ज़रूर उठेंगे...इसकी वे गारंटी दे रहे थे।

घंटे-डेढ़ घंटे ही वह बैनरवाली पार्टी कैम्पस में चीख़ी-चिल्लाई होगी। लेकिन ऐसा लगा कि जैसे उफनते दूध पर किसी ने ठंडा पानी उड़ेल दिया हो। पूरा उत्साह ही भंग हो गया। बाबा की हालत तो जैसे अब रो देंगे, तब रो देंगे। प्राचार्य महोदय ने फ़ोन पर कलक्टर साहब से लम्बी बातचीत की। हर तरह के सहयोग का आश्वासन मिला। तनाव कुछ कम हुआ। धीरे-धीरे फिर सब अपने-अपने कामों में लगे। लेकिन शाम होते दूसरा उत्पात।

इस बार हरे झंडे और यूथ विंग ऑफ पॉपुलर फ्रंट ऑफ इंडिया का लम्बा-चौड़ा बैनर था। अब की धमकी थी कि हम कमज़ात सूफ़ियों को शिउड़ी नहीं आने देंगे। बड़े नापाक लोग हैं...न ख़ुदा को मानते हैं न शरीयत को। इन्हें हम कैसे बर्दाश्त कर सकते हैं। इनका मंसूर कहता था कि 'अनल-हक़ मैं ही सत्य हूँ।' एक और सूफ़ी सरमद वह कलमा के बस शुरुआती दो लफ़्ज़ पढ़ता था...'ला इलाह' यानी कि 'नहीं है कोई इबादत के लायक़।' इनमें से ही एक था फ़ख़रुद्दीन जो पाक कलमा के लफ़्ज़ों में जबरन इश्क को घुसाता 'ला इलाह इलल्लाह इश्क़' के नारे लगाता था। एक से बढ़कर एक कम्बख़्त-कमज़ात इनमें हुए हैं। इनकी पूरी बिरादरी इस्लामी शरीयत के ख़िलाफ़ आचरण करती है। हमारे यहाँ बुतपरस्ती हराम है, ये मक़बरे और क़ब्रों को ही बुत मान कर पूजते हैं। ये ख़ुदा-अल्लाहताला-मौला को पुकारने के बदले अपने गुरु-मुर्शिद-पीर को ही टेरते रहते हैं। ऐसे नापाक इनसान जो ख़ुद को ही सच, इश्क़ को ख़ुदा माननेवाली रवायत से हैं, इनकी छाया भी हम इस शहर पर नहीं पड़ने देंगे। हमें कोई फ़र्क़ नहीं पड़ता कि वे अजमेर से आ रहे हैं कि इस्लामाबाद से।

अब तो हद ही हो गई। जिसे देखिए वह प्रोग्राम बन्द करवाने की धमकी देता फिर रहा है। कॉलेज कैम्पस को दो-चार दिनों में इनकी आदत पड़ गई। अब तो कोई नज़र भी उठाकर नहीं देखता कि रैली किसकी है, राष्ट्रवादी छात्र संघ वालों की कि पॉपुलर फ्रंट वालों की। शहर को भी तुरन्त पता लग गया कि दोनों बैनरों के पीछे अधिकांश बाहरी लोग हैं। चार-पाँच टाटा सूमो गाड़ियाँ हर दूसरे दिन चटर्जी गली के पुराने ख़ाली बँगलों में रुकती हैं। वहीं से छात्र संघ वाले बैनर-झंडे सजा कर शहर को

थर्राने निकलते हैं। दूसरी ओर दो पुरानी मिनी बसें न जाने कहाँ से पुरानी सैयद टोली में घुसती हैं। फिर आधे घंटे बाद पॉपुलर फ्रंट के सजे-धजे बैनर नारों के साथ शहर की सड़कों का फेरा लगाने लगाते हैं।

लेकिन शहर, कॉलेज, प्रशासन कहीं से तवज्जो न मिलने से दोनों गुट बेचैन हो उठे। नतीजतन बम पटक-पटक कर जबरन दुकानें बन्द कराई जाने लगीं। मिठाई और फलों की दुकानों पर कुछ लोग घायल हुए, कुछ को बम के टुकड़े- छर्रे लगे। नतीजन भगदड़ मच गई। शहर एक सौ चौवालिस धारा के कंटीलों तारों के बीच काँपने लगा। हालात कुछ ऐसे हो गए कि कलक्टर साहब को 'शिउड़ी-जुटान' के ठीक पन्द्रह दिन पहले कार्यक्रम स्थगित करने का आदेश जारी करना पड़ा। लेकिन बाबा माननेवाले नहीं थे। चहारुम के दिन सुआर्यन वाले, चालीसवें पर राष्ट्रवादी छात्र संघ और पॉपुलर फ्रंट...मज़ाक बना कर छोड़ दिया है। एक शहीद को, अपने भाई की मिट्टी को...इतनी सी इज़्ज़त भी बख़्शने के लायक़ भी हम नहीं रहे। यह तो नहीं हो सकता। वे कॉलेज कैम्पस के खेल मैदान के कोनेवाले बरगद पेड़ के नीचे आमरण-अनशन पर बैठ गए।

फ़ाइनल इयर के सारे बच्चे-बच्चियाँ भी बाबा के साथ मरते दम तक खड़े रहने की क़समों के साथ आ जुटे। दूसरे दिन बाबा से प्यार करनेवाले शिक्षक भी आ जुटे। टेंटों की संख्या बढ़ती गई। जयदेव केन्दुली-मोनेर मानुष अखाड़ा से बीस-बाईस बाउल भी अनशन पर। वर्धमान ज़िले से नामी-गिरामी कव्वाल भी अनशन पर...। दो-चार दिनों में लगा कि उस छोटे से मैदान में टेंट लगाने की जगह ही नहीं बचेगी। चौथे दिन के बाद से बाबा की तबियत ख़राब होने लगी थी। वज़न तेज़ी से गिर रहा था। रक्तचाप भी काफी कम हो गया था। कलक्टर-एस.पी., सारा शहर भारी तनाव में था। आख़िर सेन्ट्रल पुलिस फ़ोर्स की टुकड़ियाँ बसों में भर-भरकर आने लगीं। सातवें दिन जब बाबा की आँखें भी नहीं खुल पा रही थीं, रक्तचाप को डूबने से बचाने को जबरन पानी चढ़ाया जाने लगा था। कलक्टर और एस.पी. लाव-लश्कर के साथ कैम्पस में पधारे। प्राचार्य-कार्यकारणी के लोगों से बातचीत की। सबों ने मिलकर बाबा और सारे अनशनकारियों को जूस पिलाकर अनशन तुड़वाया। तय हुआ कि हर हाल में 'शिउड़ी जुटान' होगा। उत्पातियों को देख लिया जाएगा।

कैम्पस में ख़ुशी की लहर दौड़ गई। बच्चे कुछ ज़्यादा ही ख़ुश हो गए। अबीर-गुलाल से सब लाल हो गया।

लाव-लश्कर लौट गया। बाबा भी एकाध केला-पपीता खाकर डेढ़-दो घंटे में बैठने-चलने की स्थिति में आ गए। गाड़ी में बैठा घर पहुँचाने के लिए चार-पाँच लड़के उन्हें थामे आगे बढ़े। अभी सात-आठ कदम बामुश्किल चले होंगे कि कॉलेज की दीवारों पर बम पटके जाने लगे। चारों ओर धुआँ ही धुआँ। भगदड़-सी मच गई। इसी बीच दीवारें फाँद-फाँदकर दोनों गुटों के लफ़ंगे मैदान में आ गए। लगभग साठ-सत्तर लोगों की भीड़ ने बाबा को घेर लिया। उनमें कौन राष्ट्रवादी छात्र संघ का था...कौन यूथ विंग ऑफ पॉपुलर फ्रंट ऑफ इंडिया का यह पता लगाना मुश्किल था। सबके सब एक साथ चीख़ रहे थे। मानो जंगली भेड़िये आकाश की ओर थूथनें उठाकर गुर्रा रहे हों। बाबा को पसीना आ रहा है...बाबा बायीं छाती मसले जा रहे हैं,...बाबा थरथरा रहे हैं...खड़े होने में दिक़्क़त हो रही है...। साथ के बच्चे इन सारी बातों को पूरी शिद्दत से महसूस कर रहे थे। वे पूरा दम पूरी ताक़त लगाकर बाबा को उस भीड़ से निकालकर गाड़ी तक पहुँचाने की कोशिश कर रहे थे। लेकिन भेड़ियों के झुंड की मर्ज़ी तो बाबा को नोचने-चीथने की थी वे रास्ता क्यों देते? बाबा धीरे-धीरे होश खोने लगे। बेसुध देह धरती पर गिर पड़ी। छाती मसलते-एड़ी रगड़ते बाबा को भीड़ ने अपनी साँसें बचाने भर की भी मोहलत नहीं दी।

37

रो-रोकर पूछती हैं बानो शह-ए ज़मन से,
कड़ियल जवाँ की मैयत किस तरह लाये रण से।

—**नोहा** की पंक्तियाँ

इन दिनों अम्मू और 'मौसीक़ी-मंज़िल' के आँसू और ग़म एकसार हो इस ख़ानदान के सुख-दुख के इतिहास में डूबते-उतराते रहे। उस शाम ऑफिस से लौटकर मैं और श्रावणी अम्मू-शब्बो भाभी के पास बैठे थे। कमोल दा की तेरहवीं की तैयारी करनी थी। अन्तिम संस्कार और बाउल रवायतों के अनुसार सारे अनुष्ठान पुश्तैनी गाँव धूरिशा में ही हुए थे। तेरहवीं भी वहीं होनी थी किन्तु ख़रीदारी यहाँ की जाए या शिउड़ी बाज़ार में बात बराबर थी। अम्मू फिर से कुछ बोल पाने की स्थिति में नहीं थीं। शब्बो भाभी भी बस हाँ-हूँ किए जा रही थी। हाँ! बुलबुल अपनी श्रावणी आंटी के पास बैठी लिस्ट में कुछ-कुछ जोड़ती, टिक मार्क लगाती जा रही थी। समय से बहुत पहले समझदार हो गई थी हमारी बिटिया। हादसे जो न कराएँ।

तभी आश्रम के एक बच्चे के संग मैडम नीलोफ़र परवीन आती दिखीं। बहुत बेचैन-ग़मज़दा। उनकी भर्राई आवाज़ और टूटी-फूटी... सहमे-सहमे से लफ़्ज़ों से यह पता चला कि उस दिन ट्रेन में कमोल-दा

के साथ कालिन्दी मैडम भी थीं। अभी कोलकता के एक बड़े हॉस्पिटल में आई.सी.यू. वार्ड में हैं। हालात क्रिटिकल हैं। लेकिन जब कभी होश आता है तो कमोल...कमोल, छोड़ दो-छोड़ दो...और डायरी...डायरी... बस यही तीन लफ़्ज़ बड़बड़ाती हैं।

कालिन्दी उसी ट्रेन से शिउड़ी जा रही है जिससे कमोल जा रहा है यह नीलोफ़र को पता था। उसे उस डायरी के बारे में भी बताकर गई थी शायद जिसके पन्नों में नानू, अब्बू और कमोल-बाबा की हत्या-हादसे के राज़ छुपे थे। रास्ते में उस पर बातें करनी थी और डायरी कमोल को सौंपनी थी। अब चूँकि छुट्टी का आवेदन दिया था तो मैनेजर साहब को भी पता था।

इस हादसे के पहले से ही शहर में बी.बी. गुप्ता का कहीं अता-पता नहीं था। अब स्पेशल टास्क फ़ोर्स उठा कर ले गई कि अंडरग्राउंड हो गए थे, किसी को कानोकान ख़बर नहीं थी। लेकिन कमोल दा की हत्या किसने की...करवाई? किसके इशारे पर आत्महत्या वाली कहानी फैलाई जा रही है, कुछ समझ में नहीं आ रहा था।

बाबा की भीड़ के हाथों हत्या की प्राथमिकी शिउड़ी थाना में कमोल दा ने दर्ज करवाई थी। राष्ट्रवादी छात्र संघ और पॉपुलर फ्रंट वालों के कुछ नाम भी बाबा के शिष्यों के पहचानने-बतलाने के आधार पर डाले थे। गिरफ़्तारियाँ भी हुईं। किन्तु बस चार-पाँच महीने बाद ही सबों को हाईकोर्ट से ज़मानत मिल गई। शिउड़ी बाज़ार में उनके संगठनों ने अपने-अपने आरोपियों को माला-वाला पहनाकर जुलूस-वुलूस भी निकाला था।

ख़बर यह भी थी कि बाबा ने लगभग साल-भर पहले बोगी में मारपीट करनेवालों जिन ज़ालिमों के ख़िलाफ़ रेल थाना में प्राथमिकी करवाई थी, वे आरोपी भी ज़मानत पर थे और उनकी पुरानी चाल-ढाल में कोई फ़र्क़ नहीं पड़ा था।

भले ही बी.बी. गुप्ता अंडरग्राउंड हों किन्तु सुआर्यन और भगवान कच्छप रक्षक सेना तो देश-भर में पहले की तरह ही सक्रिय थी। मयंक के रिएल इस्टेट टायकून ससुर साहब और वैभवी मैडम की नज़रें आज भी 'मौसीक़ी-मंज़िल' और आश्रम की ज़मीन पर गड़ी थीं। फाइव स्टार होटल का सपना अभी भी क़ायम था। उसे ज़मीन पर उतारने के लिए वे कई-कई मोर्चों पर आज भी एक्टिव थे।

लेकिन इन सबों में कमोल दा का हत्यारा कौन था, यह तो कालिन्दी मैडम ही बता सकती हैं। लेकिन वे तो...। नीलोफ़र ने बताया कि कमोल दा की मृत देह के थोड़ी दूर आगे ही पटरी पर कालिन्दी की देह पड़ी थी। साँसें चल रही थीं इसीलिए किसी भले मानस ने उनके ही मोबाइल से आई. कार्ड पर छपे ऑफिस के नम्बर पर फ़ोन कर न केवल हमें ख़बर भर दी बल्कि उन्हें शिउड़ी अस्पताल भी पहुँचाया।

बैंक से मैनेजर दो सीनियर कुलीग और नीलोफ़र के साथ शिउड़ी अस्पताल पहुँचे थे। वहाँ उसी बोगी के दो-तीन सहयात्रियों से भी भेंट हुई। उन लोगों ने ऑफ द रिकार्ड कुछ-कुछ बताया था।...बोगी के दरवाज़े के पास सटी 'यात्री-सूची' में कमोल दा का नाम के. कबीर प्रिंट रहने, हाथों में शायर वली दकनी का दीवान और फ़क़ीराना वेश-भूषा, साथ ही दाढ़ी-वाढ़ी बढ़ी देख उसे विधर्मी-दुश्मन समझ लफंगों का एक झुंड उसे घेरकर बैठा हुआ था। न जाने किस स्टेशन पर वे चढ़े थे...लग तो लोकल पैसेंजर्स की तरह ही थे...लेकिन कौन जाने...? कोई विशेष पहचान वे बुज़ुर्ग बता नहीं पाये थे। खाना खाने के वक़्त कमोल ने जब टिफिन खोला तो मानो उस झुंड को मनचाहा बहाना मिल गया हो...कमोल-कालिन्दी लाख समझाते रहे कि यह कटहल-कोफ्ता है किन्तु वे चीखे जा रहे थे कि भगवान कच्छप महाराज का गोश्त है। फिर मारपीट शुरू हो गई थी।...उन बुज़ुर्गों को भी यह लगा था कि मारपीट के मूड में तो वे सब पहले से ही थे...कुछ-कुछ उल्टा-पुल्टा...गन्दा-शन्दा कमेंट्स तो पहले से ही कर रहे थे लेकिन कमोल-कालिन्दी ने रिएक्ट नहीं किया था...कटहल-कोफ्ते ने उन्हें वह मौका दे दिया...। केवल मारपीट कर नहीं छोड़ा...स्टेशन आने के थोड़े ही पहले...गाड़ी धीमी हो उसके पहले...पहले कमोल को फिर उसे हर हाल में बचाने के लिए लड़ रही कालिन्दी को गेट के बाहर फेंक दिया...। कमोल का सिर बिजली के खम्भे से टकराया था...इसीलिए...।

कहने-सुनने के लिए अब कुछ बचा नहीं था। अब्बू की वह बात याद आ रही थी कि हमारे संगी नमक थे...शायद गल गए...अब हमारे आँसुओं के नमक में...। जाते-जाते नीलोफ़र ने यह बतलाया था कि वह डायरी नहीं मिली थी जिसे देने कालिन्दी उस ट्रेन में गई थी। शायद वहीं पटरियों के आसपास की झाड़ियों में पड़ी हो। आँसू और ग़म में डूबी अम्मू और

शब्बो भाभी चाह रही थीं कि गुम गई 'शिउड़ी-जुटान' की उस लम्बी-चौड़ी सूची की भी तलाश हो।

...अब सब मुझे ही करना था। डायरी और उस सूची की तलाश... कालिन्दी मैडम के इलाज के हर सम्भव उपाय...। वे अच्छी हो वापस आएं...'शिउड़ी-जुटान' हो...मौसीक़ी-मंज़िल और आश्रम आगे बढ़े...।

...और 'शिउड़ी-जुटान' का अधूरा सपना, इसे तो पूरा ही पूरा करना है। जिस प्रकार कमोल दा के अन्तिम संस्कार में धूरिशा में, अजय नदी के तट पर समूचा शिउड़ी शहर उमड़ पड़ा था, उससे तो यही लगता था कि न केवल 'मौसीक़ी-मंज़िल' और संगीत महाविद्यालय बल्कि पूरा शिउड़ी शहर ही इस सपने को सच होते देखना चाहता है।...वहीं महाविद्यालय के कैम्पस में विशाल क्षितिज तक पंडाल...घराने के सारे के सारे मौसीक़ीकार, बाउल, सूफ़ी गायक सबके सब शोभा बढ़ाते। अम्मू फिर से गायें...राग मारवा के धीर-गम्भीर सुर सजें...षड्ज...गन्धार...पंचम तक आते-आते सुर के पखेरू सातों आसमान के पार नानू, अब्बू, बाबा...कमोल दा तक जा पहुँचें। फिर वहाँ से उस जुटान में एक-एक कर पधारें...सारे पुरखे... हिन्दुस्तानी मौसीक़ी के सभी पूर्वज...गोपाल नायक, अमीर ख़ुसरो, स्वामी हरिदास, बैजू बावरा, तानसेन, मुहम्मद शाह रंगीले, अदारंग, सदारंग, ख़ुशरंग, अख़्तरपिया, गुरु गोरखनाथ, लालोन फ़क़ीर, बड़े ग़ुलाम अली ख़ाँ, अल्ला बंदे ख़ाँ डागर, विष्णु दिगम्बर पलुस्कर, बड़ो बाबा अल्लाउद्दीन ख़ाँ, ओंकारनाथ ठाकुर, हीराबाई बड़ोदेकर, गंगूबाई हंगल, नानू महताबुद्दीन ख़ान, अब्बू, बाबा...अपना कमोल दा...सबके सब...।

38

यह कैसी खंडित छाया,
मेरे साथ-साथ चलती है?
ये आँखें हैं या अग्निकुंड?
या आधी रात कछारों पर
दो साथ चिताएँ जलती हैं?

—कुँवर नारायण

कमोल-माँ को मानो सब भूल ही गए थे। उनकी तो दुनिया ही उजाड़ हो गई। वज्रपात ही तो हुआ था। सब कुछ जलकर खाक़! वर्तमान-भविष्य दोनों। रोते-रोते आंसू सूख गए। बस आँखें जलती रहतीं। नींद घोंसला छोड़ उड़ी चिड़िया की तरह ग़ायब हो गई थी। आँखें मूँदकर लेटतीं तो बिस्तर के दोनों तरफ़ दो चिताएँ जलती दिखतीं। उनकी आँच महसूस होती। तेज़ छाँह अन्तरमन तक झुलसाती हुई। चट-चट की आवाजें और चिरायँध गंध। घर मणिकर्णिका घाट में तब्दील हो जाता। चैत्र शुक्ल सप्तमी का मणिकर्णिका घाट, महादेव मन्दिर का जीर्णोद्धार उत्सव और बनारस की सारी गणिकाएँ मानो वहाँ नाच-गा रही हों। अजब-ग़ज़ब के रंग चेहरे-मुख पर मले हुए। सब भयावह-डरावना।

सब पर भारी चट-चट की ध्वनि। कभी-कभी उन्हें लगता कि कोई और भी है उस घर में। कितना विशाल-कितना बड़ा तीन मंज़िला वह शिवड़ी

बाज़ार का घर। छोटी-मोटी हवेली-सा। कहाँ-कहाँ ढूँढ़तीं। कितनी-कितनी तो कोठरियाँ, बड़े-बड़े हॉल। लेकिन वह था तो ज़रूर शीर्ण-पाद वाला प्रथम मृतक, यम। पिता की दासी छाया पर पद प्रहार करने से शापित पाँवों में फोड़े लिए कमोल-माँ के घर में ही भटकता। पैरों के घसीटने की आवाज़ें और फ़र्श पर फोड़ों से टपके रक्त-पीन कमोल-माँ को साफ़-साफ़ दिखते। दिन-भर फ़र्श साफ़ करती रहतीं और रात भर घी के दीये हर कोठरी के कोनों में जलाती रहतीं। उनके लिए हर रात छोटी दीवाली हो गई थी, यम के दीये वाली रात।

घर की साफ़-सफ़ाईवाली दाई ने पहले कमोल-माँ को सँभालने की कोशिश की। दूधवाले और माछ-भाजी वाले दादा लोगों ने भी उनका मन दूसरी ओर लगाने के कितने-कितने जतन किये। पड़ोस की उनकी हमउम्र सहेलियों ने आना-जाना बढ़ा दिया किन्तु कमोल-माँ की नींद और चैन मानो दोनों बहनें कुम्भ के मेले में बिछुड़ गई हों और इस घर का रास्ता ही भूल गई हों। थक-हारकर शिउड़ी बाज़ार ने धूरिशा गाँव को ख़बर भिजवाई। कमोल के काका-काकी, भाई-बहन सब गाड़ी लेकर हाज़िर। कमोल-माँ घर छोड़ जाने को तैयार नहीं। वो जो कभी-कभी कमोल-बाबा उन्हें डाकते हैं...अपर्णा...अपर्णा...चा खाबो...उसका क्या?

धूरिशा में कमोल-माँ, अपर्णा-बौदी का घर लिपा-पुता, एकदम साफ़-सुथरा। सब चकाचक। आँगन की तुलसी भी गदराई हुई, दरवाज़े की जवाकुसुम फूलों-कलियों से लदी-फदी। रातरानी, बेली-चमेली, गेंदा-गुलाब सबके सब हरे-भरे अपने गंध-सुगंध से मदमाते। पीछे केले के गाछ और छोटी-सी पोखरी। लगता है कमोल काका ने मछली जीरा थोड़ा ज़्यादा ही डाला था। रोहू-कतला-भेटकी-चेंगरी सबके सब छोटी-सी पोखरी में गद्गद। रह-रहकर कोई-कोई उछल-उछल अपनी ख़ुशी का एहसास करा रही थी।

कमोल काका को अपनी बौदी की हाथ की रसोई बहुत भाती थी। ख़ासकर रोहू-रुई माछ, सरसों तेल की हिलसा और सबसे बढ़कर डाब भाँपा चिंगारी। इस बार सब का स्वाद लेना था यहाँ तक कि लौकी-पोस्तो का भी। पोते-पोतियों से भरा हुआ घर। कमोल-माँ का आँगन भी किलकारियों से भर गया। मानो उनका आँगन केन्दुली गाँव हो और वहाँ

रोज जोयदेव मेला लगता हो। बच्चों की किलकारियाँ बाउल गायन की तरह लगतीं। तरह-तरह की राग-रागिनियाँ उन किलकारियों से निकलकर हवा में तैरती हुई महसूस होतीं। राग-भैरवी, विभास, रामकरी-गुणकरी, मालवगौड़, गुर्जरी, वसंत, कर्णाट, श्याम कल्याण, यमन, हंसध्वनि, हमीर, केदार और शिवरंजनी...। फिर लगा कि कमोल-माँ का मन धीरे-धीरे अपनी केंचुली उतार रहा हो।

पोते-पोतियों, नाती-नतिनों के संग खेलते-खेलाते, गप्प-गल्प सुनते-सुनाते, उनकी पसन्द की रसोई राँधते महीने चुटकियों में बीत गए। कमोल-माँ की ठठरी हो गई देह पर थोड़ी चमक आई। सफ़ेद कपास से बालों में तेल-वेल दिखने लगा। शिउड़ी बाज़ार वाले घर में जबरन घुस आए प्रथम मृतक यम की याद धुँधली पड़ने लगी। उसके फोड़े भरे पैरों के दाग़दार पदचिह्नों पर आगे बढ़ने की चाह बिला गई। तभी न जाने किस काली रात में कमोल काका के मन में एक काला चोर घुसा कि बौदी अगर यहीं बस गईं तो...अपना हिस्सा माँगेंगी तो...? धनहर खेत, अनाज भरी कोठरी, बाग़-बग़ीचे, पोखर-पोखरी सब में आधा हिस्सा...बाबा रे! सारी आमदनी आधी...। इतना बड़ा परिवार पोती-पोतियाँ...सबका लालन-पालन...पढ़ाई-लिखाई...शादी-ब्याह...सब कैसे? पहले वह शक का काला चोर, उनके मन के कोने में स्थिर हो आलथी-पालथी मारकर बैठ गया। फिर अमावस की काली रात की कालिमा की तरह फैलने लगा। काका से काकी के मन में फिर बेटे-बहुओं के मन में। मन तक ही रुकता तो फिर भी एक बात होती, वह तो चेहरे से, आँखों से झाँकने लगा। पहले बोली-बानी बदली, फिर आना-जाना कम हुआ। हद तो यह हो गई धीरे-धीरे बच्चों ने भी बड़ी दादी-कमोल-माँ के आँगन में खेलना-कूदना छोड़ दिया। पहले दरवाज़े के जवाकुसुम पर असर हुआ। उसने फूलना बन्द कर दिया। धीरे-धीरे सारी पत्तियाँ झर गईं फिर चम्पा-चमेली-बेली सबके सब मुरझाने लगीं। जब आँगन की गदराई तुलसी सुबह-शाम जल ढालने के बाद भी मुरझाने लगी तो कमोल-माँ ने समझ लिया अब यहाँ रहना ठीक नहीं। चुरूलिया बड़े दादा को फोन किया। उसी रात पिछवाड़े की पोखरी में मरी हुई बिल्ली न जाने किसने फेंकी और सवेरे सारी की सारी मछलियाँ मरकर उपलाई हुई। शीर्ण-पाद यम की आहट सुनाई पड़ने लगी थी।

उसी दोपहर चुरूलिया से गाड़ी आ गई। दो-दो भतीजे भी साथ में। शाम तक अपने मैके पहुँचकर कमोल-माँ ने राहत की साँस ली। यहाँ भी ढेर सारे बच्चे, गाय-गोरू, फूल-पत्ते, बाग़-बग़ीचे, पोखर और मछलियाँ। कमोल-माँ...अपर्णा...बुआ का मन फिर से खिलने लगा। किन्तु जैसे ही बड़ी बौदी दिखतीं तो उनकी भतीजी कालिन्दी की भी याद आ जाती। मन में एक अपराधबोध-सा, एक पाप घुटनों के बीच सिर छुपाये बैठा दिखता। लगता कालिन्दी की दुर्दशा की कारण वही हैं। अगर वे ज़िद ठान लेतीं तो कमोल से कालिन्दी का ब्याह कौन रोकता? कितनी अच्छी जोड़ी। कालिन्दी कब की माँ बन गई होती...शायद कमोल भी आज साथ होता...। आँखें डबडबाने लगतीं, छाती में कुछ फँसा-फँसा सा लगता और रुलाई का ज्वार उठने लगता। वे अपनी बड़ी बौदी से नज़र मिलाने से बचतीं। किन्तु बड़ी बौदी के मन में कोई ख़लिश नहीं थी। जब तक कालिन्दी की शादी नहीं हुई थी तभी तक उनके मन में अपनी छोटी ननद अपर्णा के लिए थोड़ा ग़ुस्सा था किन्तु उसकी शादी होते वह ग़ुस्सा कब का धुल-पुँछ गया था। अब कालिन्दी की गोद नहीं भर सकी तो यह उसका भाग्य-सौभाग्य। आजकल तो उन्हें अपनी दुखियारी, भाइयों की सबसे प्यारी, छोटी ननद अपर्णा को हर हाल में ख़ुश रखने का ख़याल ही आठों पहर घेरे रहता था।

लेकिन धूरिशा में जला हुआ कमोल-माँ का मन चुरूलिया में भी बहुत दिन नहीं रुकना चाह रहा था। तभी 'शिउड़ी-जुटान' की ख़बर मिली। कमोल और उसके बाबा के संगी-साथियों ने असम्भव को सम्भव कर दिया। कमोल-बाबा की लिस्ट के एक-एक कलाकार शिउड़ी में जुटनेवाले थे। तैयारी के लिए कमोल के संगी-साथी दस दिन पहले से ही शिउड़ी आने लगेंगे, इसका अन्दाज़ा उन्हें था। उनके इतने बड़े घर के रहते उन्हें होटल में रहना पड़े...यह हो नहीं सकता।...और अपनी नानी-मम्मी संग बुलबुल भी तो आएगी। उनकी अपनी बुलबुल...कमोल की बुलबुल... उसकी देह से भी हूबहू कमोल की गंध। नाक-आँखें भी कमोल जैसी। बोल-चाल-स्वभाव सब कमोल जैसा। दादी की हाथों की डाब भापा चिंगरी कितना पसन्द बुलबुल को। उन्हें शिउड़ी जाना ही पड़ेगा।

'शिउड़ी जुटान' की तैयारी के लिए दस-ग्यारह दिन पहले मेरे पहुँचने के पहले ही मोबाइल पर कमोल-माँ, हमारी माँमोनी का सन्देशा आ गया

था कि उन्हीं के घर ठहरना है। बहुत विशाल घर किन्तु चहल-पहल की गूँज से लबालब। माँमोनी के अनुरोध पर संगीत महाविद्यालय के शिक्षकों-बच्चों ने आयोजन समिति का वहाँ कार्यालय खोल रखा था। एक-दो दिनों में यह लग गया कि न केवल संगीत महाविद्यालय बल्कि पूरा शिउड़ी बाज़ार ही उस आयोजन की तैयारी में एक बार फिर से तन-मन-धन से लगा था।

मैं और माँमोनी रोज़ अपनी प्रिय अम्मू, शब्बो भाभी और बुलबुल की प्रतीक्षा कर रहे थे किन्तु उनके पहले पधारीं कालिन्दी, एकदम सबेरे वाली छह बजिया रेल से। न जाने माँमोनी के सपने कालिन्दी भाभी के सपनों से कब मिले थे, कब बोला-बतियाया था कि एकदम नवबोधु के वेश में उन्होंने कमोल दा के घर में पग धरा। एकदम माँमोनी के सपनों वाली बोंग बोधु...केवल सिर पर माँगटीका के ऊपर मुकुट नहीं था और न ललाट पर चन्दन-कुमकुम की सजावट और हाँ! पान पत्तों की ओट भी मुखड़े के सामने नहीं थी। बाक़ी सारे के सारे सौभाग्य चिह्न मौजूद थे। सोलहों श्रृंगार के साथ। नागझुंड की भाँति एड़ी को चूमते लम्बे-घने घुँघराले केश। मैरून रंग की भारी बनारसी साड़ी पीताभ किनारों वाली। सेन्दूरफल की भाँति दीप्तमुख, गुड़हल की रक्तकुसुमों से भरी डाल-सी देह, आलता रचित पगतल और करतल पर मेहँदी के खिले हुए अलौकिक फूल। नीरडोल, शाँख काँकन, मोयूरमुख बाला, रत्नाचुर, पायल सम्मिश्रित रुनझुन से माँमोनी की वह हवेली तानपूरे की तरह झंकृत होने लगी। एक अजब तरह के उजास से घर का कोना-कोना दमक उठा। माँमोनी को तो अपनी आँखों पर विश्वास नहीं हो रहा था।

चाय-वाय के बाद गप्प-शप्प के दौरान ही मालूम चला कि गुप्ता जी से तलाक़ का मामला निपटाकर आई हैं। कमोल-बाबा की हत्या में सुआर्यन-सेना के लड़कों की भागीदारी की भनक मिलने के बाद ही कोर्ट में अर्ज़ी दाख़िल कर दी थी। बी.बी. गुप्ता की डायरी और कमोल के संग चुरूलिया में खींचे एक पुराने फोटो को सँजोये हुए वे शिउड़ी पहुँच गई थीं। दोपहर एकान्त में माँमोनी के सामने अपना हृदय खोलकर रख दिया। दशकों पहले चुरूलिया में सीढ़ी के कोने में जब पलकें उठाकर कमोल ने उन्हें देखा था उसी अपूर्व क्षण में एक तीव्र चुभन का एहसास हुआ था।

मानो कोई सूई चुभी हो और उनके अपने ही रक्त के सूत्र में हृदय को गूँथ दिया गया हो। तब से अपने ही नाड़ी-तंत्र में विष की तरह प्राण घुलता रहा था ताकि कमोल के प्राण से एकमेव हो सके। दूध में पड़े केसर की तरह सुवासित नेह मन-प्राणों में खीर की तरह खदकता रहा। वह सदा-सदा के लिए उनके हृदय में इस तरह रच-बस गया जैसे चकोर के मन में स्वाति नक्षत्र का मेघ रहता है। शायद इसीलिए गुप्ता जी को मन से कभी स्वीकार नहीं कर सकीं। शायद इसीलिए उनके बच्चे की माँ नहीं बन सकीं। चूँकि गुप्ता जी उनके मन-प्राणों को बाँध न सके, उन पर अपनी मर्दानगी की छाप न छोड़ सके शायद इसीलिए दुनिया को अपनी मर्दानगी दिखाने लगे। उनके भीतर की स्वतंत्र-स्त्री को मार न सके तो घृणा के झूठे बहानों से औरों को मारने-मरवाने लगे।

किन्तु जब उनकी घृणा और हिंसा की आँच कमोल के घर तक पहुँची तो बर्दाश्त की सारी सीमाएँ ख़त्म हो गईं और वह भुरभुरे घरौंदे की दहलीज़ को ढाहकर बाहर निकल आई। बहरहाल बैंक ने उनकी पोस्टिंग शिउड़ी बाज़ार की शाखा में ही कर दी है किन्तु वह कुछ अनाथ बच्चे-बच्चियों को गोद लेना चाहती हैं ताकि उनकी गोद और इस घर का आँगन किलकारियों से भर सके। वे इस छोटी-सी हवेली की कुछ कोठरियों में ग़रीब बच्चों के लिए स्कूल भी संचालित करने की छोटी-सी इच्छा भी लेकर आई थीं। समाज के एक हिस्से ने उनके प्रियों को मृत्यु दी थी, दुख दिया था। माँमोनी-अम्मू के वर्तमान-भविष्य पर वज्रपात किया था। कालिन्दी भाभी उसी समाज को सात-सहस्त्र रंगों से भरा बसंत लौटाने का सपना देख रही थीं।

न जाने दादी-पोती के बीच टेलीपैथी थी कि कुछ और दोपहर की रसोई में बुलबुल के पसन्दीदा व्यंजन राँधे जा रहे थे। लूची, मालपुए, मोचार घोंटो, चरचरी, भेटकी पातूरी और बुलबुल की सबसे पसन्दीदा डाब भापा चिंगरी। रसोई पूरी होते-होते ठीक एक बजे के क़रीब बुलबुल की कार दरवाज़े पर आ लगी। अम्मू तो सदा की तरह अपनी गरिमा की तेज़ दीप्त दिख रही थीं। सदा की तरह रेशम की क्रीम कलर की साड़ी, नये-नवेले कंगन और ललाट पर बड़ा-सा टीका। किन्तु आँखों से झाँकती उदासी थी। हाँ! शब्बो भाभी ने ससुरबाड़ी आने के लिए विशेष तैयारी

की थी। कॉटन सिल्क की धानी रंग की साड़ी और बोंगो बोधु के सारे आभूषणों ने मिलकर उनके व्यक्तित्व को अलग दमक से भर दिया था। माँमोनी ठीक कहती थीं, ग़ौर से देखने पर सच में बुलबुल के नख से शिख तक, बातचीत चाल-ढाल सबमें कमोल दा की झलक दिख रही थी। लग रहा था कमोल दा ने फिर से बालरूप धारण किया हो और इस बार छेली रूप में। अब माँमोनी का घर 'घर' लग रहा था। उनकी ख़ुशी तो समाते न समा रही थी। सब को कहाँ बैठाएँ, कहाँ उठाएँ उन्हें समझ में नहीं आ रहा था। अम्मू के गले लगीं तो देर तक दोनों डबडबाई आँखों और भरे हृदय से एक-दूसरे को छोड़ ही नहीं रही थीं। बुलबुल को चूमना शुरू किया तो चूमती ही गईं।

उधर कालिन्दी भाभी और शब्बो भाभी एक-दूसरे से कट रही थीं। एक-दूसरे से नज़र ही नहीं मिला रही थीं। फिर न जाने क्या हुआ, दोनों की आँखें एक साथ डबडबाने लगीं। फिर रुलाई का आवेग दोनों के तन-मन प्राणों को आलोड़ित करने लगा। दोनों की रुलाई रुक ही नहीं रही थी। मानो सघन वेदना का वेग लम्बी अवधि से बाँध तोड़ने की प्रतीक्षा कर रहा हो। अन्त में माँमोनी ने शब्बो भाभी को और अम्मू ने कालिन्दी भाभी को छाती से लगाकर सहलाना-पुचकारना शुरू किया। धीरे-धीरे दोनों शान्त हुईं। एक-दूसरे की हथेलियों को थाम बहुत देर तक बैठी रहीं। दोनों कमोल दा की स्मृतियों में डूब-डूब कर रही थीं। कमोल दा भी यहीं आसपास मँडरा रहे होंगे। बुलबुल भी भरी आँखों से सारे नज़ारे देख ही रही थी।

बुलबुल की कार के पीछे-पीछे ही दो ट्रकें सामानों-मशीनों के बॉक्सों से लदी-फद़ी दरवाज़े पर आ खड़ी हुई थीं। शब्बो भाभी ने बतलाया कि नीचे के बड़े कमरों-हॉल में साउंड रिकार्डिंग का स्टूडियो खोलना है। अब्बू-बाबा और कमोल का वर्षों का सपना था। माँमोनी को लग रहा था जागती आँखों से वे कोई सपना देख रही हैं। सब कुछ इतनी तेज़ी से घटित हो रहा था कि विश्वास करना कठिन हो रहा था। कहाँ तो एक बोधु के लिए तरस रही थीं और कहाँ दो-दो बोधु। उन्हें लग रहा था कि वे गौरांग-चैतन्य महाप्रभु की माँ शचिमाता हैं। गौरांग की तो पहली बोधु लक्ष्मीदेवी सर्पदंश से स्वर्ग सिधार गई थीं तब दूसरी पत्नी विष्णुप्रिया

आई थीं। यहाँ तो दोनों एक साथ मौजूद। दंश तो शब्बो भाभी ने भी कम नहीं सहा था। किन्तु उन्होंने सारे विष को पचाना सीख लिया था। समझ लिया था कि पहचान की राजनीति केवल घृणा और घृणा को ही जन्म देती है जिसकी हिंसा की आग हर कहीं हर किसी को झुलसा रही थी। लेकिन इस राजनीति को अपनी उँगलियों से नचानेवाले दुनिया-भर में फैले वैभवी और उसके डैडी जैसे छोटे-बड़े चेहरे को कोई पहचानना नहीं चाहता।

दिन के चौथे पहर माँमोनी की तीसरी मंज़िल की कोठरियाँ तानपूरे की झंकार से गूँजने लगीं। 'शिउड़ी-जुटान' के लिए रियाज़ ज़रूरी था। शब्बो भाभी ने राग मारवा में ख़याल के विलम्बित एकताल से आलाप लिया...'पिया मोरें अनत देश गैलवा ऽऽ...'